Bats of British Columbia

Also from the Authors of *Bats of British Columbia*

Spotted Owls: Shadows in an Old-Growth Forest
by Jared Hobbs and Richard Cannings

Rodents and Lagomorphs of British Columbia
by David Nagorsen

Carnivores of British Columbia
by David F. Hatler, David W. Nagorsen and Alison M. Beal

COMING IN 2023
Shrews and Moles of British Columbia
by David Nagorsen and Nick Panter

Royal BC Museum Handbook

BATS

OF BRITISH COLUMBIA

Second Edition

CORI L. LAUSEN, DAVID W. NAGORSEN,
R. MARK BRIGHAM AND JARED HOBBS

ROYAL **BC**
MUSEUM

VICTORIA, CANADA

Published by the Royal BC Museum, 675 Belleville Street, Victoria, British Columbia, V8W 9W2, Canada.

The Royal BC Museum is located on the traditional territories of the Lekwungen (Songhees and Xwsepsum Nations). We extend our appreciation for the opportunity to live and learn on this territory.

Substantive editing by Annie Mayse
Cover design, interior design and typesetting by Jeff Werner
Index by Stephen Ullstrom

Library and Archives Canada Cataloguing in Publication

Title: Bats of British Columbia / Cori L. Lausen, David W. Nagorsen, R. Mark Brigham and Jared Hobbs.
Names: Nagorsen, David W., author. | Lausen, Cori Lorraine, 1971- author. | Brigham, Robert Mark, 1960- author. | Hobbs, Jared, 1971- author.
Series: Royal British Columbia Museum handbook.
Description: Second edition. | Series statement: Royal BC Museum handbook | First edition authored by: David W. Nagorsen, R. Mark Brigham. | Includes bibliographical references and index.
Identifiers: Canadiana (print) 20210353503 | Canadiana (ebook) 2021035352X | ISBN 9780772679932 (softcover) | ISBN 9780772679949 (EPUB)
Subjects: LCSH: Bats—British Columbia. | LCSH: Bats—British Columbia—Identification.
Classification: LCC QL737.C5 N34 2022 | DDC 599.409711—dc23

10   9   8   7   6   5   4   3   2   1

Printed and bound in Canada by Hignell.

Contents

Cori Lausen examines the radio transmitter glued to this SPOTTED BAT before releasing it. Using radio receivers and a helicopter, researchers tracked this bat to a rock crevice high in a cliff wall along the Fraser River—the first SPOTTED BAT maternity roost discovered in this area.

Preface

The first edition of *Bats of British Columbia*, by David W. Nagorsen and R. Mark Brigham, was published in 1993. After three printings, it went out of print. Since then, an explosion in field studies of the province's bat fauna, applying new tools, such as genetic techniques and acoustic bat detectors, has added a wealth of new knowledge. Additionally, bat distributions shift and new species have been documented in the province. It is therefore time for a new edition, updating British Columbia's species list and range maps, and describing new ecological, genetic and behavioural findings. We present new keys for differentiating species morphologically and acoustically, and have incorporated a whole new section on bat echolocation, using bat detectors as tools for differentiating species and monitoring populations.

As with the 1993 handbook, much of the information in this edition is directed toward a general audience, biologists new to the study of bats, and naturalists, with emphasis on identification, natural history, distribution and conservation. As terminology may be unfamiliar to some readers, we have included an extensive glossary, with glossary terms in coloured font the first time they appear in the text. Although the book is focused on the bat fauna of BC, most of the species covered occur in other parts of the western United States, Canada and Alaska, and some also occur in eastern North America. One major change in this edition is the use of colour images throughout the book; unless otherwise noted in a photo credit, all of the photos in the book were taken by Jared Hobbs before the COVID-19 pandemic.

We have made many changes to the text. The introductory General Biology chapter has been completely revised to reflect new information about bats in BC. We've expanded the Conservation section to describe new threats from the white-nose syndrome fungus and bat fatalities at wind energy sites. The Identifying BC's Bats chapter has been enhanced with colour images of diagnostic traits. With the integration of bat detectors and mobile devices, such as smartphones, recording bat sounds is now possible for citizen scientists. We have therefore included an entirely new section on echolocation to guide readers on the use of acoustic sounds recorded with bat detectors, and each species account now has a subsection on acoustic identification. Other revisions within the species accounts include updated colour range maps, spectrograms illustrating the species' echolocation call characteristics, and conservation status. In addition to the 15 bat species that occur in BC, three bats (two only recently discovered) are covered in an Accidental Species section with their own species accounts.

While there is something in the book for all audiences, it should be stressed that live bats and bats found dead should only be handled (e.g., for purposes of species identification, including measurements) by qualified individuals who have been vaccinated for the rabies virus (see Disease and Bats, page 52).

We hope this book will create an appreciation for this fascinating group of mammals and provide impetus for their conservation.

GRAY-HEADED FLYING FOX is a megabat endemic to forested areas of southeastern Australia.

Introduction

Folklore generally portrays bats negatively. Their close association with the darkness of night has undoubtedly fostered this negative image. Unfortunately, bats are all too often regarded as blood-sucking, parasite-ridden, disease-carrying vermin; all of these assertions are incorrect. As our understanding of bat ecology has improved, we have also gained an understanding of bats as "keystone" species—species that play key roles in shaping the ecosystems of which we are a part. Around the globe, bats fulfill several important ecological roles—controlling insect populations, pollinating plants, dispersing seeds and even providing humans with medicines (e.g., the vampire bat's saliva is used as an anticoagulant to treat human stroke victims) and avenues for medical research (e.g., bat longevity is being studied to understand how humans might live longer). Yet despite their importance to the planet's ecosystems, there remains more misinformation than fact and more fear than respect for these diminutive guardians of the night.

Bats are a diverse group of relatively long-lived, slow-reproducing mammals. There are more than 1,400 species of bats worldwide. They occupy every continent except Antarctica and can be found in virtually every type of habitat, from desert to forest. Although bat diversity is highest in tropical and subtropical regions, bats have been incredibly successful at colonizing a diverse array of ecological niches over almost all parts of the globe, with the exception of the polar regions.

Although the vast majority of bats are small, weighing less than 50 grams (equivalent to seven loonies; all BC bats fall into this category), they do come in a large range of sizes. The largest are the flying foxes of Asia, Africa and Australia, which may attain a body mass of more than 1 kilogram and a wingspan of 2 metres (see image on facing page). Despite their formidable size, flying foxes are harmless fruit-eaters. The smallest bat in the world is the rare BUMBLEBEE BAT of Thailand, with a mass of about 2 grams and a wingspan of 15 centimetres. About three-quarters of the world's bats consume insects and other invertebrates, but there are species in the tropics that prey on vertebrates, such as frogs, reptiles, fish, birds and small mammals, including other bat species. The most specialized of all the mammalian predators are the three species of vampire bats of the New World continents (North and South America), which feed exclusively on the blood of birds and mammals.

It could be argued that using the word *bat* has been counterproductive to bat conservation. Use of this broad term, encompassing such a diverse group of animals, may draw attention away from the differences that exist among bat species in their foraging and drinking habitat requirements and, most importantly, in their selection of day roosts both in summer and winter. By comparison, we rarely refer to "ungulates" or "hoofed mammals" when talking about horses, giraffes, deer, elk and elephants. We know these animals are very different, with different physiology, diets and habitat requirements, and we typically call ungulate species by name rather than by "ungulate." But for most people, it does not seem odd to say "bat," and rarely do they refer to LITTLE BROWN MYOTIS or BIG BROWN BAT by their species names. It seems that both the large diversity of Chiroptera and the cryptic nature of these creatures keeps society from needing to identify these species by name.

Origins and Classification

Bats are the only flying mammals. They are also nocturnal, foraging for food at night. These traits have afforded bats an ecological and evolutionary ability to diversify, capitalizing on foraging opportunities available only to nocturnal flying mammals. Some species fly fast, typically high above the forest canopy, while others fly slowly, just above the forest understorey. Some species restrict their foraging to relatively open environments, while others nimbly manoeuvre through densely cluttered forest environments. They are not only diverse but plentiful: approximately 20% of the world's mammals are bats with more than 1400 species worldwide.

In contrast to the diversity of bats in tropical areas, the bat faunas of the United States and Canada may appear relatively mundane; at first glance, many species have evolved a similar morphology. Some species of the genus *Myotis* look so similar that only an expert can tell them apart, even when the bat is examined in the hand. Acoustic characteristics based on recorded bat echolocation calls can also be remarkably similar, which further confounds accurate species identification. Despite similar morphology, their ecology sets them apart, and we explore this fascinating field of study in this book.

The origin of bats remains obscure and controversial. A genetic study using molecular clocks placed the origin of bats around 66 to 70 million years ago, just before the mass extinction that eliminated the dinosaurs. Proto-bats were likely tree-dwelling insectivores with rudimentary gliding capabilities. Although studies have long suggested that bats evolved in a group composed of primates, colugos and tree shrews, recent molecular genetic studies refute this and instead place bats in the group Laurasiatheria, which includes shrews, whales, carnivores and even-toed ungulates. What is clear is that despite the popular perception of bats as "flying mice," they show no close relationship to rodents. While bats are among the most diverse groups of extant mammals, they are among the least common groups in the fossil record. Nevertheless, bat fossils have been found on every continent.

One of the most important deposits of bat fossils in the world is in Green River, Wyoming. Remarkably well-preserved bat skeletons from the Green River Eocene formation (53 to 49 million years old) belonging to the genus *Onychonycteris* appear to be among the most ancestral bats yet found. Their wing bones are consistent with some form of powered flight, and their teeth suggest that they ate insects, but their preserved ear bones indicate that they were incapable of using echolocation. Other intriguing features include their long limbs, the presence of claws on all their hand digits, and their robust hind limbs, so they were probably agile climbers. Wing and tail shape suggest that these early bats retained some ability to glide in addition to flapping their wings for sustained lift. While the eye morphology of these ancestral bat fossils could not be assessed, there are living bats that fly successfully at night using eyesight rather than echolocation (most Megachiroptera—see below), so we assume they could have successfully navigated at night, although the lack of echolocation would have made it hard to catch aerial insects. They may have detected their prey using vision, smell or listening for prey-generated sounds. By the middle Eocene (approximately 45 million years ago), the diversification of bats was well underway, and many of the modern families are represented among fossil forms from this time.

Today, bats are a highly successful group and are widespread, diverse and numerous. They are distinct enough from other mammals that taxonomists classify them in their own order, Chiroptera, which means "hand-wing." The living species of Chiroptera were traditionally subdivided into two major groups: the Microchiroptera, or microbats, which typically use echolocation, and the Megachiroptera, or megabats, of the family Pteropodidae, found on the continents of Asia, Africa and Australia, which have large eyes, feed on fruit and do not possess laryngeal echolocation abilities (see image on page viii). However, recent genetic research has shown that these are not natural groups. The order Chiroptera is now split into two different groups: the Yinpterochiroptera, including the Pteropodidae and six other families formerly grouped with the microbats, and the Yangochiroptera, a group that includes the other 14 families of microbats.

Beyond the relatively narrow focus of this guide, in other parts of the world, bats have evolved to succeed in many different niches. In many tropical and subtropical regions, fruit-eating bats are important dispersers of plant seeds, which they transport in ingested fruit and deposit during their nightly forays, and many species play a vital role as pollinators. Although we do not have any of these exotic forms in BC, one BC species, PALLID BAT, has been known to transport pollen among night-flowering cactus in the Sonoran Desert.

Across the United States there are approximately 47 species of bats, and less than half of these make it into Canada. In BC there are 18 species, the highest diversity of anywhere in the country. These include three accidental (irregularly occurring) species: BIG FREE-TAILED BAT, BRAZILIAN FREE-TAILED BAT and CANYON BAT. The remaining 15 species are regular residents in at least parts of

BC. These 15 native species belong to the family Vespertilionidae, a large family that ranges farther into temperate regions than any other bat family. CANYON BAT, which we consider accidental, is also in the family Vespertilionidae. By contrast, the other two accidental species, BRAZILIAN FREE-TAILED BAT and BIG FREE-TAILED BAT are both members of the family Molossidae (free-tailed bats).

Vespertilionid bats are relatively small-bodied and almost exclusively insect-eating, with some notable exceptions, including PALLID BAT, which has been found preying on scorpions, in addition to its relatively newly discovered tendency to eat nectar in some parts of its range. They are a fascinating group, as many have evolved special adaptations to cope with the severe conditions of temperate winters. In this book, we describe BC's 18 species and present our current knowledge of the distribution and ecology of these bats in the province.

Taxonomy and Nomenclature

Biologists use a system of classification to describe all life on earth. This system uses a hierarchy of taxonomic categories ranging from the kingdom (the most general category) to the species (the most basic). Species are grouped into higher taxonomic categories based on their presumed relationships. The 1,400 or so known species of bats are classified by taxonomists into 21 families; only two of these families, the Vespertilionidae and Molossidae, are represented in BC. All bats belong to the mammalian order Chiroptera.

CANYON BAT approaches insect prey. PHOTO: MICHAEL
DURHAM/MINDEN PICTURES (BAT CONSERVATION INTERNATIONAL)

Each species has a unique scientific name, or binomen (Latin for "double name"), consisting of the genus followed by the species name. By convention, the binomen is italicized, with the genus capitalized and the species name in lower case. For example, the scientific name for LITTLE BROWN MYOTIS is *Myotis lucifugus*. Closely related species that share similar morphological traits and a close genetic relationship are usually grouped in the same genus. About 130 species are recognized in the genus *Myotis*; 8 occur in BC. A further subdivision into subspecies, although considered relatively subjective, has traditionally been used to describe subgroups within a species that have different traits. These distinct geographic races or subspecies are recognized formally by taxonomists with a trinomen. *Myotis lucifugus alascensis*, for example, is a dark subspecies of LITTLE BROWN MYOTIS associated with coastal regions of the western United States and BC. The use of the subspecies category to name distinct geographic races of a species is controversial among taxonomists. Many of the subspecies or races listed in this book were described decades ago based on colour or physical traits; some are inconsistent with the groups revealed by genetics. For example, genetic data suggest that coastal and Interior populations of TOWNSEND'S BIG-EARED BAT in BC, once treated as separate subspecies, are members of a single subspecies. The boundaries and validity of the three subspecies of LITTLE BROWN MYOTIS originally thought to occur in the province are now in doubt (see What Is a Species?, page 6). More details on taxonomic status and subspecies can be found in the individual species accounts in this book.

The scientific and common names of bat species used in this book are based on *Bats of the World: A Taxonomic and Geographic Database* (Nancy Simmons and Andrea Cirranello, batnames.org) as this source is the authority on bat names and classification, and is kept up to date. This is important in light of the taxonomic changes rapidly being proposed for bats, stemming from an increasing number of molecular analyses. It's important to remember that the common names for many bats are somewhat contrived and are rarely used by scientists. Moreover, recent attempts to standardize English common names has led to some confusion, and several species retain alternative common names that are still used. For example, in older publications NORTHERN MYOTIS is listed as NORTHERN LONG-EARED MYOTIS, and CANYON BAT is called WESTERN PIPISTRELLE.

Taxonomy is a dynamic science. Since the 1993 edition of *Bats of British Columbia*, there has been an explosion in the application of new genetic techniques, such as the sequencing of mitochondrial and nuclear DNA in systematic and taxonomic studies. Genetic profiles have revealed new insights into our understanding of the relationships among bat species and their classification. Although this genetic work has given rise to recommendations to split some species into multiple new species (see What Is a Species? below), none of the bats found in the province have actually been subdivided into new species. However, the subspecies of WESTERN SMALL-FOOTED MYOTIS found in BC has been elevated to a species by authorities (DARK-NOSED SMALL-FOOTED MYOTIS), and we treat it as a full species. KEEN'S MYOTIS, recognized as a species in the 1993 edition, has insufficient genetic difference to be recognized as a valid species and is treated in this edition as a coastal race of LONG-EARED MYOTIS. Several species have undergone generic name changes. For example, TOWNSEND'S BIG-EARED BAT is now placed in the genus *Corynorhinus* instead of *Plecotus*, a genus now restricted to the Old World.

What Is a Species?

Until recently, the "biological species concept" largely dominated the way we define a species—a group of interbreeding individuals living in populations reproductively isolated from other populations. With the development of powerful genetic techniques applying analytical DNA methods, more definitions of *species* have arisen. The "phylogenetic species concept" is less restrictive than the biological species concept, requiring only that individuals share a unique evolutionary history, and breeding between members of different species does not pose a problem. A species represents a branch of ancestor-descendant populations that maintain their genetic identity from other such lineages. The "genetic species concept" defines a species as a group of genetically compatible interbreeding natural populations that is genetically—but not necessarily reproductively—isolated from other such groups. And more species definitions exist! In other words, defining species has become increasingly fuzzy.

How important it is to define *species* based on degree of interbreeding, and morphological variation versus phylogenetic ancestry; how much genetic differentiation is enough to warrant a species-level categorization; and which species concepts should be used under which situations—these are questions underpinning debates in countless papers and books. Some scientists argue that species need to be differentiated based on some recognizable trait (physical, ecological, behavioural), rather than just genetic signatures. Indeed, traditional management and conservation strategies rely on our being able to identify and delineate species. It has been argued that a new system of recognizing groups with genetic differentiation or uniqueness may be needed, separate from the traditional classification of species that recognizes breeding patterns, geography, morphology and ecology.

A case in point is LITTLE BROWN MYOTIS, a species for which five subspecies were thought to exist, although extensive geographic overlap, interbreeding and ecological mixing has occurred since the last glaciation (during which time substantial genetic variation accumulated in the isolated groups of this species— today's subspecies). A study completed in southern Alberta and north-central Montana confirmed disparate mitochondrial genomes identifying two otherwise indistinct subspecies of LITTLE BROWN MYOTIS present in the same roosting clusters in buildings, breeding and raising young together, with no morphological way to distinguish between them. The researchers concluded that although there was significant retained genetic variance from the last glaciation present in the mitochondrial genome of these two groups of bats, no morphological, geographic or behavioural trait could be used to determine which roost-mate was technically which subspecies, and as such recommended that at least one of the subspecies designations be dropped. The authors instead supported the idea of a new "barcode-based" species concept to recognize genetic differences (e.g., genetically significant units) that could be useful in categorizing variation in life forms, while leaving intact a taxonomic system relevant to conservation and management. Subsequently, a group of genetic researchers proposed instead to elevate all five subspecies of LITTLE BROWN MYOTIS to species status based on their evolutionary past. While taxonomic authorities have not changed species and subspecies categorizations for LITTLE BROWN MYOTIS to date, these disparate studies highlight the importance of defining what is meant by *species* to appropriately interpret and apply findings from genetic studies.

Checklist of BC Bats

Bats represent nearly 20% of small mammal diversity in BC. There are 15 species of bats that are reasonably well documented in the province and an additional 3 for which there are sparse records to date.

Below, families, genera and species within a genus are ordered alphabetically. Names of the authority who described the species follow the scientific name. If the species was originally described under a different genus, the authority is given in parentheses.

In addition to species accounts, there are three identification keys in this book to describe and differentiate these species based on their general morphology (Appendix 3), their skulls and teeth (Appendix 2), and their sounds (Appendix 4).

Order Chiroptera: Bats

Family Vespertilionidae: Vespertilionid Bats

Antrozous pallidus (Le Conte)	PALLID BAT
Corynorhinus townsendii (Cooper)	TOWNSEND'S BIG-EARED BAT
Eptesicus fuscus (Palisot de Beauvois)	BIG BROWN BAT
Euderma maculatum (J.A. Allen)	SPOTTED BAT
Lasionycteris noctivagans (Le Conte)	SILVER-HAIRED BAT
Lasiurus cinereus (Palisot de Beauvois)	HOARY BAT
Lasiurus borealis (Müller)	EASTERN RED BAT
Myotis californicus (Audubon and Bachman)	CALIFORNIAN MYOTIS
Myotis evotis (H. Allen)	LONG-EARED MYOTIS
Myotis lucifugus (Le Conte)	LITTLE BROWN MYOTIS
Myotis melanorhinus Merria	DARK-NOSED SMALL-FOOTED MYOTIS
Myotis septentrionalis (Trouessart)	NORTHERN MYOTIS
Myotis thysanodes Miller	FRINGED MYOTIS
Myotis volans (H. Allen)	LONG-LEGGED MYOTIS
Myotis yumanensis (H. Allen)	YUMA MYOTIS
Parastrellus hesperus (H. Allen)	CANYON BAT*

Family Molossidae: Molossid Bats

Nyctinomops macrotis (Gray)	BIG FREE-TAILED BAT*
Tadarida brasiliensis (I. Geof. St.-Hilaire)	BRAZILIAN FREE-TAILED BAT*

*Accidental occurrence—no current evidence of breeding populations and/or no specimens/captures

Bats in BC

Encompassing some 950,000 square kilometres and spanning 11 degrees of latitude and 25 degrees of longitude, British Columbia has the most diverse physiography and climate of any Canadian province. A series of north-south–oriented mountain ranges dominates the landscape and plays a major role in the province's climate, intercepting Pacific weather systems as they move eastward, creating alternating wet-dry belts. The wettest regions are associated with the Pacific coast, especially the western slopes of the coastal mountain ranges and the outer coasts of Vancouver Island and Haida Gwaii. East of the Coast Mountains, rain-shadow effects create a large arid region, the Interior Plateau. More extreme arid conditions are found in some of the southern Interior valleys, such as the Okanagan and Thompson River valleys. Other wet-dry belts are associated with the Cassiar Mountains, Rocky Mountains and Columbia Mountains (Cariboo, Monashee, Selkirk and Purcell ranges).

The vegetation of the province is predominately coniferous forest, although deciduous forest is associated with northern boreal regions and riparian habitats along rivers and lakes. Grassland and shrub-steppe habitats occur in some of the arid southern Interior valleys. Grassy alpine tundra and scrubby willow-birch habitats are common in northern BC and at high elevations in southern parts of the province. (For more information on the ecological classifications of BC, see Distribution, page 130.)

British Columbia supports the highest bat diversity (at least 15 species) of any Canadian province, a fact that can be largely attributed to the province's ecosystem diversity. Because of their mobility, bats are less impeded by physical barriers, such as water bodies (e.g., lakes and rivers), than terrestrial mammals. In contrast to small rodents and shrews, bat distributions in the province are not defined or constrained by major rivers like the Fraser, Thompson and Skeena. Bats have also managed to colonize most of the islands off the BC coast, including Haida Gwaii. In fact, on some BC islands, bats are the most diverse group of small mammals: Haida Gwaii has only one native shrew and one native mouse, but supports at least four bat species (LITTLE BROWN MYOTIS, LONG-EARED MYOTIS, CALIFORNIAN MYOTIS and SILVER-HAIRED BAT); further work might reveal more. Similarly, Vancouver Island has only six native species of mice and shrews but at least nine bat species (LITTLE BROWN MYOTIS, LONG-EARED MYOTIS, LONG-LEGGED MYOTIS, HOARY BAT, SILVER-HAIRED BAT, TOWNSEND'S BIG-EARED BAT, YUMA MYOTIS, CALIFORNIAN MYOTIS and BIG BROWN BAT).

On a provincial scale, bat diversity is greatest at low latitudes and elevations. Bats are most diverse in zones defined by shrub-steppe grassland and PONDEROSA PINE forest. With 14 summer resident species, the arid south Okanagan Valley has the highest diversity. In fact, the Okanagan has the greatest known variety and population density of bats in Canada. The number of species declines at high

Top to bottom, left to right: Shrub-steppe habitat north of Kamloops Lake. Coastal rainforest habitat on Vancouver Island. Sage grassland habitat in the South Okanagan. Northern (boreal) forest near Fort Nelson. The Fraser River, near Lillooet, is a biodiversity hotspot for BC's bat species. The Kootenay region, near Elk Lake Provincial Park. The Interior DOUGLAS-FIR forest along the Stein River exemplifies this habitat type, which occurs widely across BC. But tracts of old-growth mature forest, as shown here, are becoming increasingly rare as they are lost to logging.

latitudes. For example, there are records of eight species (SILVER-HAIRED BAT, LONG-EARED MYOTIS, BIG BROWN BAT, LITTLE BROWN MYOTIS, LONG-LEGGED MYOTIS, HOARY BAT, EASTERN RED BAT and NORTHERN MYOTIS) in northern BC, although more may be arriving over time, with recent acoustic records suggesting YUMA MYOTIS in the Atlin area. Similarly, lower bat diversity is evident with increasing elevation. Even in southern regions, few species are found at elevations above 1,500 metres.

Climate and the availability of roosting sites are major factors determining the distributional patterns and species diversity trends for bats. Roosting sites are likely scarce in subalpine or alpine habitats, and this may contribute to the low diversity of bats at higher elevations. In contrast, the Okanagan, with its cliffs, abundant rock crevices and mudstone erosion holes, and open forests, has a rich assortment of potential roosting sites, promoting a diverse fauna. Temperature, however, probably has the greatest impact on bat distributions in the province. Summer is a critical season because breeding female bats must give birth to, and raise, young in a limited window of time when insect prey are abundant. Roost temperatures need to be sufficiently warm to support pup growth. In late summer, both adults and young must accumulate sufficient fat reserves if they are to successfully hibernate over the winter. Environments at high latitude or elevation, with cool summer night temperatures, cooler roosts and a shorter growing season, make life more difficult for bats, and this likely accounts for the reduced species diversity in these areas.

Similarly, the winter range of BC bats is likely tied to temperature and the availability of suitable hibernacula. Bats are known to hibernate in the province as far north as Williston Reservoir (greater than 56°N), and some species likely hibernate at even higher latitudes. Maternity colonies of LITTLE BROWN MYOTIS have been found as far north as 60°N in northern BC, 63.5°N at Mayo, Yukon, and at 65°N at Fairbanks, Alaska. There are reports of LITTLE BROWN MYOTIS north of the Arctic Circle. These northern populations of this widespread species presumably also overwinter in northern regions, based on records of seasonal migrations of only hundreds of kilometres. The most northerly winter observation of LITTLE BROWN MYOTIS was in coastal Alaska, at 65.5°N, and hibernation of this species has now been well documented in rock crevices and tree root wads in southeast Alaska. What limits the northern extent of hibernation is not well understood, but because underground conditions can reflect surface temperatures, hibernation is likely to occur only in areas where underground temperatures reliably remain above freezing. These conditions may change with climate change, which may also shift bat hibernation habitats over time. Cold northern hibernacula may provide refuge from the fungal disease white-nose syndrome, as the fungus does not grow well at temperatures just above freezing.

References

Baker and Bradley (2006); Blejwas et al. (2021); Burgin et al. (2018); Frick, Heady and Hayes (2009); Gunnell and Simmons (2005); Haase et al. (2021); Hranac et al. (2021); Humphries, Thomas and Speakman (2002); Jung and Kukka (2016); Lausen et al. (2008); Lausen et al. (2019); McClure et al. (2020); Meredith et al. (2011); Morales and Carstens (2018); Simmons and Cirranello (2020); Simmons et al. (2008); Slough et al. (2022); Tessler, Snively and Gotthardt (2014); Wheeler and Meier (2000).

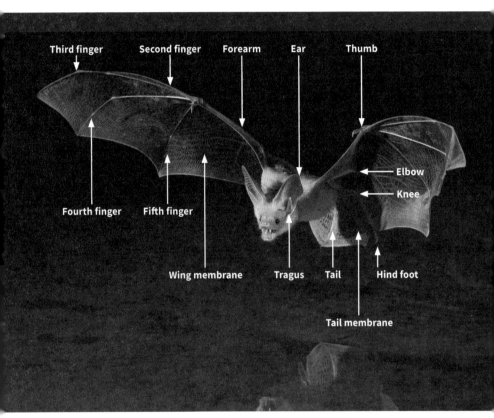

PALLID BAT in flight. Labels denote morphology referred to in this book.

General Biology

Morphology

Bats are the only mammals that can fly. All have forelimbs modified for flight, though wing size and form vary among species. Their wings possess exceptional load-carrying capability and, depending on the species, they can hover, fly exceptionally fast or be remarkably manoeuvrable. The wing consists of a thin, double-layered membrane of skin stretched between the arms, hands and fingers. The skin of bat wings is unique among vertebrates in its abundant and distinctive nerve endings. It is also significantly thinner than the skin of other comparably sized mammals and is thus low in mass despite its large surface area. Another flight membrane, the tail membrane, extends between the hind legs and tail. These membranes contain elastin fibres, making them elastic and flexible, and in adults are relatively tough and resistant to tearing. The skin contains blood vessels that are important for thermoregulation, and muscles that stretch and relax the flight membranes. In most bat species, the surfaces of the wing and tail membranes are devoid of hair, which reduces drag when the bat is in flight, although the regions around the upper arm and base of tail are often furred. The bones of the arm, hand and fingers provide the internal support for the wing. They follow the usual mammalian structure of an upper arm, forearm, wrist, and hand with a thumb and four fingers. In Pteropodidae (flying foxes, see image on page viii), the thumb and the first finger (second digit) after the thumb have a claw, but in the rest of the families only the thumb is clawed. Clawed thumbs are used for moving around in the roost or sometimes on the ground, climbing and grooming. The clawed second finger in Pteropodidae may additionally facilitate handling of fruit for consumption.

The finger and hand bones in a bat's wing are greatly elongated in comparison to those of humans. Compared to the wings of other vertebrate flyers, like birds and pterosaurs, the bat wing has many more bones and joints. While resting, bats draw the finger bones together and hold the arms against the body, probably to reduce the risk of injury to the wing. When the bat is in flight, the arms are held out to the sides with the fingers spread apart. Bat fingers have among the thinnest and most delicate of mammalian bones, and, unlike all other vertebrate wing bones, they are not hollow. This architecture promotes bending, which helps the bat's wings act as an airfoil to produce lift to keep the animal aloft and thrust to push it forward. The inside portion of the wing,

These images of a PALLID BAT show how wing shape changes with the upstroke and downstroke to adopt a lift-enhancing cambered shape.

between the body and the fifth finger produces most of the lift; movement of the wing tip (from fifth finger to the edge) generates most of the thrust. Because the wing skin is so flexible, the aerodynamic forces experienced during flight readily change the three-dimensional shape of the membrane, which has a far less structured form than the wings of birds. The membrane of the wings deflects when flapped and passively adopts a lift-enhancing cambered shape.

The complex movement of the wing in straight flapping flight generally resembles the motion of a bird's wing. The downstroke provides the main propulsion and results in the body being pushed forward and up. During the upstroke, the wings move upward and backward, resulting in a forward and downward force. During this phase of the wing cycle, the leading edge of the wing is turned up to increase lift and reduce the magnitude of the force pushing the bat downward. The power that moves the wing through the down stroke, and thus propels the bat, comes principally from the chest muscles. Unlike birds, bats lack a well-developed keel on the breastbone. This gives bats a relatively narrow profile through the chest and enables them to squeeze into narrow openings to access roosting sites.

Depending on their size and flight speed, most bats typically beat their wings 10 to 20 times per second, a slower rate than for a similar-sized bird. Flight speed is highly variable, but it probably ranges from about 7 to 36 kilometres per hour for BC species. Some species, such as PALLID BAT, interrupt flapping flight with brief bouts of gliding, holding their wings outstretched. Turns are executed by extending and turning the surface of the flight membrane in the direction of

The downstroke (top) lifts the bat up by pushing on the air below.
A CANYON BAT in flight (above) shows the downstroke and upstroke.

the turn while the other wing performs a normal flapping stroke. Bats that can turn quickly are described as "agile," whereas species that can turn sharply in a small space are described as "manoeuvrable." Agility and manoeuvrability are not necessarily linked. Fast-flying species, which are characterized by relatively long, narrow wings, tend to be highly agile but not very manoeuvrable. Slow-flying bats with short wings tend to be highly manoeuvrable.

Two measures can be used to characterize flight styles and are directly related to foraging habits: aspect ratio—a measure of wing shape (length divided by width)—and wing loading—the ratio of a bat's mass to its wing area. The higher the wing loading, the faster the bat must fly to generate lift, and, conversely, the lower the wing loading, the slower the bat can fly; the higher the aspect ratio (that is, the longer and narrower the wing), the more aerodynamic the bat will be. Bats with high aspect ratios and high wing loading tend to fly quickly and forage in the open (e.g., HOARY BAT); bats with low aspect ratios and low wing loading are slow and manoeuvrable, foraging in cluttered habitats (e.g., TOWNSEND'S BIG-EARED BAT). Bats that have low and high aspect-ratio/wing-loading combinations carve out separate niches; for example, EASTERN RED BATS have a high wing loading and low aspect ratio, making them fast flyers in cluttered habitats.

Flight is an expensive mode of locomotion. Flying bats consume energy at a rate three to five times that of a similar-sized running terrestrial mammal. But although flight is expensive, it has its advantages. Flying a unit of distance—for example, 1 kilometre—requires about a quarter of the energy it would take a terrestrial mammal to move the same distance on the ground. Although bats use energy quickly while flying, they can cover a large distance for a relatively low cost.

Because bats do not walk on their hind legs, these are relatively small and weak. Their usual resting position—hanging upside down by the feet—has led to some peculiar features in the hind legs. The knee points backward rather than forward. The five toes each end in a sharp claw for gripping the surface that bats hang from, which is also used extensively in grooming. A tail membrane, if present, provides support for flight, capture of prey, and/or catching young as they are born. All bats in BC have tail membranes and a long cartilaginous spur called a calcar, which extends from an ankle bone along the outer edge of the tail membrane. Unique to bats, the calcar provides support for the tail membrane. A diagnostic feature used to distinguish some species is the presence or absence of a distinct keel on the calcar (see image on facing page).

Bat heads are dominated by the ears. Two of BC's species, TOWNSEND'S BIG-EARED BAT and SPOTTED BAT, have enormous ears that are nearly half the body length. Large ears are capable of hearing quieter sounds—not only the faint echoes of ultrasonic signals used in echolocation but also soft sounds produced by prey, such as the fluttering of moth wings or movement of insects along vegetation. Ear length varies greatly among bat species and can vary within a species to some extent.

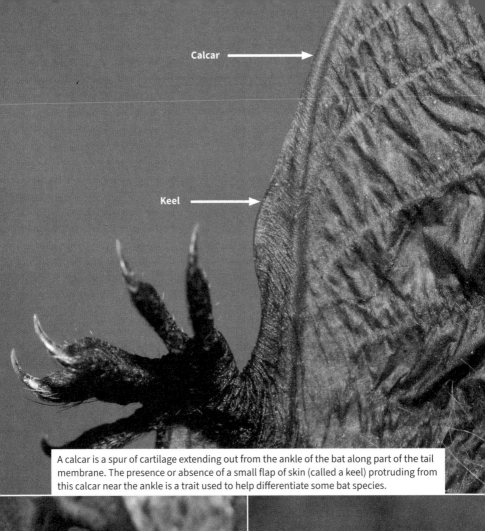

Calcar →

Keel →

A calcar is a spur of cartilage extending out from the ankle of the bat along part of the tail membrane. The presence or absence of a small flap of skin (called a keel) protruding from this calcar near the ankle is a trait used to help differentiate some bat species.

SPOTTED BAT is one of two "big-eared" bat species in BC. PHOTO: MICHAEL PROCTOR

TOWNSEND'S BIG-EARED BAT.

The Nubby-Ear Mystery

Ear length varies greatly among bat species and can vary within species to some extent. One noteworthy trait is something dubbed nubby ear or "square ear," where some individuals are mysteriously missing the tips of one or both of their ears. Many hypotheses have been offered, including frostbite, disease, birth defects, and burns that might have been acquired while roosting under a hot tin roof. Lausen and Heather Gates examined a large dataset of bat ear measurements (14,087 bats of 15 species) from BC and Alberta and found this phenomenon in only six species: BIG BROWN BAT (0.1% of 1,160), SILVER-HAIRED BAT (0.3% of 339), DARK-NOSED and WESTERN SMALL-FOOTED MYOTIS (0.2% of 1,182), LONG-LEGGED MYOTIS (0.5% of 211), LONG-EARED MYOTIS (0.1% of 689), and LITTLE BROWN MYOTIS and YUMA MYOTIS (1.5% of 9,060). There is a statistically significant difference among species, indicating that this phenomenon occurs most in the two myotis species commonly found roosting in buildings—YUMA and LITTLE BROWN. It is difficult to differentiate these two species morphologically (see LITTLE BROWN and YUMA MYOTIS species accounts), but for individuals whose identification could be resolved, LITTLE BROWN MYOTIS had the highest incidence of nubby ear (3.3% of 2,850). Evidence of these oddly shortened ears in both adult (1.4% of 6,603) and young-of-year (0.5% of 2,228) LITTLE BROWN and YUMA MYOTIS rules out frostbite as a possible cause (or at least as the only cause), because young-of-year will not yet have experienced a winter and potential exposure to freezing conditions. Among YUMA and LITTLE BROWN MYOTIS, nubby ear is found more often in females (1.6% of 6,542), but not statistically more than in males (1.1% of 2,471), and it is not clear if this is something that could be happening at maternity roosts, including buildings, where roosting bats are known to pack into the corrugations of a tin roof, inviting potential for burn-scarring of bats in direct contact with hot metal. Leah Rensel, Heather Gates and Susan Dulc have captured nubby-eared bats flying out of maternity roosts with fresh wounds on the tips of their ears, supporting the notion that nubby ears occur post-birth. Further study is needed to solve the nubby-ear mystery!

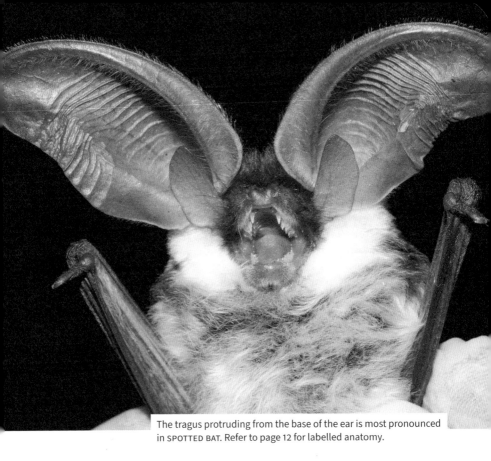

The tragus protruding from the base of the ear is most pronounced in SPOTTED BAT. Refer to page 12 for labelled anatomy.

All BC bats have a tragus, or "earlet," a fleshy protrusion from the inner base of the ear (clearly visible in the image above); this is used in echolocation, associated with acuity. Because its size and shape can vary among species, the tragus often provides a useful trait for identification.

Most bats outside of the Pteropodidae have small eyes that can sometimes be obscured by the fur. Presumably this led to the misconception that bats are blind, but while there is no doubt that all bats can see, we know little about the acuity of their vision or how much they rely on it. The size of bats' eyes varies by species, and the importance of their vision is also likely to vary.

Juvenile bats are born with deciduous milk teeth that are shed and replaced by a permanent set of teeth by two to three weeks of age. Their milk teeth are highly specialized, with tiny sharp points that enable a suckling bat to attach to its mother's nipple. The replacement of the milk teeth occurs when the juvenile bat is weaned and begins to eat solid food. The adult dentition of BC bats consists of well-developed teeth designed for chewing the hard bodies or exoskeletons of invertebrates. There are four basic types of teeth in the adult skull (see page 303): front teeth (incisors), eye teeth (canines) and cheek teeth (premolars and molars). The number of incisors and premolars varies among BC species, and this is another characteristic useful in identification (see Appendix 2). Size and structure of the teeth is linked to diet; species that prey on large, hard-shelled invertebrates are usually equipped with more robust teeth and stronger jaw musculature.

The bodies of most bats are covered with fur. Bat fur is typically uniform in length and not differentiated into long outer guard hairs and fine underfur, as is seen in many mammals. The thickest fur is found on migratory tree bats that roost in open situations (e.g., in foliage) where they are exposed to considerable variation in temperature; the furry tail membrane can be folded over the body like a blanket for insulation.

Although most bats in BC are dull brown or grey, a few of our species are beautifully coloured. For example, EASTERN RED BAT is rusty-red (see image on page 180), SPOTTED BAT is black with three white spots on its back (see image on page 170), and HOARY BAT (see image on page 187) and SILVER-HAIRED BAT (see image on page 197) have silver-tipped hairs that give their fur a striking frosted appearance. Species that are widespread across the province can vary considerably in fur colour, although one consistent pattern is that populations associated with humid coastal areas tend to be darker than those that inhabit arid environments in the dry Interior. The conventional explanation for this trend, which is called Gloger's rule, is that mammalian fur colour generally matches the background colour of the environment to provide camouflage. Mammals living in humid coastal areas tend to be darker to blend in with the dark dense vegetation. This explanation is not totally convincing because bats are active at night and spend the daytime hidden in dark roosting sites. Despite their rather conspicuous markings, the fur colour of tree bats does appear to be an adaptation for camouflage. EASTERN RED BAT, for example, appears remarkably similar to a dead leaf, and HOARY BAT resembles lichen-covered bark, with white or yellow spots and neck collars on each of these bats to break up their coloration for hiding among leaves.

References

Kurta and Kwiecinski (2007), Norberg (1987), Norberg and Norberg (2012), Norberg and Rayner (1987), Santana et al. (2011), Swartz and Konow (2015).

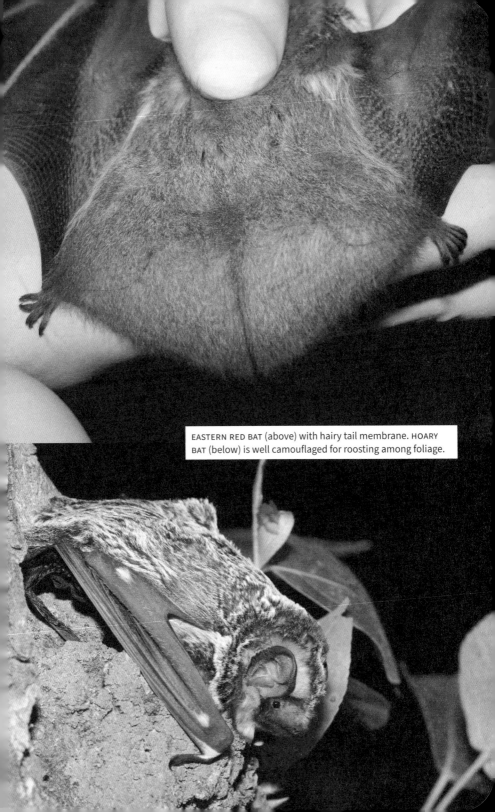

EASTERN RED BAT (above) with hairy tail membrane. HOARY BAT (below) is well camouflaged for roosting among foliage.

Using Sound to Locate Prey and Navigate in the Dark

Bats use their well-developed sense of hearing and tremendous neurological capacity for processing complex sound information in two distinct ways. One way is to listen for sounds generated by others, such as other bats or insect prey. Some large-eared species, like PALLID BAT, found in south-central BC, forage by listening for sounds made by prey on the ground, such as scorpions and crickets, before landing to scurry along in pursuit. Several other species of long- or big-eared bats (e.g., TOWNSEND'S BIG-EARED BAT and LONG-EARED MYOTIS) in BC similarly have evolved to listen for prey-generated sounds while they hover, homing in on insects that they glean off the surface of vegetation. But approximately two-thirds of all bats in the world have also evolved a highly sophisticated way of locating prey and navigating their environments: echolocation—location through use of echoes.

This orientation technique typically employs high-frequency sounds produced in the muscular "voice-box," or larynx, and emitted through the mouth or nose in a beam in front of the bat. When the sounds hit an object, they are reflected to the bat in the form of an echo. Results from laboratory studies suggest that these returning echoes provide the bat with an acoustic "image" of its environment that includes incredibly detailed information about the size, shape and movement of objects. Echolocation enables bats to navigate in the dark and to detect moving prey. All bats in BC echolocate, and some BC species, particularly those with large or long ears, take advantage of both echolocation and prey-generated sounds when foraging.

The frequency of most bat echolocation is above the threshold for human hearing: most bats produce sounds greater than 20,000 hertz (20 kilohertz), which humans cannot hear (see Acoustics: Echolocation and Species Identification, page 103). Frequencies above 20 kilohertz are thus referred to as ultrasound, or ultrasonic. For perspective, we humans have relatively pathetic hearing capabilities; most adults can only hear sounds up to approximately 10 kilohertz, though technically our brand new and highly sensitive ears at birth are capable of hearing twice this frequency. Not all bats go unheard by the human ear; several North American species echolocate in the audible range of human hearing. In BC, HOARY BAT can be heard by some listeners with sensitive hearing, as it dips to 15 kilohertz when flying in the open, and SPOTTED BAT is heard by many, as its echolocation calls typically end at an easily heard frequency of 8 kilohertz. Some bats in North America produce fundamental frequencies as high as 120 kilohertz, and in other parts of the world, some bats can echolocate at frequencies above 200 kilohertz! The vast majority of bats around the world generate the sounds used for echolocation using vocal cords in the larynx, although there are a couple of species that echolocate using sounds generated by tongue-clicking.

Echolocating bats adapt their acoustic calls through manipulation of frequency, intensity and harmonics (see Acoustics: Echolocation and Species Identification, page 103), and patterns of calls and call structure vary depending on the situation. The amount of time they spend producing a pulse of sound (call duration) varies with situation and among species, as does the amount of time they spend between calls listening for echoes. We are still studying the extent to which these echolocation signals are also used for communication, but there is mounting evidence that bats use others' signals to some extent (e.g., to "eavesdrop" on potential competitors).

Some insects have evolved strategies to avoid predation by bats. Certain noxious species produce sounds that may act as a warning signal to experienced bats that have learned to associate these sounds with bad-tasting prey. Tympanate moths, lacewings, praying mantids and crickets have ears that are sensitive to ultrasonic bat calls. Tympanate moths hear bats long before bats detect them because the moths' sensitive ears can hear bats from up to 100 metres away, while bats may only detect the moth from up to 10 metres away. Research on bats that glean their insect prey from surfaces has shown that their echolocation is adapted to use higher frequencies (i.e., greater than 50 kilohertz) and shorter-duration echolocation pulses (less than 1 millisecond) than can not be heard by tympanate moths. Other bats, such as SPOTTED BAT, have evolved echolocation calls at frequencies audible to humans, as these are likely not detected by their primary prey—noctuid moths—that hear the high frequencies of bat ultrasound. In fact, encounters between bats and some insects resemble the tactics of high-tech warfare between modern aircraft. When a bat is detected, the insect takes evasive action by moving away from the bat or, if it gets close, flying in a zigzag pattern or dropping to the ground to avoid capture. A few species, such as some tiger moths, have evolved a step further. Not only can they detect many bats' echolocation calls, but they can produce their own ultrasonic sounds as a defensive mechanism. These calls have been shown to interfere with the bat's echolocation system (termed "jamming"). Some bats will even "jam" other bats by altering their echolocation, causing their competition to miss their insect prey targets.

On the surface, echolocation sounds appear quite simple compared with sounds like bird song. In BC species, each pulse of sound generally begins at a high frequency and then rapidly drops to a lower frequency. This is called a frequency sweep, or frequency-modulated call, and the greater the difference between the highest and lowest frequencies in the call, the broader its bandwidth (see Acoustics: Echolocation and Species Identification, page 103, for further detail).

Whether a bat captures its prey on the wing (aerial hawking) or is able to snatch it from a surface (gleaning) depends on its morphology and ecology.

The structure and frequencies of bat echolocation calls vary among a large number of species, but variation within a species and even within an individual can be significant, depending on the context in which the echolocation occurs. Calls differ among populations depending on the nature of the habitat, and even within an individual as they respond to the objects in their air space. We can make some generalizations: the nature of echolocation calls is usually related to a species' hunting strategy and the type of habitat it occupies. Bats that detect prey at long distances in open areas tend to have relatively low-frequency calls, because low-frequency sounds travel farther than high-frequency sounds; higher-frequency calls are most effective at short range, and all bats generally take advantage of these as they approach objects closely.

Individual bats also vary their echolocation calls. When they are searching for insects or flying to a roost along a familiar route, they often emit only a few calls each second, but when closing in on a flying insect or approaching an unknown obstacle they can make hundreds of calls per second. Besides changing the duration and repetition rate of calls, bats can also modify their frequency, beam width (span of degrees on either side of the head) and intensity.

Echolocation has evolved with the form and ecological function of each different species of bat. As such, bat size, wing shape, prey type, behaviour and habitat selection are often tightly aligned with acoustic traits. For more on echolocation and using acoustics as a tool for bat species identification, see Acoustics: Echolocation and Species Identification, page 103.

References
Corcoran, Barber and Conner (2009); Corcoran and Conner (2014); Faure, Fullard and Dawson(1993); Fenton (1982); Fenton (2011); Fullard (1987); Griffin (1958); Jakobsen, Brinkløv and Surlykke (2013); Miller and Surlykke (2001).

Food and Water

All vespertilionid bats found in Canada feed exclusively on arthropods, an immense group of invertebrates that includes spiders, scorpions, harvestmen, centipedes, millipedes and insects. However, nocturnal flying insects are by far the most important prey for BC's bat species, and the variety of insects taken (including moths, flies, caddisflies, midges, beetles, lacewings, sawflies, grasshoppers, ants and termites) is impressive. Recent studies from Haida Gwaii, Yukon and the Northwest Territories have also provided increasing evidence that spiders are eaten by bats more often than once thought.

To obtain the energy needed to fuel flight, most bats must consume large quantities of food. During the summer, nursing females of temperate insectivorous species probably consume their own body mass each night! This rate of consumption necessarily translates into huge numbers of insects, hence the importance of bats as control agents. In an experiment done in the 1960s,

LITTLE BROWN MYOTIS released into a room of flying mosquitoes ate as many as 600 per hour. It has been estimated that the 20 million or so BRAZILIAN FREE-TAILED BATS that inhabit Bracken Cave in Texas consume about 100,000 kilograms (100 metric tonnes) of insects nightly. Estimates of the economic value of bats to humans in the United States suggest bats are worth billions of dollars annually to the agricultural industry.

Insectivorous bats employ several strategies to capture prey. They may hunt while flying or they may hang from a perch and wait for a passing insect to come within range. Some species use one of these strategies, whereas others have the flexibility to use both depending on the availability of prey and the time of night. Most BC bats hunt while continuously flying. Although this strategy probably ensures a high encounter rate with potential prey items, it also requires considerable energy. The high energy requirement has resulted in bats evolving efficient methods to capture and consume large numbers of insects. Many species are remarkable in their ability to detect and exploit rich ephemeral patches of food, such as a hatch of winged ants or termites. In addition, bats chew their food extremely quickly, up to seven times per second. BIG BROWN BAT has the ability to mount an attack on an insect every three seconds. This is an amazing feat when you consider that those three seconds includes the time required to chew captured prey and search for the next target.

Bats catch insects by scooping them with their tail membrane or wing and then biting them, or by catching prey directly with their mouth. Sometimes the motion of taking an insect from the tail membrane results in the bat doing a somersault in mid-air. An interesting observation was made by Alison George of Crawford Bay, BC, who witnessed a myotis bat hanging very close to a spider's web in her window, picking insects out of the web as they became entrapped.

Biologists have attempted to classify bats by the type of insects they eat, and labels like "moth specialist" or "beetle specialist" can be found in many publications; however, prey choice varies not only between species but also among populations of the same species and even on different nights for the same local population. For example, BIG BROWN BAT, found across much of North America, has often been classified as a beetle strategist or specialist, yet in the southern Okanagan Valley it was found to eat mainly soft-bodied caddisflies. The high incidence of aquatic insects in the diet can be attributed to the enormous abundance of these insects over various lakes and rivers in the area on summer nights. Interestingly, studies of eastern bat communities, following mass die-off of LITTLE BROWN MYOTIS due to white-nose syndrome, have reported substantial shifts in diet; for example, in southern Ontario, the diet of BIG BROWN BAT shifted to include a wider breadth of prey, including many of the insect species that were once largely consumed by LITTLE BROWN MYOTIS prior to their populations plummeting in that area. Food habits are specific to the local area and local bat assemblages; extrapolating information collected from other regions needs to be done with care. Research on diets and hunting strategies is essential to determine the role of bats in BC ecosystems. Information on diets for BC populations is based on a few species and has been obtained mostly from the Okanagan Valley. To what extent dietary data from the Okanagan can be extrapolated to other arid habitats in BC is unknown. Even less is known about the diet of bats associated with forested habitats in the province, such as the coastal old-growth forests. To date, few studies have focused on these regions. One BC study found that forest bats responded to WESTERN SPRUCE BUDWORM outbreaks, eating both the flying moth and dangling larval stages. A recent Investment Agriculture Foundation–sponsored genetics study by Felix Martinez and Patrick Burke found that myotis bats (YUMA MYOTIS, LITTLE BROWN MYOTIS and CALIFORNIAN MYOTIS) from Creston had ALFALFA WEEVIL in their guano. This suggests that bats likely play important roles in controlling a multitude of forest and agricultural pest insects. In BC, much effort goes into combatting forest insect pests through the BC Pest Management Plan, including wide-scale spraying of insecticides. Bats are likely important in keeping these costs lower than they would be otherwise, and the use of insecticides may be a detriment to bat populations that may otherwise provide more efficient natural insect control (see Conservation and Threats, page 57).

Bats typically emerge from their roosts around dusk to drink and forage. Some bats will come out earlier or later depending on local conditions, including sources of disturbance or perceived predation risk (e.g., presence of an owl, human disturbance). Some species—for example BIG BROWN BATS—seem to emerge at higher light levels (i.e., earlier) than others. As a rule of thumb, bats in BC typically emerge at civil twilight—after sunset, when there is still some daylight. Bats typically feed during one or several foraging bouts, sometimes roosting to rest and digest in between bouts (called night roosting; see Summer Roosting Sites, page 36). There are often two defined peaks in foraging activity during the night: one that lasts for a few hours after dusk and another later in the night before dawn. Depending on the temperature and the resulting activity levels of insects, bats may forage throughout the night. If the temperature cools to a point where aerial insects are no longer available (e.g., below 8°C to 10°C, but this is variable among locations), some bat species cease foraging, whereas those capable of finding and eating non-flying insects from surfaces like the ground or vegetation (i.e., gleaning bats, such as NORTHERN MYOTIS) may continue to forage in these cooler conditions.

Bats often seek water immediately after emerging from their roosts, especially following a hot day. This is particularly true of females nursing young. Opportunities to access drinking water might seem plentiful in BC, with the large number of drainages descending from mountaintops, but bats

Bats drink while in flight by dropping their bottom jaw into the water, thus requiring a calm surface. This PALLID BAT approached the water multiple times to get several mouthfuls of water.

need to drink on the wing. To do this, they approach the water's surface closely, dropping their bottom jaw to scoop water. They will typically repeat this several times, and depending on the reproductive stage of the bat, the level of humidity in their day roost (highest when there are many bats clustering together in a small space) and ambient temperature, they may drink several times throughout the night in summer. Nursing females will often drink multiple times in the night to offset water loss associated with milk production. Water that is moving too quickly or is too rough on its surface (e.g., turbulent from water moving over rocks, or disturbed by wind) is likely avoided by bats, as they risk being knocked into the water when approaching it. Additionally, rushing water is typically loud, producing not only audible sounds but sounds in the ultrasonic range that interfere with the bat's ability to hear the echoes of its echolocation calls, preventing accurate detection of the water's surface.

Different bat species appear to gravitate to different sizes of water bodies. This may be influenced by a combination of perceived predation risk and the bat's flight capabilities. More manoeuvrable bats (e.g., NORTHERN MYOTIS) are typically slower and less likely to outfly a predator in open air space, so a small puddle in a forest may be a more suitable drinking source than an open lake, which is more likely to be used by large, fast-flying, less manoeuvrable bats (e.g., HOARY BAT).

References

Boyles et al. (2011), Burles et al. (2008), Constantine and Blehert (2009), Kaupas and Barclay (2017), Kellner and Harestad (2005), Maclaughlan (2017), Morningstar et al. (2019), Rambaldini and Brigham (2011), Wilson and Barclay (2006).

Reproduction, Young and Longevity

Generally, small mammals (e.g., mice) tend to reproduce prolifically: females produce many young, often with multiple litters each year, and usually begin breeding in the same summer as their birth. Vespertilionid bats, however, do *not* follow this trend, and it is generally accepted that these are the slowest-reproducing mammals for their size. Canadian species generally produce only one litter each year, usually consisting of a single pup. Among BC species, foliage-roosting bats, such as EASTERN RED BAT and HOARY BAT (Lasiurines), are an exception, often producing a litter of two and sometimes as many as four young. Females of most species do not breed until they are more than a year old and may not successfully raise a pup each summer, depending on food availability, water supply and roost temperatures.

Some temperate bats mate in potential hibernation sites, such as mines or caves, during late summer or autumn, just before hibernation. For many species, the sexes roost separately and the periods just before and after hibernation are the only times of year when males and females are together. There is increasing evidence that some species will also mate in spring, although most mating probably occurs in autumn. Species that hibernate in mixed-sex groups have been found to mate mid-winter during periodic arousals from hibernation. In migratory species, such as HOARY BAT (see image of mating bats on page 193) and EASTERN RED BAT, mating takes place on the wing during migration, and discoveries of coupled carcasses under wind turbines (see Conservation and Threats, page 57) in autumn support this hypothesis.

The LITTLE BROWN MYOTIS mating system has been well studied. Males are promiscuous, mating apparently randomly with as many females as possible. Females may also mate with several males, with apparently little courtship behaviour. Males initiate mating by mounting and restraining the female. Females often struggle during the early stages of copulation, and males produce audible calls (5 to 12 kilohertz) that are hypothesized to pacify females. Most mating occurs before the hibernation period, when bats are still active. However, some mating occurs late in the season when the occasional active male attempts to copulate with torpid individuals, many of whom are other males.

In BC, Lausen and others have documented evidence of TOWNSEND'S BIG-EARED BAT, SILVER-HAIRED BAT and CALIFORNIAN MYOTIS mating during winter, and these same species, and YUMA MYOTIS, mating in spring. We do not fully understand when mating begins in BC each summer, but a video of what appears to be either two LITTLE BROWN or two YUMA MYOTIS mating on the ground among rocks was captured a few hours before dusk on August 25, 2020, by a Crawford Bay landowner with a maternity roost of these myotis in a building on their property (as reported by Kootenay Community Bat Project).

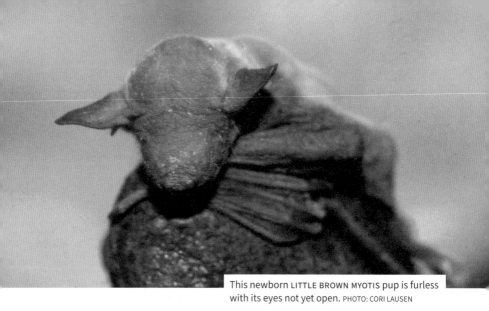

This newborn LITTLE BROWN MYOTIS pup is furless with its eyes not yet open. PHOTO: CORI LAUSEN

The testes of male bats in BC typically become scrotal mid-summer, and this involves the swelling and consequential descending of testes into the tail membrane (see Studying Bats, page 73). As with other mammals, sperm is produced and stored away from the body cavity so that they remain cooler than active body temperature. During sperm production, testosterone levels are high. After sperm production is complete, typically in late summer, the testes shrink and largely disappear back into the abdominal cavity, and testosterone production plummets. The decline in testosterone is associated with the onset of mating behaviour in bats, the exact opposite of most other male mammals, for which a spike of testosterone stimulates mating. Sperm is stored in long, narrow tubes called cauda epididymides (see Studying Bats, page 73), and the stored sperm is used when mating proceeds.

Temperate bats delay fertilization to ensure that their young are born at the appropriate time the following spring. Instead of fertilization occurring immediately after mating (the usual pattern for mammals), sperm is stored and actually nourished in the uterus of the female over winter. The following spring, females leave the hibernaculum and fly to the summer roost, where they usually form maternity colonies with other females of the same species. Ovulation and fertilization take place after the females have left the hibernaculum. The gestation period ranges from 7 to 10 weeks, depending on environmental conditions, with cold temperatures prolonging fetal development. Insects are low in calcium, and female bats need approximately 10 times more calcium to grow their fetus than is available from their diet. Female bats use calcium from their bones to produce and nurse their pups, and calcium supply constrains the size of the pups. It is not surprising that reproductive females and flying young-of-year have been found to drink at water sources that offer higher calcium content.

In Canada, baby bats (pups) are usually born in June or July, although pregnant females have been reported as late as early August in Yukon. Birth dates vary among years, among populations and even among females in the same colony. This variation in the parturition period results mainly from local climatic differences, although the age of a female may also affect the birth date. Newborns are large, often 25% to 30% of the mother's mass, but they are altricial (not fully developed) and helpless. The skin is pink with no fur, the eyes are closed and the ears are limp. Growth is rapid, however, and within a few days the eyes open, the ears become erect, the skin develops pigmentation, and the fur begins to grow. Juveniles tend to have darker, duller and shorter fur than adults. Juvenile pelage is replaced within one or two months. Young bats are equipped with sharp recurved milk teeth used to attach to the mother's nipple; this is an important adaptation when the mother flies with the pup, which must hold on via the milk teeth latched onto the teat, as the mother has no means with which to hold the pup during flight. The milk teeth are replaced by permanent dentition about the time young first begin flying and taking solid food. Although timing varies geographically and temporally, and is different among the species, young are typically adult size and flying on their own after three weeks of nursing. Weaning (the time when young begin to eat solid food) is typically at six weeks of age for many BC species, and is linked to proficient use of echolocation, mastering of flight and having the ability to feed on insects.

The age of sexual maturity is known for only a few species. In BC and Alberta, there is evidence of young-of-year males producing sperm, suggesting they can breed in their first year. This has been seen in HOARY BAT, LITTLE BROWN MYOTIS, SILVER-HAIRED BAT, CALIFORNIAN MYOTIS, NORTHERN MYOTIS, FRINGED MYOTIS, LONG-LEGGED MYOTIS and YUMA MYOTIS. Females may also be capable of breeding in their first summer, although this is often more difficult to discern in hand unless the bat was banded (see image on page 84) in the previous year to verify its age. There is mounting evidence that many female YUMA MYOTIS mate before they are one year old (see YUMA MYOTIS species account, page 271).

In vespertilionid bats, parental care is the sole responsibility of the female, and males are typically not present in the maternity colony. A strong bond develops between a mother and her young, with both producing a variety of calls for communication. During the day, the pup remains attached to its mother and frequently nurses; at night it is left behind in the roost while the mother forages. In some species, including BIG BROWN BAT, and LITTLE BROWN, YUMA and FRINGED MYOTIS, there is evidence that a few adult females will remain behind in the roost to act as babysitters. One of the more intriguing aspects of mother-infant relations is how a mother recognizes her own young, even in large colonies that may contain hundreds or even thousands of pups. Evidently

Pre-volant pup being carried by adult female (netted in flight).

a mother can identify its baby based on its position in the colony, calls (called isolation calls) and odour. There is some evidence that in a few species, such as LITTLE BROWN MYOTIS, infants can also recognize the echolocation calls of their mothers. If disturbed, most female bats can fly to a new roost site with pups attached, even those close to adult size. This demonstrates the ability of bat wings to lift considerable mass.

Most vespertilionid bats in temperate regions have remarkably long lifespans. For example, a lifespan of 19 years has been recorded for wild BIG BROWN BATS, and there are records of LITTLE BROWN MYOTIS living more than 38 years (see LITTLE BROWN MYOTIS species account, page 227). Although individual bats can potentially live a long life, many factors, in addition to low reproductive rates, limit the population size of bats. Mortality is probably greatest for hibernating juveniles during their first winter. This is not surprising, given that in the first three months of life juveniles must learn to fly and master echolocation to the extent that they can detect obstacles and prey. Moreover, they must consume enough food to accumulate large fat reserves and survive hibernation after they find an appropriate site for overwintering. Many do not survive.

In Canada, predation appears to be relatively uncommon. Even with the diversity of bat species and relatively high natural abundance of some BC bat species, there are relatively few predators that commonly eat bats. There are, however, records of predation by several species, including snakes, hawks, owls, cats, raccoons, skunks, weasels and marten. For example, Susan Dulc and others observed a medium-sized WESTERN SCREECH OWL taking bats at a bat box (also referred to as a bat house) in BC; in Alberta, Lausen observed a maternity colony of BIG BROWN BATS switching roosts each time a SHORT-EARED OWL was present at the time of their dusk emergence. Despite a lengthy list of potential predators, the most detrimental factors for bat populations are the direct and indirect effects of human activities (see Conservation and Threats, page 57).

References

Adams et al. (2003), Baxter et al. (2006), Booher (2008), Crichton and Krutzsch (2000), Jung et al. (2011), Lausen (2007), Preston et al. (2012), Schowalter (2001), Solick et al. (2012), Talerico (2008).

Torpor and Roost Selection

Bats are small and relatively poorly insulated, and they lose a great deal of heat and water through the skin of their wings and tails. Maintaining a normal mammalian body temperature of about 38°C requires considerable energy to compensate for a bat's high surface area to volume ratio. In general, bats have high energy demands to combat heat loss and to meet the demands for locomotion. As such, when bats are not eating, they are likely to make use of energy-saving strategies.

Torpor is an adaptation for conserving energy during periods of unfavourable conditions. It involves slowing the rate of metabolic reactions occurring in cells, which leads to body temperature decreasing to nearly as low as ambient temperature, thus using less energy for basic metabolic processes. In animals, energy is stored as fat. Most mammals, including bats, have two different kinds of fat: white and brown. White fat is well supplied with blood vessels and serves as an energy reservoir and insulator. Brown fat serves as an energy reservoir, but it also has a high capacity for producing heat and water as by-products of metabolism.

If a bat is trying to perform important body functions, such as digestion, milk production, healing or flight, then it must have an "active" or normal body temperature for cellular reactions to occur optimally. Maintaining optimal body temperatures requires energy; the bat will either generate its own body heat by burning fat or roost in a warm space using the environmental heat source, or some combination of these. Some bats cluster together while roosting, an energy-saving behavioural strategy that reduces heat and water loss. Even species that typically don't cluster together can be observed doing so when conditions are unfavourable (see image on page 204). Other strategies include squeezing into tight crevices, as opposed to roosting in more spacious roost locations, and selecting roosts that are warmed by the sun. In fact, roost selection can be highly strategic and critical to a bat's survival.

Throughout much of the spring and early summer, adult males have a different roosting and thermoregulatory strategy than females, as males have little to do during this time besides eating and gaining body mass. During the day, males generally seek out cool roosts that allow them to drop their body temperature and save energy. Sometimes males will select roosts that warm up in the sun late in the day, passively rewarming their bodies, reducing the amount of fat they need to use to reach an optimal operating body temperature for flight. At certain times in their reproductive cycle, female bats will also select cool roosts and take advantage of passive rewarming. However, when raising a pup, female bats typically seek out hot (about 35°C to 40°C) roost site locations, because their bodies must remain at normal (active) temperatures to efficiently develop a fetus (gestation) and then subsequently produce milk (during lactation) for their young. A pup's body must also stay warm so that the cells can divide for growth. It is no surprise that some reproductive female bats have adapted to roosting in attic spaces of houses, or under tin roofs of buildings, where temperatures can be high even on relatively cool but sunny days. Some female bats have additionally evolved to cluster in large maternal groups to reduce heat and water loss from their small bodies and thus additionally save energy, so that as a group they can more easily retain heat in their bodies for gestation and lactation.

Bats that have adapted to living in human-built structures in BC are primarily LITTLE BROWN MYOTIS, YUMA MYOTIS and BIG BROWN BAT. Buildings can provide safe, warm roosts, often with plenty of thermal options to choose from, thus allowing bats to avoid spots that are too cold or too hot (i.e., spots that could cause heat stress), and instead seek locations that are optimal for keeping their bodies and their pups' bodies at normal (active) body temperature without having to burn much of their own stored fat. In some cases, adult female bats may select slightly cooler roost locations at times when they do not need to maintain a high metabolic rate. During their short time in these cooler roost sites, the bat will reduce its metabolism and allow its body temperature to fall into a state called daily torpor. Even a slight lowering of metabolism, and thus of body temperature, below "normal" reduces the energy consumption of cellular processes. Complex roost structures likely provide a range of temperatures for varying use of torpor daily. It has been shown that roosts in buildings, because of their typically large size, thermal continuum, and protection from predators, may provide energy advantages to bats that use them; some individuals from maternity colonies roosting in buildings have been found to have higher reproductive success than in colonies roosting in nearby natural crevice roosts (note that natural crevices typically provide a narrow range of thermal options, necessitating roost switching to find optimal conditions throughout the reproductive season).

After a female bat has weaned her young, the pup continues to forage on its own and will often remain in the warm nursery roost to finish growing. Post-lactating adult females, while they will spend some days in the nursery roost with pups, will often move away to roost in cooler locations. After weaning, a mother bat has little reason to use energy to keep her body warm during the day, given that she no longer needs to produce milk or keep her pup's body warm. Instead, she will seek a roost to enable her to reduce metabolic rate, drop body temperature and save energy. Although little is known about male roost selection, males typically roost in cooler locations than females until late in the summer, when post-lactating females also seek cool day roosts, saving energy in preparation for hibernation. Females of many species do not occupy high-elevation habitats, presumably because these sites do not offer enough food resources or are too cool for females to reproduce successfully. Males are more likely to roost in these cooler high-elevation sites, using daily torpor and exploiting the insects that are available at these elevations.

References
Lausen and Barclay (2003); Rambaldini and Brigham (2008); Rintoul and Brigham (2014); Solick and Barclay (2007); Thomas, Dorais and Bergerson (1990).

NORTHERN MYOTIS is thought to depend largely on old-growth trees for summer roosts.

Tree crevice roosts used by bats. PHOTOS: CORY OLSON

Summer Roosting Sites

Depending on the species, bats use a large variety of roost sites in summer, ranging from rocks, cliffs, trees, snags and stumps to buildings, bat boxes, bridges and more. Their preferences are largely dictated by internal roost temperatures and the benefit of using torpor (relative to food supply and reproductive stage), but there are other factors at play. For example, perceived predation risk, the possibility of parasite infestation, the size of a cavity in relation to colony size, and proximity to drinking water and productive foraging habitats may also impact roost selection and roost switching.

Availability of suitable roosting sites is one of the most important factors that determine the distribution and abundance of bats. Roosts provide shelter from predators and inclement weather, and environmental conditions appropriate for raising young. Although bats are probably best known for using caves, vespertilionid bats seek shelter in almost every conceivable type of structure: trees (under bark and in hollows and crevices, and in foliage), rock crevices and under rocks, animal burrows, storm sewers and abandoned mines, in buildings and under bridges. Considerable information on the choice of roost sites by bats in BC has been reported over the past several decades (see individual species accounts).

Roosting sites fall into three general types: day roosts, night roosts and winter roosts. Day and night roosts are occupied by active individuals in the summer; winter roosts, known as hibernacula, are used by bats for prolonged periods

The concrete surfaces under some bridges (left) can provide excellent night roosts for many bat species. This bridge in the West Kootenay is used by at least three species. Piles of guano under the concrete girders and guano pellets stuck on the concrete surfaces where the bats roost, visible in this photo, are evidence of extensive use by bats. PHOTO: MICHAEL PROCTOR. BIG BROWN BATS (right) roosting in the roof of a building. PHOTO: CORY OLSON

of hibernation during winter months (see Hibernation and Winter Ecology, page 45). Regardless of the season in which a roost is used, individuals often return to roost sites. For example, the same bat may roost in the same spot in a cave each winter, and females typically return to their birth roost each summer to raise a pup, a practice called natal philopatry. Natal philopatry is associated most with females, though male philopatry to a natal roost or roosting area has been documented; there have been multiple observations of juvenile male BIG BROWN BATS and YUMA MYOTIS returning to natal roosts in spring, although by the time the current year's pups were born, these returning juvenile males were no longer observed in the nursery roost.

Most BC species spend summer days in crevices in trees, buildings, cliffs or talus slopes. The two Lasiurines (HOARY BAT and EASTERN RED BAT) roost in the foliage of trees and, occasionally, in shrubs. Foliage-roosting Lasiurines roost singly or in small family groups composed of a female and her young. These species demonstrate several adaptations for roosting in exposed sites. They tend to be coloured to blend in with their background, and they have dense fur that better insulates them from cool temperatures. All other BC species roost in crevices of some form. Large crevices and hollows tend to be exploited primarily by adult females that more typically congregate in large maternity colonies to bear and raise young (see Torpor and Roost Selection, page 32). The largest recorded maternity colonies have been found in buildings or in

This elevated bat condominium (artificial roost structure for bats), measuring roughly 4×4 metres, is located in the Creston Valley Wildlife Management Area. It was built to replace a collapsing barn that was a maternity roost for thousands of YUMA and LITTLE BROWN MYOTIS. PHOTO: CORI LAUSEN specially constructed bat condominiums (e.g., at the Creston Valley Wildlife Management Area). In BC, there are several known large YUMA MYOTIS maternity roosts in human-built structures, many of which host thousands of individuals. Some of these colonies are composed of both YUMA and LITTLE BROWN MYOTIS. Other bat species that have also been confirmed roosting in either buildings or bat boxes in BC include BIG BROWN BATS, LONG-LEGGED MYOTIS, TOWNSEND'S BIG-EARED BAT, CALIFORNIAN MYOTIS, and LONG-EARED MYOTIS. Temperatures inside summer nursery roosts can be extremely high, reaching 35°C to 40°C, a characteristic that promotes the rapid growth of pups.

Some insectivorous bats also use one or more night roosts. These sites are separate from the day roost and are often relatively exposed. Examples of night roosts include the underside of rock overhangs, building eaves, or concrete bridges. Night roosts are places to rest, digest food between periods of feeding, and retreat from inclement weather, and they may also serve as communal roost locations. Gathering in groups at night roosts may be beneficial for thermoregulation (clustering bats keep each other warm so they can digest without expending much energy to maintain body temperature), and perhaps to share information about foraging and roosting locations. Bats will often briefly swarm at some night roosts soon after emergence, leave to forage, and then return later in the night after the first major foraging bout. Night roosts are often used by multiple species, although typically night roosts are not used by lactating females, who instead return to the nursery roost periodically throughout the night to nurse.

The use of buildings as roosts often brings bats into conflict with humans. Large numbers living in the attic of a house can be a nuisance that many people won't tolerate. Unlike mice, bats do not chew through building materials; however, they do urinate, and this can result in a strong smell (from the ammonia in the urine) and cause staining at the entry and exit points. Bats also produce guano; this is strikingly similar in appearance to mouse droppings. But while mouse droppings tend to be pointed on their ends and difficult to crush because of the plant material they contain, bat guano pellets are typically round on the ends and crumble easily when crushed, often producing rather shiny dust (the exoskeletons of insects, see image next page) or fluffy dust (the scales of moths). Bat guano, unlike mouse feces, is also typically found stuck to walls or windows after being deposited by flying bats. Because of the increasing threats that bats face, and the knowledge that building roosts provide ideal conditions for reproduction (and thus recovering populations; see Conservation and Threats, page 57), there is a growing movement to allow bats to remain in buildings as long as human living quarters are not being accessed by the bats. Many small colonies, particularly in well-insulated buildings, may remain undetected for years. When guano accumulation, odours or noise from large colonies motivate the need for a remedy, eviction by appropriately timed and humane methods of exclusion may be desired.

In an attic, bat guano accumulates where bats roost (left). Bat guano size differs—the larger pellets left of the Canadian 25-cent coin (for size) are from a BIG BROWN BAT, and the pellets right of the coin are from LITTLE BROWN MYOTIS (top right). PHOTO: CORY OLSON. A crushed guano pellet revealing small shiny bits of insect carapace. PHOTO: MICHAEL PROCTOR

There is no way to successfully move or translocate a colony of bats, nor is it legal. In BC, bats are protected under the provincial Wildlife Act, and it is illegal to kill them. Capture, even for research purposes, requires a special permit, and there is a process in place to scrutinize methods to ensure that bats are not harmed. Given this protection, eviction (when necessary) is best carried out after the young bats are flying and ideally after bats have left for the winter season to avoid inadvertently trapping them inside. The BC Community Bat Program (bcbats.ca) provides detailed resources for safe eviction, in addition to providing information about how to suitably replace lost roosting habitat. Following successful eviction, bats will most likely try to return to the roost site in subsequent years and will thus seek any nearby suitable alternative roost sites following exclusion. To maintain neighbourly relations, it is recommended that you warn your human neighbours about any bat exclusion activities. An experiment conducted near Ottawa, Ontario, revealed that female BIG BROWN BATS excluded from building roosts used as maternity colonies moved to the nearest available structure, usually a neighbouring house, and this scenario has also been documented by the BC Community Bat Program.

It is possible to invite bats into your neighbourhood without having to share your house. Bat boxes are popular around the globe. However, in some places,

These back-to-back multi-chamber bat boxes studied by Tanya Luszcz are equipped with temperature dataloggers (small white tube with wires visible, on post) to monitor internal roost conditions. A radiant shade has been hung on the far bat box to reduce solar radiation on hot Okanagan days. PHOTO: CORI LAUSEN

This bat box in Metro Vancouver is unusual in having more than the standard four chambers. Providing many chambers potentially accommodates more bats but, most importantly, can offer more microclimate options. PHOTO: JOHN SAREMBA

such as Spain, Australia and BC, mass mortality of bats has been associated with overheated bat boxes. There is growing concern that strategic plans for the design and placement of these boxes may be needed to ensure the safety of bats in a changing climate and where natural roosts are increasingly limited. Most bats use natural crevice roosts, such as rock cracks or tree hollows, and natural roosts can also overheat when in direct sunlight for long periods of the day, reaching lethal temperatures (during the summer, extended exposure to temperatures hotter than 40°C to 44°C can result in death for many bat species). To date, however, mass mortality events due to overheating have only been observed in artificial roosts, which suggests that our designs or placements of these structures can in some situations create ecological sinks, luring bats to use unsuitable conditions.

As explained in Torpor and Roost Selection (page 32), females need a specific set of thermal conditions to raise a pup successfully, and these conditions are likely to vary across the spring and summer months. When one crevice roost gets too hot, mother bats can switch to an alternative roost, one that was perhaps too cool earlier in the season but is now "just right." This "Goldilocks approach" to roost selection is critical for all bats and often motivates roost switching. Bats that roost under bark, such as CALIFORNIAN MYOTIS, may switch between a small subset of trees with loose bark, each with different solar exposure and thus varying in available roosting conditions from day to day.

Bats that roost in rock crevices, such as DARK-NOSED SMALL-FOOTED MYOTIS, will also adaptively select roost sites within a small patch of rock crevices or within a talus slope. An aggregation of crevice roosts used by bats is sometimes referred to as a roosting area, and in most studies where reproductive females are followed using radiotelemetry (radio-tracking using a radio transmitter) they are found to switch roosts for reasons related to thermal needs and energy conservation, social networking or avoidance of predation. A building attic offers a range of microclimates for bats to choose from, akin to the variety of tree cavities or rock crevices available across a natural roosting area; in other words, a bat will find an optimal location either by shifting around inside a complex roost like a building attic or by moving among a collection of crevices. Insulated buildings can offer safety from predators and stable and warm temperatures day and night (good for pup growth). In an Alberta study, it was shown that bats roosting in a building did better than those in rock crevices, because they gave birth to young earlier, and those young fledged earlier, giving them additional time to prepare for hibernation.

In natural roosting scenarios, a maternity colony of bats will use many roosts throughout the reproductive season, switching roosts every day or two. In Alberta, a LITTLE BROWN MYOTIS colony was found to use approximately 60 different trees over the course of a summer, and a BIG BROWN BAT colony used more than 70 rock crevice roosts within a 4-kilometre stretch of river. Although the BIG BROWN BAT rock crevice roosts were found to sometimes overheat, with internal temperatures as high as 50°C, bats were not roosting in these crevices in these conditions. We don't yet understand why some bats remain in overheating bat boxes and don't switch to alternative roosts when temperatures exceed safe limits, but the leading hypothesis is that these bats lack alternative roosts from which to choose. This can happen when, for example, a colony is evicted from a building roost (offering myriad temperatures from which to choose) that it has depended on for a long period of time. Especially in our urban centres with increasingly energy-efficient buildings, alternative building and natural roosts may be hard to find after eviction. A single bat box consisting of a few chambers is likely to provide only a fraction of the temperature ranges that a colony of reproductive females needs throughout the entire pup-raising season.

The term *bat condominium* (see image on page 38) usually refers to a large structure (perhaps 4 metres by 4 metres) that resembles a tree house on posts, containing banks of roosting chambers inside. Mini-condos are similar but smaller structures. Although these artificial roosts are less likely to offer ideal conditions than building roosts, as they typically are not insulated, they still offer a larger range of temperatures than a bat box. Even multi-chambered bat boxes tend to mirror outside temperature fluctuations, reaching hotter and colder temperatures than a more thermally stable roost in a rock crevice or attic.

Just as we would not expect a single tree cavity or a rock crevice to meet the needs of a nursing colony of bats throughout the summer, we should not expect this of a single bat box. If bats are excluded from building roosts, equivalent roosting habitats that offer a range of microclimate options should be provided, especially if other building roost sites are limited in the immediate vicinity.

Construction of many bat boxes, installed in a variety of solar exposures, might mimic a natural roosting area in an urban setting where a colony of bats has likely lost all suitable natural roost options. In the Metro Vancouver region, a mass mortality of adults and large non-flying pups due to overheating was observed by John Saremba and Leah Rensel in 2018 (see Conservation and Threats, page 57, for photos). Large pups may have been too heavy for mothers to fly with them, preventing them from fleeing the hot roost during the day. In the Creston area, Susan Dulc observed a colony of pregnant bats fleeing from an overheating bat box mid-afternoon in June 2019, seeking refuge on the trunks of nearby trees. In a heat wave that covered much of southern BC in the summer of 2021, the BC Community Bat Program and others sent out wide-reaching communication asking people to cover bat boxes with white sheets or awnings, which apparently many people did, and no mass mortalities of bats were reported, despite record-high temperatures in the province; BC Community Bat Program representatives also reported that many bats moved out of bat boxes in response to the extremely hot weather. It may be important to strategically place multiple bat boxes with varying solar exposure (and thus different internal temperatures) adjacent to one another, to enable easier roost switching, especially during daylight hours when overheating can occur and predation risk from birds is high. Simulating a natural crevice roosting area with bat boxes in an urban environment may require collaboration among neighbours to achieve the necessary Goldilocks approach to providing sufficient choice of roost conditions.

This is just one strategy for becoming a bat-friendly community. Once roosts are established, box maintenance is required to keep boxes free of wasp nests and to replace rotting boards. These actions will continue to help bats to reproduce successfully. It should be noted that different bat species prefer different box characteristics, so consulting the plans available through reliable sources will help determine what is best for your area. And despite differing designs of bat boxes, only a small number of bat species roost in these types of artificial structures.

References

Barclay and Brigham (2001); Bideguren et al. (2019); Brigham and Fenton (1987); Brigham et al. (1997); Flaquer et al. (2014); Griffiths (2021); Johnson et al. (2019); Lausen (2001); Lausen and Barclay (2006b); Olson and Barclay (2013); Ormsbee, Kiser and Perlmeter (2009); Psyllakis and Brigham (2006); Rueegger (2016); Vonhof and Barclay (1996); Vonhof and Barclay (1997); Willis and Brigham (2004).

Hibernation and Winter Ecology

Insect-eating bats have limited choices when faced with winter food shortages: migration, hibernation, or some combination of the two. Bats can move seasonally to warmer climates where insects are available at least some of the time, remaining active with possibly some intermittent use of torpor or short bouts of hibernation. Alternatively, bats can hibernate for many months, subsisting only on energy reserves stored in the form of fat. Between late summer and early winter, bats in BC are typically on the move, either migrating south out of BC for warmer climates, or headed to hibernacula where they can find stable, non-freezing winter temperatures in which to roost. Most BC species rely on hibernation to cope with winter, using extended periods of deep torpor (see Torpor and Roost Selection, page 32).

How far, and along what migration routes, populations of the different BC species move seasonally is largely unknown. Based on data from studies of banded individuals (see image on page 84) in eastern North America, we know that some species will move up to several hundred kilometres between summer roosts and winter hibernacula. For example, band recovery records of LITTLE BROWN MYOTIS in Alberta, analyzed by Dave Hobson, revealed bats flying up to 240 kilometres between summer maternity roosts and a cave hibernaculum in the Rocky Mountains. SILVER-HAIRED BATS, while often considered migratory across much of their North American range, do not seem to always migrate long distances in BC, and in fact, based on recaptures of banded individuals, Lausen and others have found SILVER-HAIRED males who are year-round residents in the vicinity of some West Kootenay mines.

However, with more bat detectors being used across the province, temporal and geographic patterns showing peaks of activity are likely to emerge as datasets are shared and combined. Substantial bat activity in late summer and early fall was detected by Lausen at the province's highest mountain highway pass, Salmo-Creston (Kootenay Pass), suggesting that at least some species move up and over mountain ranges during seasonal movements. In BC, two species—EASTERN RED BAT and HOARY BAT—migrate south, while the rest are thought to overwinter by hibernating. But to date there is direct evidence for only the following species overwintering in BC: TOWNSEND'S BIG-EARED BAT, SILVER-HAIRED BAT, CALIFORNIAN MYOTIS, DARK-NOSED SMALL-FOOTED MYOTIS, BIG BROWN BAT, YUMA MYOTIS, LONG-LEGGED MYOTIS, LITTLE BROWN MYOTIS, and PALLID BAT.

Bats typically arrive at their hibernation site in late summer or autumn (September to November). Unlike some other hibernating mammals, such as ground squirrels, bats cannot store gathered food as a source of energy. Before entering hibernation, they accumulate body fat to use as an energy source through the winter. If their body fat reserves become depleted, they starve. Overwinter survival depends on a strategic energy budget limited by the amount of fat they can carry while flying, making hibernation a physiologically challenging time for bats. The percentage of body fat that bats take into hibernation seems to vary widely across species and regions, presumably according to the length of the hibernation period, which occurs when insect food is absent. In BC, pre- and post-hibernation body mass is only known for some species, and it has been found that masses in autumn are approximately 9% to 50% higher than in spring (see species accounts). Unplanned arousals due to human disturbance (e.g., humans entering cave hibernacula in winter) reduce the fat stores available for bats to finish the winter. It is best not to disturb bats during hibernation, as this could decrease their likelihood of overwinter survival.

To reduce energy consumption during hibernation, bats lower their metabolism. LITTLE BROWN MYOTIS, for example, has a resting heart rate (a good proxy for metabolism) of 100 to 200 beats per minute, but when actively flying its heart rate increases to more than 1,000 beats per minute. In comparison, the heart rate of a torpid or hibernating individual may decline to as few as 10 beats per minute; at the same time, their breathing rate will decrease to as little as one breath per hour. Using torpor, a bat can regulate the decline in its body temperature to just a few degrees above freezing; hibernacula must presumably be selected to provide optimal temperatures for keeping cellular reactions as low as possible. Optimal conditions for hibernation can vary widely based on geography and species. Populations of the same species at different latitudes can have different adaptive physiological set-points, meaning that they differ in which temperature and humidity conditions result in the least amount of fat consumption. This is not surprising, given that even humans acclimate to their local climate, with people who live in tropical climates, for example, being less comfortable in cold weather.

Like all mammals, bats cannot survive their bodies freezing; if they are exposed to temperatures lower than 0°C, they must expend energy to ensure that they do not freeze. Selecting appropriate winter roosts is critical. In Alberta and the Northwest Territories, LITTLE BROWN MYOTIS do not start increasing their metabolism and burning fat to stay warm until their surroundings are colder than 2°C. This is similar to SILVER-HAIRED BAT and CALIFORNIAN MYOTIS in BC, which also do not expend fat to keep warm until their surroundings are between 0°C and 2°C. YUMA MYOTIS and TOWNSEND'S BIG-EARED BAT in BC start defending their body temperature by burning fat once their surroundings drop below 4°C and 5°C, respectively. Based on species-specific physiology, bats should select winter roosts that provide optimal energy savings throughout the winter and do not freeze, although in reality they use a large range of hibernation roost conditions, with different species in different geographic areas using different thermal profiles; roost availability and changing weather conditions may complicate roost selection, so preferences will vary across a species' range. For example, LITTLE BROWN MYOTIS across their North American range have been found to hibernate in temperatures from –4°C to 13°C, but in Alberta and the Northwest Territories, government-collected microclimate data in two large LITTLE BROWN MYOTIS cave hibernacula showed stable temperatures between 2.0°C and 2.5°C. These caves also have saturated air (relative humidity 100%), which would undoubtedly keep hibernating bats from losing too much water through their large wing skin surfaces. In contrast, Lausen measured microclimates in BC hibernacula: a mine hibernaculum of CALIFORNIAN MYOTIS and SILVER-HAIRED BAT had temperatures ranging from 6°C to 7°C and humidity from 84% to 100%; at the largest mine hibernaculum known for TOWNSEND'S BIG-EARED BAT in BC (located between Grand Forks and Greenwood), bats hibernate between 2°C and 4°C and 62% and 98% relative humidity. These roost temperatures are all well below the optimal growth temperature (approximately 13°C to 14°C) of the fungus that causes white-nose syndrome, which may be helpful in preventing the continued spread of this disease (see Conservation and Threats, page 57).

Bats, like virtually all mammals that hibernate, naturally arouse from hibernation several times throughout winter. When they need to, hibernating bats can warm their bodies to normal temperature in about 30 minutes, using heat generated from brown fat. This process is called arousal. Hibernation bouts of extended deep torpor are days or weeks in length, with more than 80% of fat stores being used for the short arousals between bouts. The function of these energetically expensive arousals is not well understood. Numerous physiological reasons have been proposed, including to drink water, to sleep (for maintenance of neural circuitry), and to allow the immune system to function normally. While most mammalian hibernators are relatively dormant during these periods of arousal, bats are atypical in that they may fly during arousals, spending additional energy for flight inside or outside the hibernaculum.

Could bats be seeking new roosting locations as conditions change? Perhaps. Hibernacula appear to be selected based on temperature and humidity, but precisely how bats choose is unknown. Each species appears to have its own ideal conditions, cool enough to allow the metabolism to remain low, yet warm enough to avoid freezing or burning large amounts of fat to avoid freezing. Some natural arousals appear to be stimulated by water loss, and bats in humid sites hibernate for longer periods. Bats may also cluster in groups to reduce water loss. But as weather conditions change, bats may need to switch roosts throughout the winter. If the bat is roosting in a large cave or mine, this may simply entail moving to a new location in the underground structure; however, if the winter roost is a rock crevice, switching roosts may require the bat to exit the roost and fly in cold conditions to relocate to a different crevice or underground space. Lausen documented the demise of a CALIFORNIAN MYOTIS and SILVER-HAIRED BAT hibernating in the same rock crevice together in January in the West Kootenay. Necropsy by the BC Animal Health Lab concluded that the cause of death was exposure to the cold. The bats had not switched to a warmer roost because the opening of their crevice had iced over completely, preventing escape. Roost switching is not always the reason for winter flight. In Alberta, BIG BROWN BATS roosting in rock crevices of Dinosaur Provincial Park have been studied extensively. Here, the ground and main water sources remain largely frozen throughout winter, with no insect prey available. Use of temperature-sensitive radio transmitters and PIT tags (passive integrative transponders; see Studying Bats, page 73) has shown that BIG BROWN BATS arouse on average every 9 days, with an average arousal rate per individual of 17 times per winter. An average of 6 arousals per winter were associated with flight outside the rock crevice roosts, but few of these flights ever resulted in switching of roosts, nor were there any signs of bats drinking from the only available open water source in the park (an experimentally heated water tank; see image on facing page). Periodic capture and sampling showed that the bats were becoming progressively dehydrated throughout the winter. Elsewhere in Alberta, Cory Olson determined that 36% of recorded hibernal arousals inside a cave hibernaculum of LITTLE BROWN MYOTIS were associated with flight and movement between roost sites within the cave. Bat detectors at the entrance to this cave did not record bats throughout the winter—evidence that all mid-winter flights occurred within the confines of the cave.

Lausen and others have studied the winter ecology of CALIFORNIAN MYOTIS and SILVER-HAIRED BATS in the West Kootenay extensively using temperature-sensitive radio transmitters. They found that bats took flight outside their mine, tree or rock crevice hibernacula during approximately 60% of arousals, and that flight was not always associated with roost switching (see species accounts). Some captured bats would accept drinking water, but most did not. Bats that did drink were willing to lap at melting snow. All captured bats offered food would accept it, but there was little evidence of insect food available to them naturally, other than some overwintering arthropods in some mines (e.g., harvestmen, flies). Interestingly, all low-elevation mines monitored by bat detectors at night in the West Kootenay area during winter (Lausen and others examined more than 20 sites) yielded echolocation calls of flying bats; however, not all of these mines were found to house hibernating bats when examined during the day. While some mines allow bats to hide in crevices during the day, many have smooth rock surfaces with shallow drill holes, and Lausen and others proposed that bats were flying into the mines at night, but not using them as hibernacula for roosting. To test this, they performed an experiment at two West Kootenay mines where dual stereo microphones on a bat detector allowed direction and timing of flight to be recorded, confirming that CALIFORNIAN MYOTIS (the most common species detected) would fly into mines at some point during the night, stay for a few minutes or hours, and then leave the mine, not using it as a winter roost. It was proposed that the bats visited these mines to feed on hibernating arthropods,

This modified hot tub in Dinosaur Provincial Park is approximately 200 metres from a known BIG BROWN BAT hibernaculum (rock crevice), and was designed by Leroy Lausen (pictured here) to allow Cori Lausen and later Brandon Klüg-Baerwald to determine if bats drink water in winter. The hot tub kept water liquid throughout winter and pumped it up into the water tank on the top, available for bats to drink. The box mounted on the top by the rubber water tank contained a bat detector, which triggered a trail camera when a bat approached, with the goal of capturing any drinking event in winter. A submersed PIT-tag reader in the water tank could also record a bat's visit if it was PIT-tagged. PHOTO: CORI LAUSEN

but study of the guano refuted this (for details, see CALIFORNIAN MYOTIS species account, page 207). Instead, it may be that mines offer a safe refuge for obligate winter flights; further research would be needed to test this hypothesis.

Other than to drink water or to switch roosts, bats may also fly during winter to mate. Males and females of a given species may or may not hibernate in the same sites. For example, cave hibernacula of LITTLE BROWN MYOTIS in Alberta and the Northwest Territories are biased toward males. Lausen and others have repeatedly captured free-flying male and female CALIFORNIAN MYOTIS, TOWNSEND'S BIG-EARED BATS and SILVER-HAIRED BATS in winter in the West Kootenay, confirming that most sites have males and females roosting together or at least in the same vicinity. Captured individuals have shown evidence of recent mating, including reddened female genitalia, sperm being discharged from vaginal tracts, erect penises, and diminishing sperm stores in males recaptured across the winter season.

Winter bat flight activity levels vary geographically, and different species are active in different areas. Over a span of 10 years, Lausen and others placed bat detectors outside potential roosts, along potential or known flyways (linear corridors like rivers), and at open winter water sources (e.g., reservoirs, hot springs) across much of BC. These recordings revealed at least some bat activity in all winter months across most of southern BC, ranging from Radium Hot Springs and Columbia Lake in the east to various locations on Vancouver Island in the west. Winter bat activity was also extensive on Haida Gwaii, and as far north as the Nass River in the northwest and Dawson Creek in the northeast. Bat activity during winter was not detected on the Stikine River at Telegraph Creek and Dease Lake, nor at Liard Hot Springs or the "warm springs" in the Atlin Lake area, suggesting that in these northern latitudes there may be some sort of climatic boundary, where bats either do not overwinter or do not fly outdoors during arousals from hibernation.

In southeast Alaska, radio-tracking of LITTLE BROWN MYOTIS late in the fall led researchers to crevice hibernacula in talus slopes and within root systems of trees (root wad roosts). Using motion cameras, Karen Blejwas and others recorded mating activity in fall at these crevice hibernacula. Additionally, winter acoustic recordings have confirmed the presence of SILVER-HAIRED BATS in southeast Alaska, presumably in rock crevice hibernacula. It is likely that many species in BC, especially along the coast, use rock crevices or root wads to hibernate, but this has not been confirmed. The mild conditions of the coastal environment may also lure bats for overwintering; bats have been observed flying over the St. Elias Mountains and glaciers, suggesting migration of some Yukon bats over the coastal mountains for hibernation. Twenty-five bats were found frozen in a glacier in Yukon, supporting the notion that bats will migrate over high elevations even where roosting and foraging habitats do not exist. Lausen observed the coldest temperature documented during bat flight in BC at approximately −14°C (in South Okanagan), although most bat activity occurs at temperatures warmer than −10°C, and smaller bats (e.g., myotis species) tend to be recorded flying in warmer winter conditions than larger-bodied bats (e.g., SILVER-HAIRED BAT and BIG BROWN BAT).

Clearly, periodic flight during hibernation is important and may be ubiquitous among hibernating bats. But why do bats fly in winter if not to find remnant morsels of insect food, switch roosts, drink water or mate? It seems that the energetically costly, and in many cases risky, activity of flying in sometimes extremely cold temperatures must serve one or more fundamental purposes that have not yet been identified. As with many aspects of bat behaviour, we still have much to learn about hibernation.

References

Blejwas, Lausen and Rhea-Fournier (2014); Blejwas et al. (2021); Dunbar and Brigham (2010); Klüg-Baerwald and Brigham (2017); Klüg-Baerwald et al. (2016); Klüg-Baerwald et al. (2021); Lausen and Barclay (2006a); McGuire et al. (2021); McGuire et al. (2022); O'Farrell and Studier (1970); Slough and Jung (2008); Thomas, Dorais and Bergerson (1990); Verant et al. (2012); Webb, Speakman and Racey (1996).

Winter Roosting Sites (Hibernacula)

Bats use caves, mines, storm sewers, buildings, tree cavities, tree bark and rock crevices as winter roosting sites, with the choice depending on the species and location. Moreover, unless disturbed, bats show a strong degree of loyalty to roosting sites, with individuals returning to the same sites for summer and/or winter roosts over many years or even decades. And yet, despite this loyalty, most winter roosting locations in BC are not known. This is likely due in large part to the difficulty in radio-tracking these small free-flying animals (see Studying Bats, page 73), especially when they roost underground or in rock crevices where the radio signal is difficult to detect. In fact, once a bat with a radio transmitter has gone deep into the ground to find stable microclimates, detecting it from the surface is usually impossible. Most hibernating bats in BC are probably underground, and pinpointing precise locations to discern which species select which types of roost will require further research.

One effective study by Lausen and others used temperature-sensitive radio transmitters on SILVER-HAIRED BATS and CALIFORNIAN MYOTIS over multiple winters near Castlegar and Nelson to determine roost selection and hibernation patterns (see species accounts). These species have been successfully radio-tracked, as they have been found hibernating in shallow crevices, mines or trees. SILVER-HAIRED BATS were found under bark of live WESTERN REDCEDAR and DOUGLAS-FIR trees; in snags of aspen, DOUGLAS-FIR and PONDEROSA PINE; and in rock crevices or mines. Roost switching occurred frequently. SILVER-HAIRED BAT also depends on trees for roosting in summer, and a preliminary study by Emily de Freitas has found that trees selected in summer differ from those used in winter. CALIFORNIAN MYOTIS roosted mainly in rock crevices and occasionally in mines, although one individual was found roosting in the root wad of an upturned tree. Bat detectors recorded CALIFORNIAN MYOTIS bats flying during winter across their BC range, and they likely hibernate in crevices where they can get below the frost line.

Overwintering bats also roost in buildings, although the full extent of this is not known. Winter records of bats inside buildings are mainly of YUMA MYOTIS and BIG BROWN BAT, although LONG-LEGGED MYOTIS, SILVER-HAIRED BAT and LITTLE BROWN MYOTIS have also been found. Lausen captured free-flying YUMA MYOTIS in late autumn and early winter in the Creston area, determining that many bats, especially young ones, remain in nursery-roost buildings for the winter, relocating to use micro-sites around chimneys, in insulated areas of attic floors. There are likewise many winter records of BIG BROWN BAT in buildings, reflecting this species' tolerance of cold and fluctuating conditions. However, the species is commonly recorded in winter flying where there are no buildings. Radio-tracking of this species during winter in the Alberta prairies has shown that it also uses rock crevice hibernacula, including erosion holes in mudstone of river valleys.

Extensive underground monitoring using specially designed bat detectors for use within roosts (roost loggers), has uncovered few significant bat hibernacula in BC. Of the more than 200 underground bat detectors placed in mines and caves by Wildlife Conservation Society Canada's BatCaver program, roughly half have not recorded any bat activity. Bats may be scattered widely across and within the province's cave systems; detecting the presence of bats in large and often complex underground spaces is confounded by the short detection range of roost loggers (often less than 15 metres), and bats on tall cave ceilings may therefore evade detection, as do bats that use unmonitored exits. The West Kootenay region has numerous abandoned mines, and together with the mild winter climate, this may account for the high level of winter bat activity detected in that region. Hibernation records from caves and abandoned mines in BC are limited to individuals of LITTLE BROWN MYOTIS and/or YUMA MYOTIS, DARK-NOSED SMALL-FOOTED MYOTIS, BIG BROWN BAT, CALIFORNIAN MYOTIS, SILVER-HAIRED BAT, LONG-EARED MYOTIS, LONG-LEGGED MYOTIS, and TOWNSEND'S BIG-EARED BAT. The sizes of these winter populations range from a single individual in many mines and caves to an estimate (based on mark recapture statistics by John Boulanger) of up to 3,000 individuals of mixed species in one West Kootenay mine. In contrast, in eastern Canada, at least up until the arrival of white-nose syndrome, colonies of 10,000 to 15,000 bats were known to hibernate in caves and abandoned mines. With the large number of caves, crevices, abandoned mines, and suitable trees available in BC, it is likely that bats overwinter in small numbers or in isolation in many, if not most, areas of the province. This would explain why almost all bat detectors deployed in winter in southern BC record bat activity at some point during the winter (see Hibernation and Winter Ecology, page 45).

References

Brigham (1987); Halsall, Boyles and Whitaker (2012); Lausen and Barclay (2006a); Neubaum, O'Shea and Wilson (2006).

Disease and Bats

In North America, very few diseases are transmittable to humans by bats, and bats in Canada represent an exceedingly small risk to human health. Like most wild mammals and domestic pets, bats harbour a variety of ectoparasites, including bat-bugs, ticks, mites and fleas. Fortunately, most of the parasites associated with bats are highly specific to bats and are rarely at home on or in humans. Ectoparasites of temperate Vespertilionid and Molossid bats are not known to transmit any diseases to us.

While some bats in other parts of the world are associated with transmission of increasingly well-known viral diseases (e.g., Ebola, Hendra, SARS-COV and SARS-COV-2), only two conditions associated with bats require public awareness in North America: histoplasmosis and rabies. Histoplasmosis is caused by a soil-dwelling fungus (*Histoplasma capsulatum*) that is found worldwide, especially in warm humid regions. The growth of the fungus is enhanced by feces from both birds (usually pigeons or poultry) and bats. Humid caves appear to provide ideal conditions for this fungus to flourish. Humans are infected by inhaling the fungal spores when they disturb dry fecal deposits. The infection usually affects the lungs, but symptoms vary greatly. Many infections are overlooked because they produce such mild symptoms or none at all. However, histoplasmosis can be severe in some cases, producing symptoms similar to tuberculosis. Histoplasmosis associated with bats is extremely rare in the Pacific Northwest, and the risk of contracting this disease from bats in BC is minimal, with no cases reported to date. The best precaution for persons entering a bat roost that may harbour the fungus is to spray the area with some water to reduce dust, and to wear a mask with a HEPA filter to remove particles as small as 2 microns in diameter.

By far the most negative image associated with bats is that they can transmit diseases. Rabies is a viral disease that is fatal if left untreated. Rabies can infect any mammal, but carnivores (such as skunks, foxes and raccoons) and bats seem to be most susceptible. In BC, all cases of rabies in wild animals have, to date, been associated with bats, with the exception of a rabid skunk in 2021. One of the most frightening symptoms of the disease is paralysis, especially of the hind limbs and throat muscles, prior to death. Paralysis of the throat muscles prevents the animal from swallowing and the accumulation of saliva gives the animal the appearance of frothing at the mouth. The inability to swallow water gave the disease its historical name, hydrophobia. The virus is transmitted through the saliva of an infected animal by a bite. Once in the host, via a bite, the rabies virus progresses along nerves to the spinal cord and brain, eventually invading all nervous tissue and the salivary glands. Presumably, bats infect one another through bites while in day roosts.

The incubation period (time from exposure to development of symptoms) is usually several weeks, although in a few cases it may be up to a year or more. Bats in fact do *not* act as asymptomatic carriers of the rabies disease; instead, they will succumb to the disease once symptoms set in, just as all other mammals will. Some mammals may develop an excitable or "furious" form of rabies in which they become aggressive and engage in attacks. In the majority of cases of bat rabies in North America, individuals appear normal except for a gradual weakness and loss of flying abilities from the developing paralysis. Lausen has observed aggressive behaviour in a rabid BIG BROWN BAT (in Montana), as have others. Another known exception to this is CANYON BAT,

This bat-bug (above) resembles a bedbug in appearance, but it is an ectoparasite specific to bats. Orange ear "chigger mites" (below) are among the most common ectoparasites seen on bats in BC.

which has been reported to be rather aggressive when rabid (see CANYON BAT species account, page 295). Even in large colonies containing thousands of bats, infections seem to involve only a few individuals. This may be in part due to natural immunity that seems to exist in some bat populations.

In the western United States, bats commonly submitted for rabies testing and found to be rabid include BIG BROWN BAT, BRAZILIAN FREE-TAILED BAT and CALIFORNIAN MYOTIS. However, the bat species most associated with human cases of rabies is SILVER-HAIRED BAT. Of 32 human deaths caused by bat rabies in North America between 1958 and 2000, 8 were associated with the rabies virus variant found in SILVER-HAIRED BATS. TRICOLORED BAT, an eastern species, accounts for the largest number of bat-related human rabies cases overall in the United States during the same period (16 cases). Surprisingly, both bat species are rarely submitted for rabies testing, and rarely found to be rabid, and this may be due to their tendency to roost in trees and less often in anthropogenic structures. As such, infected animals are less likely to be encountered relative to building-roosting bats, such as BIG BROWN BATS, a species frequently reported rabid in the United States. However, it is also possible that rabies viruses associated with a particular species of bat (e.g., SILVER-HAIRED variant) are transmitted to humans via other bat species. For example, the SILVER-HAIRED rabies virus variant has been found in other bats, and often the bat associated with the rabies case is not found but rather deduced from genetic sequencing of the virus in the infected human. Bat rabies variants have in fact also been found in non-bat species, including skunks, evidence of cross-species transmission. This supports the fact that analysis of rabies variants in humans may not accurately identify the animal that directly transmitted the disease.

The British Columbia Centre for Disease Control reports that 1,949 bats were tested for rabies at the Rabies Laboratory of the Canadian Food Inspection Agency in BC between 2004 and 2018. Of these, 133 (6.8%) tested positive for rabies. This is similar to US data from 2001 to 2009, when 205,439 bats were submitted for rabies testing and 6.7% were positive. In the BC submissions, the species of bat could be determined in 1,873 (96%) of the submitted specimens, and the most common species tested for rabies was YUMA MYOTIS, of which 386 specimens were tested and 4% were positive. The species most commonly found to be rabid was BIG BROWN BAT (17% of 341 bats submitted tested positive). Since 1950, there have been two human deaths from bat bites in BC. The species implicated in these deaths were an unknown myotis species in the 2003 case, and SILVER-HAIRED BAT in the 2019 case. However, the bats were not actually identified or sampled; instead, the species was inferred based on the rabies variant, as determined through monoclonal antibody and real-time polymerase chain reaction testing for the 2003 case and genome sequencing for the 2019 case. Similar SILVER-HAIRED virus variants were responsible for the human cases in 2000 in Quebec and in 2007 in Alberta, and, as discussed above, this is the most common cause of bat-derived human rabies in the United States.

Less than 7% of bats in BC and across the United States that are submitted for rabies testing actually turn out to be rabid. A bat is turned in for testing typically because it is found not hiding for some reason, including being found on the ground. For example, bats that are wounded by cats, lured into houses with lights on that attract insect prey, or found roosting in exposed locations (which young-of-year or migrating bats are more likely to do) may be seen as suspicious and turned in for testing. In reality, the actual percentage of the wild population of bats in North America that has the rabies virus is poorly known and seems to vary geographically and between species. The overall prevalence seems to range between less than 0.1% and 1.3%.

While both the prevalence of rabies in bats and the chances of humans contracting rabies from bats are low, once it has been transmitted to a human the disease is fatal unless treatment is administered before symptoms appear. Symptoms can develop within weeks or months, and this extended incubation period means that the exact source of exposure might not be recalled.

If a person is bitten or scratched by a bat, or a bat has come into contact with human skin, medical attention should be sought. Be particularly wary of bats that are on the ground or behaving unusually. Children should be warned about the dangers of touching bats or any unfamiliar wild animal. If a bat has been in the same room with a human who may be unable to report an incident, such as a baby or a person with a disability that impairs awareness or communication, seek medical advice.

Pets, especially cats, can be a problem as they sometimes bring disabled bats indoors. Vaccination of dogs and cats against rabies is strongly recommended. If it is necessary to handle bats, take precautions. When handling live bats, wear leather gloves to avoid being bitten. Dead bats should be picked up while wearing disposable rubber gloves; you can improvise by covering your hand with a plastic bag.

The development of rabies can virtually always be prevented after an animal bite (bat or otherwise) if post-exposure treatments begin shortly (within days) after exposure. Pre-exposure vaccination for the rabies disease is also available as an intramuscular vaccine (delivered as three injections in the upper arm over a period of three weeks), but this is costly.

A persistent myth is that the rabies treatment post-exposure is given through multiple injections to the abdomen. The reality in all Canadian jurisdictions is that, like the vaccination process, post-exposure treatment is just a short series of intramuscular injections; following the potential rabies transmission event, individuals who have not previously received pre-exposure vaccination will receive a combination of human rabies immune globulin and rabies vaccine, administered as soon as possible following exposure.

If you are concerned about possible exposure to a rabid bat, contact a local health unit; if you are concerned that an unvaccinated pet has been exposed, contact your local veterinarian.

References

Bonwitt et al. (2018); Brass (1994); Constantine and Blehert (2009); Fenton et al. (2020); Franka et al. (2006); Leslie et al. (2006); Messenger, Rupprecht and Smith (2003); Messenger, Smith and Rupprecht (2002); Parker et al. (2003); Patyk et al. (2012); Pybus (1986); Shankar et al. (2004); Turmelle et al. (2010).

Conservation and Threats

Bats are threatened worldwide—nearly 1,000 species have been identified by the International Union for Conservation of Nature as needing conservation or research attention. There is evidence of a disturbing trend of population declines for many species in Europe and North America. All 18 species native to the United Kingdom are considered vulnerable or endangered. Seven bats in mainland United States appear on the federal list of endangered species, and in Canada three species—TRICOLORED BAT, LITTLE BROWN MYOTIS and NORTHERN MYOTIS—are listed as Endangered by the federal Species at Risk Act (SARA) because of the impacts of white-nose syndrome. LITTLE BROWN MYOTIS and NORTHERN MYOTIS occur in BC, as do PALLID BAT (nationally listed as Threatened) and SPOTTED BAT (Special Concern).

In the early 21st century, two new major threats to North American bats have emerged—fatalities from wind turbines and mortality from white-nose syndrome (WNS). These add to the myriad other human-caused threats, including habitat loss, pesticide use, sound pollution, persecution, climate change, and various other indirect sources of human-caused mortality, such as vehicle collisions and predation by domestic cats. As the longest-living and slowest-reproducing of all small mammals, bat populations cannot rapidly rebound from mass die-offs, such as those caused by WNS. North American populations of several species have declined dramatically, especially in eastern reaches, with recovery estimated to take hundreds of years, if it occurs at all.

While WNS is a major threat to North American bats that hibernate, the wind energy industry mostly threatens migratory species. With growing concern over the rising costs and long-term environmental impacts of fossil fuels, wind energy has become an increasingly important means of generating electricity. Millions of bats have been killed at wind energy sites in North America; 21 of the approximate 47 species of bats occurring in the United States have been killed at turbines, but fatalities at most sites are skewed toward the three species of bats that typically migrate to Canada annually—HOARY BAT, EASTERN

RED BAT and SILVER-HAIRED BAT. These three species account for more than three-quarters of carcasses found under turbines, largely during the late summer and autumn migration period. North American estimates of fatalities at wind energy sites have all been in excess of 500,000 bats per year, and the number of wind development facilities continues to rise. With this heavy death toll each year, and the geographic coverage of wind turbines increasing, estimates of cumulative effects paint a dire outlook for migratory bats on this continent. One study predicted that HOARY BAT populations will decline by 90% in the next 50 years. A western US study confirmed population declines of this species through analysis of a long-term survey dataset. These fatalities raise important concerns about long-term cumulative impacts of current and proposed wind energy development on bat populations. A review of 20 years of data from Cypress Hills, Saskatchewan, determined there had been no declines in HOARY or SILVER-HAIRED BATS, suggesting population impacts may differ across the continent, perhaps associated with migration routes, and the presence of wind turbines along these corridors. Collisions at turbines do not appear to be chance events—bats are attracted to turbines.

It has been proposed that turbines attract insect prey and so bats could in turn be attracted to turbines to exploit these rich food resources, but Erin Baerwald has refuted this hypothesis based on a meta-analysis of bird fatalities. Baerwald found that insectivorous birds—specifically nighthawks, which are active at dusk—did not experience higher mortality than non-insectivorous birds, concluding that increased insect densities are not likely to explain attraction of bats to turbines. It is possible that turbines may resemble roost trees, and these tree- or foliage-roosting bats, migratory across much of their North American range, are attracted to them during the autumn migration, when most fatalities occur. However, at the wind energy sites in northeastern BC, most fatalities are SILVER-HAIRED BAT and some myotis species, including the endangered LITTLE BROWN MYOTIS and NORTHERN MYOTIS, with only a few HOARY BAT and EASTERN RED BAT fatalities. Carcasses of the myotis species are most frequently found in the summer, suggesting that these species are not necessarily migrating. Currently, we do not know what causes this attraction to wind turbines.

Research on acoustic deterrents continues, but the most likely feasible solution to the problem of turbines to date appears to be a cessation of power generation in late summer and early autumn on nights with low wind speeds, when bats are most likely to be migrating. Clearly there will be an economic cost to this, but to reduce the significant risk of extinction for species demonstrating high fatalities, this is a necessary conservation action. At the time of writing this book, all three migratory tree bats in Canada—HOARY BAT, EASTERN RED BAT and SILVER-HAIRED BAT—were in the process of a conservation assessment review by the Committee on the Status of Endangered Wildlife in Canada

Wind turbines near Dawson Creek, BC. PHOTO: DAVE NAGORSEN

(COSEWIC). The threat of energy development is especially potent for LITTLE BROWN MYOTIS and NORTHERN MYOTIS, which are also at risk of another major source of mortality: white-nose syndrome.

White-nose syndrome (WNS) is an infectious fungal disease that has killed millions of hibernating bats since it was first discovered in eastern North America in 2006. The condition is named for a distinctive growth on the muzzle and wings caused by a pathogenic fungus, *Pseudogymnoascus* (formerly *Geomyces*) *destructans,* often referred to as PD. The fungus seems to have been introduced, inadvertently from Eurasia, illustrating the problem of global movement of pathogens by humans. By 2019, the fungus had been reported from across the eastern United States and Canada, as far west as Manitoba and Wyoming. In 2015 NORTHERN MYOTIS was listed as Endangered in the United States, and in 2014 LITTLE BROWN MYOTIS, NORTHERN MYOTIS and TRICOLORED BAT were listed as Endangered in Canada. Both of these endangered myotis species are found in BC, although at the time this book went to print, the fungus that causes WNS had not yet been reported in BC. In 2016 the fungus jumped to the Pacific Northwest and was first confirmed in a LITTLE BROWN MYOTIS in Washington State. The fungus was subsequently found on a SILVER-HAIRED BAT that same year. Since then, WNS has also been found in LONG-EARED MYOTIS, YUMA MYOTIS and possibly FRINGED MYOTIS. The disease has now also been reported on the east side of the Cascade Mountains.

While there has been considerable and rapid research on WNS and much about the disease is now understood, there are no obvious ways to limit the spread of the fungus and no effective treatment options ready to deploy to reduce mortality rates. Several hibernating species in North America are threatened with extirpation because of this disease. Fortunately, the hardest-hit eastern bat populations are beginning to recover, at least in some areas. Populations of some species have declined by more than 90% within five years of the disease reaching a site.

WNS is spread from bat to bat but may also be spread by human activities. To counter this, many jurisdictions have implemented a moratorium on caving activities, and there has been much outreach with cavers, recommending that clothing and equipment be decontaminated after each use. Nevertheless, other major contributors to disease spread, such as accidental bat translocations, have not been ruled out. We don't know how PD jumped to Washington, but there are a few caves in the northwest part of the state where it showed up, roughly 50 kilometres from the major port of Seattle. Using genetics, the source of the Washington PD case was traced back to Kentucky, and while we may never know how this fungal disease jumped from Kentucky to Washington, bat translocation cannot be ruled out.

A review of accidental bat translocations revealed many known cases of aircraft, shipping containers and other long-distance vessels moving bats. In 2012, several Canadian bat biologists were contacted by the Canadian Food Inspection Agency following the discovery of numerous individuals of a species of Asian pipistrelle found in a Chinese cargo ship docked in the port of Vancouver. Karen Blejwas and Tory Rhoads, through multiple interviews in the western United States and Canada, compiled a list of known bat translocations, including discoveries during imports of Christmas trees and lumber shipments, as well as bats hitchhiking on coastal vessels. Hundreds of cross-continent, long-haul semi-trucks drop cargo at the port of Seattle every day, so it is possible that a bat infected with PD or having full-blown WNS arrived in the west as a stowaway from the east.

Dave Hobson in Alberta and others have received reports of bats being translocated in the awnings of camper vans, and the Canadian Wildlife Health Cooperative launched a campaign to educate RV campers in the west to close up awnings and umbrellas at night to reduce the chances that bats would be accidentally moved while they day roost. Regardless of the mechanism of transfer, it is likely inevitable that WNS will eventually spread across the continent. Western North America has roughly twice the number of bat species found in the east, and it is not yet known which species will be most impacted by this disease, but the building-roosting LITTLE BROWN and YUMA MYOTIS account for the highest numbers of WNS cases to date in the west. Wildlife Conservation Society Canada (WCS Canada) worked collaboratively with Thompson Rivers University and McMaster University to develop a potential prophylaxis for WNS, a cocktail of anti-PD bacteria naturally found on some BC bats' wings and also known to occur in Canadian soils. As this book goes to print, this probiotic cocktail has successfully been tested on captive YUMA MYOTIS and piloted at bat boxes and building roosts used by three colonies of YUMA and LITTLE BROWN MYOTIS in southwest BC.

Six of BC's bats are currently listed by the B.C. Conservation Data Centre as being on the Red List or Blue List as Endangered or Threatened species, respectively: PALLID BAT (the only Red-listed species), TOWNSEND'S BIG-EARED BAT, SPOTTED BAT, DARK-NOSED SMALL-FOOTED MYOTIS, NORTHERN MYOTIS and FRINGED MYOTIS. With no long-term data on population trends, we have no clear indication if numbers are stable or declining for these species in BC. Fortunately, the North American Bat Monitoring Program (nabatmonitoring.org) is currently being implemented in the province (since 2016). This is a collaborative initiative of WCS Canada, the Ministry of Environment and Climate Change Strategy, BC Parks and many other organizations, including naturalist groups and regional community bat programs. Colony counts of building-roosting bats conducted by BC citizens are being coordinated by the BC Community Bat Program, and acoustic surveys across the province are being coordinated by WCS Canada. The goal of these long-term datasets is to track population and species trends over time to inform bat conservation and management.

Destruction of roosts and disturbance of roosting bats are serious threats in BC. Large maternity colonies in buildings are considered, by some, as a nuisance and their roosts are often destroyed with little or no concern for the impact on bat populations. In BC, bats are protected under the provincial Wildlife Act, and handling or killing bats requires special permits. However, this law is not always known about or abided by, and inappropriate evictions occur. The BC Community Bat Program provides online resources on proper eviction methods. It is often argued that bats associated with buildings are the "common" species, but we know so little about population numbers that it is difficult to know which species are common. It is also predicted that the building-roosting species (LITTLE BROWN MYOTIS) is likely to be hit hardest by WNS, based on reports in eastern Canada, where few large maternity roosts in buildings remain. YUMA MYOTIS is a similarly common building-roosting bat in BC, and this species, together with LITTLE BROWN MYOTIS, has the highest WNS-caused mortality rates in Washington, the only jurisdiction in the west to have this disease to date. In addition, not all building-roosting bats in BC are YUMA MYOTIS, LITTLE BROWN MYOTIS or BIG BROWN BATS; some bats that roost in buildings may be relatively rare and considered to be potentially endangered or threatened, such as TOWNSEND'S BIG-EARED BAT, PALLID BAT and FRINGED MYOTIS. For example, the only known maternity colony in BC for FRINGED MYOTIS, a species on the provincial Blue List, was found in the attic of a house near Vernon.

Because of their position in the food chain as insect eaters, bats are obvious candidates for pesticide poisoning. Over the years, there have been multiple studies showing a build-up of toxic organochlorines in bats, and although many of these types of pesticides are no longer used in Canada or the United States, they remain in use in other countries and are still travelling to North America via atmospheric exchange. There has been little study to date on the effects of new types or use patterns of pesticides (e.g., neonicotinoids) on bats, and this research is urgently needed. Forest management and agricultural industries in BC incorporate various pest-control strategies, including the use of various pesticides. BC's Integrated Pest Management Plan for forestry would greatly benefit from the inclusion of strategies for retaining the natural pest control services afforded by bats.

Chemical and biological pest control may be contributing to the well-documented insect declines around the world. The impact of substantial declines in insect abundance on insect-eating animals, including bats, has yet to be determined. In addition to chemical pesticides, there are biocides like BTI, which targets mosquitoes. Because BTI can additionally cause significant declines in midges, it is likely to reduce food availability for bats.

Habitat loss, especially the loss of roosting sites, continues to threaten bats around the globe. Large tracts of bat habitat, including forests and wetlands, have been, and continue to be, lost through rapid urban development. Unfortunately, at least in BC, the highest development pressures largely occur in the low-lying river valleys where humans prefer to live and where all species of bats raise young. Valley-bottom forests and extensive riparian rock habitats continue to be lost from flooding for hydroelectric dams in some areas (e.g., BC Hydro's Site C dam in the Peace River valley). Most of these habitat changes represent a permanent loss of bat habitat, and although several species have adapted to roosting in human-built structures, the ephemeral nature of these roosts, as property ownership changes, buildings are renovated and more land is developed, works against the conservation of these long-lived mammals (see discussion on bat boxes in Summer Roosting Sites, page 36).

Mine closures threaten bat hibernacula in many areas of BC. Many abandoned mines in this province, especially those that are deep and/or at low elevations, are used by bats in winter (see Winter Roosting Sites—Hibernacula, page 51). Instead of blasting a mine portal shut, sealing it off completely, mines can be safely closed to human entry, while enabling bats to continue to fly in and out. This can be done through the installation of a steel grate, sometimes in combination with a concrete or metal culvert. These grates, also called gates, need to be robust to prevent human access and have appropriately spaced horizontal bars to be "bat-friendly." While a few mines have been gated in BC to protect hibernating bats, many have been closed without the requisite long-term acoustic monitoring needed for a proper assessment of winter use.

In BC, timber harvest operations probably have the most wide-scale, and possibly the most severe, impact on bat habitat. Forests are used by many bat

Cori Lausen descends to the lower entrance of a mine hibernaculum in the West Kootenay to retrieve research instrumentation that has been monitoring hibernating bats. The mine was gated to protect the three species of bats that regularly use it each winter. Lausen wears a Tyvek suit as standard practice at bat hibernacula across North America to ensure that there is no accidental transmission of the fungus that causes white-nose syndrome. PHOTO: FLORIAN GRANER (SEALIFE PRODUCTIONS, WA)

Two "old-growth tree" mimic roosts being erected near Burges James Gadsden Provincial Park in fall 2020 by a team led by Darcie Quamme. BrandenBark (artificial bark) is wrapped around a pole to create the roost on the right, and layers of DOUGLAS-FIR bark have been screwed together to form a matrix of crevices to create the roost on the left. The former is expected to last 30 years and was used as a LITTLE BROWN BAT maternity roost in its first summer of deployment; the longevity of the latter, designed and constructed by landowner Sigi Liebmann, is unknown. Monitoring of these artificial roosts began in spring 2021. PHOTO: CORI LAUSEN species for foraging and roosting, but bats use these habitats in different ways. Some species roost alone under bark, others roost in large maternal colonies in tree hollows, and still others roost in foliage. During winter, roosting requirements appear to shift, with bats finding shelter inside tree cavities that are insulated and unlikely to freeze. In BC and Alaska, bats have even been found using tree root wads as winter roosts. In addition to the obvious impacts associated with clear-cutting of large tracts of forest habitat, removal of standing dead trees (snags), intensive management of secondary forests and increasing concern over high fuel loads has led to prescriptions for forest fire management that favour removal of important snag or wildlife trees (and thus habitat) for bats. Managing forests for the availability of roosting sites is complicated by the sheer diversity of bats in BC, many of which select different characteristics in tree roosts.

The use of the term *bat* makes it harder to remember that different species have different habitat requirements, and this needs to be considered when addressing threats like habitat loss. Quick fixes for habitat loss often include suggestions to install bat boxes, for example, even though only a few bat species in BC use these structures for roosting, and there has been no study of how natural assemblages of bat species are affected by the installation of them. "Artificial bark" roost structures using poles are now being erected in the Kootenay region, with the goal of mitigating habitat loss for a larger number of bat species, but these old-growth/snag mimics are costly and labour-intensive to create. Other tree roost mitigation experiments are taking place largely in the Kootenay region, employing an approach that creates crevices for potential roost sites (most widely implemented by Todd Manning) by making strategic slices in trees with a chainsaw. The lack of knowledge of species-specific roosting requirements (for winter and/or summer use) continues to hamper attempts to identify and thus retain a suitably large and representative portion of roost trees during forestry operations (e.g., wildlife habitat feature designations).

Although wildlife biologists have paid considerable attention to how large mammals and some smaller mammals (e.g., rodents) use forests of different ages, relatively little research has been done concerning the detrimental effects of forestry and timber harvest practices on bats, especially on their foraging behaviour. In the mid-1990's, Scott Grindal undertook groundbreaking research on the impact of forest harvesting on some species of bats near Nelson, BC. He used acoustic bat detectors to eavesdrop on the echolocation calls made by bats to assess activity and found that levels were consistently highest along the hard edges between cut-blocks and intact forest; based on the nature of their echolocation calls, he determined that bats were commuting and not feeding. Audrey Lauzon repeated this study at precisely the same location 25 years later and found that although the edges had "blurred" (i.e., were less abrupt due to vegetation that had grown in), the results were similar, and she concluded that

Two Provincial Designations—Not Enough to Protect Bat Habitat

Bats present a challenge for the development of habitat protection policies because of differing habitat requirements among species, their cryptic nature and their need to use roosts with specific physical and microclimate characteristics (exemplified by roost switching throughout the summer and often during winter). To partially address bat habitat protection, in 2018 the BC government passed an order (M213) under the Forest and Range Practices Act to protect a specific list of wildlife habitat features (WHFS) on Crown land in the Kootenay-Boundary Region. The list includes bat maternity roosts and hibernacula where they occur within "natural features" (i.e., a cave used by bats can be designated as a WHF but a mine used by bats cannot).

For a bat roost site to be afforded protection, the order requires WHFS to be identifiable without the use of "scientific tools." This has prevented several confirmed tree hibernacula that had been located using radiotelemetry from being recognized as WHFS. Birds may be better suited for protection under this order as they at least produce a nest that is generally visible (and typically used for the duration of the young-rearing period)—in contrast to bats, which hide, do not create any type of structure, and typically need to switch roosts during the maternity season. For example, some maternity colonies have been documented using up to 60 roosts in one summer. It is likely that a different, larger-scale approach will be needed to achieve effective legislation for protecting bat habitat in BC.

To date, the only existing option for larger-scale habitat protection for bats (also regulated under the Forest and Range Practices Act and thus also applying only on Crown lands) is designation of a wildlife habitat area (WHA). Through a formal consultation process, species-specific habitat management (i.e., conservation) can be granted to a short list of identified species (commonly referred to as "Identified Wildlife"). At the time this book was being written, only two currently recognized species of bats in BC qualified for habitat management under this policy: FRINGED MYOTIS and SPOTTED BAT. This policy therefore does not provide habitat protection for the two bat species recently listed as Endangered by COSEWIC (LITTLE BROWN MYOTIS and NORTHERN MYOTIS) because they have not yet been added to the Identified Wildlife list under the Forest and Range Practices Act. At the time we were writing this book, the Identified Wildlife list had not been updated since 2006.

This LITTLE BROWN MYOTIS (above) in Alberta died after becoming entangled in the burrs of an invasive burdock plant. PHOTO: NATHAN DEBRUYN. This desiccated BC bat of unknown species was found in Salmon Arm entangled in burdock (below). PHOTO: KEN DZINGAL temporal aspects need to be considered when assessing the effects of habitat disturbance on these long-lived mammals. To help the forestry industry develop practices sensitive to bat populations, it is imperative that further research be carried out to determine the impacts of such commonly applied practices as harvesting, tree thinning and snag (or wildlife tree) removal.

Sources of bat mortality associated with human activities, other than harm from evictions and habitat loss, can also include inadvertent death traps, such as irrigation pipes, forest insect traps, barbed wire and upright buckets, rain barrels or watering tanks—and even invasive plants. Because bats that are not in flight depend on their clawed thumbs to climb and manoeuvre on the ground, they are vulnerable to slippery surfaces that offer no grip. Many bat species do not easily take flight directly from the ground, and when they do they cannot gain height quickly. A bat that accidentally drops into a bucket, or approaches water in a rain barrel too closely and falls in, can become trapped if the sides of the container are too slippery or lipped, thus preventing escape. In some cases, the distress calls attract other bats, resulting in multiple mortalities (see image on page 145).

These situations can be easily prevented by either turning buckets upside down or ensuring that there is some sort of rough-surfaced ramp bats can use to crawl out to safety. This also applies to cattle drinking tanks, which can be an inviting water source for bats in dry areas but can also be deadly to a bat that accidentally hits the water surface. The animal may be stuck swimming around and around the tank, unable to escape. While bats are good swimmers, they do need to be able to crawl out of the water to regain flight. Similarly, insect traps may pose a danger to some bats. Large tracts of forest in BC are monitored for insects, specifically forest pests. Traps to capture insects are occasionally found to contain LONG-EARED MYOTIS, a gleaning bat that is presumably lured into the trap by the prey-generated sounds being emitted by arthropods in the trap (see image on page 224). Also noteworthy are multiple observations of bats becoming entangled in invasive plants in BC: burdock and FULLER'S TEASEL have entangled bats in BC, including CALIFORNIAN and LONG-EARED MYOTIS on Salt Spring Island. This may happen when low-flying bats approach vegetation closely, foraging or looking for roost opportunities, and the robust burrs of the seed pods snag their fur. The BC Community Bat Program has records of LONG-EARED MYOTIS, TOWNSEND'S BIG-EARED BAT, HOARY BAT, SILVER-HAIRED BAT and various unidentified myotis species that have succumbed to entanglement in burdock. While this program has not received observations of bats impaled on barbed wire, there are records of this in Alberta and elsewhere.

As described in preceding sections, all bats in BC navigate through their environment and find prey using sound. As most people can attest to, our landscapes are becoming louder. Even once-quiet grasslands are today being inundated with white noise associated with industrial activities, including resource extraction, transportation (i.e., road noise) and agriculture. Multiple studies have shown negative impacts of noise on foraging success for bats. For example, PALLID BATS, which depend on hearing prey-generated sounds when hunting for terrestrial arthropods, avoid areas of noise; their foraging is negatively impacted even 640 metres away from a major road (see PALLID BAT species account, page 135). This may have conservation implications in the south Okanagan, where this and other bat species may be inundated with competing night-time sounds associated with orchards, highways, agriculture and tourism. Tourism in summer in the popular Okanagan valley is associated with constant sound emanating from highways, concentrated in the low-elevation valley where adult female bats of up to 15 species raise young.

Another threat that can be associated with roads is light pollution. How lights impact bats is also poorly studied, with species-specific differences stemming from the tendency of some bats to forage for insects that congregate around lights, while others are seemingly repelled by lights. Outdoor lighting can impact use of roosts and commuting zones, in addition to changing foraging behaviours. Multiple studies have shown that red light impacts bats less than other colours or white light.

Climate change is likely to impact animals around the globe. It will impact bats in complex ways through shifts in insect densities and diversity, changing availability of water sources, altered summer and winter roosting conditions, and even potential changes in body size stemming from changing evolutionary forces. As small-bodied mammals with high surface-to-volume ratios, bats have specific roosting requirements both in summer and in winter, and their use of torpor as an energy-saving strategy is closely linked to ambient conditions. So it stands to reason that temperate zone bats are likely to be impacted in many ways as the climate changes—in both summer and winter periods. There is already some evidence that extended droughts reduce reproductive success in bats because nursing mothers do not have enough water to produce sufficient milk.

Mass mortality events related to heat stress have been reported in several countries and in different species of bats, ranging from mass mortality in overheating bat boxes in Spain to multitudes of dead bats in Australia during recent extreme heat waves. In fact, several extreme heat events in Australia have been associated with the deaths of tens of thousands of flying foxes, including an event in 2018 that killed 23,000 SPECTACLED FLYING FOXES, approximately one-third of the global population. Reports of overheating bat boxes have come from various locations, including California and Florida; in these hot latitudes, overcrowding can also lead to heat dissipation problems (see image on page 70). In BC, there have been multiple reports of bats experiencing heat-related stress, including Susan Dulc's observation in the Creston area of bats fleeing a hot bat box in daylight, Gillian Sanders and Steve Latour's report

Collisions with Cars

Highways may be a significant source of direct mortality for bats through collisions with vehicles. This is not well studied in Canada but is an increasing focus of research in the United States, where only 17% of the landscape is more than 1 kilometre from a road, and in Europe, where bat overpasses and underpasses are being installed with successful use by bats. In BC, although no formal study has taken place, monitoring of WESTERN TOAD where they must cross a highway between a lake and their upland terrestrial habitat resulted in several observations of bat collisions with vehicles. Over 21 nights spent monitoring toads on roads, Kim Frederiksen observed four road-killed bats (later identified as either LITTLE BROWN MYOTIS or YUMA MYOTIS), each on separate nights, along a 12-kilometre stretch of highway in the West Kootenay. Attuned to the

Dead bat found in car radiator.
PHOTO: MATHIEU LAURIAULT

possibility of colliding with bats, she also observed her own vehicle hitting three bats outside of the monitoring area, despite slow driving speeds.

Collisions with bats may be more likely in some areas, such as highways that bisect species' home ranges. This may be expected in greater frequencies where busy roads follow river valley bottoms and bats need to fly across the roads to get from a roost (e.g., in rock outcrops along the perimeter of valleys) to drinking and foraging areas elsewhere in the valley. Not easily noticed by drivers, unlikely to make a sound on impact, small-bodied and thus likely to ricochet into ditches, or easily scavenged from road surfaces—all these are reasons why the impacts of roads on bat populations may be overlooked.

Free-tailed bats (top left) bulging out of the bottom of a bat box in Florida. This behaviour can result from overcrowding or overheating, or a combination of these conditions. PHOTO: LAURA FINN (FLY BY NIGHT, INC.). YUMA MYOTIS (top right) congregate at the opening of this bat box in the West Kootenay during hot weather. To solve this problem, the owner began raising and lowering an awning each day to keep the sun directly off the box. Both adults and pups experienced heat stress, and some bats have died at this roost during overheating events. PHOTO: STEVE LATOUR. A bat box in Port Coquitlam reached more than 42°C on July 4 and 5, 2018, coinciding with a mass mortality of more than 70 adults and pups (bottom left and right). Overcrowding occurred at a time of high ambient temperatures. PHOTOS: JOHN SAREMBA

of "bulging bats" trying to vent themselves at the opening of a hot bat box in the Twin Bays area in July, and Leah Rensel and John Saremba's discovery of a pile of dead and overheating pups and adults underneath hot bat boxes in Port Coquitlam (see also Summer Roosting Sites, page 36).

While dry hot summers are at one end of the spectrum for climate change impacts on bats, winter hibernation is also likely to be impacted. Underground temperatures usually reflect mean surface temperatures, and shifts in hibernation conditions over time can therefore also be predicted. As outlined above (see Hibernation and Winter Ecology, page 45) temperatures measured at known western Canada hibernacula are cooler than the optimal growth range of the fungus that causes white-nose syndrome, and the geographic impact of this disease may therefore shift over time as hibernaculum conditions change. On the other hand, winters are likely to shorten, enabling bats to emerge from hibernation earlier in some areas. The interactions of climate change, bat hibernation and white-nose syndrome will be complex.

Education to change negative perceptions of bats is critical to ensuring the survival of these enigmatic and ecologically important animals. One of the most important contributions to aid bat conservation is simply to be more tolerant of these mammals. For interested individuals, we recommend joining Bat Conservation International. This non-profit organization does an excellent job of promoting bat conservation and it provides a wealth of educational material about bats in general. Locally, the BC Community Bat Program is a useful source of information and provides opportunities for citizens to become involved in bat conservation efforts. Other opportunities to engage with bat conservation include the BatCaver program, where cavers and mine enthusiasts help locate and monitor underground habitat for bats in western Canada. Bat conservation efforts and strategies in BC are overseen by the British Columbia Bat Action Team (BCBAT), a group that provides input into development of provincial bat survey standards, best management practices for various sectors that have impacts on bats and bat habitat, conservation and recovery of bat species at risk, education and outreach, and identification of bat research and conservation priorities. The number of people advocating for bats in BC continues to grow, and it is this increasing support from citizens that is needed to safeguard bat biodiversity in the province.

References

Adams (2010); Adams et al. (2015); Altringham and Kerth (2016); Ancillotto, Serangeli and Russo (2013); Baerwald and Barclay (2011); Bailey et al. (2019); Bat Conservation International (2020); Blejwas et al. (2021); Boyle et al. (1997); British Columbia Community Bat Program (2020); Brühl et al. (2020); Bunkley and Barber (2015); Constantine (2003); Frick, Kingston and Flanders (2019); Frick et al. (2010); Frick et al. (2015); Frick et al. (2017); Gonsalves et al. (2013); Green et al. (2020); Grindal and Brigham (1998); Grindal and Brigham (1999); Hallmann et al. (2017); Hein et al. (2017); Jones et al. (2009); Loeb et al. (2015); Mineau and Callaghan (2018); Olson and Barclay (2013); Ommundsen (2020); Racey (1982); Rodhouse et al. (2019); Sherwin, Montgomery and Lundy (2013); Stone, Harris and Jones (2015); Straka et al. (2019); Straka et al. (2020); Thapa, Turner and Roossinck (2021); Voigt and Kingston (2016); Weaver (2019); Wildlife Conservation Society Canada (2021); Zimmerling and Francis (2016).

Susan Dulc and Cori Lausen erect a mist-net over a stream near Lillooet. It will be opened at dusk. PHOTO: IAN ROUTLEY

Studying Bats

Biologists can study bats directly or indirectly. Indirect study can involve collecting guano, observing and counting individuals as they emerge from roost sites, or recording echolocation sounds. Guano can be used to genetically identify bat species, to look for micro-organisms like the fungus that causes white-nose syndrome or viruses that can be shed under stress, or to examine diet. Counts of bats emerging from roosts is becoming a popular citizen science contribution to our understanding of population changes as bats face unprecedented threats (see Conservation and Threats, page 57). Because bats in BC produce sound to navigate their environment and capture prey, these sounds can be used to confirm, and in some cases quantify, their presence in the night sky. Spectral analysis of the sounds they produce can be used to differentiate many species (see Acoustics: Echolocation and Species Identification, page 103).

Biologists can also study bats directly by capturing them. Bats can be captured with thin mesh nets, a method similar to that used for capturing birds. However, a mist-net for bats is typically made of thinner threads and has shallower pockets. Mist-netting bats involves placing a net across a potential flyway; by the time a bat detects the net, it has a hard time avoiding it. Once it hits the net, the bat falls into a pocket and is not easily able to fly out of it. The challenging part of netting bats is knowing where to place nets, how high or low to set them, and what arrangements of nets to use to maximize the chance of a bat flying into them. The answers to these questions depend largely on the landscape and the species being targeted. Different net deployments target different species. For example, when targeting high-flying SPOTTED BATS, biologists set nets high above a valley bottom; when targeting species that spend a lot of time foraging over water, like YUMA or LITTLE BROWN MYOTIS, the nets are placed in a valley bottom near or over the water. Slow flying and/or manoeuvrable species may be most likely to avoid capture by flying around a net once detected by its echolocation. And high-flying species may evade nets when they are deployed close to the ground. Most bat nets are 2.6 metres tall, although nets can be vertically joined to create a high "wall" that extends 10.4 metres into the air. In forest habitats, nets can also be strung in the canopy.

Another common way to capture bats is by using harp traps. As the name implies, these traps typically look like harps, with double or triple layers of vertical fishing line strung on a square frame. Each row of vertical strings is called a bank; a triple-bank harp trap means there are three rows of vertical strings, each slightly offset from the others. As the bat flies, it will have a difficult time manoeuvring through the closely spaced strings and, after hitting strings, will fall into a bag below the trap that has flaps to reduce captured individuals' ability to crawl or fly out.

Cori Lausen (top) scans a "quad mist-net" for bat captures. This wall of net consists of four standard-sized nets tied together; it is raised and lowered using a flagpole system developed by Bat Conservation and Management. Jared captured this image using a long exposure and "light painting" techniques. LONG-EARED MYOTIS (bottom left) captured in a mist-net during a BC inventory. PHOTO: CORI LAUSEN. Small and large harp traps (bottom right) are set up outside an abandoned cabin that houses a large maternity roost of YUMA MYOTIS in the West Kootenay. As bats fly out the cabin window and door, they run into the vertical fishing lines of the trap and drop into the bag below. PHOTO: SUSAN DULC

Authors Jared Hobbs and Cori Lausen set a mist-net to target SPOTTED BATS in Lillooet. PHOTO: IAN ROUTLEY

A bat in hand can be measured. The most useful measurement is of bat forearm length (image on page 93), which can provide an index of age in pups and often aids in species differentiation in adults (see In-Hand Differentiation, page 92). Forearm length may vary within a species between males and females, with females of many species being slightly larger. Length can also increase with latitude, with larger individuals in more northerly and colder locations, a phenomenon known as Bergmann's rule. The principle is that larger individuals are better equipped to reduce heat loss. This holds for LITTLE BROWN MYOTIS in both BC and Alberta: there are substantial forearm measurement records of this geographically widespread bat, and while the same pattern holds on each side of the Rocky Mountains—larger forearms in northerly locations (i.e., Yukon and the Northwest Territories)—overall, LITTLE BROWN MYOTIS west of the Rocky Mountain Continental Divide are smaller than those on the east side. Similarly, bat size can vary according to landscape. In BC, there is a trend among some bat species to be smaller on the coast than inland. This is the case for CALIFORNIAN MYOTIS and for LONG-EARED MYOTIS,* two species for which there are a substantial number of morphometric records (see next two pages).

---

* See Lausen et al. (2019), graph on page 276.

Species	Source of measured bats	Forearm lengths (millimetres)		Larger females— statistically significant?
		Females	Males	
CALIFORNIAN MYOTIS	BC	33.2 (n = 250)	32.8 (n = 303)	yes
LITTLE BROWN MYOTIS	BC, Yukon (west of Rocky Mountains Continental Divide)	36.5 (n = 921)	36.2 (n = 284)	yes
	BC, Alberta, Yukon, Montana, Northwest Territories (east of Rocky Mountains Continental Divide)	38.2 (n = 560)	37.9 (n = 944)	yes
LONG-EARED MYOTIS	BC	38.3 (n = 150)	37.3 (n = 81)	yes
LONG-LEGGED MYOTIS	BC	38.6 (n = 75)	38.4 (n = 33)	no
NORTHERN MYOTIS	BC	36.7 (n = 31)	35.9 (n = 18)	yes
SILVER-HAIRED BAT	BC	41.9 (n = 33)	41.4 (n = 180)	yes
TOWNSEND'S BIG-EARED BAT	BC	44.4 (n = 129)	43.1 (n = 151)	yes
YUMA MYOTIS	BC	35.0 (n = 935)	34.2 (n = 446)	yes

Comparisons of male and female mean forearm lengths are listed for species where sample sizes exceeded 45 bats (with at least 15 of each sex). In all species that could be examined, females were significantly larger than males, with the exception of LONG-LEGGED MYOTIS, which showed only a small difference between male and female forearm lengths across BC.

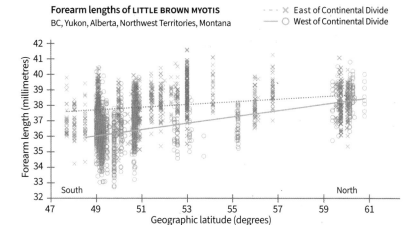

Forearm lengths of LITTLE BROWN MYOTIS
BC, Yukon, Alberta, Northwest Territories, Montana

- - - ✕ East of Continental Divide
——— ○ West of Continental Divide

Forearm length (millimetres)

Geographic latitude (degrees)

South — North

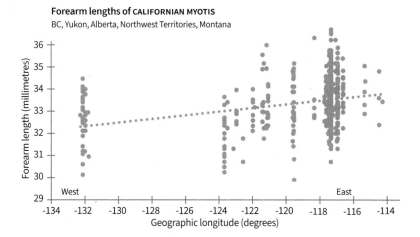

Forearm lengths of CALIFORNIAN MYOTIS
BC, Yukon, Alberta, Northwest Territories, Montana

Forearm length (millimetres)

Geographic longitude (degrees)

West — East

Morphological traits can also be used to differentiate species (see In-Hand Differentiation, page 92) and the sexes. As typical mammals, a male has a penis and females have a vaginal opening (see images on next page), so genitalia may be used to differentiate the sexes. The tip of the penis can have very different shapes among bat species (see page 79, e.g., PALLID BAT has a flat, wide penis, in contrast to most other bat species), although this is not typically used to differentiate bats in BC. Female bats have mammary glands with nipples, and in BC all but the Lasiurines have just two; HOARY BATS and EASTERN RED BATS have four.

While a bat is in the hand, its age can also be assessed. Knowing approximate age can help define population vital rates to better understand the impact of

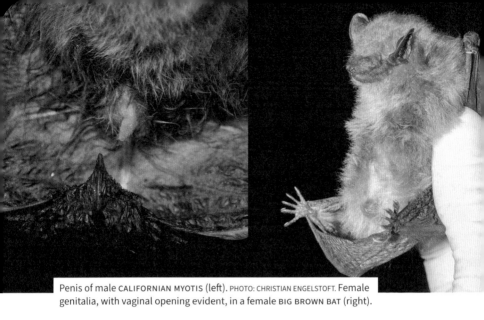

Penis of male CALIFORNIAN MYOTIS (left). PHOTO: CHRISTIAN ENGELSTOFT. Female genitalia, with vaginal opening evident, in a female BIG BROWN BAT (right).

threats to these long-lived mammals. Traditionally, assessing the ages of bats has involved determining whether they are young-of-year or adult, but we now encourage further age estimation descriptions, even if they are relative and specific to a particular species in a specific area, largely because an adult bat can live for many years or even decades. Monitoring populations appropriately may require a further breakdown of the adult cohort. While an individual's exact age cannot be known without tracking it through its life (e.g., through mark-recapture), a relative ranking of age within the adult cohort of a species in an area can be achieved by assessing the degree of tooth wear. Different classes of tooth wear have been developed for different species in different areas, all reflecting the fact that permanent adult teeth, which replace the jagged milk teeth of nursing pups, wear over time. The fraction of the upper canine teeth worn down is typically used to quantify tooth wear. For example, Susan Holroyd presented a seven-class tooth wear code for BIG BROWN BATS in southern Alberta, where class 1 means sharp, pointed canines, and class 7 indicates that less than three-quarters of the tooth is remaining. Bats that eat harder-bodied insects are likely to wear down their teeth faster than those feeding more on softer-bodied insects. Teeth are small and may require magnifiers to examine, and the degree of wear of the upper canines is relative and does not provide an absolute age. Although this method is not precise, estimating tooth wear is worthwhile.

Assessing reproductive status can provide extremely valuable information for the monitoring of these long-lived mammals. To describe male reproductive status, you must determine whether there are testes present and/or stored

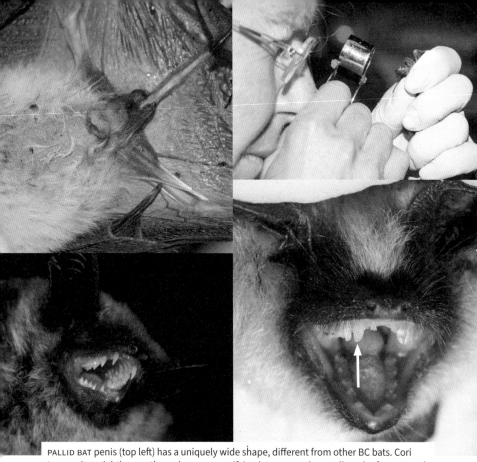

PALLID BAT penis (top left) has a uniquely wide shape, different from other BC bats. Cori Lausen (top right) peers through a 10× magnifying lens to see the small teeth of a captured bat. Categorizing relative degree of tooth wear (tooth class) of multiple captures can help describe population age structure for a species in a given area. Sharp canine teeth (bottom left) of a young LONG-EARED MYOTIS. PHOTO: CHRISTIAN ENGELSTOFT. The worn upper canine teeth of this older DARK-NOSED SMALL-FOOTED MYOTIS (bottom right) look almost flattened, the result of tooth wear from a lifetime of crunching insect exoskeletons.

sperm. Bats are scrotal when the swollen testes have descended into the tail membrane and are producing sperm. During this period, sperm is stored in the cauda epididymides, located on either side of the tail near the body. The cauda epididymides are black when empty and generally easy to observe during the summer when there is not much stored body fat. If the male has never produced sperm in its life (i.e., is a young-of-year), these black organs are short and thin, and often hard to see because they occur close to the base of the tail, up near the abdomen. However, in an adult male that has reproduced but is not currently storing any sperm, these organs will look wide and stretched out, often obvious and extending along both sides of the tail. During sperm production, the large,

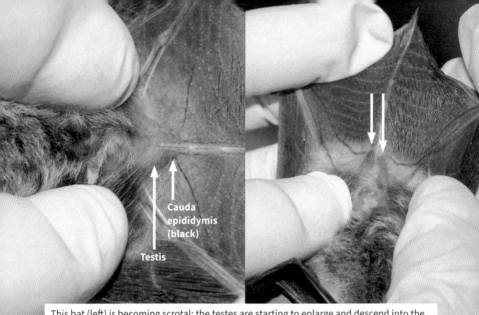

Cauda
epididymis
(black)

Testis

This bat (left) is becoming scrotal: the testes are starting to enlarge and descend into the tail membrane. The empty cauda epididymides are underneath the testes, and as the testes enlarge and produce sperm, the sperm will be stored in the epididymides (see facing page top left). When completely empty of sperm prior to becoming scrotal, the cauda epididymides look stretched and deflated along the sides of the tail (right).

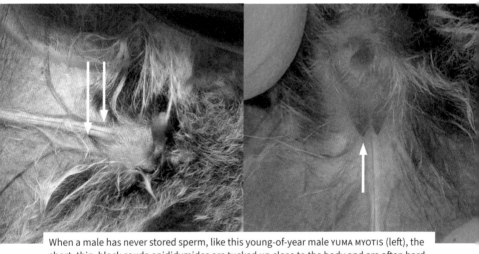

When a male has never stored sperm, like this young-of-year male YUMA MYOTIS (left), the short, thin, black cauda epididymides are tucked up close to the body and are often hard to find (in contrast with a male that has stored sperm previously—see image above right).
RIGHT PHOTO: CHRIS CURRIE

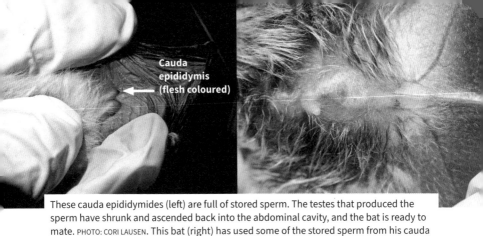

Cauda epididymis (flesh coloured)

These cauda epididymides (left) are full of stored sperm. The testes that produced the sperm have shrunk and ascended back into the abdominal cavity, and the bat is ready to mate. PHOTO: CORI LAUSEN. This bat (right) has used some of the stored sperm from his cauda epididymides, and they therefore show a small portion of black where the epididymides are empty. The amount of stored sperm left can be estimated to indicate the progression of mating activity. For example, this bat might be described as having approximately 85% remaining sperm.

swollen testes usually obscure the thin black cauda epididymides. After sperm production is complete and the testes shrink back up into the body cavity, the cauda epididymides are a creamy flesh colour when filled with sperm. The sperm will stay relatively cool in the tail membrane, to survive and be ejaculated over an extended period. In this full state, cauda epididymides can be mistaken for swollen testes. As mating proceeds and stored sperm is ejaculated, the cauda epididymides shrink and their margins return to a black colour, indicative of a lack of sperm. Much can be learned about timing of mating if the amount of stored sperm remaining is estimated.

Once the fetus beings to develop, females will have a slightly distended abdomen, though in early pregnancy this can be difficult to differentiate from a stomach full of food. However, by late spring in much of BC, pregnancy is relatively easy to assess either visually or using gentle palpation of the abdomen. When the pup is born and starts to nurse, the female will show an obvious ring of missing fur around her nipples (also called teats; see image next page), and gentle squeezing is likely to excrete a drop of milk. The nipple will also generally look reddened and elongated during the nursing phase. Once the pup starts to nurse less, the mammary gland produces less milk, and the weaning process begins. Hair will start to regrow around and even on the end of the nipples, and the nipple may look scabbed over and/or not yield milk when gently squeezed. A female that is post-lactating is no longer nursing a pup, and if this is observed too early in the season, while other members of the colony are still lactating, this can mean that the female's pup has died.

As pups grow, their long bones elongate, and the relative age of non-flying pups can be determined by measuring the length of the forearm. To determine

The bare teats of this SPOTTED BAT (left) indicate that she is currently nursing a pup. The bare area around the teat of this lactating female LITTLE BROWN MYOTIS (above) is evidence of nursing.

if a bat is young-of-year or an adult, researchers examine the shape and degree of ossification of the finger joints in the wing. Round finger joints indicate an adult, while a long joint indicates a juvenile. Sometimes it is also necessary to backlight the joint to observe it. As a pup grows, the cartilage of the finger joints is converted to bone. Light passes through cartilage, and thus backlighting a finger joint in a young-of-year individual will reveal one or two gaps (called epiphyseal gaps) in an elongated joint where cartilage still exists, and light thus passes through. This gap can even be measured over time to compare relative ages of young-of-year. It will look like one long gap in newly flying pups and will start to look like two distinct gaps in older young (see image facing page). In contrast, adult joints will look very round, and light will not pass through the joint (see image on facing page). It varies as to how long a young-of-year bat will be recognizable using this technique; in many cases, joints are fully fused prior to hibernation.

A bat's exact age can be determined if it is permanently marked and recaptured over its life span. Although labour-intensive, marking bats is also highly valuable for studying other behaviours, like migration, roost fidelity and relationships. Examples of marking are wing branding, tattoos, forearm bands and PIT tags. Bands and PIT tags are used most often.

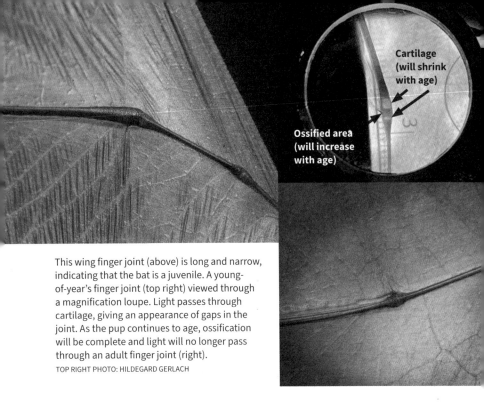

Cartilage (will shrink with age)

Ossified area (will increase with age)

This wing finger joint (above) is long and narrow, indicating that the bat is a juvenile. A young-of-year's finger joint (top right) viewed through a magnification loupe. Light passes through cartilage, giving an appearance of gaps in the joint. As the pup continues to age, ossification will be complete and light will no longer pass through an adult finger joint (right).

TOP RIGHT PHOTO: HILDEGARD GERLACH

Unlike bands, PIT tags are not visible on the outside of the body. These tags, approximately the size of a grain of rice, are microchips that are injected under the skin that can be scanned with appropriate equipment. This technology is popular with domestic animals, such as dogs and cattle, and works well for bats, especially females, because of their high roost fidelity. As they return to their roost, they pass by a PIT tag reader, which scans the tag and records the bat's presence.

Marking and then recapturing individuals can be useful for estimating population sizes, studying roost fidelity and roost switching, quantifying survivorship, documenting movement patterns, and more. Research on new methods that use visual matching of collagen–elastin bundle patterns for recognition of individuals has been published, but it is not yet clear if this technique will prove logistically feasible for widespread use. Wing or tail membrane venation patterns have proven useful in Europe to distinguish between similar species.

When a bat is captured, samples can be collected. Hair can be used for isotope analysis, skin for genetic analyses, or blood for physiological study. These samples can provide information about the individual or the population more generally. An example is the use of isotopes to investigate movement patterns of bats. With this technique, concentrations of stable (not radioactive) isotopes of carbon, nitrogen and hydrogen, which reflect the prey and water consumed,

This female YUMA MYOTIS has a numbered forearm band to allow individual identification for monitoring purposes. Bands are lipped to prevent any damage to the wing, and they are loose enough for the bat to groom under the band.

A long antenna scans PIT tags in bats as they enter or exit under the wood siding of this building roost at Stave Lake. The bats must pass close to the antenna for their PIT tag to be read, and each detection is logged by the receiver in the waterproof case mounted under the stairs. PHOTO: LEAH RENSEL

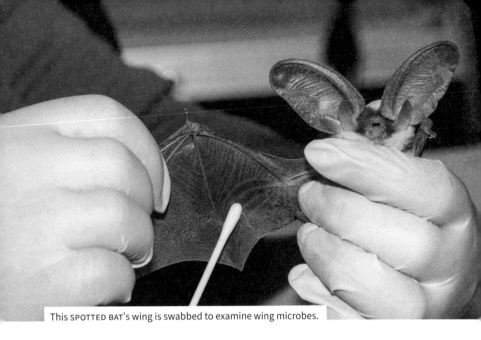

This SPOTTED BAT's wing is swabbed to examine wing microbes.

are commonly measured; "isoscape" maps are then used to match bat isotope concentrations to landscape isotope patterns, illustrating bat movement. Skin samples may be used to evaluate a bat's relationship to other bats in the region or across the continent. Blood can be used to look for signatures of dehydration or hormone concentrations. Of increasing importance is swab sampling of wing membranes to test for the fungus that causes white-nose syndrome. Wing swabs are also proving valuable for other uses, such as describing the microbial diversity on bat skin and using skin cells as sources of genetic material for species identification. Trained biologists handling bats can take a fresh tissue sample from a strategic location on the wing, using small biopsy punches (see image on page 136), or, if the bat is dead, snip off a small piece of wing or tail skin. In all cases, the tissue sample can be taped to a paper index card and dry-stored temporarily at room temperature (eventually freezing or using other storage techniques).

It's a good idea to wear gloves when handling bats, dead or alive, even if you have been vaccinated for rabies. Carcasses should be double-bagged and then placed in the freezer. Similarly, guano of bats should be collected using gloves, and then placed into a paper envelope and left at room temperature in a dry location, although freezing may be most appropriate for long-term storage (months or years). Contact the BC government's Animal Health Centre laboratory or the BC Community Bat Program for further information and questions about bat carcasses, samples or guano.

Radiotelemetry is a specialized and relatively more expensive method of tracking many animals, including bats. This method involves attaching

Female SPOTTED BAT with radio transmitter glued to her back. This allowed the bat to be tracked using a combination of helicopter and on-the-ground radiotelemetry, leading Cori Lausen and Jared Hobbs to a cliff maternity roost in the Lillooet area.

a tiny battery-powered radio transmitter to a bat. For most small species, transmitters are glued to the skin between the shoulder blades. At some point after deployment (typically a few days to weeks) the transmitter intentionally falls off and the fur grows back in. During deployment, the transmitter emits a pulsed signal detectable with a portable radio receiver and directional antenna. This technology has been evolving over the years, and there are now radio transmitters suitable for use on even the smallest species in BC. The transmitter must be small enough that bats can still fly, and this requires a very small battery to power the units. Commercially available transmitters can be as small as 0.27 grams. As a rule of thumb, transmitters should not exceed 5% of the bat's body mass, especially in the middle of summer when the bat would be flying nightly to forage. The emitted radio signal does not travel far, nor does it last long, typically running out of power after one to eight weeks. Radio transmitters are attached using non-toxic glue and may not stay attached to the bat for as long as the battery lasts; this is especially true for bats that repeatedly rub against rock as they move in and out of their crevice roosts. Some programmable radio transmitters can turn on and off on a set schedule to conserve battery power and thus last longer.

Radiotelemetry has advanced our understanding of many aspects of bat ecology, including migration, roost selection, foraging behaviour, movements between roosts, home range size and more. There are also transmitters with temperature sensors that change the pulse rate of the emitted signal with temperature—they beep faster when warmer and slower when colder. This has been particularly useful for understanding torpor patterns of bats both in summer and during winter hibernation (see Torpor and Roost Selection, page 32).

Bat echolocation signals (see Using Sound to Locate Prey and Navigate in the Dark, page 22) are also used to study bats. For example, bat detectors that record ultrasound can be deployed to record bat calls as an index of relative abundance, as an indication of foraging or commuting activity, to survey for species diversity, and more. We do not detail this aspect of studying bats in this book, but we recommend Fraser, Silvis and Brigham's *Bat Echolocation Research: A Handbook for Planning and Conducting Acoustic Studies* (second edition) to interested readers.

Using bat detectors, reference recordings of captured bats can be made to learn about the sounds they make. To ensure quality recording of a bat's echolocation calls, bats can be tethered to keep them close to a bat detector while they fly. There are two basic types of tethering techniques: bat-kiting and zip-lining. Bat-kiting, a nickname coined by Erin Baerwald, allows a bat to fly freely on an elastic thread tether held by a researcher, generally gaining substantial height during flight (see images next page). For species that are particularly manoeuvrable, this often results in quite acrobatic performances, with the bat flying up high and then suddenly swooping down. This "natural flight" can often produce better reference calls than that of a bat that is recorded using the zip-line method. A zip-line, as the name implies, is somewhat like a laundry line. It is usually made of fishing line tautly strung between two posts at least 1 metre off the ground, and the bat is tethered to the fishing line using an elastic thread; the bat's flight is restricted to back and forth along the length of the line, its height limited by the elastic thread. The advantage of zip-lining a bat is that a person does not have to constantly hold the tether, and the bat can fly fast and in a straight line. Some species of bats (fast-flying, less manoeuvrable ones, like HOARY BAT) produce high-quality calls on zip-lines, while other species (small manoeuvrable ones, like LONG-EARED MYOTIS) produce high-quality calls using bat-kiting.

Reference recordings can also be achieved by recording free-flying bats as they are released. These can present more of a challenge, as a bat can quickly fly out of range of your detector and spotlight. However, if the bat circles back around, or if you have several people positioned with bat detectors and the bat flies by one of these detectors after it has risen several metres above the ground, good-quality reference calls, uninfluenced by the clutter of vegetation, can be recorded (see Acoustics: Echolocation and Species Identification, page 103). It is important not to lose sight of the bat while it is being recorded, and to

A bat can be tethered on a thin elastic thread to keep it within range of a bat detector—this is one way to obtain reference recordings that underpin species identification (e.g., in auto-identification software). Michael Proctor (above) "bat-kites" a bat during an inventory in Mongolia, allowing it to fly freely on the end of a thread. This bat quickly leaves his hand, stretching the elastic thread. More thread is then let out to allow the bat to fly higher, at which time optimal low-clutter reference calls can be recorded. PHOTO: HUNTER CAUSEY, DURING BAT INVENTORY IN MONGOLIA

Cori Lausen (left) releases a bat that is tethered using a thin elastic thread to a zip-line (fishing line strung between two thin green poles, one visible in this image). Once airborne, this bat will fly well above the zip-line, where low-clutter echolocation pulses will be produced. In both photos, the person holding the bat detector to record the echolocating tethered bat is outside of the photo frame.

use a highly directional microphone, so that you know the call recorded is in fact being emitted by the bat that you released. Tiny coloured glow sticks can be temporarily glued onto bats just prior to release so that the bat might be seen later in the night, identified to species and recorded, but the 5% mass limit guideline should be followed. Ventral gluing of these sticks is best to view from below as the bat flies by, but often they will land and groom the sticks off their bellies.

We reiterate here that only trained individuals with pre-exposure rabies vaccinations and the appropriate permits should handle bats. In BC, the Resources Information Standards Committee outlines methodologies to use and protocols to follow to ensure bat safety and standardized data collection across the province. More generic information on methodology for the study of bats can be found in sources such as *Ecological and Behavioral Methods for the Study of Bats* (second edition), by T.H. Kunz and S. Parsons.

References

Amelon et al. (2017); Brunet-Rossinni and Wilkinson (2009); Dokuchaev (2015); Fraser et al. (2020); Kunz and Parsons (2009); Pavlinić, Tvrtković and Holcer (2008); Player (2017); Walker et al. (2016).

Identifying BC's Bats

Many bat species in BC are difficult to differentiate from one another, and sometimes a combination of tools may be needed. Before we dive into the more technical approaches to identifying bats, we stress that many of the bat species in BC can be identified using the photographs in the species account, and this does not require touching bats. When you are trying to identify a roosting or downed bat, there are several strategic parts of the body that you should photograph or observe: the front of the head, the side of the head, and the tail. Additional photographs of the bat's back and underbelly, if visible, may assist in identification using fur colour or other defining traits. (See In-Hand Differentiation, page 92.)

Some species, however, are difficult to identify without close inspection. This is particularly true of the myotis species. Even when a bat can be closely examined in the hand, final species determination may require analysis of echolocation calls, genetics (DNA), examination of dentition, or even consideration of skeletal structure. Mist-net or harp trap capture to observe a bat directly in the hand remains one of the best ways to differentiate species, but even that may involve some uncertainty. Genetic tools for differentiating bat species are becoming more common as more techniques have become available, including greater ability to examine more areas of the genome. In some cases, entire genomes are being sequenced. The greater the extent of the genome that can be examined, the more likely it is that a reliable species differentiation can be made. To date, a number of species have been difficult to resolve using genetic techniques based on the small sections of the genome that are typically sequenced. For example, researchers have shown that CALIFORNIAN MYOTIS cannot be differentiated from WESTERN SMALL-FOOTED MYOTIS using common genetic markers of the mitochondrial genome; Wildlife Genetics International (David Paetkau) in BC has confirmed this to also be the case for CALIFORNIAN MYOTIS versus DARK-NOSED SMALL-FOOTED MYOTIS and for LONG-EARED MYOTIS versus some LITTLE BROWN MYOTIS in the province.

All handling of bats must be done by people with pre-exposure rabies vaccinations who have been trained in this field. Training procedures will provide specific details not included in this book, but here we describe the various measurements and traits most commonly used in species identification. This chapter explains how to differentiate bats using two main methods: in-hand examination and acoustic analysis.

In-hand examination uses morphology and measurements. This process requires measuring tools, such as vernier calipers, plastic rulers and precise weigh scales. Body traits and size can be used to differentiate most species of BC bats. Skull and dentition keys, which may also be helpful in differentiating species, are available in Appendix 2.

Acoustic analysis uses acoustic signatures of free-flying bat echolocation. This requires a bat detector. Bat detectors can be active (the user actively holds the device while recording bats), passive (the user may leave the device unattended to remotely record bats at scheduled intervals), or both. Some bat detectors, generally those used for active recordings, have a display screen either built in or viewable on an attached mobile device that allows users to visualize bat calls as spectrograms (representations of frequencies produced over time), and most detectors will record sound files for subsequent analysis. Recordings can be analyzed later using computer software. This chapter explains key features of bat echolocation pulses, how to interpret the recordings, how some species of bats can be identified using acoustics, and limitations of using acoustics to determine species presence.

In-Hand Differentiation

When a bat is first examined, obvious features, such as colour and relative ear length, may allow immediate identification. For example, a SPOTTED BAT (see species account, page 169) is uniquely black with three white spots on its back and pinkish ears nearly the same length as the rest of its body. Other easily identifiable species in BC include PALLID BAT, EASTERN RED BAT, HOARY BAT and TOWNSEND'S BIG-EARED BAT. However, other BC species are less obvious, such as the eight species of myotis—all small bats in varying shades of brown. Measuring limb bones and ears and determining the relative steepness of the forehead of the skull (morphometrics), looking for the presence or absence of certain traits or features (diagnostic characters), and in some cases testing bats' ultrasonic signals (e.g., frequencies of sound produced) will assist in differentiation. For example, body features used for differentiation of myotis species include the presence or absence of a keeled calcar (see page 17), the shape of the tragus, and the presence or absence of obvious hairs along the edge of the tail membrane or in the armpit area under the wings (see image on page 264).

If you are photographing an unknown bat for later identification, we recommend taking the following photos:

1. Front head shot to show shape of nose and any facial mask that might be evident around the eyes
2. Side profile of head showing the ear and tragus clearly
3. Entire tail area, including at least one hind foot so that the calcar and edge of the tail membrane can be examined (ideally the tail membrane would be stretched out to more clearly see features)

These photos, together with a forearm measurement (from elbow to wrist), will provide key information used to identify bats, but further photos (such as of the underside of the wing, or of dorsal fur) and measurements of ear length may help in some cases. These diagnostic traits are illustrated in the accounts for each species.

Because genetic tools are increasingly available and affordable, species of bats can also be identified from small pieces of tissue or from guano pellets (see Studying Bats, page 73).

Morphometrics

Forearm length
This is the most standard measurement taken for bats. Accurate forearm measurement requires the use of vernier calipers, with tips that have been ground off to remove sharp points. Measure the length of the ulna bone, aligning the calipers from the wrist to the elbow. Typically, the right forearm is measured.

Ear and tragus length
These are measured using a small ruler with the zero measure at the edge. Place the ruler gently into the ear, approaching from the outside (distal), and nestle the base of the ruler *into* the base of the ear. The base of the ear, which generally aligns with the base of the tragus, may be difficult to see, and you may need to move the head and fur. Gently lay the ear against the ruler. As this is a difficult measurement to make consistently, three independent measures are generally made and averaged.

Tragus length is also challenging to measure. Apply the ruler in the same way as described above, but carefully align the ruler alongside the tragus, again from the base, manipulating the head and fur to be able to see clearly. Ear and tragus measurement can be useful for differentiating "long-eared" bat species (such as LONG-EARED MYOTIS, FRINGED MYOTIS and NORTHERN

MYOTIS) from species with short ears (such as LONG-LEGGED MYOTIS and BIG BROWN BAT). For detailed information about ear length, see measurements in individual species accounts.

Foot length

Isolate the hind foot. The best way to do this is by holding the bat in such a way that it stands on a ruler and allowing the bat to bend its leg as though it were going to crawl on the ground. Measure from the heel to the tip of the longest digit, including the length of the claws. This measurement can be useful for differentiating several of the myotis species, as some have a small hind foot (e.g., CALIFORNIAN, LITTLE BROWN and YUMA MYOTIS) while others have a large hind foot (LONG-LEGGED MYOTIS, LONG-EARED MYOTIS and FRINGED MYOTIS). For more information, see foot measurements in species accounts.

Tibia length

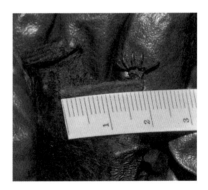

The tibia can be measured using a ruler or calipers. As with the foot length measure, this is often best accomplished by allowing the bat to bend its leg while standing on a surface, such as your finger or a table. Use the calipers or ruler to measure the tibia—the main leg bone between the ankle and the knee. This measurement can be useful for identifying LONG-LEGGED MYOTIS.

Snout length and width

The snout can be measured using a ruler. Approaching from the top, measure both the width and the length. The base of the snout is where the hairline ends, and you may need to move the fur until the line can be seen. Length is the measure from hairline to the tip of the nose at the nostrils. The width of the snout is also measured at the hairline. The relative width to length of the snout can be useful for differentiating CALIFORNIAN MYOTIS from DARK-NOSED SMALL-FOOTED

MYOTIS, and the width of the snout can be useful for differentiating FRINGED MYOTIS from LONG-EARED MYOTIS.

Thumb length

Align a ruler at the base of the thumb and measure to the tip of the claw. While all of the thumb measurements in this book include the claw, sometimes two measurements are made, one with and one without the claw, to account for the fact that some individuals have far greater curvature of the claw than others. It is therefore important to record whether a thumb measurement includes the claw. This measurement can be useful for differentiating CALIFORNIAN MYOTIS from DARK-NOSED SMALL-FOOTED MYOTIS.

Diagnostic External Features

We can use the presence of certain features in combination with morphometrics to confidently arrive at an identification. Below are some of the typical features that are inspected when differentiating bats. Many of these features are referred to in the species accounts and in Appendix 3.

Tail membrane

Keeled calcar: Look for presence or absence of a flap of tissue on the outside of the calcar (the cartilaginous spur off the ankle (see image on page 17). This small flap is called a keel, and is important in differentiating many species, especially various myotis species. However, some species have only partial keels, and some individuals may have an indistinct keel on one side of the body and not on the other; partial keels are often found on LONG-EARED MYOTIS. For other species, such as CALIFORNIAN MYOTIS, DARK-NOSED SMALL-FOOTED MYOTIS and LONG-LEGGED MYOTIS, the keel is obvious and distinct, and is important in differentiating them from myotis that do not have keeled calcars, such as LITTLE BROWN MYOTIS and YUMA MYOTIS.

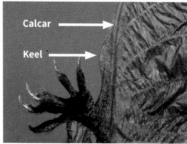

Calcar

Keel

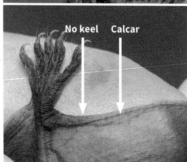

No keel   Calcar

A calcar with a keel (top) and without a keel (bottom).

Fringe of hair: A comb of stiff hairs along the outer edge of the tail membrane is a trait pronounced in FRINGED MYOTIS. However, LONG-EARED MYOTIS can also have a subtle fringe of sparsely spaced hairs, especially in young individuals.

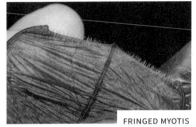
FRINGED MYOTIS

Dorsal surface hairy: Most bats have little hair on the dorsal (top) surface of the tail membrane; however, SILVER-HAIRED BAT is usually partially furred there, and HOARY and EASTERN RED BAT have fully furred tail membranes (see image on page 21).

Vertebrae extend beyond membrane edge: The tip of the tail extends several vertebrae past the end of the tail membrane in DARK-NOSED SMALL-FOOTED MYOTIS, but not in the similar CALIFORNIAN MYOTIS (see image on page 208). BRAZILIAN FREE-TAILED BAT has a tail that extends well beyond the edge of the tail membrane.

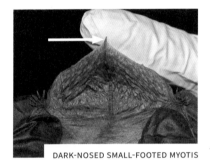
DARK-NOSED SMALL-FOOTED MYOTIS

Wing membrane
On most bats, the underside of the wing membrane has sparse hair, with the bulk of the fur ending at the edge of the body. But on LONG-LEGGED MYOTIS, the hair is rather thick, extending all the way out to an imaginary line between the elbow and the ankle. This species is often said to have "hairy armpits" (see image on page 264).

Shape of ear and tragus
The shape of the ear and tragus can be important for differentiating some species. For example, NORTHERN MYOTIS has a pin-point sharp tragus that is straight. This is used to differentiate it from the similar LITTLE BROWN MYOTIS, whose tragus is blunt and sometimes curved or even notched (see images in species accounts). CANYON BATS have a unique paddle-shaped tragus. Some

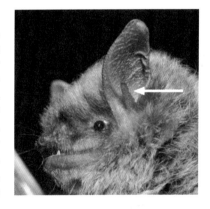

bats, like LONG-LEGGED MYOTIS, have round-tipped ears, whereas others, like CALIFORNIAN MYOTIS, have more pointed ear shapes.

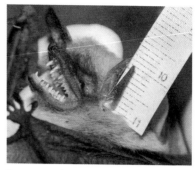

To measure the length of the tragus, a plastic ruler is gently set into the base of the ear.

Head

While skulls of the various species differ (see Appendix 2), this is not always obvious on a live bat. One rather subjective feature that can be assessed is the slope of the forehead. By feeling the forehead with the tip of your finger, you can develop a sense of "steep" versus "shallow," traits that can help differentiate YUMA MYOTIS (steep) from LITTLE BROWN MYOTIS (shallow). Coloration of the skin and fur on the head can also help with species identification—for example, DARK-NOSED SMALL-FOOTED MYOTIS appears to have a dark "mask" over the eyes, whereas the similar CALIFORNIAN MYOTIS usually does not. Likewise, LONG-EARED MYOTIS typically has a dark mask over the eyes, whereas NORTHERN MYOTIS, another myotis with relatively long ears, does not.

Morphological Key to BC Bats

The following key is based largely on external features. Diagnostic characteristics are arranged into descriptive pairs, or couplets; each couplet offers the user two mutually exclusive choices (labelled *a* or *b*). To identify a bat, begin with couplet number 1 and select a or b. This will either give you a species name or direct you to another couplet in the key. By working through the various steps in the key, you will arrive at an identification. We have tried to avoid subjective traits (e.g., "slightly darker than" or "slightly larger than") and instead emphasize presence or absence of features or absolute size measurements; however, in some cases, these relative traits are helpful, and they may be provided in addition to other, less subjective traits. To simplify the key, the diagnostic criteria in a couplet (decision between two options at each branch of the key) are limited to a few characteristics. Once you have made an identification, consult the description in the appropriate species account to see if it is consistent with the determination from the key.

Many identification keys incorporate locality information (e.g., "found only in the Okanagan Valley"), but we deliberately avoided geography in the keys, given that species ranges are not completely known and may shift over time. We also advise you to take photographs to allow subsequent confirmation of your species identification. Note that due to the extreme difficulty in telling

YUMA MYOTIS apart from LITTLE BROWN MYOTIS based solely on external features and measurements, we recommend the use of a bat detector to aid in differentiating these species. A biologist might also consider confirming species identification by using genetic samples (e.g., from a biopsy punch or wing or cheek swab) supplementing the use of acoustics and morphometrics.

Each couplet includes the number of the previous determining couplet. If you arrive at an unlikely or incorrect identification, use these numbers to navigate backward through the key.

| 1 | 1a | More than one-third of the tail extends beyond the outer edge of the interfemoral membrane (see image on right): Go to **2** |  |
| | 1b | Tail enclosed in the interfemoral membrane (e.g., see images on p. 96 and p. 208): Go to **3** | |

BRAZILIAN FREE-TAILED BAT. PHOTO: MICHAEL DURHAM/MINDEN PICTURES (BAT CONSERVATION INTERNATIONAL)

| 2 (L1) | 2a | Ears joined at the base, forearm length 58–64 mm: BIG FREE-TAILED BAT (p. 291) |  |

BIG FREE-TAILED BAT. PHOTO: MICHAEL DURHAM/MINDEN PICTURES (BAT CONSERVATION INTERNATIONAL)

| | 2b | Ears not joined at the base, forearm length 36–46 mm: BRAZILIAN FREE-TAILED BAT (p. 285) | 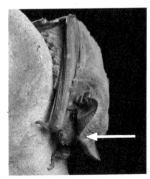 |

BRAZILIAN FREE-TAILED BAT. PHOTO: MICHAEL DURHAM/MINDEN PICTURES (BAT CONSERVATION INTERNATIONAL)

| 3 (↳1) | 3a | Ear length greater than 28 mm: Go to **4** |
| | 3b | Ear length less than 28 mm: Go to **6** |

| 4 (↳3) | 4a | Fur on back black with three prominent white spots on rump and shoulders: SPOTTED BAT (p. 169) |
| | 4b | Fur on back not black and lacking white spots: Go to **5** |

| 5 (↳4) | 5a | Nose with two prominent bumps (see p. 148 in TOWNSEND'S BIG-EARED BAT species account), forearm length 40–50 mm: TOWNSEND'S BIG-EARED BAT (p. 147) |
| | 5b | Nose lacking two prominent bumps, forearm length 48–58 mm: PALLID BAT (p. 135) |

| 6 (↳3) | 6a | Fur orange or reddish orange in colour: EASTERN RED BAT (p. 179) |
| | 6b | Fur not orange or reddish orange: Go to **7** |

| 7 (↳6) | 7a | Fur on back with frosted or silver tipped hairs, at least part of the dorsal surface of the tail membrane thickly furred: Go to **8** |
| | 7b | Fur on back without frosted or silver-tipped hairs, dorsal surface of tail membrane has few hairs: Go to **9** |

| 8 (↳7) | 8a | Upper surface of tail membrane completely covered with fur, yellowish-brown fur around head, forearm length 50–57 mm: HOARY BAT (p. 187) |

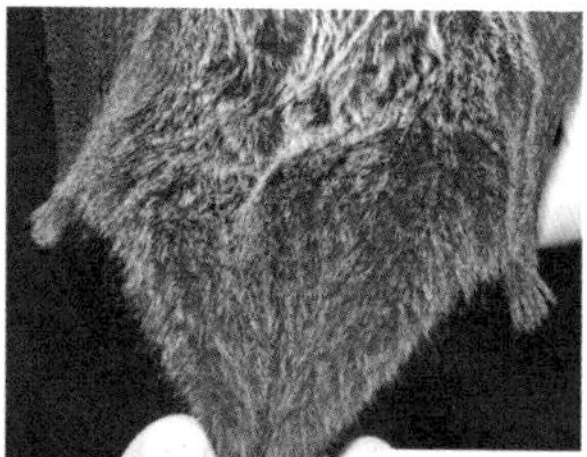

HOARY BAT

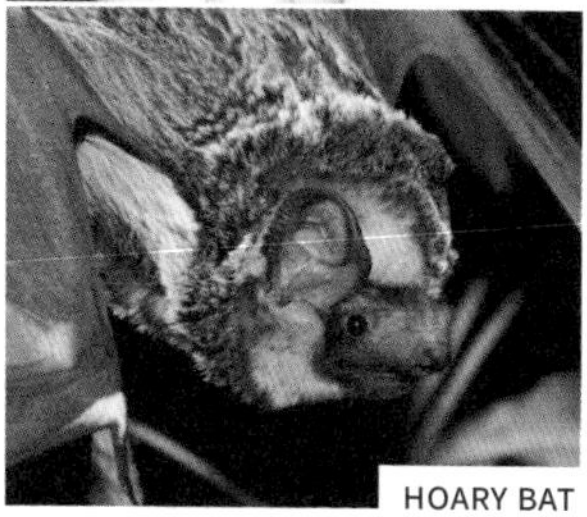

HOARY BAT

	8b	Upper surface of tail membrane furred only at its base, forearm length 38–45 mm: SILVER-HAIRED BAT (p. 197)

SILVER-HAIRED BAT

9 (t7)   **9a**   Tragus is paddle shaped, and there is a dark mask over the eyes: CANYON BAT (p. 295)

       9b   Tragus is not paddle shaped: Go to **10**

CANYON BAT. PHOTO: JOSE MARTINEZ

10 (t9)   **10a**   Distinct fringe of hairs on outer edge of tail membrane (see image on p. 96), forearm length greater than 38 mm: FRINGED MYOTIS (p. 255)

       10b   Lacking a distinct fringe of hairs on outer edge of tail membrane: Go to **11**

11 (t10)   **11a**   Prominent keel on each calcar (see image p. 95): Go to **15**

       11b   Indistinct or no keel on each calcar: Go to **12**

12 (t11)   **12a**   Forearm length to ear length ratio less than 2.6, ear length equal to or greater than 14.5 mm (see image on p. 93 for comparison): Go to **13**

       12b   Forearm length to ear length ratio greater than 2.5, ear length less than 15 mm: Go to **14**

| 13 (ι12) | 13a | Ears darker than fur and when fur is parted at shoulder, dark bases are evident (dark shoulder patches); tragus rounded at tip, ears greater than 15 mm and typically greater than 17.5 mm: LONG-EARED MYOTIS (p. 217) |  |

LONG-EARED MYOTIS

| | 13b | Tragus is sharp, ears about the same colour of brown as the fur, ear length less than or equal to 17.5 mm but typically less than 16 mm; when fur is parted at shoulder, darker "shoulder patches" are not evident: NORTHERN MYOTIS (p. 247) |  |

NORTHERN MYOTIS

14 (ι12) **14a** Forehead feels relatively steep, fur looks short and dull brown, forearm equal to or less than 36 mm: likely YUMA MYOTIS (p. 271)

14b Forehead feels shallow, fur looks glossy brown and hairs are relatively long, forearm greater than 35 mm: likely LITTLE BROWN MYOTIS (p. 227)

Morphology may not differentiate these two species. The use of an acoustic bag test is recommended (see YUMA and LITTLE BROWN MYOTIS species accounts). For biologists, a skin sample for genetic testing may also be useful (see Studying Bats, p. 73).

15 (ι11) **15a** Underwing furred outward to a line extending from knee to elbow ("hairy armpits"; see image on p. 264): LONG-LEGGED MYOTIS (p. 263)

15b Underwing not furred outward to a line extending from knee to elbow: Go to **16**

16 (ι15) **16a** Forearm length greater than 40 mm, snout has slight glandular swellings visible on each side: BIG BROWN BAT (p. 159)

BIG BROWN BAT

16b Forearm length less than 36 mm: Go to **17**

17 (ι16) **17a** Fur on back pale blonde to yellow, contrasting sharply with blackish ears, face, and wings; slight dark mask across eyes; long thumbs (greater than 4 mm); several tail vertebrae extend past edge of tail; length of bare area on snout rectangular in shape, approximately 1.5 times width across nostrils: DARK-NOSED SMALL-FOOTED MYOTIS (p. 239)

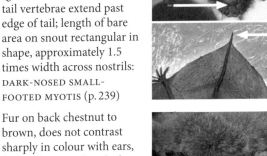

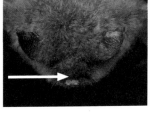

17b Fur on back chestnut to brown, does not contrast sharply in colour with ears, face and wings; thumb short (less than 5 mm); tail ends flush at edge of tail membrane (see image p. 208); bare area on snout square in shape, approximately equal length to width across nostrils: CALIFORNIAN MYOTIS (p. 207)

References

British Columbia Ministry of Environment, Lands and Parks (1998), Kunz and Parsons (2009), Lausen (2005), Rodriguez and Ammerman (2004).

Acoustics—Echolocation and Species Identification

Echolocation is the use of reflected sounds (echoes) to locate objects, such as prey, water, and obstacles or features of the landscape (see Using Sound to Locate Prey and Navigate in the Dark, page 22). To generate echoes for echolocation, bats must produce sounds, and all echolocating bats do this through their mouth or nose. In areas where insects are present, bats will use echolocation in foraging bouts throughout the night, whether capturing insects that are free-flying (aerial hawking) or taking insects from surfaces of vegetation or even from the ground (gleaning).

Bats adapted for foraging by gleaning are most often adept at flying amidst vegetation, typically with shorter and wider wings that favour high manoeuvrability, allowing them to closely approach vegetated surfaces. Insects can generate sounds when moving around on surfaces, such as leaves, and some bats (generally "long-eared" or "big-eared" species) are adapted to listen for these prey-generated sounds. These gleaning bats (e.g., NORTHERN MYOTIS) will use the prey-generated sounds to home in on an insect on a surface, which is often more effective than echoes in differentiating between insects and other objects like leaves or grass. Bats that are less manoeuvrable, such as the migratory tree bats with longer, slimmer wings, will tend to fly higher, straighter and faster, capturing insects through aerial hawking and spending more time in open areas rather than highly vegetated ones. The environments that bats occupy and the way bats search for food influence how they use echolocation.

Sound travels in wave patterns through air and bounces off objects, and bats interpret the returning echoes. Long wavelengths of sound (low frequencies) travel far, but only reflect from large objects. For example, a high-pitched human voice could have a frequency of 3,000 hertz, or three kilohertz (as the fundamental frequency; see Additional Terminology, page 113). Sound at this frequency has 3,000 waves passing by a given point each second, and at 343 metres per second (the usual speed of sound), this equates to a wavelength of 11.4 centimetres. A sound wave can bounce off an object with a diameter of at least half the wavelength, so in theory, echoes of that 3 kilohertz voice would be generated by any object that is 5.7 centimetres or bigger. If bats were only interested in avoiding obstacles or finding objects 5.7 centimetres or larger, they too could simply produce sounds at this frequency. However, flying at night, as all bats do, requires the ability to detect objects much smaller than 5.7 centimetres, especially the insects that they hunt! To put their prey size into context, beetles and moths are often less than two centimetres in size, and mosquitoes can be less than 0.5 centimetres. Many are even smaller. Generating an echo off an insect 3 millimetres long (e.g., midges have a wingspan of 2 to 3 mm) requires a frequency of 57,000 hertz, or 57 kilohertz, much higher than the human voice in our example.

The higher the frequency of sound produced, the smaller the insects a bat can detect, so most bats produce high-frequency sounds. In contrast to the relatively low-frequency sounds produced by a human, these high frequencies provide a higher level of detail to the bat about its surroundings, effectively allowing bats to "see" with their ears, which act as directional antennae picking up returning echoes. As with any good thing, though, there is a trade-off. The higher the frequency, the shorter the distance the sound travels. Some of the higher frequencies that bats produce travel less than a metre before they are too weak to return a detectable echo. For a bat that flies fast through open areas, such as a BRAZILIAN FREE-TAILED BAT moving at 14 metres per second, much lower frequencies are necessary to act as "high-beam headlights" so that the bat has sufficient reaction time to avoid obstacles.

Broadly speaking, echolocation employs ultrasound, defined as sound above what the human ear can hear—frequencies greater than 20 kilohertz. Most bats that echolocate use ultrasound, but echolocation can also be accomplished with sound that is audible to humans, and generally this is used by bats that feed on bigger prey, such as large moths. Bats that echolocate in the audible range of human hearing are often referred to as audible bats. There is only one bat species in BC that is easily heard by the human ear: SPOTTED BAT. By using low-frequency sounds to hunt for large moth prey, this bat feeds on tympanate ("eared") moths, which "hear" ultrasound—moths that have evolved to evade most other species of bats that echolocate using ultrasound. Some bats also use quieter calls so that tympanate moths cannot sense them from as far away as other louder bats.

This recording of a bat's echolocation, made up of a series of pulses of sound, is displayed as frequencies (y-axis, in kilohertz) produced over time (x-axis, in seconds). Each frequency-versus-time graph is referred to as a spectrogram. The top spectrograms in A, B and C are full spectrum, with colour representing the intensity of frequencies within each call (red has the highest amount of energy, or amplitude). The bottom spectrograms in A and C are zero-crossing displays of the same recording. In this case, the full-spectrum recording has been zero-crossed in the acoustics software package Insight (Titley Scientific), so that both formats can be viewed as separate spectrograms at the same time. Each pulse of sound looks somewhat like a hockey stick in shape, and this is most noticeable at high magnification (in this case F8, a setting in the software). Each pulse can also be referred to as a bat "call"; the entire series of calls is an "echolocation sequence." A is in "Compressed Time Mode," meaning that the time between calls has been removed to visualize many pulses at once with sufficient detail. This means that the accuracy of the time axis is only relevant within the duration of each pulse, not the time between the pulses. This is in contrast to D and C, showing the same call sequence in true time, such that the time scale is accurately depicting how much time elapsed during the production of each pulse and between pulses. When zoomed out at a magnification of F5, in true time, spectrograms in C show the entire 2.8-second call sequence. An asterisk marks the same pulse in each view to orient the call sequence.

OSCILLOGRAM

80 FULL-SPECTRUM SPECTROGRAM   **Harmonics of pulse**

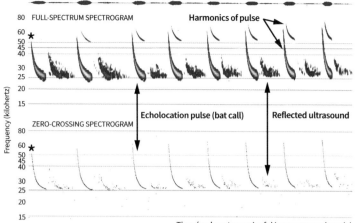

Echolocation pulse (bat call)   **Reflected ultrasound**

ZERO-CROSSING SPECTROGRAM

Frequency (kilohertz)

A. Compressed time (magnification F8)   Time (scale not meaningful in compressed mode)

OSCILLOGRAM

FULL-SPECTRUM SPECTROGRAM

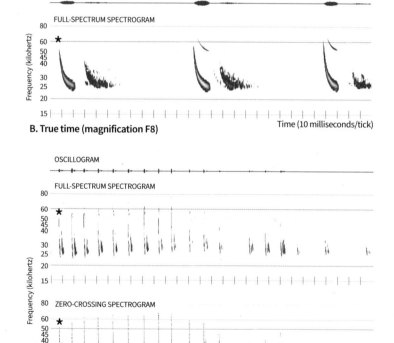

B. True time (magnification F8)   Time (10 milliseconds/tick)

OSCILLOGRAM

FULL-SPECTRUM SPECTROGRAM

ZERO-CROSSING SPECTROGRAM

C. True time (magnification F5)   Time (100 milliseconds/tick)

Bats that echolocate in the ultrasonic range are heard using bat detectors, which convert ultrasonic signals into those audible to human ears, generally producing sounds of less than 5 kilohertz for a pleasant pitch. Most bat detectors allow us to hear bats, but detectors that also sample and transform ultrasound for analysis on computers are increasingly affordable, with various models available that differ in functionality.

Digitized sound has revolutionized the way we survey for bats. Bat echolocation can now be recorded onto digital media such as SD cards and uploaded onto computers where sound is then parsed into its component frequencies (plotted against time) to be depicted in a graph called a spectrogram. The properties of the bursts of sounds that bats produce while navigating through their environment searching for prey often allow us to differentiate between species, providing an invaluable survey tool that does not require capture. However, because the sounds that bats generate are functional—they are used to navigate and hunt—similar bats eating similar-sized insects in similar habitats will produce similar echolocation calls, and species may not always be identifiable.

Over time, biologists studying bat echolocation have identified when and how some species can be differentiated, but we are still learning new things about how bats echolocate in certain circumstances. As a rule of thumb, we generally try to record bats when they are in the open, searching for prey, and try to avoid recording them when they are reacting to obstacles. This is because many bat species produce similarly broadband high-frequency sounds in rapid succession when they are navigating and foraging in cluttered environments. Although there are some exceptions, most species of bats are most identifiable when they are producing search phase calls in the open. Unfortunately, some species are less likely to be recorded in open environments than others.

Bats in North America regularly vary the frequencies that they produce (frequency-modulated, or FM, call types), typically starting each echolocation pulse at a high frequency and sweeping progressively through lower and lower frequencies. This change in frequencies over time can be depicted graphically in a spectrogram (a graph of frequency versus time). Bats in North America produce pulses of ultrasound so that they have time to listen for returning echoes between the emitted pulses. Pulses of sound are also referred to as calls, and a series of calls, separated by pauses to listen for echoes (time between calls), is referred to as a sequence (see spectrogram B on previous page). The lowest frequency that a call reaches is one of the most important parameters used to differentiate species. Almost all bats in North America echolocate using an FM call type (i.e., their echolocation pulses sweep through multiple frequencies), separated by relatively long periods of listening (sometimes referred to as low duty cycle). Pulses that sweep through a large range of frequencies are referred to as broadband (broad bandwidth), while pulses that sweep through few frequencies are narrowband. Some calls can even approach constant frequency.

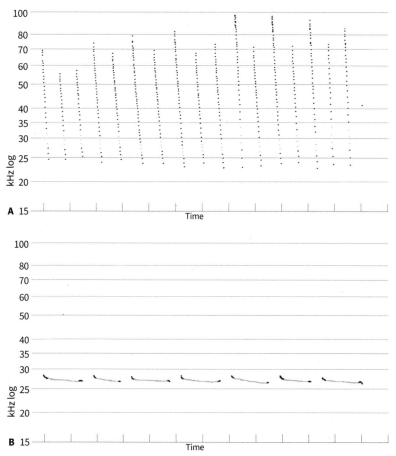

Echolocation pulses (in zero-crossing format). A. A large range of frequencies in a short duration (broadband pulse). B. A narrow range of frequencies over a longer duration (narrowband pulse). Blue represents call bodies (see next page).

Calls that sweep through many frequencies quickly (short-duration calls) look steep (see spectrogram A above) and are said to have a high slope (sometimes measured in octaves per second); calls that are lower in slope change frequencies more gradually (see spectrogram B above) and can even become flat as they achieve a constant frequency over time. If the rate with which the bat sweeps through frequencies suddenly changes, the call appears to have a bend at the point in time where this rate changes, and this is often referred to as a knee or elbow; along with call slope in general, the presence of this knee/elbow can be a useful feature for differentiating between some species. Also useful in differentiating species is the presence and shape of a toe; the toe (sometimes

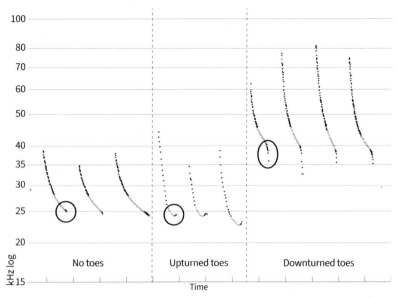

A toe is a pulse feature that may not always be present in a recording. The pulse on the left has no toe; the middle pulse shows an upward-facing toe; the pulse on the right has a downward-facing toe.

referred to as a tail) is a possible extension of a call, and it can either turn up or down (see spectrogram above).

Biologists typically assign a species to a frequency category or group, such as "40 kilohertz bats," which means that calls typically end around 40 kilohertz (though for some, calls could end between 35 and 45 kilohertz, depending on the level of clutter the bat is responding to). Often, call sequences are assigned to a group of species based on the end frequencies of the majority of the pulses—this is typically done when complete diagnostic information needed to classify to species is lacking. The "end frequency" of a call is generally defined as the lowest frequency in a call *excluding* the toe, and this can be called the characteristic frequency, to distinguish it from the minimum frequency, which could be lower if a toe is present. The flattest part of the call is usually the loudest and lowest frequency, and is referred to as the call body (shown in blue in zero-cross spectrograms); a toe, if present, extends past this. When we measure the slope of a call for species differentiation, it is usually the slope of the call body. In this book we typically refer to "end frequency" generically but in cases where a substantial toe is present, characteristic and minimum frequencies can be quite different.

Because high-frequency (short-wavelength) sounds do not travel far, bats need to vocalize as loudly as they can each time they produce an echolocation pulse to maximize the distance it will travel. Some bats produce sounds louder than

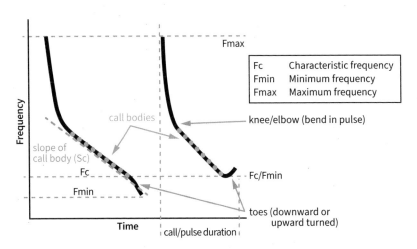

Several key measurements (call parameters) of a pulse can be used in describing differences, and statistical comparisons can be used to differentiate species.

jet engines (up to 140 decibels). As you can imagine, this constant "screaming" is exhausting, as is flying, and in fact each of these activities requires about the same amount of energy. Bats have evolved to synchronize these activities to save energy, belting out an echolocation pulse with each wing beat as they exhale, sometimes even skipping a few pulses if they are out in the open with no obstacles in their way. This wingbeat-pulse synchronization can sometimes help identify bat species, as big bats with slower, more powerful wingbeats (such as HOARY BAT) are likely to produce fewer pulses of ultrasound per second when flying in the open. When a large, high-flying bat like a HOARY BAT is commuting in open night skies, it may produce an echolocation pulse every one to two seconds, while a small bat like a CALIFORNIAN MYOTIS flying in a forest may flap its wings with synchronized pulses of echolocation 10 times per second.

As a bat approaches an object, such as a flying moth, it needs to quickly calculate how far away the moth is so that it can close in and grab it, using its tail, a wing or its mouth. These calculations are done by the bat as a series of complex neural processes using the returning echoes. Information from echoes bouncing off insect prey needs to be received more rapidly as the bat gets closer to the insect, and that is when the wingbeat-echolocation synchronization is decoupled; at this time, the bat produces more than one echolocation pulse per wingbeat as it rapidly approaches the insect and assesses the position and trajectory of the target. This increasingly rapid production of echolocation pulses as a bat approaches and then captures its insect prey occurs in two phases: the first is called an approach, and it is followed by an even faster series of pulses called a buzz, named for the way it sounds when heard through a bat detector. Aerial-hawking bats have evolved echolocation patterns such that call frequencies, intensity of the sound they produce, and the wingbeat period (amount of time between flaps) all interact to match the detection range of insect prey. This means that for most bats, an echo off an insect being targeted for prey is received before the next echolocation pulse is produced. Maximum detection distances for prey items correspond to the speed of the wingbeat, with larger bats pursuing insect prey farther away from them than smaller bats, which react to closer prey. Bats typically detect prey 3 to 12 metres in front of them, resulting in a sudden change in their echolocation calls as they transition from "search" to "approach" to "buzz." This transition is usually associated with a substantial change in the frequencies being produced and the repetition rate with which those sounds are generated.

These differing echolocation patterns in reaction to objects can be thought of as a clutter continuum. On one end of the clutter continuum, the bat produces echolocation pulses that will travel far to maximize its search distance. No echoes are detected, so no response is initiated by the bat. An echo might be received from a distant object, perhaps a background surface, such as the ground or forest canopy, which is important for navigating around obstacles while searching for prey. As a bat detects an echo reflected from a surface or object (clutter), it reacts. A bat searching for prey may approach the object that has caused the reflection, and it will adjust its production of echolocation calls to better perceive the object. This generally requires use of higher frequencies because the smaller wavelengths will provide a finer scale of detail, including an estimate of distance to the object. If the object is an insect, the bat will pursue it and, as mentioned above, this will require that the bat receive echoes rapidly, increasing its rate of pulse production, to as high as 100 or more pulses per second (buzz; see spectrograms on page 111). A buzz indicates close approach to an object, and while this is often an insect, and thus called a feeding buzz, this can also occur as a bat approaches the surface of the water, a drinking buzz. There is thought to be a trade-off between call intensity (loudness) and repetition rate, such that if an object like an insect is close, quieter and less energetically expensive calls can be used more frequently.

There are no hard and fast rules that apply to body size and echolocation, but some general patterns have evolved. Larger high-flying bats typically emit low-frequency sounds as these sounds travel further. They will also typically produce long-duration pulses and may even skip some pulses when flying in unobstructed airspace. Their naturally longer wing-beat stroke will result in a longer listening period between pulses. Large bats producing infrequent low-frequency sounds are less able to detect small insect prey, but their echolocation is well-suited for commuting or migrating. Bats with small body sizes will typically produce higher-frequency, shorter-duration pulses at a more rapid repetition rate. Their echolocation does not operate over as great a distance because of the attenuation (weakening) of high-frequency sounds. By completing

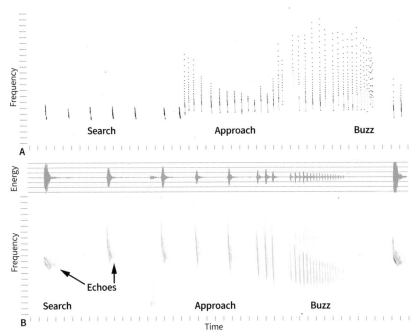

The top zero-cross recording (A) shows a sequence of calls as a bat forages (search), approaches (approach), and captures (feeding buzz) an insect. The shape of the calls changes to look steeper as the duration of each call shortens and bandwidth generally increases; the time between calls shortens so that the bat receives reflected sounds more often and can process this information to home in on the insect prey. This same sequence is seen in the bottom full-spectrum spectrogram (B), where a bat approaches the surface of the water, culminating in a drinking buzz. Sometimes a near-double image of a pulse can be recorded as a bat approaches calm water, because the ultrasound reflected off the water has a delayed arrival at the microphone (sometimes referred to as a specular echo).

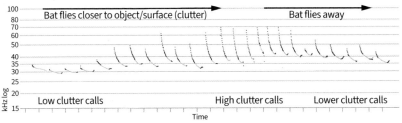

A bat changes its echolocation pulses in response to receiving echoes. The source of the reflected sound, whether that is a leaf, insect, another bat, and so on ("clutter"), causes the bat to alter its echolocation. The range of pulse shapes that a bat produces, from when it is not responding to reflected sound to when it is closely approaching an object, can vary widely in duration, frequency, repetition rate and bandwidth. This range is sometimes referred to as a "clutter continuum" (Chris Corben, personal communication) and highlights the inherent difficulty in differentiating species using echolocation, given the huge range of overlapping call shapes bats can have when responding to clutter. This recording is of an EASTERN RED BAT.

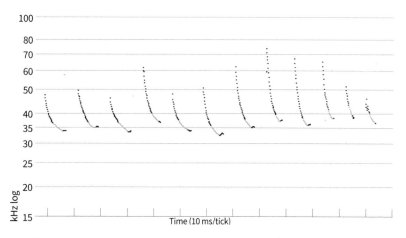

100
80
70
60
50
40
35
30
25
20
15

kHz log

Time (10 ms/tick)

Zero-cross spectrogram showing calls of an EASTERN RED BAT flying through clutter.

a pulse quickly, the bat avoids overlap between producing sound and receiving echoes. However, large high-flying bats may experience issues with call-echo overlap—that is, an echo originating from its first call may travel a long distance and could be received after the bat has produced its second call, and so forth. This mismatch in timing presents possible confusion in call-echo assignment, but many large fast-flying species have evolved to keep track of which echo originates from which echolocation pulse. This echo-call assignment can be accomplished through use of alternating call types, including varying the energy levels of certain frequencies or sweeping through a different suite of frequencies. Another strategy is to skip some calls altogether, increasing the time window in which to receive the echoes before another call is produced. HOARY BATS are known to use both of these strategies under different circumstances; sometimes they skip calls when flying in the open as this increases their chance of hearing an echo reflected from a distant surface, but when flying quickly among clutter they will vary their echolocation call frequencies. In fact, all Lasiurines (e.g., HOARY BATS, RED BATS) typically produce a "random undulating minimum frequency pattern" of calls with upturned toes (hooked calls; see above zero-cross, and see HOARY BAT and EASTERN RED BAT species accounts) when flying quickly among clutter. Pulses appear to randomly end at different frequencies, such that each pulse appears unique in minimum frequency, perhaps facilitating the recognition of corresponding echoes. Complex neural processes allow these bats to assign echoes to originating pulses while navigating quickly through cluttered environments.

To demonstrate the extreme variation of calls that one individual can make depending on the level of clutter it is flying through, the image on page 111 shows the clutter continuum of an EASTERN RED BAT flying in an open environment (the lowest-sloped and lowest-frequency calls on the bottom of page 111), approaching sound-reflecting clutter and producing steeper, higher-frequency and larger-bandwidth calls in response, and finally returning to a more open environment, resulting in lower-frequency calls again. HOARY BATS similarly range through an extreme range of low- and steep-sloped calls with large changes in frequency, in response to degree of clutter (see HOARY BAT species account). The image on page 114 shows clutter continuum spectrograms of BIG BROWN BAT and SILVER-HAIRED BAT. While the high- and low-clutter sequences of these two species look almost identical, the open environment calls differ, with SILVER-HAIRED BAT producing flat or nearly flat calls—something that BIG BROWN BATS do not do (see SILVER-HAIRED BAT and BIG BROWN BAT species accounts). Unique call features that allow some species to be differentiated are most often observable when the bats are recorded searching, rather than responding to echoes. As such, bat detectors that record passively are typically best deployed in areas where bats are likely to be echolocating in the open rather than responding to clutter.

Additional Terminology

To make full use of the acoustic descriptions provided in each of the species accounts in this book, you will need some additional terminology.

Sound is made of a mix of frequencies of varying intensities (loudness). Because bats typically scream during echolocation to ensure that the signal travels far enough to facilitate foraging, once the bat is close enough to the microphone it becomes louder than the ambient "noise." Ambient noise includes sounds like wind-blown grass, rustling of leaves, birds, insects and more. Ambient sounds can be recorded by any standard sound recorder, but special equipment is needed to record high-frequency ultrasound and to properly sample sound with short wavelengths. Bat detectors allow ultrasonic frequencies to be sampled, and some provide options for sampling different ranges of ultrasonic frequencies. To sample the complete range of fundamental harmonic (see page 116) frequencies produced by bats in North America, a device must be able to record frequencies between 7 and 120 kilohertz. Recording frequencies as high as 120 kilohertz requires a sampling rate of 256 kilohertz (256,000 samples per second). Digitized sound must be processed (using fast Fourier transform) to parse out the mix of frequencies that it contains and display a spectrogram of frequency against time (e.g., see full-spectrum spectrogram on page 111). Spectrograms, by way of colour, can illustrate which frequencies were louder; often red or orange is used to denote the loudest frequencies.

Larynxes (voice boxes) are like stringed instruments. Plucking a guitar string generates sound because the string vibrates, and vocal cords vibrate in the same

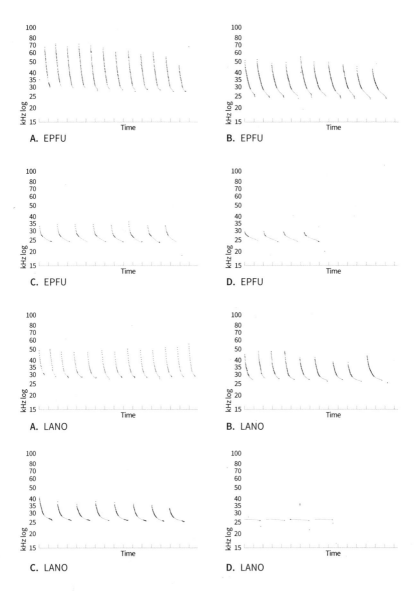

Four zero-cross spectrograms each of BIG BROWN BAT (A–D EPFU) and SILVER-HAIRED BAT (A–D LANO), demonstrating similarity in call structure for all but the lowest level of clutter (bottom right spectrogram D for each species). Despite this high degree of overlap in call structure, these species are sometimes acoustically differentiated (see species accounts). Time axis represents 10 milliseconds per tick.

A HORSESHOE BAT (left) has an interesting nose leaf structure that plays a role in altering its echolocation calls. This type of bat is not found in BC. The TOWNSEND'S BIG-EARED BAT (right) is the only bat in BC with an unusual nose (see page 147).

way. Similarly, bats use their larynxes to produce ultrasound. The sound may exit their mouth, their nose, or both. Bats that echolocate out of their nose may further manipulate the sound by directing or focusing the signal. Bats with leaf-noses (see image above) or other notable nasal structures produce echolocation calls that have multiple harmonics. Although no BC bats have a true nose leaf, TOWNSEND'S BIG-EARED BAT does emit sounds out of its rather intricate-looking nose (above), and its second harmonic is often recorded in full spectrum (or split harmonic pattern in zero-cross; see below).

Sound waves emanating from a guitar string or a vocal cord are the same length as the string or cord that generates them. The length of the wave (number of wave cycles per second) dictates the frequency, as discussed above. Frequencies change as wavelengths change, and wavelengths change as the effective length of the string or cord changes. For example, a higher frequency is produced by a guitar string when the string is shortened by pushing on a fret, and vocal cords are adjusted by musculature in the larynx. The wavelengths that match the length of the string or cord are called the fundamental frequencies, or first harmonic. Other wavelengths, however, are generated at the exact same time as the fundamental, and they are proportional, such that the second harmonic is half the wavelength of the fundamental, the third harmonic is one-third the wavelength of the fundamental, and so forth. This means that the second harmonic is twice the frequency of the fundamental; the third harmonic is three times the frequency of the fundamental, and so forth. This mix of frequencies that are whole-number multiples of the fundamental (or first harmonic) is a basic property of sound.

Because lower-frequency sounds travel farther than higher frequencies, we most often record only the fundamental harmonic of bats. However, if the bat is close enough to the microphone, and the detection equipment is capable of recording very high-frequency sounds, a second, and sometimes even a third

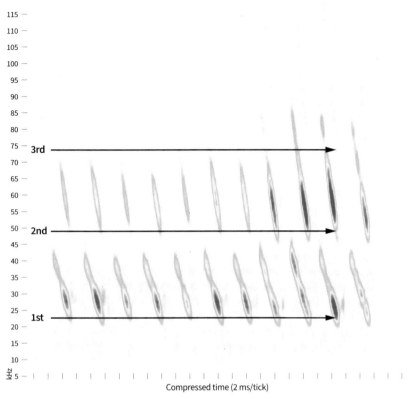

Second and third harmonics are present for some calls in this full-spectrum recording of a TOWNSEND'S BIG-EARED BAT.

harmonic can be recorded (see part A of the spectrogram on page 105, and harmonics of pulse label). Some bats, such as species of the genus *Corynorhinus*, typically put a lot of energy into their second harmonic, and this is visible in full-spectrum spectrograms as loud sections within each of the first and second harmonics of a pulse (see red portion of pulses in spectrogram above, and pulses of part A of spectrogram on facing page). In BC, TOWNSEND'S BIG-EARED BAT is one of these *Corynorhinus* species, and generating sound out of its nose may give the species its unique acoustic signature. Multiple harmonics are likely to be used by bats to exploit the benefits of higher frequencies at close range to an object, allowing better resolution of detail and distance.

Harmonics of sound provide options for bats to use higher frequencies in echolocation, even though their vocal cords may naturally produce lower-frequency sounds. An interesting example is CALIFORNIAN LEAF-NOSED BAT (not found in Canada), a big bat whose large larynges (vocal cords) produce a

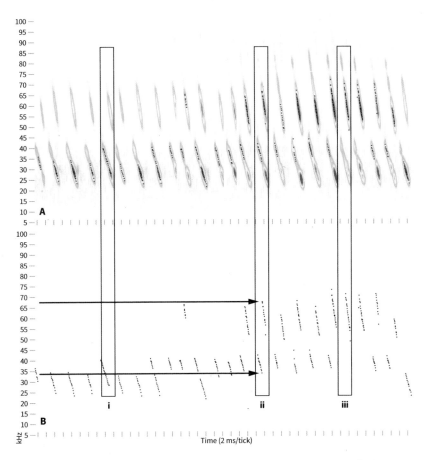

In the full-spectrum recording of a TOWNSEND'S BIG-EARED BAT in A, the loudest (high amplitude) part of each call is indicated by the red colour. The black overlay of dots is Kaleidoscope (Wildlife Acoustics) software's non-enhanced zero-crossing rendering of these full-spectrum calls. The spectrogram in B shows the zero-cross dots without the full-spectrum background. For the first series of calls, the first harmonic is loudest, and therefore only the first harmonic zero-crosses (example outlined in i). In the middle part of the sequence, the second harmonic increases in loudness (see facing page), such that now the loudest part of some of the calls shifts mid-pulse into the second harmonic, such that the first part of the first harmonic zero-crosses during the time when it is the loudest signal, and then the second part of the second harmonic zero-crosses when it is loudest; this produces what is called a split-harmonic in zero-crossing (example outlined in ii). In this example, the first part of the first harmonic stops zero-crossing at approximately 35 kilohertz, and because a second harmonic is twice the frequency of the first, we see the second part of this split harmonic start at approximately 70 kilohertz (see arrows). Near the end of this sequence, the second harmonics of several pulses are louder than the first harmonics throughout the entire pulse duration, so only the second harmonic component zero-crosses (example outlined in iii).

x-axis Time (s)	y-axis Frequency (Hz)	N	1	
0.0000	37915	Fc	30.95	kHz
0.0002	36697	Sc	116.00	OPS
0.0005	35477	Dur	4.02	ms
0.0007	34409			
0.0009	33613	Fmax	37.91	kHz
0.0012	32922	Fmin	24.58	kHz
0.0014	32193	Fmean	29.86	kHz
0.0017	31558			
0.0019	30948	Ntbc	0	
0.0022	30246	TBC	0.00	ms
0.0025	29466			
0.0028	28571	Fknee	32.92	kHz
0.0031	27634	Tknee	1.17	ms
0.0034	26667	Ok	3.43	%
0.0037	25600	S1	213.06	OPS
0.0040	24578	Tc	1.94	ms
		Qual	0.12	%

(Left axis, kHz log, plotted against Time: 100, 80, 70, 60, 50, 40, 35, 30, 25, 20, 15)

Zero-cross rendering of a TOWNSEND'S BIG-EARED BAT pulse summarizes the frequencies in a bat call, with each dot making up the spectrogram being an x-y coordinate (grey shaded box of data points that underpin the graphed pulse), where x is time (seconds) and y is frequency (hertz or kilohertz). This window is also showing various call measurements (blue shaded box) of this one pulse, similar to what is displayed in AnalookW software.

long-wave (low-frequency) fundamental harmonic. This bat is somewhat unusual in its foraging behaviour: despite its large size, it gleans prey off surfaces, including the ground, much like PALLID BAT. But unlike PALLID BAT, CALIFORNIAN LEAF-NOSED BAT uses its unique nasal structure to adjust its echolocation calls to emphasize (louder, more energy) higher-frequency components of their sound (higher harmonics). Bats that forage in high clutter typically have low-intensity, high-frequency echolocation calls. Although CALIFORNIAN LEAF-NOSED BAT's fundamental harmonic is low frequency (approximately 25 kilohertz), it shifts the energy of its calls into the higher-frequency components, thus benefiting from the higher resolution provided by shorter sound waves. This bat will regularly emphasize its higher-frequency second and third harmonics—so much so that in zero-cross recording (see below), you may not record any of its 25 kilohertz calls (fundamental frequency), instead seeing only evidence of the 50 kilohertz (second harmonic) and 75 kilohertz (third harmonic) components of the echolocation signal. TOWNSEND'S BIG-EARED BAT is a BC species that also takes advantage of multiple harmonics during foraging: it will hover in front of objects, a perfect opportunity to take advantage of the better resolution provided by higher frequencies in higher harmonics.

Some researchers prefer to view only the loudest frequencies produced by a bat at any point in time, because this gives the call more definition; this is called a zero-crossing analysis of the pulse (e.g., see spectrograms on page 114). The advantage of zero-crossing is the less ambiguous call shape compared to full spectrum, but the disadvantage is that only the loudest sounds will be represented. If the bat call is not the loudest sound, it will not be represented. This may be the case, for example, if there is a calling insect close to a bat detector's microphone. In this case, insect-generated frequencies may be plotted in the zero-cross spectrogram instead of the quieter underlying bat call. Fewer bat calls may be rendered in the zero-crossing recording. Some bat detectors allow you to record directly to zero-crossing rather than recording the full complement of frequencies making up the sound environment. This is called native zero-crossing. Advantages of recording in native zero-crossing instead of full spectrum is the low digital memory requirements of zero-cross recordings (approximately 1/1000 of the memory is required), and in most cases, lower energy consumption by the detector. If the loudest frequencies of a bat's call are split across more than one harmonic, only the loudest component of each harmonic is shown, resulting in what's called a split-harmonic pattern (see example ii in spectrogram on page 117; see also TOWNSEND'S BIG-EARED BAT species account). Because of the frequency division process in zero-crossing analysis, a time series of the loudest frequency is plotted in a zero-crossing spectrogram. The dividing factor that is used can often be user-controlled, and this is called the division ratio. For example, a division ratio of 8 loosely means that every eighth sound wave triggers a data point in a zero-cross spectrogram. This counting of waves associated with measured time intervals creates a frequency-versus-time data table that, when plotted on a frequency-versus-time graph (see image on facing page), gives a clear outline of loudest frequencies produced by the bat during its echolocation pulse; thus zero-cross spectrograms often look like a string of dots, depending on the selected division ratio and how quickly the bat is changing frequencies. Lower division ratio (e.g., a division ratio of 4, which is a good setting for recording SPOTTED BATS) results in a higher density (resolution) of dots making up the spectrogram, because time measurements associated with counts of waves are made more frequently. The downside of lower division ratio is that higher-frequency bat calls, such as those of most myotis species, will be oversampled, and this may produce a fuzzy assemblage of dots rather than a clear linear pulse shape.

When to Use Acoustics to Differentiate Species

Unlike birdsong, the primary purpose of bat echolocation is to navigate and find food, not to convey species-identifying information. Different species' echolocation calls are notoriously difficult to distinguish, especially for similar species, and there are exceptions to all rules and definitions. Intra-individual, intra-species and environmentally induced variation all contribute to extreme overlap among species and even species groups, and echolocation calls should be categorized with the understanding that there is always some degree of potential error associated with this process. While it is beyond the scope of this book, there are numerous software packages available for the analysis of bat calls. Most acoustics software programs provide spectrograms to visualize the bat recordings. Some also allow manual processing, such as call measurements and appending file metadata. Several commercially available computer software packages are available that attempt to automatically classify recordings of bats to the species level, providing a quantitative measure of confidence.

All bats in North America that use a frequency-modulated call type use higher frequencies of sound when approaching an object to resolve distance and detail. This means that as bats approach objects they may start to produce steeper, higher-frequency calls; this often results in different species having similar-looking spectrograms, confounding species identification. The complexities of recording bats and interpreting their spectrograms, especially if the behaviour of the bat was not observed at the time of recording, makes species identification solely based on acoustic parameters difficult, to say the least. It is not impossible to tell species apart, especially species that echolocate using different frequency ranges or with markedly different pulse shapes; however, to differentiate species that have extensive call parameter overlap, it is highly recommended that additional tools be used to determine species' presence.

Caution should always be taken when interpreting bat calls that have been recorded by a passively deployed bat detector and automatically identified using software. Because the bat was not seen at the time of recording, its behaviour in relation to clutter and distance from the microphone cannot be known. The plasticity of echolocation among and within species and even individuals makes species identification based on acoustic recordings challenging. Auto-identification software packages all rely on a reference call library, most of which consist of calls produced by captured bats recorded as they are released from someone's hand, usually close to the ground and thus near a source of clutter. Though it is often advisable to record in open (uncluttered) areas to maximize the chance of differentiating many species, it is not always possible to achieve these types of reference recordings. Because of this, most auto-identification software algorithms or models have been developed with a large portion of high-clutter calls and in most, if not all, cases represent only a subset of calls that a species produces, especially for wide-ranging species that may have regional acoustic differences. While there are a variety of uses for auto-identification software, it is advisable to have an expert review all species assignments if the data are to be used for inventory purposes or to inform management decisions. Experts are more likely to group similar species together (e.g., BIG BROWN BAT or SILVER-HAIRED BAT) when a unique or diagnostic species-specific trait is not present, unlike most auto-identification software, which assigns species labels based on statistical probabilities or degree of pattern matching.

Bat detectors that record echolocation are just one tool that can be used to differentiate bat species. Other tools, as mentioned previously, include genetic sampling (e.g., from wing biopsies or guano collected at roosts) and mist-net or harp trap capture. If a bat can be seen flying, it may also be possible to see its colour using a spotlight. But for the most part, acoustically recording bats is the simplest method and, thanks to affordable bat detectors, such as those that can plug into smartphones or tablets, is often the cheapest method of detecting bats. And anyone can do it. Bat detectors are the binoculars of the bat world and have the potential to make "backyard batting" just as popular as backyard birding. There are smartphone apps that will automate acoustic identification, using the same principles as automatic classification in computer software.

Although there are many reasons why automatic classification may provide an erroneous species identification, listening to the ultrasound of bats overhead is still fun, engaging and informative. There are many detectors on the market; the cheapest only allow listening (e.g., heterodyne detector; see top detector in image on page 122), while more expensive models allow you to listen, visualize spectrograms, record and analyze (e.g., Echometer and Walkabout; see bottom two detectors in image on page 122). Just be cautious in interpreting species labels generated by automated acoustic identification software or applications.

Categorizing Bats Using Acoustic Traits

The first step in trying to identify a bat that has been recorded is to determine which species could produce the observed range of frequencies. Bats are typically categorized according to the lowest frequency that they typically produce. For example, in BC three species of bats fall within a frequency guild of 45 to 50 kilohertz: CANYON BAT, YUMA MYOTIS and CALIFORNIAN MYOTIS. These species typically produce calls that end in the 45 to 50 kilohertz range, although it is possible for them to produce calls that end outside of this range under some conditions. Approximate ranges of ending frequencies for all bats in BC can be a coarse guide for those new to acoustic analysis (see page 123). However, this frequency guild "map" should be considered an estimate of what these species do; behaviour, species assemblages (communities) and local environmental parameters can influence the echolocation calls produced by bats. Bats can also influence each other's ultrasound production, because the presence of another bat is a source of reflected sound (echoes), and bats respond to objects by altering their echolocation calls. Acoustic identification of species should ideally be restricted to cases in which only a single bat is present. Similarly, ideal recordings should capture bats flying in open spaces,

An increasing number of bat detectors are available, differing in functionality. Top is a simple handheld heterodyne detector for listening only (Pettersson D100); bottom left is a Wildlife Acoustics Echometer Touch II bat detector plugged into an iPad, allowing listening, visualization, full-spectrum recording and application of auto-identification through an app; bottom right is a Titley Scientific Anabat Walkabout, which allows listening and simultaneous recording and visualizing in full-spectrum and zero-crossing formats, recording to an SD card.

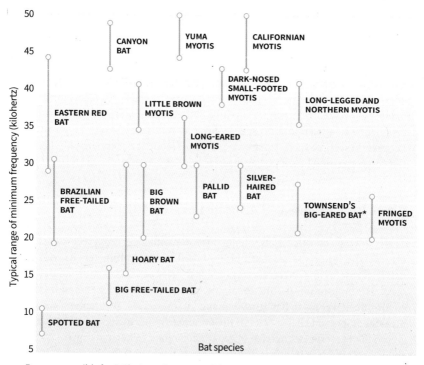

Frequency guilds for BC bat species, categorizing species based on the lowest frequency or range of frequencies that they tend to produce. This does not reflect the entire repertoire of the species across its range but provides a typical range of lowest echolocation frequencies. The asterisk refers to fundamental harmonic only; in zero-crossing spectrograms, a diagnostic split harmonic pattern is generally observed (see spectrogram on page 150 in TOWNSEND'S BIG-EARED BAT species account).

not navigating through clutter. Habitat is likely to influence the amount of clutter that a bat will encounter while searching for prey (e.g., open grassland versus dense forest), and this will influence echolocation call frequencies as a function of time. Some species are identifiable when responding to clutter (e.g., Lasiurine species, such as HOARY BAT, which has a diagnostic undulating minimum frequency pattern when flying through clutter), but most are best differentiated through search phase calls that are not influenced by returning echoes. In reality, bats produce a range of calls, even in seemingly uncluttered environments, because of their awareness of other bats, the ground, the bat detector microphone, and so on. There is no complete reference library of recordings for all species under all conditions.

It is important to remember that because of acoustic overlap among species, echolocation categories may be more appropriate than species-level categorization, to reduce false positives. For example, BIG BROWN BATS and SILVER-HAIRED BATS often overlap in acoustic call parameters, necessitating a combined category of BIG BROWN/SILVER-HAIRED BATS. In areas where BRAZILIAN FREE-TAILED BATS are found, this dyad category may need to be expanded into a triad of BIG BROWN/SILVER-HAIRED/BRAZILIAN FREE-TAILED for some recordings because of extreme call overlap between these three species. As such, if a recording were made that had characteristics of all three of these species, the recording would be labelled as a triad and no species-level identification would be possible. Because these three species share a typical end frequency of about 25 kilohertz, this category could be simply labelled "25 kilohertz bats."

Key to BC Bats Based on Acoustic Characteristics

The following acoustic key is intended for use with zero-cross recordings to identify species or species assemblages based on call parameters as seen in native zero-crossing. Acoustic keys are less diagnostic than morphological ones, as echolocation is functional and can be substantially altered by the environmental context, bat behaviour and, in some cases, geography. This key includes all possible bat species in the province of BC, including accidentals, although not all species overlap in geographic range. When making decisions about potential species identifications, you should consider the distribution maps included with the species accounts in this book, as well as any known range expansions beyond what is described here.

This key focuses largely on echolocation calls made by bats navigating through their environment in search of prey; in other words, this key assumes that the calls being examined are search phase calls produced by bats flying in an open environment and not responding to objects (no clutter). If the bat was not viewed during the recording, you cannot be certain that this assumption is correct. Also, while it would be nice to think that we know enough about call variation among individuals of all species to consider all possible circumstances and possibilities, this is not the case. Exceptions are bound to arise, as with any aspect of the natural world.

For additional call parameters in full spectrum and in different levels of clutter, see individual species accounts and the acoustic species summary table in Appendix 4. Call frequencies listed in the criteria for species differentiation refer to the frequencies at which calls typically end, not including toes and not accounting for split harmonics. For example, if a call is split between the first and second harmonic, the "end frequency" refers to where the first harmonic ends, even if the full spectrogram of the first harmonic is not complete (i.e., the end frequency of the first harmonic of a split harmonic call can be deduced by dividing the end frequency of the split second harmonic by two; see the arrows in B in the spectrogram on page 117). This key also assumes that a single bat has been recorded and the recording is of high quality and of a sufficiently long sequence that species-specific diagnostic call patterns are evident.

Once you have a potential identification, consult the acoustic descriptions and figures in the appropriate species account to determine if it is consistent with the result from the key. It is generally good practice to have an expert review acoustic data and, where possible, to use additional methods of identification, such as mist-net capture or genetic identification from guano. If the call sequence being investigated does not fit into any identification category in this key, the call sequence may be unsuitable for species-level classification; however, species group classification, such as "myotis" or "25 kilohertz myotis," may be appropriate. Alternatively, if it is a sequence of calls that have been produced in response to clutter, this key does not apply. See species accounts and Appendix 4 for descriptions of echolocation calls in response to varying levels of clutter.

This key also assumes that there are no WESTERN RED BATS in BC. This is relevant in the comparison of CANYON BAT and YUMA MYOTIS (couplet 15).

1	1a	Most of the pulses end below 15 kHz: Go to **2**
	1b	Most of the pulses end at or above 15 kHz (if at 15 kHz, pulses are flat): Go to **3**
2 (t 1)	2a	Most or all pulses end below 10 kHz: SPOTTED BAT (p. 169)
	2b	Most or all pulses end above 10 kHz: BIG FREE-TAILED BAT (p. 291)
3 (t 1)	3a	Social directive (very long tail extending below 20 kHz from a call that has approximately 25 kHz characteristic frequency) present (see spectrograms on p. 138): PALLID BAT (p. 135)
	3b	Social directive not present: Go to **4**
4 (t 3)	4a	Most or all pulses end below 20 kHz: HOARY BAT (p. 187)
	4b	Most or all pulses end above 20 kHz: Go to **5**
5 (t 4)	5a	Sequence of calls has pulses that undulate in minimum frequency, have upturned toes, and include low-sloped (less than 25 octaves per second, or OPS) pulses, with most ending at or above 30 kHz or slightly lower: EASTERN RED BAT (p. 179)
	5b	Sequence is not as described in *a*: Go to **6**

6 (↳ 5)	**6a**	Most or all pulses end below 35 kHz: Go to **7**
	6b	Most or all pulses end above 35 kHz: Go to **13**
7 (↳ 6)	**7a**	Calls are low in slope, including flat or near flat, or with a low sloped component following a short broadband sweep: Go to **8**
	7b	Pulses have a broad frequency sweep, giving them a relatively steep straight appearance: Go to **11**
8 (↳ 7)	**8a**	At least some pulses end below 23 kHz: Go to **9**
	8b	All pulses end above 23 kHz: Go to **10**
9 (↳ 8)	**9a**	Pulses are flat or nearly flat (5 OPS or less): BRAZILIAN FREE-TAILED BAT (p. 285)
	9b	Pulses are not flat: BIG BROWN BAT (p. 159)
10 (↳ 8)	**10a**	At least one pulse is nearly flat (5 OPS or less): SILVER-HAIRED BAT (p. 197) or BRAZILIAN FREE-TAILED BAT (p. 285), but only where this species is expected (see accidental species accounts)
	10b	All pulses are greater than 5 OPS in slope: BRAZILIAN FREE-TAILED BAT (p. 285), BIG BROWN BAT (p. 159) or SILVER-HAIRED BAT (p. 197)
11 (↳ 7)	**11a**	Broadband short-duration pulses end between 20 and 27 kHz: Go to **12**
	11b	Broadband short-duration pulses end between 30 and 35 kHz: LONG-EARED MYOTIS (p. 217)
12 (↳ 11)	**12a**	Split-harmonic pattern is present (between first and second harmonics; see spectrogram on p. 117), and/or there is an upsweep into the calls (social component; see spectrograms on p. 150), and/or a slight concave or arched curvature (first pulse of spectrogram A p. 150 and first and second pulses of spectrogram B p. 150): TOWNSEND'S BIG-EARED BAT (p. 147)
	12b	Split-harmonic pattern is not present: FRINGED MYOTIS (p. 255), TOWNSEND'S BIG-EARED BAT (p. 147) or PALLID BAT (p. 135)

13 (t 6)   **13a**   Pulses end below 38 kHz and have relatively low slope (less than 50 ops, and as low as 25 ops); a distinct elbow/knee may be present: LITTLE BROWN MYOTIS (p. 227)

         13b   Pulses are not as in *a*: Go to **14**

14 (t 13)   **14a**   Most or all pulses end at or above 43 kHz: Go to **15**

         14b   Most or all pulses end below 43 kHz: LITTLE BROWN MYOTIS (p. 227), DARK-NOSED SMALL-FOOTED MYOTIS (p. 239), NORTHERN MYOTIS (p. 247), LONG-LEGGED MYOTIS (p. 263); possibly CANYON BAT (p. 295) or CALIFORNIAN MYOTIS (p. 207). See species accounts for possible further differentiation.

15 (t 14)   **15a**   Average pulse slope of sequence is low (30 ops or less) and calls often flatten at end and may have an upturned toe: CANYON BAT, or possibly YUMA MYOTIS (see species accounts for possible further differentiation)

         15b   Average pulse slope of sequence is greater than 30 ops: YUMA MYOTIS (most likely to have pronounced elbows/knees in calls) or CALIFORNIAN MYOTIS (less likely to have pronounced elbows/knees in calls). See species accounts for possible further differentiation.

References

Barclay (1999), Bell (1985), Brigham et al. (2002), Cvikel et al. (2015), Fraser et al. (2020), Holderied and Von Helversen (2003), Jakobsen et al. (2018), Jones (1999).

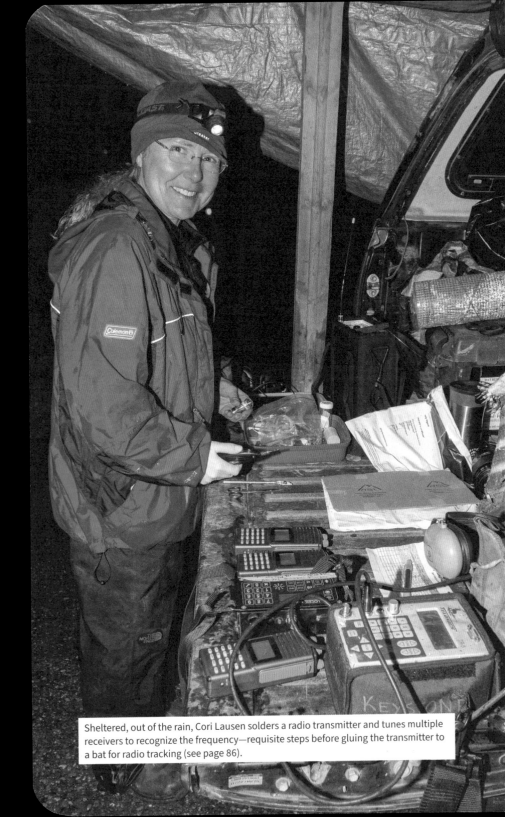

Sheltered, out of the rain, Cori Lausen solders a radio transmitter and tunes multiple receivers to recognize the frequency—requisite steps before gluing the transmitter to a bat for radio tracking (see page 86).

Species Accounts

Here we provide a detailed species account for each of British Columbia's 15 bat species. We do not include full accounts for BIG FREE-TAILED BAT, BRAZILIAN FREE-TAILED BAT or CANYON BAT, as these species are known from only a few occurrences/recordings, so their status in BC is essentially unknown. As such, they are covered in the Accidental Species section, which follows the other species accounts. Wherever possible, we have used species information from studies of BC populations or populations from bordering provinces, territories or states, but it's important to remember that there is considerable variation in the amount of information available for our bat species.

The name of the species is given as the common name and the genus and species (following accepted names as listed at batnames.org in 2021). Information in each account is presented in 12 categories.

DESCRIPTION provides an overall description of the bat, including colour of fur, ears and wing membranes; ear size; tragus size and shape; and the presence or absence of a keel on the calcar. One or more colour images illustrate the species. A subsection on Morphologically Similar Species provides a detailed summary of diagnostic traits that are used to distinguish a species from other similar species. Although a few BC bats can be reliably identified from photographs, most of these diagnostic traits can only be applied to captured bats or specimens held in the hand.

ACOUSTIC CHARACTERISTICS summarizes the frequencies and general structure of the species' echolocation calls recorded by bat detectors, with examples of typical spectrograms. The species is placed in a frequency group, defined by the lowest frequency that most calls may reach. This excludes call toes (or tails, as they are sometimes called). Refer to Acoustics, page 103, and the glossary for definitions. Unless otherwise noted, spectrograms in this book are displayed using acoustic software as follows: all zero-crossing recordings are in AnalookW (©Chris Corben), and all full-spectrum recordings are in Kaleidoscope (©Wildlife Acoustics). In each zero-cross spectrogram, the y-axis scale is 12 to 120 kilohertz (logarithmic), except for the SPOTTED BAT account, which starts at 8 kilohertz; the time (x-axis) magnification setting is F7. In the full-spectrum spectrograms, the frequency scale is linear from 5 to 120 kilohertz, and with a single exception (specified in the species account), all recordings were made at a sampling rate of at least 256 kilohertz, ensuring that frequencies of 128 kilohertz or lower could be recorded when the bat was within range of the microphone. Colour of the full-spectrum spectrograms ranges from green (quiet/low amplitude) through yellow (moderate amplitude) to red (loud/highest amplitude). An oscillogram (waveform) is shown in blue above all full-spectrum recordings, with a scale of +/–20,000 decibels. All spectrograms are shown in compressed mode, meaning that the time elapsed between calls is largely removed to allow more pulses to be shown in the spectrogram; the duration of time along the x-axis is 90 milliseconds in all cases. This means that the time axis (x-axis) is only accurately displaying the time *within* the pulse (where each tick on the axis in the full-spectrum spectrograms represents a duration of 2 milliseconds); time between pulses is *not* representative of the true time that elapsed. All reference recordings were of bats identified through capture and then recorded on release, unless specified, in which case bats may have been spotlighted, bat-kited or zip-lined (see Studying Bats, page 73). All recordings were made by Cori Lausen unless otherwise specified. Not all recordings were made in BC, but all are representative of echolocation calls that could be emitted by bats in BC. The entire repertoire of a species cannot be represented here, but in most cases a small sample of the variability—high-, low- and/or moderate-clutter pulse shapes—is provided, and in some cases a social call recording is included if it can aid in species identification. A subsection, Acoustically Similar Species, lists species with similar echolocation calls.

DISTRIBUTION includes a description of the provincial range and an associated range map showing known species records from the province. Species range maps are based on ecosection polygons, to be consistent with the B.C. Conservation Data Centre's species range mapping method. Ecosections are part of the ecoregion classification system in BC, which stratifies the province according to geographical units. The three levels (ecoprovinces, ecoregions and ecosections) are progressively more detailed categorizations of the ecosystem characteristics. Categories are based on similar climate, physiography, hydrology, vegetation and wildlife potential. An ecoregion is an area with major physiographic and minor macroclimatic variation. There are 38 pure terrestrial ecoregions in BC. Ecosections are areas with "minor physiographic and macroclimatic variations." There are 139 ecosections in BC, ranging from pure marine units to pure terrestrial units. The map shows terrestrial ecosection boundaries within the ecoregions.

For the range maps, we selected ecosections using a combination of confirmed records, acoustic records and expert opinion. We used confirmed records (vouchers and observations, and acoustic records for SPOTTED BAT and HOARY BAT) to identify the ecosection(s) where the species was considered present, and these are represented with dark grey shading. To identify the ecosection(s) where the species is considered "expected," represented with light grey polygons,

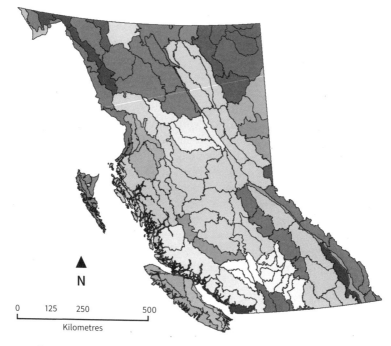

Ecosections—Ecoregion

Ecosystem Classification of British Columbia

Ecosections are shaded by ecoregion

- Boreal Mountains and Plateaus
- Boundary Ranges
- Central Alberta Upland
- Chilcotin Ranges
- Chugach Mountains and Icefields
- Coastal Gap
- Columbia Highlands
- Central Canadian Rocky Mountains
- Eastern Continental Ranges
- Eastern Hazelton Mountains
- Eastern Vancouver Island
- Fraser Basin
- Fraser Plateau
- Georgia-Puget Basin
- Gwaii Haanas
- Hecate Continental Shelf
- Hyland Highland
- Hay-Slave Lowland
- Inner Pacific Shelf
- Interior Transition Ranges
- Liard Basin
- Lower Mainland
- Muskwa Plateau
- Northern Continental Divide

- Northern Columbia Mountains
- Northern Cascade Ranges
- Nass Ranges
- Northern Canadian Rocky Mountains
- Northern Alberta Upland
- Okanagan Highland
- Omineca Mountains
- Outer Pacific Shelf
- Pacific Ranges
- Pelly Mountains
- Peace River Basin
- Purcell Transitional Ranges
- Southern Alberta Upland
- Sub-Arctic Pacific
- Selkirk-Bitterroot Foothills
- Skeena Mountains
- Southern Rocky Mountain Trench
- St. Elias Mountains
- Thompson-Okanagan Plateau
- Transitional Pacific
- Western Continental Ranges
- Western Vancouver Island
- Yukon-Stikine Highlands
- Yukon Southern Lakes

we used acoustic records (for species other than SPOTTED BAT and HOARY BAT) and expert opinion. Expert opinion was useful in areas where inventory had not been conducted but suitable habitat occurred. If an ecosection polygon is within a species' range, the entire polygon is shaded, even if it contains areas where the species may not be present.

We considered a record confirmed if it was a voucher or observation, or for SPOTTED BAT, an acoustic record. Vouchers are species occurrences based on museum specimens, live captures identified from a DNA sequence, or photographs of species that are reliably identified from a photograph. Observations are species occurrences based on live-capture releases (with no DNA samples or identifiable photographs) or bats observed in roosts. Species occurrences came from a database that included historical museum specimens, captures and observations, and from captures and acoustic records contributed by various researchers, naturalists and government sources, including the BC Ministry of Environment and Climate Change Strategy's Wildlife Data and Information and the B.C. Conservation Data Centre, and acoustic records from the North American Bat Monitoring Program. Because of conservation sensitivity for a few species, a small amount of capture data was not made available for use in this book.

ROOSTING describes habitat for summer day and night roosts, including female maternity roosts.

FEEDING identifies the prey species consumed, the general feeding habitats used, and hunting techniques used to capture prey.

REPRODUCTION describes the general reproductive cycle, including the timing of birth and development of young.

MIGRATION AND WINTER describes the winter biology, including migration movements and winter hibernation sites.

CONSERVATION STATUS provides conservation rankings of species at risk, including provincial listings and federal rankings under the Canadian Species at Risk Act, and summarizes potential and ongoing threats to the species.

TAXONOMY AND VARIATION lists any recognized subspecies found in BC. Unresolved taxonomic issues and results from relevant genetic studies are also reviewed in this section.

MEASUREMENTS include seven linear measurements in millimetres, and body mass in grams. The values given are the mean, range (in parentheses) and sample size (n = number of individuals measured). Measurements are based on adult bats from BC unless otherwise specified in the account. Tail vertebrae length refers to the length of the tail in its entirety, even if the tail extends past the edge of the tail membrane. Body mass is based on adult males and non-pregnant or early pregnancy adult females only. Because mass can be highly variable due to a bat's ability to consume a large amount of food relative to its body size, we made all efforts to include only mass measurements from bats that had been held for one hour if they had been captured free-flying during the foraging season; this is enough time for a bat of normal body temperature to largely void the digestive tract, allowing for a relatively accurate estimate of body mass. As such, masses presented in each account are from adults without bias from pregnancy or food in the digestive tract. An explanation of how measurements are made of some of the appendages can be found in General Biology (see In-Hand Differentiation, page 92).

REMARKS provides any interesting facts about the species, and areas for future study.

REFERENCES includes some sources cited in the 1993 handbook and new sources that support information presented in the account. We have included names of data contributors if their data are unlikely to be found in government databases, are not in publicly available reports or are not published. We have made all efforts to include references for all data used in our species accounts, including citing reports or other sources of unpublished literature when available. Occurrence records from outside of BC provide context for some species accounts, and these were obtained from the following databases: Alberta Fisheries and Wildlife Management Information System, Montana Natural Heritage MapViewer, and Saskatchewan Conservation Data Centre's Saskatchewan Vertebrate Taxa List.

References
Demarchi (2011), Simmons and Cirranello (2020).

PALLID BAT

Pallid Bat   *Antrozous pallidus*

DESCRIPTION

PALLID BAT has the largest average forearm length of any bat in BC. In mass and wingspan, it is second only to HOARY BAT. PALLID BAT has short, fine fur that is pale yellow, or blond on the back and creamy white on the underside. Its distinctive ears are large: the width of each ear at the base is almost equal to the length. The tragus is long and narrow, with a toothed outer margin. The snout is large and square, with a shallow ridge on top and a tip that is somewhat pig-like, with several glandular swellings. PALLID BAT has robust teeth for eating large prey. Compared with other Canadian bats, the eyes are relatively large. The calcar lacks a keel.

MORPHOLOGICALLY SIMILAR SPECIES

None. PALLID BAT is pale in colour, and compared with other BC bat species, possesses relatively large eyes, ears and forearms. The only resident BC species with which it could be possibly confused is TOWNSEND'S BIG-EARED BAT. PALLID BAT is much larger, its ears are not joined at the base, and it lacks the two prominent bumps on the nose. The presence of only two pairs of lower incisors is unique among BC bats.

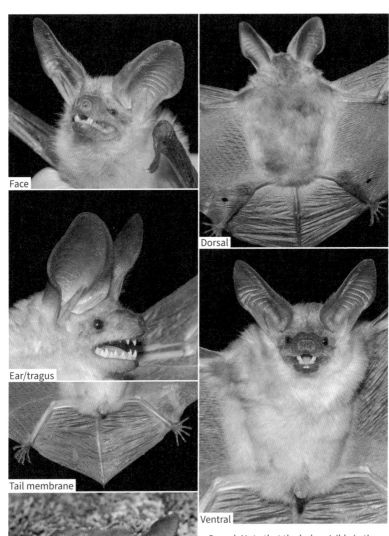

Face

Dorsal

Ear/tragus

Tail membrane

Ventral

Side

Dorsal: Note that the holes visible in the wing membrane are following genetic sampling. Genetic samples are taken strategically in locations that have little to no innervation and no major blood vessels, and therefore do not cause pain or bleeding. Sampling holes have been observed to heal over as quickly as a few days, and most often do not scar, leaving no indication that a wing biopsy occurred. Genetic samples, especially of species at risk, are important for conservation efforts.

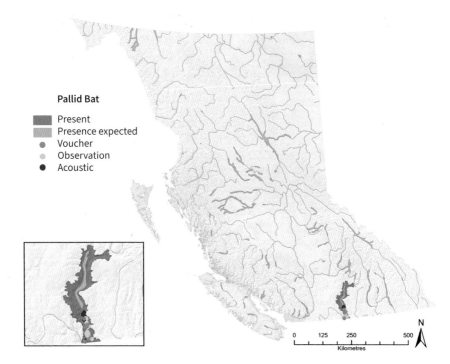

DISTRIBUTION

PALLID BAT ranges from Mexico throughout the western United States. In BC, PALLID BAT has been confirmed in the south Okanagan Valley and is suspected to occur as far west as Hedley and as far north as Kelowna or even Kamloops, based on acoustics. There are also possible detections of PALLID BAT in Grand Forks based on acoustics only. Suitable habitat exists in the Thompson-Nicola, continuing north from Lillooet to the Chilcotin-Fraser Complex and along the Chilcotin River to Hanceville. Further study may elicit detection in at least some additional areas.

ACOUSTIC CHARACTERISTICS

25 kilohertz. Because PALLID BAT has evolved to be a gleaner, it echolocates using relatively high-clutter call shapes despite its tendency to forage in grasslands and other open environments. This is attributed to its tendency to hunt ground-dwelling prey using listening for a combination of echoes and for prey-generated sounds. PALLID BAT calls often appear wavy, and always have some form of curvature to the call, even if it is subtle curvature, such as a small knee or a small foot near the end of the call. When PALLID BAT calls taper off at the end with a foot (where the lower frequencies change less over time), the foot is short in duration (less than 3 milliseconds).

ZERO-CROSS RECORDINGS

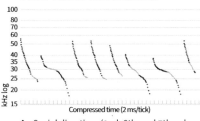

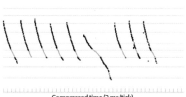

A. Social directives (2nd, 6th, and 7th pulses from left) interspersed with search phase pulses, some showing wavy nature.

B. Search phase calls with single social directive (6th pulse from left). (Winter recording by Tanya Luszcz at Vaseaux Lake in the Okanagan.)

C. Wispy social directives on a series of pulses.

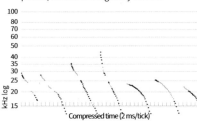

FULL-SPECTRUM RECORDINGS

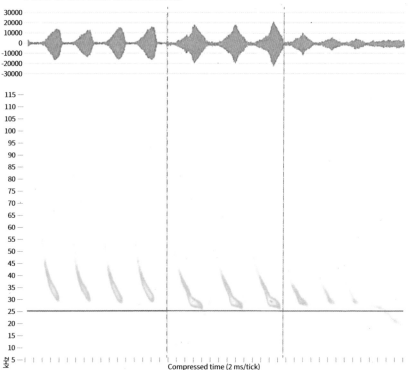

Left pane, higher-clutter pulse shapes; middle pane, lower clutter; right pane, a sequence with a social directive.

PALLID BAT makes a rather unique social call that is sometimes referred to as a social directive. This call starts like a typical echolocation call but continues lower in frequency in the shape of a stretched S or zigzag. The directive sweeps into the audible range and is often emitted several times in rapid succession. This call appears to function as a contact call, as it is frequently produced when bats return from foraging, before entering their roost. These social calls are unique between individuals.

ACOUSTICALLY SIMILAR SPECIES
FRINGED MYOTIS, LONG-EARED MYOTIS, BIG BROWN BAT, SILVER-HAIRED BAT.
FRINGED and LONG-EARED MYOTIS calls can be similar to those of PALLID BAT, as all three species produce high-clutter-type calls (i.e., short-duration broadband). LONG-EARED MYOTIS calls typically end at 30 kilohertz; however, PALLID BAT calls can also end at 30 kilohertz when they are producing their highest-frequency call types in cluttered environments. In a low-clutter foraging situation, PALLID BAT will still produce steep calls, but they tend to end closer to 25 kilohertz. This pattern invites confusion with FRINGED MYOTIS, which typically has a similar minimum frequency; however, PALLID BAT spectrograms usually do not show a starting frequency much higher than 80 kilohertz, whereas FRINGED MYOTIS, especially when close to the microphone, can have a spectrogram showing a tremendous frequency sweep, starting at 120 kilohertz and down to 25 kilohertz in less than 3.5 milliseconds on average. PALLID BAT has slightly longer-duration calls, averaging 6 milliseconds. Because of this difference in typical bandwidth and duration, FRINGED MYOTIS and PALLID BAT are usually differentiated based on overall shape of calls. FRINGED MYOTIS most often produces calls that are linear in shape, ending rather abruptly around 20 to 25 kilohertz, while PALLID BAT calls most often show some level of curvature and taper off at the end with a foot.

PALLID BAT calls can also be similar to the calls that BIG BROWN or SILVER-HAIRED BATS produce when flying in high clutter, causing confusion of identification among these three species, especially when the level of clutter that the bat is responding to is unknown. However, at least in some cases, the low-frequency social component that can extend the 25 kilohertz echolocation call sets PALLID BAT apart from BIG BROWN BAT. Lausen has observed BIG BROWN BATS occasionally producing an extension of an echolocation call that can drop below 25 kilohertz, but it is not nearly as extreme as the long wavy or zigzag extension of the PALLID BAT directive.

ROOSTING
PALLID BAT is found in arid grassland or shrub-steppe habitats where boulders, cliffs or rocky outcrops can be used as roosts. In BC, PALLID BAT is restricted to low-elevation (300 to 490 metres) habitats in areas of grassland and PONDEROSA

PINE forest, often in the vicinity of cliff faces. Although little is known about the species' biology in BC, it has been the subject of intensive study in the southern United States. Horizontal rock crevices with hot (30°C) and constant temperatures are preferred as summer day roosts, although PALLID BAT has been found roosting in tree cavities, buildings, caves, grottos and mine adits. In BC, biologists have located 16-day roosts, all used by males, who were tracked using radiotelemetry. All of these roosts were in rock crevices of cliffs. In one study, males used torpor each day (measured with temperature-sensitive transmitters) and switched roosts on average every four days (ranging from 1 to 13 days), but bats remained loyal to the roosting area. Most roosts faced south or southeast. Males did not use torpor when night roosting during this June to August study. In Oregon, female PALLID BATS exhibited a high degree of roost switching (every 1.4 days on average) while tracked. It was determined that roost switching was an adaptive behaviour to reduce ectoparasite loads; high ectoparasite levels were correlated with lower body mass in nursing females, suggesting that parasites are likely detrimental to the bats.

Outside BC, PALLID BAT is known to be gregarious, with males and females roosting together in small colonies of 12 to 100 individuals, with the largest colonies composed of females with young. Composition of the summer colonies seems to vary locally; in some areas, males and females roost separately, but in others mixed colonies containing both sexes have been found. Composition of colonies in BC is unknown; less than 16% of known captures (9 of 54) have been female, and only 7 have been young-of-year (all males). It appears that PALLID BATS frequently change the location of their day roost.

In BC, this bat typically selects rock crevices or PONDEROSA PINE for night roosts, but Mike Sarell and Daniella Rambaldini observed them using a carport, a bridge and an outdoor stairwell. In the United States, crevices, caves and anthropogenic structures, including buildings and bridges, are used. Night roosts are often in exposed sites near the day roost and are often conspicuous because of large accumulations of guano and discarded insect fragments; small prey are apparently eaten during flight, but for larger items PALLID BAT retreats to a night roost to consume its meal, often culling legs or wings. In Oregon, PALLID BATS showed fidelity to night roosts, and individuals found together at a night roost may occupy separate day roosts. As with other bat species, it has been suggested that PALLID BATS may congregate at night roosts for social reasons.

FEEDING

In BC, PALLID BAT seems to forage frequently over tracts of open grassland habitat composed of sparsely distributed BIG SAGEBRUSH, RABBIT BRUSH and ANTELOPE BRUSH. Gravel/dirt roads and vineyards may provide foraging corridors, and there are several observations of PALLID BATS flying low over roads or within vineyards in the Okanagan. PALLID BATS may commute up to

4.5 kilometres between their day roost and foraging areas, and this distance has thus been used to define critical foraging habitat in the species' federal recovery plan.

As a large powerful bat with robust teeth, this species can kill and eat large invertebrates. While it can capture flying prey, this bat is well adapted to capturing its prey on the ground or gleaning it from the foliage of trees and shrubs. On the ground, it can pursue prey by moving quickly on all four limbs. Invertebrates taken in the western United States include June beetles, moths, cicadas, praying mantids, katydids, grasshoppers, scorpions and crickets. In a South Okanagan study of PALLID BAT use of vineyards, the principal prey were scarab beetles and JERUSALEM CRICKETS. There are also records of this bat preying on small lizards and even a COLUMBIA PLATEAU POCKET MOUSE. Fecal pellets from the Okanagan Valley of BC mostly contained beetles; moths and lacewings were only minor prey items. Studies across the range of the species highlight the opportunistic nature of their foraging behaviour and suggest that the diet of this species varies substantially by area and between individuals. A study on the Baja California peninsula demonstrated that more than half of captured PALLID BATS included nectar in their diet. Video investigations revealed PALLID BATS landing on flowers and plunging their head into the flower's base to lap pooled nectar. By visiting flowers, PALLID BATS could play a role in pollination (see image on page 4). It is not known whether nectar contributes to PALLID BAT diets in BC.

In an Okanagan study, PALLID BATS were more likely to forage over native habitat relative to vineyards. The open rows in the vineyards were proposed to offer foraging opportunities for PALLID BATS to detect prey and land, but further study demonstrated that vineyards provided lower insect diversity (lower prey quality) and lower overall prey abundance. Prey quality is important, as it has been calculated that a single JERUSALEM CRICKET could provide nearly all of a PALLID BAT's daily energy requirement; the bat would have to consume up to 30 beetles for the same energy intake. Beetles were the most available ground prey in vineyards, whereas JERUSALEM CRICKETS and katydids were more readily available, in addition to various beetles and scorpions, in natural habitat. JERUSALEM CRICKETS appear to have specific habitat requirements, resulting in localized concentrations, and are not always above ground, which may affect the foraging behaviour of PALLID BATS.

While hunting, PALLID BAT flies slowly and close to the ground with rhythmic dips and rises, using a combination of echolocation for navigation and listening for prey-generated sounds, like the rustle of a large insect in the grass, to target the exact location of the prey. PALLID BATS track aerial prey with echolocation, but prey-generated sounds are essential for locating terrestrial prey. Studies in the laboratory have shown that even low levels of ambient noise affect the bat's ability to find prey among the vegetative clutter. Scientists simulated conditions of PALLID BATS foraging up to 640 metres from a major road and 320 metres from a natural gas compressor station, and found that even low levels of noise can reduce foraging efficiency two- to three-fold. This may be a conservation concern in areas where there are gas compressors, traffic or other human disturbances at night that might generate noise, thus reducing foraging efficiency in PALLID BATS. These findings may have direct implications for the Okanagan in particular, where there may be pumps, such as for irrigation, and other equipment running at night (e.g., orchards, vineyards).

Before returning to the day roost, PALLID BAT may briefly feed again before dawn, a trait shared with other bat species. PALLID BATS in the Okanagan have also been observed foraging during periods of precipitation.

REPRODUCTION

There are few known records of PALLID BAT reproduction in BC: to date, a nursing female and eight males with enlarged testes have been captured in August. In the southwestern United States, mating takes place from October through December. The gestation period is approximately nine weeks, with the young typically born in May and June. Although there are a few records of females carrying three or four fetuses, one or two young are usually produced, with twins being most common. Females are capable of breeding in their first year, but yearling females have only one young. At birth, young weigh about 3.0 to 3.5 grams and are undeveloped, with the eyes closed. At four to five weeks, the pups are capable of flight (i.e., volant), and by eight weeks they attain adult size. The age of sexual maturity for males is unknown. Adults are estimated to live to approximately 15 years in the wild.

A genetic investigation in Oregon found that while females tend to return to their birth colonies, males disperse, causing male-mediated gene flow. This pattern of male-mediated dispersal, common in bats and other mammals, has also been confirmed in several other studies of PALLID BAT.

MIGRATION AND WINTER

Winter monitoring has yielded several possible recordings of PALLID BAT in South Okanagan, but only one site, near Vaseux Lake, yielded confirmed acoustic detection of a PALLID BAT; these recordings were made by Tanya Luszcz on two occasions (December 3 and 5, 2015), verified by the production of the unique PALLID BAT social directive call, and validated by experts. They were collected near a known summer roost. This is consistent with our understanding of the overwintering ecology of this species in the western United States; PALLID BAT is thought to overwinter in the general vicinity of its summer range. Hibernating PALLID BATS have been found in buildings, rock crevices, mine tunnels, caves and a hollow post. Most of these hibernating records describe single animals or a few individuals; large winter aggregations seem to be rare. Mike Sarell made an unusual observation of a juvenile female PALLID BAT in torpor for two weeks (November 6–21, 2019) in an outside stairwell of a human-dwelling condominium in Osoyoos.

CONSERVATION STATUS

One of the rarest mammals in the province, PALLID BAT was assessed as Threatened by COSEWIC in 2010 and is listed on schedule 1 of the federal Species at Risk Act. Provincially, it is on the Red List. With a small population size and restricted range in the grasslands, loss of roosting and foraging habitat from development is a major concern for this species. More than 67% of the native foraging habitat within PALLID BAT's range has been lost, with this trend likely to continue in all but the protected sites outlined in the recovery strategy as critical habitat. Other threats include increasing levels of anthropogenic noise from transportation networks and energy development. Horticulture may also be a conservation concern in the PALLID BAT range, since it can substantially reduce hunting success for this species. In Okanagan, where vineyards and orchards have replaced much of the natural foraging habitat, there is concern that reduced prey availability has impacted and continues to heavily impact this species. A 2016 recovery plan prepared by the province identified habitat protection as a major objective.

TAXONOMY AND VARIATION

Recent genetic research on female lineages (through mitochondrial DNA) revealed three distinct non-overlapping clades of PALLID BAT in western North America, with BC individuals belonging to the same clade as Utah, Nevada, Arizona and Mexico, distinct from California and more eastern populations. However, when breeding patterns are examined, BC is somewhat isolated. Unfortunately, in these genetic studies there was a large sampling gap that did not include any samples from Washington, Oregon, Idaho or Montana; it is therefore not yet known whether BC PALLID BATS breed with bats from these adjacent states, though it seems likely given the proximity of the Okanogan Valley in Washington.

Six subspecies are recognized; these are largely based on pelage colour and skull size. One subspecies occurs in BC.

➤ *Antrozous pallidus pallidus* (Le Conte)—A variable widespread subspecies ranging from Mexico across much of the western United States to BC.

MEASUREMENTS

PALLID BAT weighs less in the early part of the season, from May to July (average 19.8 grams, range 16.8–23.5; n = 16), than later in the season, from August to September (average 29.9 grams, range 18.9–36.0; n = 15), when it is almost 50% heavier.

Total length (mm):	103.0 (55–121)	n = 7
Tail vertebrae length (mm):	43.0 (36–51)	n = 8
Hind foot (mm):	11.5 (8.5–14)	n = 9
Ear (mm):	26.0 (20.4–30.0)	n = 10
Tragus (mm):	12.0 (9.3–15)	n = 7
Forearm (mm):	54.7 (50.3–58.0)	n = 54
Wingspan (mm):	354.0 (310–372)	n = 16
Mass (g):	23.3 (16.8–36)	n = 45

REMARKS

The first occurrence of this species in BC was reported by Ian McTaggart-Cowan and Ken Racey in July 1931; an adult male PALLID BAT was found roosting in a stone pile near Boulder Creek, about 5 kilometres north of Oliver. Research in the Okanagan carried out by Brock Fenton and Robert Herd in the late 1970s and 1980s resulted in the capture of four PALLID BATS in the vicinity of Vaseux Canyon. Since then, the species has been regularly captured throughout the south Okanagan and as far north as Okanagan Falls. More surveys are required in the dry southern Interior to accurately define the species range.

A musky skunk-like odour is produced by glands on the muzzle. There have been no experimental studies to determine the function of this odour, but some have suggested that it is a defensive mechanism for repelling predators.

Mike Sarell discovered five PALLID BATS down a vertical section of irrigation pipe (from which they could not escape) in a vineyard north of Oliver. He hypothesized that the first bat was led down the slippery six-inch "Big O" pipe by the sound of a large insect rustling at the bottom of it, but then could not escape, and its distress calls lured in additional individuals. The bat on the bottom of the pile was dead, and the others were found in varying stages of poor health. Sarell also reported an incident with a PALLID BAT at a BIG BROWN BAT maternity roost. After emergence, he heard a lone adult female BIG BROWN BAT guarding pups making aggressive sounds and observed a PALLID BAT trying to gain access to the roost.

REFERENCES

Arlettaz, Jones and Racey (2001); Arnold and Wilkinson (2011); British Columbia Ministry of Environment (2016); Bell (1982); Bunkley and Barber (2015); Chapman, McGuiness and Brigham (1994); COSEWIC (2010); Environment and Climate Change Canada (2017); Frick, Heady and Hayes (2009); Fuzessery et al. (1993); Grindal, Collard and Brigham (1991); Hermanson and O'Shea (1983); Johnston and Fenton (2001); Lack and Van Den Bussche (2010); Lewis (1994, 1996); Orr (1954); Racey (1933); Rambaldini and Brigham (2008); Rambaldini and Brigham (2011); Ross (1961); Tacutu et al. (2018a); Weyandt and Van Den Bussche (2007).

PALLID BATS lured by sound down a Big O pipe in the Okanagan, from which they could not escape. PHOTO: MIKE SARELL

PALLID BAT flies away from the camera. Note the strong flight musculature in the back and the strong-looking legs, indicative of this species' ability to push off from the ground directly into flight (in contrast to many other species, which typically climb up a structure and then drop to take flight).

Townsend's Big-Eared Bat   *Corynorhinus townsendii*

DESCRIPTION

The large ears of TOWNSEND'S BIG-EARED BAT are unmistakable, enabling easy identification. TOWNSEND'S BIG-EARED BAT also has two prominent vertical, glandular swellings on the nose (the Latin for the genus means "club nose"). The tragus is long and pointed, and the calcar lacks a keel. The fur is soft brown to slate grey in colour, and the wing membranes are dark brown.

MORPHOLOGICALLY SIMILAR SPECIES

None. PALLID BAT and SPOTTED BAT are the only other species in the province with such proportionately large ears. SPOTTED BAT is readily identified by its jet-black fur and distinctive markings; PALLID BAT is larger (forearm length 45 to 60 millimetres) than TOWNSEND'S BIG-EARED BAT and lacks the bumps on the nose. Among BC's bats, only SILVER-HAIRED BAT and TOWNSEND'S BIG-EARED BAT have a combination of two upper and three lower premolar teeth on each side of their jaws (see Appendix 2). Refer to each species account for other distinguishing features.

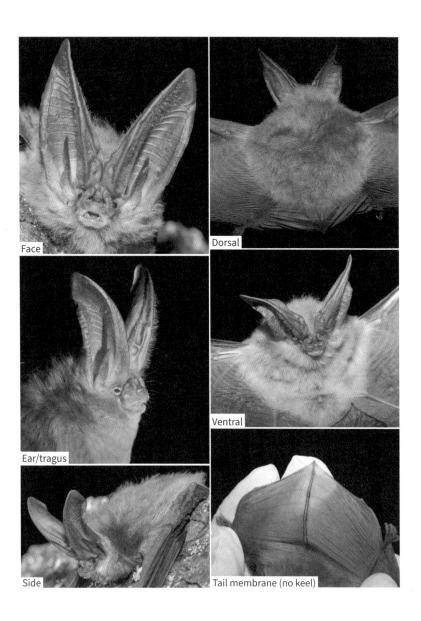

Face

Dorsal

Ear/tragus

Ventral

Side

Tail membrane (no keel)

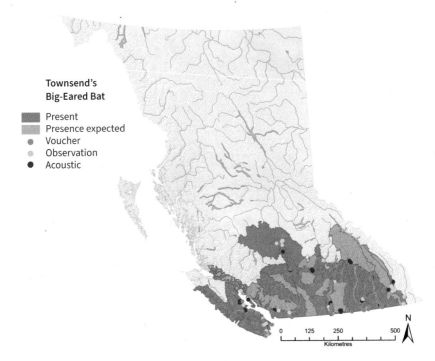

Townsend's Big-Eared Bat

- Present
- Presence expected
- Voucher
- Observation
- Acoustic

N

0   125   250   500
Kilometres

DISTRIBUTION

In the United States, TOWNSEND'S BIG-EARED BAT is found throughout the west, with isolated populations in the Great Plains and farther east. In Canada, it is known only from southern BC. On the south coast it also inhabits various islands, including eastern Vancouver Island, the Gulf Islands, and Quadra and Cortes islands, as well as the Lower Mainland. In the BC Interior, this bat ranges as far north as Williams Lake and east to Fort Steele in the Rocky Mountain Trench. Its elevation range in western Canada extends from sea level to 1,500 metres, including during winter hibernation. In summer it occupies grassland and forested habitats.

ACOUSTIC CHARACTERISTICS

25 kilohertz. TOWNSEND'S BIG-EARED BAT is a relatively slow flyer, has large ears to hear soft echoes of reflected ultrasound and prey-generated sounds, and approaches insects that may have the ability to hear bat ultrasound (e.g., tympanate or "eared" moths). As such, these bats typically do not produce loud echolocation calls. The species is accordingly often under-represented in acoustic surveys, as it is only recorded when it flies close to a bat detector.

The species' echolocation calls are typically steep, sweeping through a large range of frequencies, with minimum frequencies typically around 25 kilohertz but as low as 20 kilohertz. This species often shows a diagnostic call pattern due

ZERO-CROSS RECORDINGS

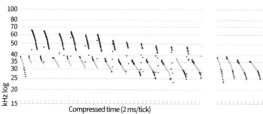
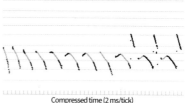

A. Typical search phase calls showing diagnostic split harmonic pattern (see page 117).

B. Typical echolocation calls interspersed with calls starting with an upsweep, a social component. The last three pulses of sequence show split harmonics (zero-crossing diagnostic pattern).

FULL-SPECTRUM RECORDINGS

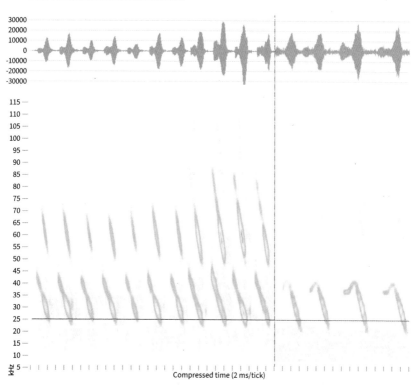

The high-amplitude second harmonic (ending at approximately 50 kilohertz) is visible in the first pane (bat was bat-kited), and the upsweep social component is present on all four pulses in the second pane (recording from the North American Bat Monitoring Program).

its tendency to put substantial energy into its second harmonic, resulting in a similar power spectrum in the first and second harmonics. This appears as two rows of calls of similar energy in a full-spectrum spectrogram, with the lowest row of pulses being the first harmonic/fundamental frequency (approximately 25 kilohertz) and the top row of pulses being the second harmonic (approximately 50 kilohertz—a minimum frequency that is twice the fundamental minimum frequency). Because the peak energy typically shifts mid-way through the call, a zero-crossing of TOWNSEND'S BIG-EARED BAT echolocation displays a distinctive pattern; the loudest (highest energy) signal is shown at any one point in time, resulting in the zero-cross spectrogram displaying the first part of the first harmonic and the second part of the second harmonic for many calls in a sequence (see spectrogram on facing page). This pattern of two rows of partial calls is called a "split-harmonic" and is a diagnostic pattern that easily differentiates this species in pure zero-crossing environment, providing that the call sequence is viewed in real time to ascertain that this is only one bat calling; if viewed in compressed mode, not taking into account the timing between calls, it is possible that this pattern could be misinterpreted as two bats—one low-frequency bat and one high-frequency bat. The relatively louder portion of the signal being in the second harmonic may be adaptive for use of higher frequencies in resolving detail and capturing prey at close distance, and to make echolocation calls less audible to moth prey. Individuals may have an upsweep in frequencies leading into a call, and it has been assumed that this is social in nature (see facing page full-spectrum recording and B of zero-cross recording).

ACOUSTICALLY SIMILAR SPECIES

FRINGED MYOTIS, and POSSIBLY CALIFORNIAN or YUMA MYOTIS. TOWNSEND'S BIG-EARED BAT and FRINGED MYOTIS may be confused, as both species produce calls that typically end at 20 to 25 kilohertz. Because both bats glean insect prey and have relatively large ears, they tend toward high-clutter call shapes, even when foraging in an open environment. Both species echolocate in the open with very fast broad-band sweeps, producing steep-looking calls; however, the regular split-harmonic pattern seen in zero-crossing is produced only by TOWNSEND'S BIG-EARED BAT and allows this species to be differentiated from FRINGED MYOTIS. In full spectrum, where all harmonics show for any bat approaching the bat detector microphone closely, these two species are not as easily differentiated, necessitating a close examination of the relative energy in each harmonic. Occasionally, TOWNSEND'S BIG-EARED BAT can produce pulses with a subtle arched shape. This can be seen in the top right spectrogram on the facing page (B)—the first three pulses drop abruptly and then take on the arched shape. All pulses show the arched shape not seen in FRINGED MYOTIS calls.

The second harmonic pattern evident in zero-cross spectrograms produces a band of split calls with minimum frequency of approximately 50 kilohertz,

The genus name *Corynorhinus* means "club nose." This unusual nose is thought to provide TOWNSEND'S BIG-EARED BAT with a unique ability to alter its echolocation calls, often visualized as a "split-harmonic" pattern in zero-cross recordings.

which invites confusion with CALIFORNIAN MYOTIS and YUMA MYOTIS; both of these species have fundamental harmonics terminating at 50 kilohertz. There is less chance of confusion with these species when viewing calls in true time, as the split calls align and are then unlikely to be misinterpreted as two bats (one low-frequency and one CALIFORNIAN/YUMA MYOTIS).

ROOSTING

TOWNSEND'S BIG-EARED BAT roosts during the day in caves, rock crevices, abandoned mines, and buildings. Because this species does not use roosts that are as hot as building attics typically used by roosting LITTLE BROWN MYOTIS and YUMA MYOTIS, its maternity roosts are often found in structures that offer cooler mid-summer microclimates, such as abandoned buildings with access to ceilings and cellars, natural cavities formed by boulders, and caves and abandoned mines.

Because TOWNSEND'S BIG-EARED BATS tend to eat a lot of moths, culled moth wings are often seen in their day and night roosts. Additionally, their guano can vary widely in colour, including grey fluffy-looking pellets when they have been consuming large numbers of moths. Here, three TOWNSEND'S BIG-EARED BAT guano pellets from a mine in West Kootenay show brown and black variation next to culled moth wings. PHOTO: MICHAEL PROCTOR

The only evidence for tree roosting in BC was a radio-tagged individual that appeared to be roosting in a BLACK COTTONWOOD tree in Creston. Maternity colonies in BC have mainly been found in buildings where this bat selects large open areas in the attics and lofts of old houses, cabins and barns, consistent with their preference to roost in the open. Unlike other building-roosting species, TOWNSEND'S BIG-EARED BAT does not appear to use crevices.

Susan Holroyd and Vanessa Craig discovered the largest known maternity roost in a building, a colony of 455 individuals found roosting in an old tractor shed on Denman Island. Studies in the Creston Valley of southern BC, and studies near Lillooet, revealed that cave-like cavities in talus slopes, and rock cliffs with warm aspects, are also used for maternity roosts.

This species is neither widespread nor common in BC, but the BC Community Bat Program is finding an increasing number of substantial TOWNSEND'S

BIG-EARED BAT maternity roosts in southern BC, occasionally with hundreds of bats. Night roosts have also been reported in mines, caves and buildings.

A maternity colony near the Cranbrook airport had unrestricted access to an entire abandoned building for suitable microclimate selection, but rejuvenation of the structure confined the bats to a small section of the attic, where the bats continue to roost through the installation of temperature-controlled air conditioning by the owners. This species has not been found to use traditional bat boxes, but a special outbuilding constructed on the same piece of land has successfully served as a secondary roost at this site.

Winter hibernacula are in old mines, tunnels and natural caves. Groups in caves and mines are generally small; clusters of up to 10 individuals have been observed in a mine with several hundred individuals distributed throughout.

FEEDING

Small moths form the bulk of the diet, with other insects, such as beetles, lacewings and sawflies, taken opportunistically. TOWNSEND'S BIG-EARED BAT has also been observed gleaning insect prey from the surfaces of broad deciduous leaves. They often perch at night roosts to consume captured prey. When feeding on moths, TOWNSEND'S BIG-EARED BAT removes the moth's wings, leaving a telltale sign of a TOWNSEND'S BIG-EARED BAT night roost. Old buildings and abandoned mines used as night roosts often have piles of culled moth wings.

In a radiotelemetry study near Lillooet, TOWNSEND'S BIG-EARED BAT appeared to maintain linear home ranges, foraging in riparian habitats along creeks and rivers for distances of up to 8 kilometres from their day roost sites. Other foraging habitat types include pastures, fields with mature grass, road corridors and low-elevation open forests.

REPRODUCTION

Mating occurs in the late fall, winter and spring. In the West Kootenay, based on signs of reproduction, mating continues throughout the winter (e.g., vaginal sperm discharge observed in free-flying bats captured in December through February outside known mine hibernacula). Remaining stored sperm in spring (March and April) suggests that mating also continues after emergence from hibernation. Males are scrotal and producing sperm again by late July. The males advertise for females using a ritualized courtship procedure. Lausen and others have observed pairs of TOWNSEND'S BIG-EARED BATS in low-elevation abandoned mines in fall in the West Kootenay; the female tended to be torpid, with some vaginal discharge, whereas the associated male was most often not torpid. This is consistent with observations by others of males mating with torpid females. The females delay implantation until spring, when they aggregate to form a maternity colony and, after a 50- to 60-day gestation period, give birth to a single pup. Pregnant females have been found from June 4 to August 3 in BC.

TOWNSEND'S BIG-EARED BATS hibernating in a mine near Nelson at the end of winter. As the bats were disturbed, they have each unrolled one ear. PHOTO: CORI LAUSEN

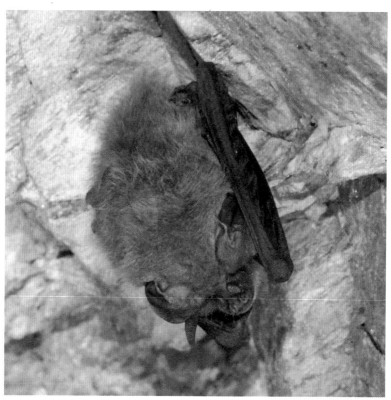

TOWNSEND'S BIG-EARED BAT hibernating in a mine in the West Kootenay. The ears are wrapped beside the body, leaving the tragi pointing out. PHOTO: MICHAEL PROCTOR

This is a visually distinct bat in hand, but it can easily be confused with roosting myotis species when observed during hibernation. While hibernating, TOWNSEND'S BIG-EARED BAT partially rolls and tucks its long ears in beside its body behind its head. This leaves the tragus sticking up well above the head, which can be mistaken for small ears (see image page 155). When disturbed during hibernation, TOWNSEND'S BIG-EARED BAT often untucks one ear first (image page 155) and may fully arouse following this, eventually untucking the second ear.

This species is regularly observed during hibernation, but this may reflect an observational bias due to the species' preference to roost on open surfaces rather than tucking into crevices like many other hibernating bat species. Winter records and hibernacula (caves, mines, concrete bunkers) are known from most of the species' range in BC, including the Williams Lake area at the northern extent of its range. TOWNSEND'S BIG-EARED BAT appears to have relatively restricted seasonal movements compared with at least some species—it does not appear to migrate long distances between its summer and winter ranges. It also tends to select drier and cooler sites for hibernation than other bats. In the Interior, typical temperatures in hibernacula range from 0.5°C to 6°C; on the coast it will hibernate in structures as warm as 9°C. Lausen and others have found that relative humidity of BC hibernacula can range from 60% to 98%. TOWNSEND'S BIG-EARED BAT often switches roost locations during hibernation; this may be associated with changes in roost microclimate conditions. It is the most frequently encountered bat species in low-elevation mines in winter in the Kootenay region, often roosting within 10 metres of mine entrances. Unlike other bat species that seek more stable microclimates, and thus deeper mines or caves, TOWNSEND'S BIG-EARED BAT will use shallow mines for overwintering. Using temperature-sensitive transmitters and dataloggers, Lausen and others have established that hibernating TOWNSEND'S BIG-EARED BATS arouse on average every three weeks (observations of hibernation torpor bouts range from a few to over 40 days); arousals from hibernation are often associated with flight either inside or outside a mine, resulting in roost switching throughout the winter.

In addition to their use of low-elevation mines during winter, a large number of TOWNSEND'S BIG-EARED BATS (more than 200) have been observed hibernating in a deep, multi-level high-elevation (1,500 metres) mine between Grand Forks and Greenwood. Based on acoustic and capture data from late fall or during winter, numbers of hibernating aggregations are thought to be substantial. Several other sites are known, including large mines near Nelway (mine elevation 870 metres) and Salmo (mine elevation approximately 1,300 metres). Both males and females show fidelity to hibernacula between years, with multiple banded individuals being recaptured at a mine in the West Kootenay.

Migration distances are assumed to be short, based on fall acoustic monitoring data. Banding and radio-tracking data led Heather Gates and others to conclude that females from a large building maternity roost near Grand Forks (650 metres) overwintered in a high-elevation (1,500 metres) mine 16 kilometres away.

CONSERVATION STATUS

This species has not been assessed by COSEWIC. BC has TOWNSEND'S BIG-EARED BAT on its Blue List, and it is designated a sensitive species in many western states. Major conservation concerns include its sensitivity to disturbance at maternity roosts and winter hibernacula. Because of a tendency to roost in drier environments, it may not be susceptible to white-nose syndrome.

TAXONOMY AND VARIATION

Coastal populations tend to be darker than Interior populations, and these two forms were traditionally treated as different subspecies: *Corynorhinus townsendii townsendii* and *C. t. pallescens*. Recent genetic studies, however, revealed no significant differences among BC populations. They are now treated as single evolutionary lineage and subspecies: *C. t. townsendii*.

▷ *Corynorhinus townsendii townsendii* (Cooper)—Ranges from northern Mexico across much of the western United States, reaching its northern limits in BC.

MEASUREMENTS

Mass of adults varies throughout the year: March–April 9.3 grams (7.7–11.0; n = 23); May–August 9.9 grams (7.5–13.6; n = 34); September–November 10.6 grams (7.7–14.7; n = 162); December–February 10.2 grams (7.7–14.0; n = 78). Bats are approximately 14% heavier in fall than in spring. Females are larger than males (see table on page 76).

Total length (mm):	100	(83–113)	n = 52
Tail vertebrae length (mm):	46	(38–57)	n = 44
Hind foot (mm):	11	(7–10)	n = 51
Ear (mm):	33	(27–40)	n = 38
Tragus (mm):	13.8	(10–16)	n = 23
Forearm (mm):	43.7	(40.1–49.2)	n = 280
Wingspan (mm):	287	(232–313)	n = 32
Mass (g):	10.3	(7.5–14.7)	n = 297

(see above for seasonal breakdown)

REMARKS

Because of their ability to manoeuvre well, fly slowly and even hover, this species may often evade mist-nets and thus be under-represented in capture-based studies.

The characteristic large ears of TOWNSEND'S BIG-EARED BAT are usually regarded as an adaptation for the quiet echolocation calls produced by this species. However, it has been speculated that they may also assist with temperature regulation by emitting heat. The distinctive glandular bumps on the nose may function as sexual scent glands.

This is one of the few species of bats that can sometimes be identified based on guano. The large component of moths in the diet can produce a light-brown or grey guano in addition to the darker guano typically produced by all other BC species (see image on page 153); the guano can be powdery and break apart readily when handled due to the high moth scale content. Light-coloured guano among culled moth wings is a characteristic of a TOWNSEND'S BIG-EARED BAT roost (either a day or night roost).

The remains of a TOWNSEND'S BIG-EARED BAT were recovered from the stomach of a PACIFIC MARTEN trapped on the Klanawa River, Vancouver Island, in mid-January.

TOWNSEND'S BIG-EARED BAT is a host to a unique type of ectoparasitic BAT FLY, *Trichobius corynorhini*. This blood-sucking fly is found more often on female bats than males.

Reports on the level of sensitivity of this species to human disturbance are mixed. While some sources report roost abandonment following disturbance, others in BC have reported that entering roosts in winter or summer has not resulted in abandonment. A more comprehensive study on the sensitivity of this species to disturbance is needed.

REFERENCES

Anderson and Racey (1991); Firman (2003); Fullard and Yack (1993); Hill et al. (2006); Hobbs et al. (2011); Hobbs et al. (2015); Kunz and Martin (1982); Nagorsen et al. (1993); Reid et al. (2010); Pearson, Koford and Pearson (1952).

Big Brown Bat

Eptesicus fuscus

DESCRIPTION

One of BC's larger bats, BIG BROWN BAT has a large, broad head, broad snout and long, dull fur. Fur colour varies from pale to dark brown; the fur tends to be oily in texture. Flight membranes and ears are black. The ears are relatively short, just reaching the nose when laid forward. The tragus is short and blunt, and the snout has a strong muscular appearance. The calcar has a prominent keel. The skull is robust, with thick heavy jaws, a flattened braincase and large teeth.

MORPHOLOGICALLY SIMILAR SPECIES

None. BIG BROWN BAT is a distinct bat that can be readily distinguished from all of BC's myotis species by its large size (forearm greater than 42 millimetres in adults), muscular-looking snout, large head and long fur. When observing just the head, this species can be differentiated from other "brown-coloured" bats in BC by the "swollen" regions on either side of the snout, which are clustered sebaceous glands, not present in myotis species.

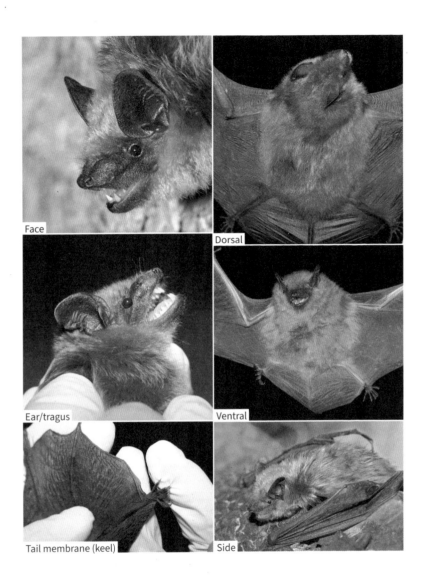

Face

Dorsal

Ear/tragus

Ventral

Tail membrane (keel)

Side

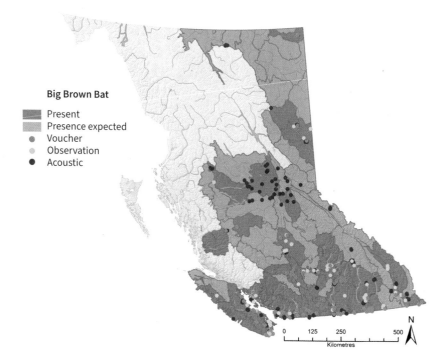

Big Brown Bat

- ▬ Present
- ▦ Presence expected
- ● Voucher
- ◔ Observation
- ● Acoustic

N

0   125   250   500
Kilometres

DISTRIBUTION

BIG BROWN BAT has a large distribution that extends from northern South America and Central America to southern Canada. In BC, it is found on Vancouver Island, on the coastal mainland north to the Bella Coola Valley, and in the Interior, where its northern limits are poorly defined. Northernmost known localities in the province are from the Prince George and the Peace River regions and likely extend throughout the northeast, based on records from the Nahanni in the Northwest Territories. Given a single record from the interior of Alaska, BIG BROWN BAT's range may also extend into extreme northwest BC. Recordings of 25 kilohertz bats in Atlin and in Yukon confirmed the presence of SILVER-HAIRED BAT, but the presence of BIG BROWN BAT cannot be ruled out, given the overlap of their call characteristics.

ACOUSTIC CHARACTERISTICS

25 kilohertz group. BIG BROWN BAT typically produces echolocation calls that drop to 25–30 kilohertz. In open environments, search phase calls have shallow slopes, though never flat. In clutter, they can produce steep-looking calls but retain a shallower component to their calls near the end of each pulse, giving them a "hockey-stick" shape.

ZERO-CROSS RECORDINGS

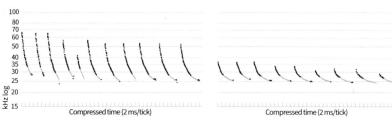

A. High-clutter pulses transitioning into moderate-clutter pulses.

B. Moderate-clutter pulses transitioning into open environment pulses.

FULL-SPECTRUM RECORDINGS

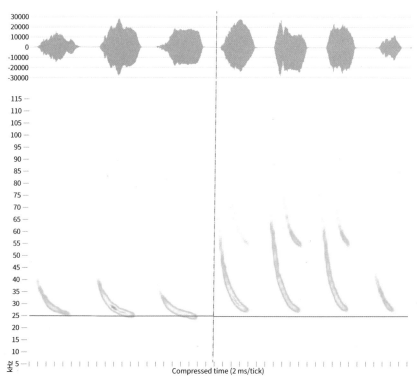

Relatively low-clutter pulses in left pane, and higher-clutter in right pane. In right pane, note that the starting frequency of the first harmonic exceeds 65 kilohertz, a trait that can help differentiate BIG BROWN BAT from SILVER-HAIRED BAT in clutter.

ACOUSTICALLY SIMILAR SPECIES

SILVER-HAIRED BAT, BRAZILIAN FREE-TAILED BAT, PALLID BAT, HOARY BAT. Differentiating BIG BROWN BAT from SILVER-HAIRED BAT is difficult, as most of the call repertoire overlaps. BIG BROWN BAT does not produce calls that have a pure constant frequency component, so the slope of its calls does not ever become flat; this sets it apart from SILVER-HAIRED BAT, which will produce calls with completely flat slopes in open environments. The slope of the call bodies (the flattest part of the call) of BIG BROWN BAT calls is typically 8 octaves per second or greater, though it occasionally drops as low as 5 OPS. Echolocation calls of BIG BROWN BAT flying in moderate to high clutter, when recorded at close range, can start at frequencies greater than 65 kilohertz, unlike SILVER-HAIRED BAT calls, which start well below this. This is a trait that can help separate BIG BROWN BAT recordings from recordings of SILVER-HAIRED BAT, whose calls generally start their sweep using frequencies lower than 60 kilohertz. Caution is advised when evaluating this trait, because if the bat does not come close enough to the detector, maximum frequency characteristics cannot be used for differentiation. The trait is apparent when a BIG BROWN or SILVER-HAIRED BAT foraging in clutter has come close enough to the microphone in a full-spectrum recording, as a second harmonic will be seen; and if it is a BIG BROWN BAT, a zero-cross recording will show calls starting at 60 kilohertz or higher. Minimum call frequency can also be used to differentiate SILVER-HAIRED and BIG BROWN BATS: calls from BIG BROWN BAT can end as low as 20 kilohertz, whereas SILVER-HAIRED BAT is not known to produce frequencies below 23 kilohertz.

BRAZILIAN FREE-TAILED BAT and PALLID BAT are also 25 kilohertz bats and can produce calls that look like BIG BROWN BAT's calls. In areas where these species overlap, it may be difficult to confidently differentiate BIG BROWN BAT based solely on acoustics. Certain call characteristics unique to BRAZILIAN FREE-TAILED BAT can be used in its identification (see BRAZILIAN FREE-TAILED BAT species account). In the case of PALLID BAT, if the recordings are made in open environments, it is likely that BIG BROWN BAT will produce low-sloped calls, which can differentiate it from the high-clutter pulse shapes that PALLID BAT produces, regardless of the level of clutter it is foraging in (see PALLID BAT species account).

Minimum frequencies of calls are typically uniform within a sequence, unlike Lasiurines, whose calls have a somewhat randomly undulating pattern, each with differing minimum frequencies. However, recordings of BIG BROWN BAT are likely to be confused with those of HOARY BAT when recording within detection range of where these bats could interact with clutter. In clutter, HOARY BAT, as a Lasiurine, is most likely to produce a call sequence that shows undulating minimum frequencies (see HOARY BAT species account) that would set it apart from BIG BROWN BAT; long enough recordings of call sequences are needed to verify a uniform call pattern and confidently rule out HOARY BAT.

ROOSTING

BIG BROWN BAT occurs in a variety of habitats in the province, including arid grassland and Interior and coastal forests. Elevation records extend from sea level to 1,040 metres. Throughout its range this bat demonstrates a strong affinity for buildings, and it is often appropriately referred to as a house or barn bat. In BC, maternity colonies have been found in the attics of houses, cabins and barns. The BC Community Bat Program reports that 10% of all monitored human-built roosts (i.e., bat boxes, building roosts) house this species, and roosts confirmed with this species are found in the following regions: Cariboo, Columbia-Shuswap, Fraser Valley/Lower Mainland, Kootenay, Okanagan, Peace, Skeena, and southern Vancouver Island and the Gulf Islands. In the Okanagan, maternity roosts are also known in PONDEROSA PINE snags and rock crevices. BIG BROWN BAT often roosts in well-lit locations and selects roosts in the temperature range of 33°C to 35°C, cooler relative to roosts of the other common building-roosting bats, such as LITTLE BROWN MYOTIS and YUMA MYOTIS. Temperatures above this will often force BIG BROWN BATS to move to a cooler site within the roost or change roosts. Maternity colonies as large as 700 individuals are known, but those associated with buildings are typically smaller, often composed of no more than 50 individuals. Tree-roosting colonies in the Okanagan contain anywhere from a few to 200 bats, with the colony size averaging approximately 100 individuals. Loyalty to roosting sites seems to depend on the type of roost being used. BIG BROWN BATS roosting in buildings or rock crevices show strong fidelity to those sites. In contrast, individuals roosting in trees seem to move regularly between several roosts, although they often have many of the same roost mates.

FEEDING

This species is regarded as a generalist that hunts in a diversity of habitats: over water, over forest canopy, along roads and clearings, and in urban areas, often around streetlights. The echolocation calls are high in intensity, and in open areas, such as forest clearings and over water, BIG BROWN BAT may first detect prey from as far as five metres. In most locations, beetles are an important part of the diet, and the species' heavy teeth and strong jaws appear to be an adaptation for chewing hard-shelled insects. Nonetheless, remains of moths, termites, carpenter ants, lacewings, caddisflies and various flies have also been identified in fecal pellets.

The only data available on feeding biology for BC come from research conducted at Okanagan Falls. There, BIG BROWN BAT emerged 30 to 40 minutes after sunset and hunted 5 to 10 metres above the water along a 300-metre reach of river. It is a relatively fast flyer, attaining speeds of up to 3 to 4 metres per second when pursuing prey. Several feeding flights of 30 to 60 minutes in duration were made during the night. Between feeding bouts, BIG BROWN BAT often used night roosts located near the feeding area. Although suitable day roost sites were located near the Okanagan River, individuals roosted during the day as far as 4 kilometres from their foraging area. During this study, the main prey item was large caddisflies; interestingly, midges were not taken, though they were the dominant insect group recorded in the area. This might be explained by the fact that echolocation frequencies produced by BIG BROWN BAT would likely restrict the detection of midges to a distance of only 1 metre, leaving inadequate time to react and capture these prey items; alternatively, the absence of these insects in the diet may be attributed to a preference for larger prey.

REPRODUCTION

Mating is believed to take place in autumn and winter. Fertilization occurs in spring after departure from the hibernaculum. Males may attain sexual maturity in their first year; females may breed in their first year, but in most populations they do not. Although twins are typical in eastern North America females, in western North America they usually have single young. Thirteen pregnant females collected in BC each carried a single fetus. Data available for BC suggest that the young are born in late June, but parturition could be as late as early July. For example, a sample of females with near-term fetuses and newborn young was collected in the Okanagan Valley on June 24, but an early pregnancy female was captured July 4 in southern Okanagan. Lactating females have been captured throughout July and into early August. Birth dates and development of the young can clearly be extremely variable, differing among roosts and even among individuals within a roost. As such, pregnant females, females with newborn young, and females with well-developed young can be found together in the same roost. In the Okanagan, biologists have observed considerable year-to-year variation, with dates for the first appearance of the young varying by as much as a month. This variation probably results from year-to-year differences in weather.

The body mass of newborn young is about three grams. They are naked and blind, though the eyes open a few hours after birth. Juveniles can fly at 18 to 35 days of age. There are longevity records showing that this species can live at least 19 years in the wild.

Scrotal males have been captured as early as late June, with fully scrotal males actively producing sperm typically by late July.

MIGRATION AND WINTER

Winter activity of BIG BROWN BAT has been documented across southern BC, as far east as Radium Hot Springs. This bat is thought to hibernate in rock crevices across its western range, but there is also evidence of use of buildings, caves and mines in BC. In caves and mines, BIG BROWN BAT often hibernates in exposed areas near the entrance where it can be found hanging from the ceiling and walls or wedged into small crevices or under rocks. It has been found hibernating in shallow (less than 50 metres deep) mines in the Okanagan and Boundary regions, likely because of its ability to survive in cold conditions. There are acoustic recordings of 25 kilohertz bats, most likely BIG BROWN BATS, flying mid-winter in the Peace River region, representing the farthest northern recordings of bats mid-winter in BC. Northeastern BC experiences extremely cold temperatures in winter, as does southern Alberta, where BIG BROWN BATS also regularly fly in winter. It is not known why bats fly in winter at freezing temperatures, or why BIG BROWN BAT is among the more common species to do so. Captured BIG BROWN BATS flying mid-winter in Alberta were sufficiently fat that it was unlikely they were seeking food. While thirst and unsuitable roost microclimates may be reasons for cold winter flight, BIG BROWN BATS hibernating in rock crevices do not typically switch roosts mid-winter and show signs of progressive dehydration; the need to fly may instead stem from a physiological requirement more directly met by the activity of flight.

Natural seasonal migrations up to 288 kilometres have been documented, but most individuals move no more than 80 kilometres between the summer and winter roosts. In fact, populations exploiting buildings may use the same site in winter and summer. An individual banded several decades earlier at a maternity roost in Idaho was subsequently captured at a mine in the West Kootenay in early November, only 50 kilometres away from the original capture point (exact year banded was unknown). Experiments have demonstrated that this species possesses a remarkable homing ability, with individuals released as far as 400 kilometres from their roost managing to find their way back.

In eastern North America, swarming behaviour often takes place at mines or caves before this species enters hibernation. BIG BROWN BAT hibernates singly or in clusters of up to 100 individuals, though large concentrations have been found in a few caves and mines. This is a hardy bat, capable of withstanding low temperatures. It selects a dry microenvironment with temperatures from –10°C to 5°C for hibernation, though temperatures below –4°C will usually stimulate arousal. Based on captures outside of BC, when BIG BROWN BAT enters hibernation in late autumn it weighs about 25 grams; when it completes hibernation in spring, it will have lost about 25% of its body mass.

CONSERVATION STATUS

BC populations of this species are secure. About 4% of the total bat fatalities at North American wind energy sites are BIG BROWN BATS. A few BIG BROWN BAT carcasses were recovered at wind energy sites in northeastern BC, but the impact of this mortality on populations is unknown. Studies in eastern North America have shown that this species is at least somewhat resistant to the fungus that causes white-nose syndrome.

TAXONOMY AND VARIATION

Three subspecies are recognized in Canada based on pelage colour and skull morphology, with one occurring in BC. Recent genetic research, however, has shown complex patterns of genetic structure across this species' range, inconsistent with the named subspecies. Two distinct mitochondrial DNA lineages (Pacific Northwest and eastern) are found in Canada, but nuclear genetic markers suggest minor genetic diversity across North America.

➤ *Eptesicus fuscus bernardinus* Rhoads—Ranges from California across Oregon and Washington to BC and possibly Alaska.

MEASUREMENTS

Total length (mm):	116	(98–131)	n = 126
Tail vertebrae length (mm):	46	(37–55)	n = 123
Hind foot (mm):	12	(8–15)	n = 115
Ear (mm):	15	(11–19)	n = 66
Tragus (mm):	7	(5–9)	n = 50
Forearm (mm):	47	(40.5–52.0)	n = 186
Wingspan (mm):	328	(205–393)	n = 62
Mass (g):	16.1	(10.1–23.0)	n = 106

REMARKS

This species may have some claim to be the "provincial bat," as it has turned up in the provincial legislative buildings in Victoria during the fall and winter. This is consistent with fall and winter observations from Alberta and Saskatchewan, where BIG BROWN BATS are also reported in brick or concrete buildings.

REFERENCES

Betts (1998); Brigham (1990); Brigham (1991); Brigham and Fenton (1991); Klüg-Baerwald and Brigham (2017); Klüg-Baerwald et al. (2016); Klüg-Baerwald et al. (2017); Lausen and Barclay (2002); Lausen and Barclay (2006a, b); Rehorek, Smith and Bhatnagar (2010); Slough and Jung (2008); Slough et al. (2022); Turmelle, Kunz and Sorenson (2011); Willis and Brigham (2004); Willis and Brigham (2007).

Spotted Bat

Euderma maculatum

DESCRIPTION

SPOTTED BAT has black dorsal fur with three large white spots on the rump and shoulder regions, making this one of the most distinct and spectacular bats in North America. There are also smaller white patches at the base of each ear. The ventral fur is largely white but looks black when parted because of black underfur. The throat has a small naked patch, although it is often hidden in the fur. The immense pinkish ears are joined basally across the forehead; the tragus is large and broad. A fringe of fine hairs extends along the top border on the back of the ears. The calcar is not keeled.

MORPHOLOGICALLY SIMILAR SPECIES

None. In BC, SPOTTED BAT is unique in its appearance. The only other bat with such proportionally large ears is TOWNSEND'S BIG-EARED BAT, which is light brown or light grey in colour and smaller in size.

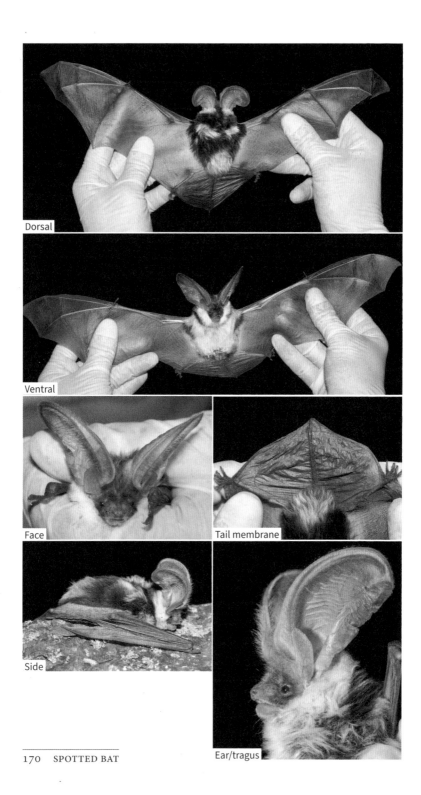

Dorsal

Ventral

Face

Tail membrane

Side

Ear/tragus

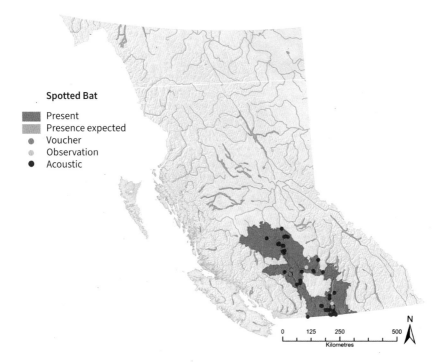

Spotted Bat

■ Present
■ Presence expected
● Voucher
● Observation
● Acoustic

DISTRIBUTION

This rare species is typically found in arid regions throughout the western United States to Mexico, with its core range defined by the extent of the Great Basin Desert region. In Canada, SPOTTED BAT occurs only in southern BC, mainly in the Okanagan, Similkameen, Thompson, Fraser and Chilcotin river valleys. However, it has also been acoustically recorded through the North American Bat Monitoring Program in the Skagit Valley, with several recordings made in 2018 and 2019 around Ross Lake, and in the Kettle River valley north of Rock Creek. In the Fraser River valley, it is found in open bunchgrass valley bottom and sparsely forested mid-bench areas dominated by PONDEROSA PINE and Interior DOUGLAS-FIR trees. Along the Fraser River, its range extends from Lytton north to near Sword Creek, west of Williams Lake. On October 1, 2021, the Wildlife Rescue Association of BC rescued an adult female SPOTTED BAT found roosting for several days on a balcony in Chilliwack, approximately 3.5 km from the Fraser River. It is not known if this was a migrating bat.

ACOUSTIC CHARACTERISTICS

Audible. In BC, SPOTTED BAT is the only truly "audible" bat, meaning that it does not echolocate in the ultrasonic range. To the unaided ear, this bat's echolocation sounds like a series of clicks. Echolocation calls can start as high as 18 kilohertz and sweep down to 7 kilohertz, and they are always broadband

ZERO-CROSS RECORDINGS

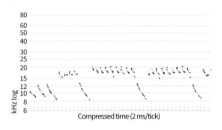

Sequence of social calls between 15 and 20 kilohertz follows all but the first two echolocation pulses (each ending between 8 and 10 kilohertz).

FULL-SPECTRUM RECORDINGS

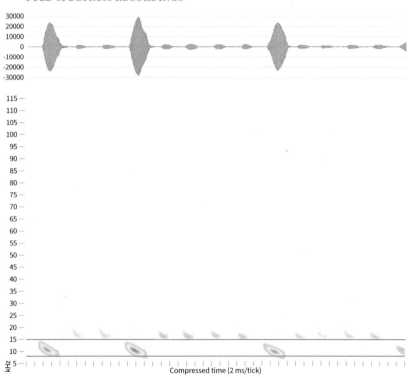

Three echolocation pulses in an open environment, each ending at approximately 8 kilohertz (lowest frequency line drawn on spectrogram and part of a fourth pulse at far right). In this particular recording, social calls were also produced, ending at approximately 15 kilohertz.

calls, regardless of clutter level. In the open, this bat's calls typically start below 10 kilohertz and rapidly sweep to 7 or 8 kilohertz; in clutter, calls start as high as 18 kilohertz and sweep quickly down to 12 kilohertz or lower.

SPOTTED BAT produces low-intensity calls relative to other bat species, and this has been shown to be effective in capturing tympanate (eared) moths. SPOTTED BAT calls are barely detectable, or completely inaudible, to eared moths. Research has shown that most eared moths do not detect SPOTTED BATS until the bat is less than 1 metre away; in contrast, BIG BROWN BAT, producing higher frequencies and louder calls, can be detected by eared moths at a distance of 20 to 25 metres, giving the moth more time to respond and avoid predation. Despite SPOTTED BAT calls tending to be low in intensity, their low frequencies travel far, and some observers report hearing SPOTTED BAT calls up to 250 metres away, although this varies by observer.

SPOTTED BAT produces a unique pattern of social calls consisting of a rapid series (time between pulses less than 10 milliseconds) of short-frequency sweeps (centring around 15 kilohertz) and short-duration (less than 2 milliseconds) pulses in between echolocation calls (see spectrograms on facing page).

ACOUSTICALLY SIMILAR SPECIES

None. Because SPOTTED BAT uses frequencies in the audible range, many sources of non-bat sounds can potentially be confused with this species. Sounds produced by wind rustling leaves or patterned insect noise, for example, can sometimes obscure acoustics recordings of this species. SPOTTED BAT's low-intensity calls mean that full-spectrum bat detectors are more likely to record this species than zero-crossing detectors, unless the bat approaches the microphone closely. Because of its low frequencies and short duration calls, zero-crossing recordings can under-represent this species if the set division ratio is too high (hence a division ratio of 4 is recommended, although 8 will suffice, especially in a quiet recording environment).

ROOSTING

In BC, SPOTTED BAT is generally found below 900 metres in dry Interior grasslands. The availability of appropriate roosting habitat is considered a limiting factor in the distribution of this species, given its preference to day roost in crevices of steep cliff faces (up to 400 metres high). This results in a discontinuous or patchy distribution throughout the species range. Roosting sites in the Okanagan Valley have been identified in cliffs at McIntyre Bluff, Gallagher Bluff, Spotted Bluff, the west side of Vaseux Lake and Vaseux canyon. In 2014 a radiotelemetry study at Lillooet found four rock crevice maternity roosts, all on the Fraser River along the east-facing valley wall. The precise crevices used were identified using a helicopter, but the crevices were not accessible and thus could not be measured or monitored. Radio-tagged bats returned nightly to the same rock crevice and were not observed switching roosts during the 16-day monitoring period. These Lillooet rock crevice roosts were used by reproductive adults with their offspring, all high above the canyon floor in the east-facing side of the Fraser River valley. Roosts have also been detected by Mike Sarell and Jared Hobbs near Big Bar, and by Francis Iredale (and others) near Kamloops. In Arizona, females select rock crevices with southern exposure, while males did not select roosts based on aspect; accessible crevice roosts have measured 2 to 5.5 centimetres wide. Use of night roosts in BC has not been documented, although in Arizona night roosting in aspen trees has been documented.

While observations of SPOTTED BATS exiting from several locations on a cliff face suggested that adult females might roost solitarily, observations from radio-tracking in Lillooet suggest that maternity rock crevice roosts were occupied by multiple bats. Radiotelemetry data collected in two separate studies in the Okanagan valley suggest some level of roost site fidelity, as radio-tagged bats returned to the same roost site daily for up to 21 days. In Lillooet, although radio-tracking only occurred in one summer, all subsequent visits to the vicinity (in following years) of four maternity roost rock crevices have documented occurrence of SPOTTED BATS, often with several bat passes heard each minute early in the evening during emergence. This suggests that the roosting area, and perhaps the same rock crevice roosts, are used each year.

FEEDING

While some studies have reported SPOTTED BAT to forage at heights of greater than 10 metres, foraging heights as low as 3 metres have been documented in BC and Oregon. Because standard mist-nets are 2.6 metres high, capture of SPOTTED BATS is challenging and generally requires that nets be raised and ideally stacked one on top of the other. Only 22 SPOTTED BATS have been captured to date in BC (2 by Leonard and Fenton 1983, 4 by Wai-Ping and Fenton 1989, 2 by Lausen in the Okanagan 2013, and 14 by Lausen and others in 2014 and 2017). Captures in the Lillooet area were in nets whose tops ranged from 4.6 to 8.0 metres above the ground (see top image on page 74).

SPOTTED BAT forages over marshes, riparian habitats, open fields, grasslands, open PONDEROSA PINE woodlands, and clearings in forest. In Arizona, the diet is primarily composed of moths, though genetic analysis of fecal samples revealed consumption of noctuid, geometrid and lasiocampid moths (Order Lepidoptera).

SPOTTED BATS have been observed hunting alone and appear to avoid each other while foraging. Some observations of foraging behaviour suggest that SPOTTED BATS may use a "trapline" foraging strategy, revisiting foraging areas along a regular route.

In 2014, triangulation of radio-tagged bats near Lillooet demonstrated that adult SPOTTED BATS foraged a maximum straight-line distance of 9.5

to 18.8 kilometres from day roosts. Based on radio-tracking five bats for two days, the study conservatively estimated home ranges to be on average 384 hectares—100-fold smaller than reported in Arizona, where foraging bats were tracked up to 36 kilometres from their roosts. We will need further study in BC to determine if the Lillooet home ranges might have been underestimated because of low sample sizes, or if this represents less commuting time as a consequence of shorter nights.

Measurements of straight-line nightly movements in Lillooet were similar to those reported in the only other foraging study of SPOTTED BAT in BC; in the southern Okanagan, SPOTTED BATS moved 6 to 11 kilometres straight-line distance between day roosts and foraging locations. In Arizona, SPOTTED BATS travelled up to 43 kilometres from their roost to foraging sites where they were captured, and they have been recorded flying at speeds up to 53 kilometres/hour.

REPRODUCTION

Little information is available regarding reproduction. In BC, young are probably born in late June or early July. In two independent studies near Lillooet, lactating females were captured in early and late July, and volant juveniles were captured mid-August. Scrotal males were captured in both late July and mid-August. The only pregnancy record for the province is June 16.

Outside BC, there are two older records of male SPOTTED BATS having stored sperm in their cauda epididymides in March and April, suggesting this species may continue to mate in spring, but mating likely starts in autumn, as with all other BC bats. Scrotal males have been captured in late June in Arizona.

MIGRATION AND WINTER

Annual movement patterns are unknown; we are unsure whether SPOTTED BAT migrates out of the province for winter. Lausen recorded a SPOTTED BAT as late as October 28 in the South Okanagan, and as early as March 12 in Lillooet, but unlike many other BC bat species, SPOTTED BAT has never been detected flying during winter despite substantial winter recording in both the South Okanagan and Lillooet areas. This is in contrast to captures of this species in Utah in November at –5°C, where it was speculated that the bats emerged from hibernation to drink.

Wherever they hibernate, overwintering roosts are likely in rock crevices on steep cliffs, similar to their summer roost sites; however, there is a single record from Albuquerque, New Mexico, of a SPOTTED BAT in late January roosting in a warehouse. The validity of an anecdotal observation of four SPOTTED BATS hibernating in a cave in Utah in 1941 is unknown; there are no other records of this bat roosting or overwintering in caves or mines.

SPOTTED BAT was assigned a status of Special Concern by COSEWIC and listed under Schedule 1 of the federal Species at Risk Act, and it is on the province's Blue List. These listings can be attributed to small population size and restricted range. Disturbance at roosts in cliffs by rock climbers, and loss of foraging habitat, were identified by COSEWIC as conservation concerns, but these threats are likely localized and infrequent. The 2013 provincial management plan prepared as a result of the COSEWIC listing identified habitat protection and population monitoring as high priorities for conservation of this bat.

TAXONOMY AND VARIATION
There are no recognized subspecies of SPOTTED BAT. Ongoing genetic studies at Northern Arizona University, and preliminary results from Faith Walker and Carol Chambers suggested SPOTTED BATS in the Pacific Northwest are more closely related to each other than to populations in the southwestern United States.

MEASUREMENTS

Total length (mm):	116	(107–125)	n = 4
Tail vertebrae length (mm):	50	(47–50)	n = 4
Hind foot (mm):	10	(9–10)	n = 4
Ear (mm):	36.5	(31–41)	n = 10
Tragus (mm):	13	(7–21.5)	n = 10
Forearm (mm):	50.2	(36.5–53.1)	n = 20
Wingspan (mm):	346	(336–355)	n = 5
Mass (g):	17.4	(12.0–21.4)	n = 16

REMARKS
This mammal was first discovered in BC in 1979, when Brock Fenton and his colleagues detected its echolocation calls near Oliver while conducting a general bat survey in the Okanagan. In 1991, Mike Sarell heard this species near Spences Bridge in the Thompson River valley, expanding its range beyond the Okanagan.

In 2010, Hobbs, Mike Sarell and Francis Iredale reported hearing SPOTTED BATS along Carpenter Lake, near Gold Bridge, the northwesternmost record for the species in BC. On May 19, 2020, Hobbs and Jessica Holden heard a SPOTTED BAT while conducting owl fieldwork at Rock Creek, which is the southeasternmost record for the species in BC.

This species is famously difficult to capture because of its high-flying nature and tendency to not access low-elevation water sources. The two main locations in western North America where captures have occurred with some reliability are near the Grand Canyon in Arizona and near Lillooet in BC.

Mummified SPOTTED BAT carcasses dating back to approximately 10,000 years were found in a cave in the Grand Canyon.

There are several records of daytime flying by SPOTTED BAT, all on hot days in the southern Okanagan and all associated with drinking. On one occasion, a BELTED KINGFISHER was observed attacking a day-flying SPOTTED BAT that was drinking from Vaseux Lake, though the bat was able to dodge the repeated attacks by the bird and finally flew off after drinking multiple times.

REFERENCES

British Columbia Ministry of Environment (2013); Chambers et al. (2011); COSEWIC (2004b); Fullard and Dawson (1997); Fullard, Fenton and Furlonger (1983); Hardy (1941); Hobbs et al. (2015); Jung (2014); Leonard and Fenton (1983); Mead and Mikesic (2001); Navo, Gore and Skiba (1992); Painter et al. (2009); Poché (1975); Poché (1981); Rodhouse, McCaffrey and Wright (2005); Siders et al. (1999); Storz (1995); Wai-ping and Fenton (1989); Watkins (1977); Woodsworth, Bell and Fenton (1981).

PHOTO: IAN ROUTLEY

Eastern Red Bat   *Lasiurus borealis*

DESCRIPTION

EASTERN RED BAT is sexually dimorphic in fur colour and size. Males have reddish-orange hair; females are duller and paler, with chestnut-coloured hair, and are slightly larger than males. Underparts are slightly paler, and white patches are found below each shoulder, extending under the neck. The wing membranes are black, with paler/red coloration on the forearm and fingers. This is a medium-sized bat with a long tail, a tail membrane that is extensively furred dorsally, and an indistinctly keeled calcar. This species, along with HOARY BAT, is a member of the genus *Lasiurus*; these are the only two Lasiurines in Canada, each having the furry tail to which the Latin genus name refers. Fur also extends partially onto the dorsal and ventral surfaces of the wing membranes near the body. The ears are short and rounded, with a blunt tragus.

MORPHOLOGICALLY SIMILAR SPECIES

None. EASTERN RED BAT is morphologically unique among BC's bats, and identification in the hand or from photographs is unambiguous. It is the only BC bat to have a rich, dense and luxuriant coat of reddish-orange fur and one of only two species in BC (in addition to HOARY BAT) to have a tail membrane completely covered with fur on the dorsal surface.

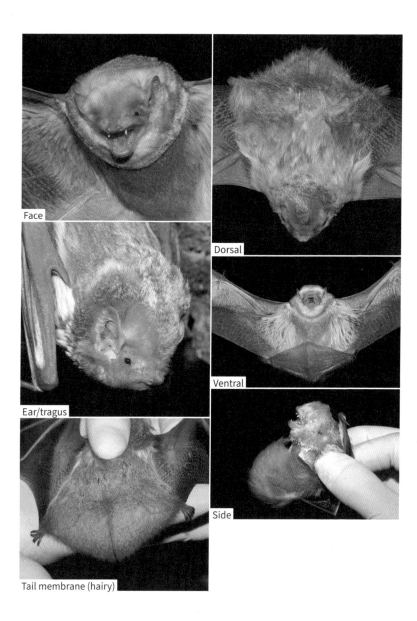

Face

Dorsal

Ear/tragus

Ventral

Side

Tail membrane (hairy)

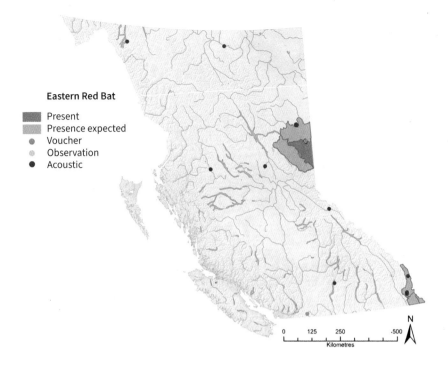

Eastern Red Bat

- Present
- Presence expected
- Voucher
- Observation
- Acoustic

0   125   250   .500

Kilometres

N

DISTRIBUTION

With a distribution that extends across eastern North America, EASTERN RED BAT reaches its western limits in Alberta, BC and the Northwest Territories. The species has only recently (2012) been verified in BC, so we know little about its actual distribution west of the Continental Divide. There is a historical (1905) museum specimen originally identified mistakenly as a WESTERN RED BAT from the Skagit River Valley in southwestern BC, and more recent records in the Peace River region of BC (five fatalities at two wind energy sites). However, the species' occurrence in the remainder of the province is largely unknown, and based only on a scattering of acoustic records: several early summer North American Bat Monitoring recordings near Vernon, Kamloops, Smithers, Terrace/Kitimat, Skagit, Fernie, Kimberley, Nicholson, Spillimacheen and Premier Lake Provincial Park; a recording from Atlin during an August bat inventory; an August 2019 recording by Hobbs, near Elkford; and a July 2020 recording by Tim Ennis at Cumberland on Vancouver Island. It is suspected that the range of EASTERN RED BAT is expanding in BC.

ACOUSTIC CHARACTERISTICS

35 kilohertz. EASTERN RED BAT is a high-flying bat, and when foraging below the treetops this species can be seen flying fast and making sharp turns. When in the open, EASTERN RED BATS produce low-sloped calls, approaching

ZERO-CROSS RECORDINGS

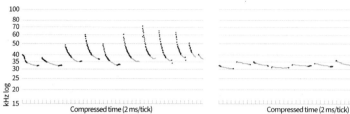

A. Low-clutter pulses transitioning into moderate-clutter pulses.

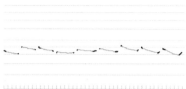

B. Sequence of pulses in an open environment.

FULL-SPECTRUM RECORDINGS

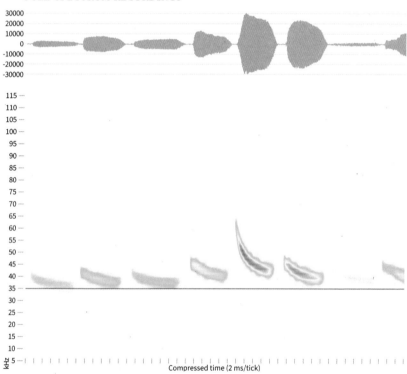

Open-environment pulse shapes start and end this sequence, with a couple of higher-clutter pulses mid-sequence.

flat (0 octaves per second) near the end, often with an upturned toe right at the end of the call. These open environment calls usually end at frequencies as low as 30 kilohertz. The minimum frequencies of EASTERN RED BAT calls often fluctuate, which is typical of a Lasiurine acoustic pattern. This is less pronounced in high-clutter habitats, where EASTERN RED BATS change their call frequencies extremely quickly, seen in spectrograms as steep, nearly vertical calls. These high-clutter calls are easily confused with myotis species in clutter, and minimum frequencies can exceed 45 kilohertz.

ACOUSTICALLY SIMILAR SPECIES

LITTLE BROWN MYOTIS. Any myotis species could possibly be confused with EASTERN RED BAT if the recordings were made in moderate to high clutter, and especially if the recording is short or of poor quality. However, it is LITTLE BROWN MYOTIS that is most likely to be confused acoustically with EASTERN RED BAT because of the low-sloped call that this myotis makes in an open environment (typically greater than or equal to 25 octaves per second; see LITTLE BROWN MYOTIS species account). The low-sloped calls of each of these two species can generally be differentiated when the sequence is long enough and of good quality, such that upturned toes of EASTERN RED BAT and a possible undulating minimum frequency pattern set EASTERN RED BAT apart from the typically uniform call sequence and downward-facing toes of LITTLE BROWN MYOTIS calls.

ROOSTING

Both BC species of *Lasiurus* bats (HOARY BAT and EASTERN RED BAT) are loosely described as "tree bats." EASTERN RED BATS roost, and even hibernate, in deciduous trees, using dead leaves and leaf litter for concealment, as do WESTERN RED BATS (not found in BC). Outside BC, hibernating EASTERN RED BATS are observed using their furred tail membrane as a "blanket" which they wrap over their body up to their head to form a tight ball. They are not known to use bat boxes or buildings but have occasionally been found in caves; although the extent of cave roosting behaviour is unknown, some observations suggest that presence in caves is associated with mortality. The reasons for this are not clear.

FEEDING

These fast-flying bats are best suited for foraging in open habitats where they feed on moths, beetles and other insects and are often observed over roads and small waterways. While they generally roost solitarily, they have been reported to hunt in groups of as many as 30 bats.

REPRODUCTION

Despite more than 50 summer or fall captures and turbine mortalities of EASTERN RED BATS in Alberta, not a single female (of 21) was found to be reproductive, and no volant juveniles have been reported from BC or Alberta. Similarly, there are no records of reproductive female EASTERN RED BATS in BC. There are a few records of reproductive female EASTERN RED BATS captured in Cypress Hills, Saskatchewan.

What is known about EASTERN RED BAT reproduction (from elsewhere in their range) is that breeding takes place in late summer and early autumn, and fertilization is delayed until spring; this is similar to all other species of bats in Canada. Findings of dead bats (mortalities at wind turbines) still coupled in mating is further evidence that these bats copulate in the air. They produce more pups per litter than most other Canadian bat species, with typical litter sizes of two to three pups, but they can have as many as five. Most Lasiurine bats, including EASTERN RED BAT, have four teats, allowing for concurrent nursing of multiple young.

MIGRATION AND WINTER

EASTERN RED BAT is thought to be highly migratory, leaving Canada for the winter. In late summer, both males and females migrate south, though nothing is known about migration routes for EASTERN RED BATS that summer in BC.

Although EASTERN RED BAT roosts solitarily in summer, it has been reported migrating in large groups, with some observations of diurnal movements. In the southeastern United States, where most EASTERN RED BATS are thought to overwinter, these bats move into leaf litter on the ground during cold periods. In periods of warmth, during winter, EASTERN RED BAT continues to forage at night.

CONSERVATION STATUS

In light of the few confirmed BC occurrences, and a lack of evidence for a resident breeding population, EASTERN RED BAT has been assigned an unknown conservation status by the province. Across North America, EASTERN RED BATS are the second most commonly killed bat at wind turbines, accounting for about 22% of the total bat fatalities. Fatalities at BC wind energy sites have been documented, albeit infrequently, but this may reflect difficulties associated with surveying for dead bats beneath turbines. The impact of this mortality source on the North American population remains unquantified but is suspected to be high.

TAXONOMY AND VARIATION

No subspecies are currently recognized. No genetic analysis has been done for individuals found west of the Rocky Mountains; however, populations in eastern

North America show little genetic structure using nuclear or mitochondrial DNA markers. This pattern is consistent with a migratory bat that undergoes long-distance movements, as there is high potential for mating and thus genetic exchange among individuals that summer in widely separated regions.

MEASUREMENTS*

Total length (mm):	108.9		
Tail vertebrae length (mm):	52.7		
Hind foot (mm):	7.9		
Ear (mm):	11.4		
Tragus (mm):	6.1		
Forearm (mm):	39.7	(36.3–42.6)	n = 30
Wingspan (mm):		(280–330)	
Mass (g):	12.9	(10.4–17.4)	n = 29

* Measurements are from Shump and Shump (1982) and van Zyll de Jong (1985), and from Alberta captures.

REMARKS

In the 1993 edition of this handbook, a museum specimen of a red bat from the Skagit Valley was misidentified as the WESTERN RED BAT, a bat that occurs from South America to northern California. This misidentification was based on consideration of geography and the subspecies designation on its specimen tag. However, DNA analysis of its wing tissue in 2012 demonstrated unequivocally that this specimen is an EASTERN RED BAT. There is currently no evidence that the WESTERN RED BAT occurs in the province.

REFERENCES

Arnett and Baerwald (2013); Lausen and Player (2014); Lausen, Waithaka and Tate (2014); Myers (1960); Nagorsen and Paterson (2012); Reimer et al. (2014); Shump and Shump (1982); Slough et al. (2022); Solick et al. (2020); van Zyll de Jong (1985); Vonhof and Russell (2015); Willis and Brigham (2003).

Hoary Bat

Lasiurus cinereus

DESCRIPTION

HOARY BAT is BC's largest bat species in terms of mass (typically between 20 and 35 grams) and wingspan (nearly 40 centimetres), although PALLID BAT has longer forearms. HOARY BAT has a soft appearance, with long fur on its back composed of dark brown and grey hairs tipped with white; hence the common name "hoary," meaning greyish white. There are small patches of yellow or white fur on its wrists, near the arm, on the underside of the wing and on the shoulders. There is also yellow fur around the face, largely on the forehead and throat. The wing membranes are black with paler coloration on the forearm and fingers. HOARY BAT has relatively large dark eyes, and ears that are rounded and relatively short. The dorsal side of the tail membrane is extensively furred. HOARY BAT and EASTERN RED BAT are the only two bats in the genus *Lasiurus* in Canada, each having the "hairy tail" to which the Latin genus name refers. The hind foot is relatively small, with a dense covering of fur on the dorsal surface. The calcar has a narrow keel.

MORPHOLOGICALLY SIMILAR SPECIES

None. HOARY BAT is morphologically unique among BC's bats and can be identified unmistakably in the hand. It has a distinctive appearance, with long, dense grey or dark brown fur and "grizzled" or greyish-white hair tips. It is

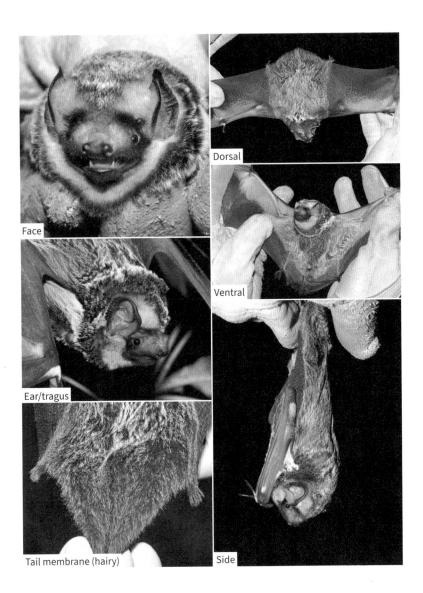

Face

Dorsal

Ear/tragus

Ventral

Tail membrane (hairy)

Side

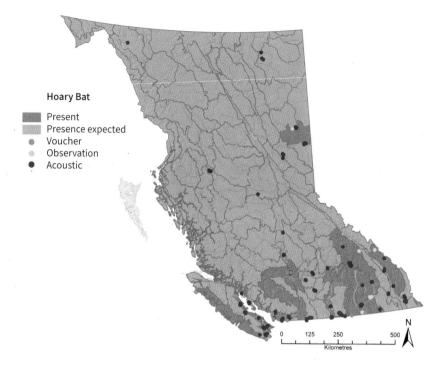

Hoary Bat
- Present
- Presence expected
- Voucher
- Observation
- Acoustic

one of only two species in BC that has a tail membrane extensively covered with dense fur on the dorsal surface. This bat is also unique in the audible vocalizations that it emits when handled—a clicking sound followed by what might best be described as a rasping hiss.

DISTRIBUTION

HOARY BAT is migratory and is the most cosmopolitan of North America's bats, with the largest range of any species in North America. In BC, HOARY BAT occupies a diversity of habitat types and is frequently associated with both forested and grassland habitats in the province. The species is found in most areas of BC, including Vancouver Island; Cortes, Denman, Hornby and Quadra in the northern Gulf Islands; and the Interior north to the Peace River region and in the northwest to Atlin. Although there are no confirmed records, this species likely also occurs along the coastal mainland north to the Prince Rupert area. HOARY BATS have also been reported from Yukon and southeast Alaska. In some regions of North America, the sexes appear to occupy separate summer ranges; based on available records, this observation has not been documented in BC—both sexes appear to overlap extensively.

ZERO-CROSS RECORDINGS

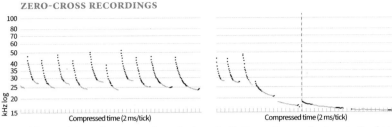

A. Undulating minimum frequency pattern of pulses is diagnostic of Lasiurines when flying among clutter, receiving echoes from nearby objects.

B. Clutter continuum of pulses starting from relatively high clutter through to an open environment.

C. Concave-shaped social call (first pulse) starting off sequence of highly variable echolocation calls.

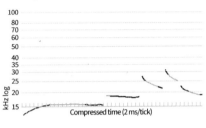

FULL-SPECTRUM RECORDINGS

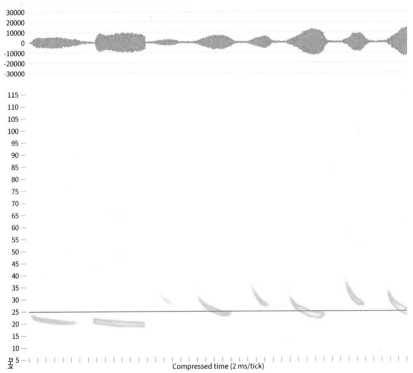

The first two pulses are typical low-sloped, long-duration, low-frequency open environment calls, followed by higher-clutter pulse shapes with the undulating minimum frequency pattern typical of a Lasiurine.

20 kilohertz. HOARY BAT can produce echolocation calls as low as 15 kilohertz, just audible to some people. It can produce the longest-duration calls (approximately 30 milliseconds) of any BC species when echolocating in an open environment, and HOARY BAT has the longest listening time between calls, which coincides with strong but infrequent flaps of the wings. Because of this low frequency, and the high energy output of the calls produced by this large bat, HOARY BAT echolocation can travel a long distance—farther than a high-powered spotlight beam, often precluding visual tracking of the bat while it flies in open night skies. If observed during flight, the long, narrow wings give this bat a shape unlike any of the other low-frequency bats in BC. It also does not need to be observed to be identified, because many aspects of its echolocation calls are unique.

In general, HOARY BAT produces low-frequency echolocation calls, but its repertoire includes a wide breadth of shapes and frequencies. In an open environment, it will produce long-duration calls (up to 30 milliseconds) that appear flat or almost flat, and often as low as 15 kilohertz. These constant-frequency-type calls are always below 20 kilohertz. Because HOARY BAT is fast-flying, recordings of HOARY BAT flying in the open often contain few pulses, and the time between each call can be up to two seconds, representative of a slow wingbeat (because of large body size). HOARY BAT does not always produce a call with each beat of the wings when in the open, where echoes are less frequent or unlikely. In high clutter, its calls sweep quickly through a large bandwidth of frequencies, starting as high as 50 kilohertz and dropping down to a minimum frequency of 30 kilohertz or lower. The spectrograms of these higher-clutter calls are steep and typically show an upturned toe or hook on the end of the call.

Like other Lasiurine bats, HOARY BAT alternates the minimum frequencies of their calls somewhat randomly throughout a sequence of pulses; this is most pronounced in clutter and may be a mechanism to better track echoes, conferring a benefit to this fast-flying bat when foraging in a cluttered environment. The other Lasiurine bat in BC is EASTERN RED BAT, and while they have this pattern in common, their calls fall into different frequency ranges and are thus never confused (see EASTERN RED BAT species account). HOARY BAT can also emit a low-frequency call with a concave spectrogram, thought to be communicative (social) in nature.

HOARY BAT also produces calls with low energy levels ("micro-calls") producing echoes that give the bats enough time to avoid an obstacle but likely not to capture prey. These micro-calls are of low-enough intensity that the bat would need to be within a few metres of the microphone to be recorded. In some cases, HOARY BATS fly without echolocating at all. Low-amplitude calls and the lack of echolocation while flying may contribute to these bats being killed by fast-turning wind turbine blades.

ACOUSTICALLY SIMILAR SPECIES

BRAZILIAN FREE-TAILED BAT, BIG BROWN BAT, SILVER-HAIRED BAT. HOARY BAT's alternating call patterns typically set it apart from non-Lasiurine bats when moving through a moderately cluttered environment; however, confusion with BIG BROWN BAT, SILVER-HAIRED BAT and BRAZILIAN FREE-TAILED BAT is possible when this pattern is not obvious.

The low-frequency, concave social call occasionally produced by HOARY BAT, and its other low-frequency calls, can also resemble the ultrasonic vocalizations emitted by flying squirrels.

ROOSTING

HOARY BAT is thought to roost primarily in trees, relying on foliage for concealment. It may use coniferous habitats more frequently than red bats, and it has also occasionally been documented roosting in caves. Summer acoustic records are few, but range in altitude from sea level to 1,775 metres (late June recordings by Lausen at Kootenay Pass). Because of its tendency to roost in the foliage of coniferous and deciduous trees, HOARY BAT is often referred to as a tree bat. Other than a few individuals found roosting in the foliage of fruit trees in the Okanagan, specific details on the tree roosts selected in BC are not available. At Delta, Manitoba, individuals roosted 8 to 12 metres above the ground, usually near the end of branches of deciduous trees, such as ash. HOARY BAT likely selects sites that afford concealment from predators while also providing an open flight path for easy access to and from the roost. In Oregon, HOARY BAT was found to be restricted to old DOUGLAS-FIR forests; this finding was attributed to its roosting preferences.

Although HOARY BAT typically uses tree foliage and branches as day roosts, there are several unusual roosting records from the province; HOARY BATS have been found in a hollowed WESTERN REDCEDAR tree and using an inactive woodpecker nest in a cavity in the bole of a tree. Although rare, there are also reports outside BC of HOARY BATS in caves and roosting on buildings.

In summer, males are solitary, and females roost in family groups composed of a mother with her young. In contrast to many of BC's other bat species, breeding females do not congregate in maternity colonies. Observations also suggest high roost-site fidelity; family groups have been observed to use the same roosting location for more than a month.

FEEDING

HOARY BAT preys primarily on moths but can eat a diverse variety of insects. It has even been reported preying on other, smaller, bat species. Large moths, beetles and dragonflies form the bulk of the diet; small insects, such as midges and flies, are less commonly taken. The tendency to prey on large insects is consistent with this bat's large skull and teeth, its swift but less manoeuvrable

HOARY BATS coupled in mating after falling to ground on the northeastern shore of Ross Lake, approximately 15 kilometres south of the BC–Washington border. PHOTO: JARED GRUMMER (ARCOIRIS PHOTOGRAPHY)

flight, and the low-frequency echolocation calls that make it most effective at detecting large prey at long range. As a large-winged fast flyer, it generally hunts over open areas, such as rivers, lakes and clearings.

Nursing females reduce their foraging time to spend more time with their young at the roost during the first few weeks of nursing. Because their tree roosts tend to be relatively exposed, females may stay with their undeveloped young for prolonged periods to insulate them from cool temperatures. As a fast-flying bat with relatively poor manoeuvrability, HOARY BAT typically forages at or above canopy height, even in open areas such as fields and forest clearings. On capture, HOARY BATS are often seen with tapeworms exuding from the anus. It is not clear what the source of this parasite would be, but this observation suggests that the bat is consuming insects or other prey that are intermediate hosts of these intestinal worms. HOARY BATS are often attracted to insect concentrations at lights around buildings; their presence at some locations in the province may be largely the result of installation of permanent outdoor lights. Where insects are particularly concentrated, HOARY BATS will establish a feeding area and appear to exclude other bats. Intruding bats may be chased, and loud chirping calls (audible to the human ear) are often emitted during these chases.

HOARY BATS have been observed on many occasions showing aggression toward other bats, including fighting and killing other species, and are attracted by echolocation calls from their own and other species, and by distress calls of myotis species.

REPRODUCTION

HOARY BATS mate in the fall or early winter and delay implantation until spring. Copulation begins in the air, determined by observations of coupled bats falling out of the night-sky, making audible squabbling sounds (see image on page 193).

During the spring migration, females are often found pregnant, so it is assumed that mating takes place during the autumn migration period or in winter. Although there are no breeding data available for BC, in other parts of Canada it appears that young are born in June. Females typically give birth to twins, though occasionally a mother will have as many as four pups, which she can nurse simultaneously; like other Lasiurines, HOARY BAT has four teats. The newborns are small and underdeveloped, with closed eyes and ears. The top of the head, shoulders, and tail membrane are covered with fine silver-grey hair, but the undersides are naked. Development is slow, with the ears opening by 3 days and the eyes at around 12 days. Normally the young are left at the roost each night, but females can carry their young until they reach approximately a week in age; they are volant within a month of birth but are well tended by the female even after they can fly. By five weeks they are capable of sustained flight, though family groups remain together for several more weeks. They are thought to live for approximately 14 years in the wild.

MIGRATION AND WINTER

Circumstantial evidence based on seasonal occurrences strongly suggests that HOARY BAT, like other "tree bats" (i.e., EASTERN RED BAT), is migratory in BC, with separate spring and late summer-autumn migration periods. There are records of HOARY BATS arriving in many areas of BC in late March and early April, and acoustic recordings of this species are less frequent by mid-October, presumably because most individuals have left the province for warmer southern wintering areas. Lausen recorded spikes of acoustic activity at 1,775 metres (Kootenay Pass) in August, ending in late September. Kyle Nelson recorded a pass of a HOARY BAT on D'Arcy Island on November 3, 2018, and Michelle Evelyn reported a cat-killed adult male HOARY BAT from Sechelt on November 10, 2019, the latest record of this species in the province. Near Victoria, Purnima Govindarajulu acoustically recorded HOARY BATS starting March 29, 2013, at Mary Hill Training Area, and Mike Farley posted a photo to the Field Naturalists of Vancouver Island Facebook group of a HOARY BAT roosting on bark about 16 m up the trunk of a mature DOUGLAS-FIR in Marigold Park on April 9, 2021. In 2020 near Courtenay on Vancouver Island, Tim Ennis acoustically recorded HOARY BATS starting March 19.

Seasonal occurrences in BC are consistent with a migratory pattern, but where the BC population overwinters is unknown. Acoustic monitoring for five months on Grouse Mountain in the southern Coast Mountains of the province detected HOARY BATS from July 3 to October 8. A migratory passage was documented there in mid-September, with numerous detections consistent with autumn migrants passing through. This migration period is more than a month later than autumn migration of HOARY BAT in southern Alberta. At wind energy sites in the Peace River region, acoustic monitoring recorded sporadic HOARY BAT activity from July to mid-September.

In BC, migration routes have not been delineated. In the Waterton Lakes area of southwest Alberta and Montana, along the Foothills migration route, 94% of 58 reproductive adult males captured between July 16 and August 21 were early scrotal, and only 6% were late scrotal with signs of stored sperm. This supports the belief that mating in this species takes place in late fall or early winter in its southern overwintering areas outside of Canada. In southwest Alberta, HOARY BATS documented migrating together were not necessarily related; this has led to the conclusion that migration in HOARY BATS is not a learned trait. Although they migrate for the winter, they may undergo short bouts of hibernation in their winter areas.

CONSERVATION STATUS

HOARY BAT is considered secure by the province. The greatest threat is likely from fatalities at wind turbines; this species shows the highest mortality rate of any bat at wind energy sites across North America, accounting for 38% of all reported fatalities. A population analysis concluded that the total population could decline by up to 90% in the next 50 years, with a risk of extinction unless this mortality source is reduced. However, searches for fatalities at four wind energy sites in the Peace River region of BC recovered only a few HOARY BATS. Nonetheless, the BC population presumably encounters wind turbines in other jurisdictions during its autumn and spring migrations, where some may be killed. Until migration routes are better understood, the impact of wind turbine fatality on the BC population is unknown.

TAXONOMY AND VARIATION

Three subspecies have been traditionally recognized in North America, South America and Hawaii, with *Lasiurus cinereus cinereus* (Palisot de Beauvois) restricted to North America. A recent genetic study has shown that the subspecies fall into three divergent genetic groups that may warrant treatment as distinct species. The authors of the study considered HOARY BAT sufficiently distinct from other Lasiurine bats to be classified as a separate genus, *Aeorestes*. More genetic research is needed to resolve this taxonomy. We follow batnames.org in retaining *Lasiurus*. A genetics study based on DNA samples from Alberta, Manitoba and Ontario showed some divergence between western and eastern HOARY BATS. We need more genetic research across North America to understand the genetic variation and structure in this species.

Total length (mm):	137 (125–144)	n = 11
Tail vertebrae length (mm):	60 (50–66)	n = 10
Hind foot (mm):	12 (10–15)	n = 12
Ear (mm):	14 (13–16)	n = 4
Tragus (mm):	9 (9–10)	n = 4
Forearm (mm):	54.2 (50.3–57.4)	n = 29
Wingspan (mm):	392 (338–415)	n = 7
Mass (g):	27.8 (15.7–37.9)	n = 47

REMARKS

The thick, dense fur covering the body and tail membrane of HOARY BAT is likely important for insulation. The hoary colour appears to provide camouflage against a background of lichen-covered bark. Because of its solitary roosting habits in trees, HOARY BAT is rarely encountered by humans and, as a result, there is still much to be learned about its distribution and roosting behaviour in the province.

BC Hydro reported a "flock" of HOARY BATS that roosted in mid-September on an industrial crane at Hugh Keenleyside Dam; most took flight during the daytime when the crane was moved, though some were injured.

A HOARY BAT was observed roosting unusually low to the ground (approximately 1 metre) in a RED-STEM CEANOTHUS in Okanagan Mountain Provincial Park on October 6, 2008.

REFERENCES

Andrusiak (2008); Baerwald (2015); Baird et al. (2015); Barclay (1984); Barclay (1985); Barclay (1986); Barclay (1989); Blejwas, Lausen and Rhea-Fournier (2014); Brokaw, Clerc and Weller (2016); Corcoran and Weller (2018); Cowan and Guiguet (1960); Findley and Jones (1964); Frick et al. (2017); Hall (1929); Holderied and Von Helversen (2003); Marín et al. (2021); Murrant et al. (2013); Myers (1960); Nagorsen, Robertson and Manky (2014a); Nagorsen, Robertson and Sarell (2014b); O'Farrell, Corben and Gannon (2000); Perkins and Cross (1988); Shump and Shump (1982); Slough, Jung and Lausen (2014); Slough et al. (2022); Tacutu et al. (2018b); Willis and Brigham (2005); Willis, Brigham and Geiser (2006); Wine, Bowen and Green (2019); Ziegler, Howarth and Simmons (2016).

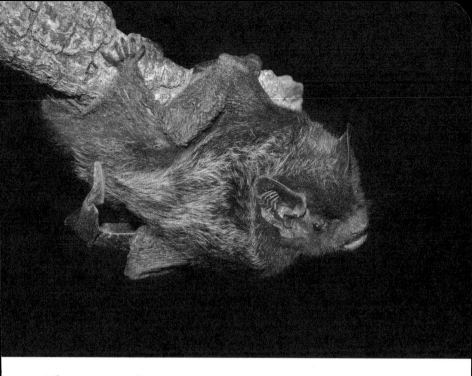

Silver-Haired Bat   *Lasionycteris noctivagans*

DESCRIPTION

SILVER-HAIRED BAT is medium-sized relative to other BC species, with rich, dark brown or black fur. In younger individuals, there are silver- or white-tipped hairs on the back and belly. These silver-white tips are less pronounced in older bats, whose fur appears more brown than black and could even have a yellow-orange tinge. The ears are short and round, with a short, blunt tragus. Ears and wing membranes are black and furless. The dorsal surface of the tail membrane is lightly furred, with hair extending about halfway to the tip of the tail. The calcar lacks a keel.

MORPHOLOGICALLY SIMILAR SPECIES

None. Based on colour, size and lightly furred tail membrane, SILVER-HAIRED BAT is distinctive. On the dorsal surfaces, the frosted hairs are most concentrated in the central area of the back (see dorsal image next page). The fur on the dorsal surface of the tail membrane is relatively thick near the body, but sparser on the distal half of the tail membrane—in contrast to Lasiurines, whose tail membranes are entirely furred with densely packed hairs, and distinct from other BC bat species whose tail membranes are largely unfurred. The ear of SILVER-HAIRED BAT is substantially shorter and rounder than in myotis species, and the leading edge of the ear (the front "rim") typically has a pinkish colour.

The only species with which this species could be confused is HOARY BAT. Silver or white-frosted tips of dorsal fur superficially resembles that of HOARY BAT, but SILVER-HAIRED BAT lacks a prominent ring of yellow around its head and lacks patches of white fur on its wrists. In addition, the wings of SILVER-HAIRED BAT are hairless, whereas HOARY BAT has yellow fur along the underside of the wing nearest the arm. SILVER-HAIRED BAT has only a light covering of fur extending out from the base of the tail membrane, in contrast to the extensively furred tail membrane of HOARY BAT.

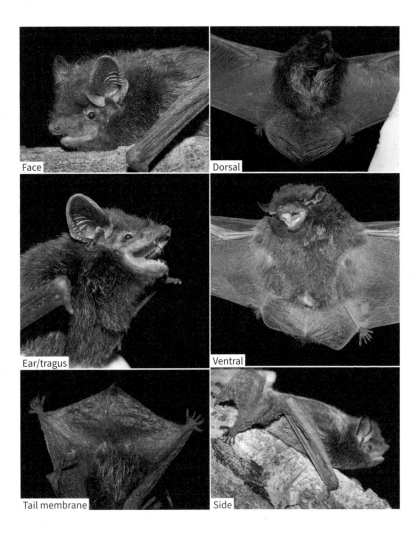

Face

Dorsal

Ear/tragus

Ventral

Tail membrane

Side

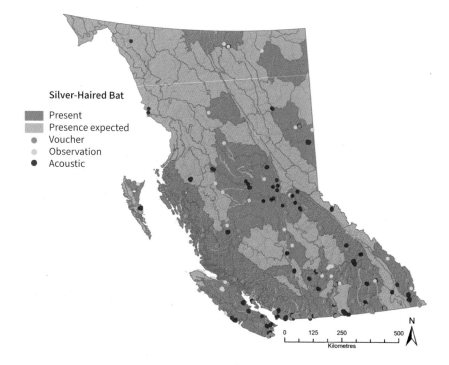

Silver-Haired Bat

- Present
- Presence expected
- Voucher
- Observation
- Acoustic

0　125　250　500
Kilometres

N

DISTRIBUTION

SILVER-HAIRED BAT is among western Canada's more cold-tolerant species. It is found in forested areas throughout BC, Alaska and much of Yukon and the Northwest Territories. To the south, the species can be found throughout the contiguous United States. In BC, it is found in Vancouver Island, Haida Gwaii, and Calvert, King and Goose Islands in the Great Bear Rain Forest; Hornby and Denman in the northern Gulf Islands; Texada Island; and across the Interior as far north as the BC-Yukon border, including Atlin in the northwest.

ACOUSTIC CHARACTERISTICS

25 kilohertz. The echolocation calls of SILVER-HAIRED BAT are typically uniform within a sequence and end in the range of 23–30 kilohertz, regardless of the level of clutter through which the bat is flying. In open (uncluttered) environments, the call shape is narrowband and can look completely flat (constant frequency), approaching 25 kilohertz in a spectrogram.

Lausen and Greg Falxa have made extensive observations of a unique series of pulses deemed a "song," produced by SILVER-HAIRED BAT (see B, C of zero-cross spectrogram next page). The purpose of this consistent pattern of pulses is not known, but the vast majority of them have been recorded in late fall and winter (in Washington and the West Kootenay), suggesting that this may be associated with mating.

ZERO-CROSS RECORDINGS

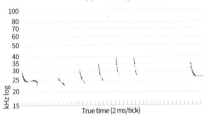

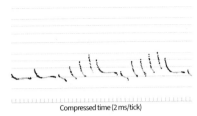

A. Sequence of calls showing the whole clutter continuum repertoire, starting with open environment pulse shapes (flat-sloped), transitioning to moderate- then higher-clutter pulse shapes, indicative of the bat approaching an object.

B. Repeated pattern of pulses, called a song, produced by SILVER-HAIRED BAT and frequently recorded in fall and winter in the Pacific Northwest.

C. The same SILVER-HAIRED BAT song as shown in B, but at a reduced magnification (F5 instead of F7), and in True Time mode such that the time (x) axis truly represents the elapsed time (in milliseconds).

FULL-SPECTRUM RECORDINGS

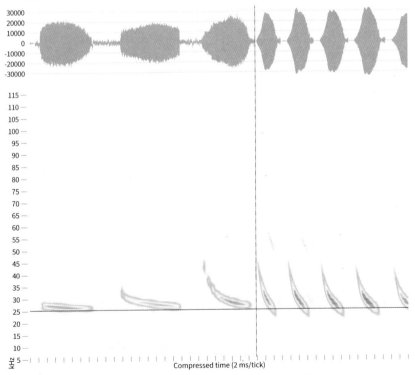

The sequence in the left pane is a recording in an open environment, with the pulse on the far left almost completely flat, but the slope increases as the bat approaches the microphone. The sequence in the right pane is of high-clutter pulses in a reference recording of a zip-lined bat.

ACOUSTICALLY SIMILAR SPECIES

BIG BROWN BAT, BRAZILIAN FREE-TAILED BAT, HOARY BAT. SILVER-HAIRED BATS are extremely difficult to differentiate acoustically from BIG BROWN BATS. However, the fact that in open environments SILVER-HAIRED BAT can produce completely flat, constant-frequency-type calls sets them apart from BIG BROWN BAT, whose lowest sloped calls are typically 8 octaves per second, though can occasionally drop as low as 5 OPS. SILVER-HAIRED BAT flat calls (less than 5 octaves per second) typically do not drop below 25 kilohertz, unlike the repertoire of HOARY BAT and BRAZILIAN FREE-TAILED BAT, which include flat calls below 25 kilohertz (see species accounts). In moderate clutter, SILVER-HAIRED BAT calls, like BIG BROWN BAT calls, take on a "hockey-stick" shape. SILVER-HAIRED BAT does not produce calls below 23 kilohertz, while BRAZILIAN FREE-TAILED, HOARY and BIG BROWN BATS will drop lower than this (see species accounts).

Another trait that might be useful in distinguishing calls of SILVER-HAIRED BATS from those of BIG BROWN BATS is that SILVER-HAIRED BAT does not start its moderate-clutter calls at as high a frequency as BIG BROWN BAT does. Some acoustic experts suggest that in moderate to high clutter at close range to the microphone (when a second harmonic is detectable), the highest recordable frequency produced by SILVER-HAIRED BAT is typically less than 50 kilohertz; BIG BROWN BAT typically produce frequencies greater than 65 kilohertz under similar conditions.

Although SILVER-HAIRED BAT can be acoustically confused with BIG BROWN BAT, experienced observers can use a spotlight to visually track the echolocating bat and identify the species based on appearance: SILVER-HAIRED BAT looks grey or brown depending on age or state of moult, whereas BIG BROWN BAT has a pale-coloured body with contrasting dark wings.

In open environments, BRAZILIAN FREE-TAILED BAT and SILVER-HAIRED BAT share calls whose spectrograms appear completely flat at approximately 25 kilohertz. Although this call pattern usually does not enable species differentiation, if a sufficient sequence of calls is recorded, differences between the species can be sometimes be detected: SILVER-HAIRED BAT will typically produce a uniform series of pulses, whereas BRAZILIAN FREE-TAILED BAT will periodically and seemingly randomly produce a call of elevated frequencies mid-sequence, often doing so several times during the sequence, with each raised pulse sometimes also showing an increased slope (see page 286 in accidental species account—BRAZILIAN FREE-TAILED BAT). BRAZILIAN FREE-TAILED BAT will produce flat calls between 20 and 25 kilohertz (see species account), which SILVER-HAIRED BAT does not do, as it does not produce flat calls below 25 kilohertz.

Unlike the calls of Lasiurines, SILVER-HAIRED BAT calls typically have the same minimum frequency within a sequence, but recordings of SILVER-HAIRED

BATS might be confused with those of HOARY BATS in locations where these bats interact with clutter. In clutter, HOARY BAT tends to produce a call sequence that shows undulating minimum frequencies (typical Lasiurine call pattern; see HOARY BAT species account), setting it apart from SILVER-HAIRED BAT; sufficiently long recordings of call sequences are needed to verify a uniform call pattern by which to confidently rule out HOARY BAT.

ROOSTING

SILVER-HAIRED BAT has been recorded in a diversity of forest types, from wet coastal temperate rainforests to dry Interior forests of PONDEROSA PINE and DOUGLAS-FIR. Biologists once believed the species to be largely solitary or to roost in pairs, but more recent evidence suggests they may roost in larger groups. Near Nelson, maternity tree roosts were found to house up to 12 individuals, consistent with similar observations in the Cypress Hills in Saskatchewan. The few records with elevation data suggest an altitudinal range from sea level to 500 metres, but during seasonal migration they have been documented at over 1,700 metres.

In summer, SILVER-HAIRED BATS generally roost under a flake of bark on dead or decaying trees, but they have also been found roosting in tight spaces on buildings (e.g., between boards or roof tiles, behind window shutters or barn doors), in crevices of tree trunks (including abandoned woodpecker holes), and less frequently under rocks or in rock crevices.

FEEDING

SILVER-HAIRED BAT is fairly common in forested areas, from treeline to valley bottom. Prey items identified in the diet cover a wide range of small insect species, including moths, midges, leafhoppers, caddisflies, flies, beetles, ants, termites and wasps. SILVER-HAIRED BATS are aerial foragers, catching their prey in mid-air using their mouth or occasionally their tail membrane, as do other aerial-hawking bats.

No information is available on the use of night roosts by SILVER-HAIRED BAT, though it has been captured entering mines at night in the West Kootenay.

REPRODUCTION

Mating starts in the fall in BC, as evidenced by decreasing amounts of stored sperm documented in captures throughout September and October. There is also evidence of mating in mid-winter in the West Kootenay, including captures of free-flying males with erect penises and observations of diminishing stores of sperm throughout winter, and free-flying females with sperm leaking from vaginal tracts. Stored sperm has been observed in cauda epididymides as late as May in BC, suggesting that spring mating is possible in BC. Spring mating in SILVER-HAIRED BAT has been confirmed elsewhere by Jeff Clerc, who observed this in New Mexico. In BC, males have descended testes in late July, suggesting that sperm production begins mid-summer. There is a record of young-of-year male SILVER-HAIRED BATS in BC producing sperm and mating in their first autumn.

As with other hibernating bats, implantation is delayed until spring and takes place after the females emerge from hibernation. After a 50- to 60-day gestation period, parturition occurs; twins are common for this species, though it is not known how often they occur in BC. The only breeding data for the province was of a female collected in the Peace River region on June 18 with two fetuses (7 millimetres), and a lactating female mid-July in the West Kootenay. Newborn young are hairless, with a body mass of 1.8 to 2.0 grams.

Males banded as juveniles have been recaptured in later years and seasons at the same mine, bringing into question how much, if any, migration this species, particularly males, undertakes in BC (see below).

MIGRATION AND WINTER

Throughout most of Canada, SILVER-HAIRED BAT is thought to be migratory, sometimes moving in groups. In eastern North America, northern populations have long been presumed to migrate seasonally to warmer latitudes to hibernate for the winter, but isotope analysis has found high variability in migration behaviour, with some bats transitioning to new areas for winter, and other individuals remaining sedentary.

Most Canadian populations are assumed to overwinter in the United States, but this is likely not the case in BC, as this species is commonly found year-round. Through banding of SILVER-HAIRED BATS at mines in the West Kootenay, Lausen gathered evidence for male SILVER-HAIRED BATS residing at the same mine in all seasons over multiple years. Females are recaptured from year to year at these Kootenay mines, but generally only in the season of initial banding. Based on these records, it is hypothesized that only females make migratory movements in BC, but the distance of these migrations is not known.

In BC, male and female distributions overlap extensively in all seasons. Spikes in acoustic activity of SILVER-HAIRED BATS on Kootenay Pass (Lausen, elevation 1,775 metres) and in the Peace River region in August and September provide evidence of some extent of seasonal migration. Additionally, August and September SILVER-HAIRED BAT fatalities under wind turbines in the Peace River region account for more than 50% of fatalities. Carcasses are also found under turbines in spring (starting in early May), even in the absence of peaks of spring acoustic activity of this species. This is consistent with observations in southwest Alberta at wind energy sites.

Winter records exist from the West Kootenay, Victoria, Vancouver, Salt Spring Island, Okanagan Valley, and north to Williams Lake. Laura Matthias, Peter Ommundsen and others have acoustically recorded SILVER-HAIRED BAT throughout the winter months on Salt Spring Island (2014 to 2020). Based on winter captures by Lausen and others in the West Kootenay and anecdotal observations of "black bats" in trees felled during winter, trees appear to be important hibernation sites in BC; SILVER-HAIRED BATS have been observed hibernating under the bark of live WESTERN REDCEDAR trees, DOUGLAS-FIR (in both snags and live trees), PONDEROSA PINE snags, and TREMBLING ASPEN snags. In hibernacula found in aspen snags, the bats were roosting in the hollow under intact but loosened bark, sometimes low to the ground. Radio-tracking in the Beasley and Syringa Provincial Park areas of the West Kootenay enabled Lausen to identify rock crevice hibernacula in addition to use of trees and mines. Using temperature-sensitive radiotelemetry, Lausen determined that most SILVER-HAIRED BATS are torpid during hibernation for an average of seven days, but hibernation bouts sometimes last more than three weeks. During arousals, more than half of the bats exited their hibernaculum, and more than half of these flights resulted in the bats switching roosts. While some bats hibernated in a mine in the Beasley area, not all bats used the mine and numbers were lowest in years when the mine was driest. In the winter of 2021, Emily de Freitas confirmed use of trees as hibernacula in the Beasley area and documented some radio-tagged bats switching trees to roost in large-diameter and hollow PONDEROSA PINE snags when temperatures dipped as low as –15°C. In 2021 it was also confirmed that SILVER-HAIRED BATS remained in deep torpor in trees as late as the end of April, likely due to the low insect food supply that is typical in spring.

While many SILVER-HAIRED BATS hibernate solitarily in the West Kootenay, Lausen and others found mixed-species clusters containing CALIFORNIAN MYOTIS, with up to six bats in a cluster. These two species were also found

A mixed cluster of SILVER-HAIRED BAT and CALIFORNIAN MYOTIS hibernating in a mine near Nelson. Mixed clusters are most commonly observed during extreme cold, dry conditions in the mine. PHOTO: FLORIAN GRANER (SEALIFE PRODUCTIONS, WA)

cohabiting in a rock crevice hibernaculum during this study. This particular rock crevice reached temperatures below freezing, and although SILVER-HAIRED BAT and CALIFORNIAN MYOTIS tried to leave the roost, the entrance had iced over and both bats froze and died. Winter records of individuals in attics, at any time of the year, are not common, though there is a record of a SILVER-HAIRED BAT in winter in a house in Vancouver, and Cory Olson (Alberta Community Bat Program) also had one observation of this in Alberta. During winter in West Kootenay, landowners regularly report finding SILVER-HAIRED BATS roosting in firewood piles or inside log houses.

SILVER-HAIRED BAT is cold-hardy and has been recorded hibernating in sites that range from –0.5°C to 7°C, and 85% to 100% humidity. The northern limits of the winter range suggest that this mammal can overwinter in regions where the average daily temperature for January is above –7°C (isotherm), although recent evidence from the Lake Michigan area suggests that this threshold might actually be closer to –12°C. SILVER-HAIRED BAT has been acoustically detected overwintering in south-eastern Alaska, still within the –7°C isotherm, though roost sites have not been identified.

The largest number of winter captures (n = 130, December to February) of SILVER-HAIRED BAT has been in the West Kootenay by Lausen and others. All bats were captured while flying during brief periods of arousal from hibernation, and there was no evidence of any feeding behaviour (no guano production). Some bats would drink when offered water or snow, and several showed signs of having just mated.

CONSERVATION STATUS

Although SILVER-HAIRED BAT is considered secure by conservation agencies, it faces several threats. Given its strong association with trees for maternity and hibernation roosts, commercial forest harvest practices likely severely impact the availability of roosts in logged areas. It is also susceptible to fatalities at wind energy sites. A survey of fatalities at 64 wind energy sites across Canada revealed that 25% of the bat fatalities were SILVER-HAIRED BATS, second only to HOARY BAT. At four wind energy sites in the Peace River region of BC, SILVER-HAIRED BATS had the greatest fatality rates of any bats, accounting for about 50% of the total fatalities. With so little known about its populations and movements in the province, the impact of these fatalities is unknown.

TAXONOMY AND VARIATION
No subspecies are recognized.

MEASUREMENTS
Adult mass varies across the seasons: March–April, 10.0 grams (9.2–12.5; n = 7); May–June, 9.6 grams (8.3–22.1; n = 8); July–August, 11.9 grams (7.9–15.2; n = 48);

September–November, 13.3 grams (11.4–15.9; n = 66); December–February, 11.0 grams (8.4–15.9; n = 70). Bats are on average 39% heavier in fall than in spring. Females are larger than males (see table on page 76).

Total length (mm):	100	(90–117)	n = 68
Tail vertebrae length (mm):	41	(31–50)	n = 70
Hind foot (mm):	9	(6–11)	n = 69
Ear (mm):	12	(9–15)	n = 17
Tragus (mm):	7	(4–8)	n = 22
Forearm (mm):	41.5	(38.4–45.0)	n = 296
Wingspan (mm):	291	(200–354)	n = 38
Mass (g):	11.9	(7.9–15.9)	n = 199

REMARKS

In the forests of coastal Oregon and Washington, SILVER-HAIRED BAT activity was measured in greatest abundance in stands of old-growth forest. This was attributed to the availability of abundant roosting sites associated with snags and old trees in these forests.

The rabies variant that infects SILVER-HAIRED BAT is associated with the greatest number of bat-transmitted human rabies cases in the northwestern and north-central United States (eight cases between 1958 and 2000). Surprisingly, this species is rarely submitted for rabies testing and rarely found to be rabid. This may be due to its tendency to roost in trees rather than anthropogenic structures, so infected animals are less likely to be encountered than building-roosting bats, such as BIG BROWN BATS, a species frequently reported as rabid in the United States. However, it is also possible that SILVER-HAIRED BAT rabies viruses are transmitted to humans via other bat species, since the rabies virus variant associated with SILVER-HAIRED BAT has been found in other bats, and often the bat associated with the rabies case is not found but rather deduced from genetic sequencing of the virus in the infected human.

REFERENCES

Barclay (1985); Barclay (1986); Barclay, Faure and Farr (1988); Blejwas, Lausen and Rhea-Fournier (2014); Bohn (2017); Cowan (1933); Cryan (2003); Falxa (2007); Franka et al. (2006); Fraser, Brooks and Longstaffe (2017); Hemmera (2013, 2014); Kunz (1982); Kurta et al. (2018); Messenger, Smith and Rupprecht (2002); Nagorsen, Robertson and Sarell (2014b); Parsons, Smith and Whittam (1986); Schowalter, Dorward and Gunson (1978); Slough et al. (2022); Szewczak (2011); Thomas (1988); Vonhof and Barclay (1996).

Californian Myotis

Myotis californicus

DESCRIPTION

CALIFORNIAN MYOTIS is the second smallest myotis species in BC and one of only three species of myotis with a prominent keel on its calcar. Fur colour varies from rusty to blackish brown; the fur is dull and lacks a glossy sheen. Ear, wing and tail membranes are black. Ears are pointy, are long relative to head and body, and extend beyond the nose when laid forward.

MORPHOLOGICALLY SIMILAR SPECIES

LONG-LEGGED MYOTIS, DARK-NOSED SMALL-FOOTED MYOTIS. There are only three myotis species in BC with a prominent keel on the calcar of the tail membrane: CALIFORNIAN MYOTIS, DARK-NOSED SMALL-FOOTED MYOTIS and LONG-LEGGED MYOTIS. LONG-LEGGED MYOTIS has hairy armpits and a much longer forearm (approximately 40 millimetres) than the smaller DARK-NOSED SMALL-FOOTED MYOTIS (forearm 29 to 35 millimetres).

Where they co-occur, DARK-NOSED SMALL-FOOTED MYOTIS and CALIFORNIAN MYOTIS are difficult to differentiate. The dark facial fur of DARK-NOSED SMALL-FOOTED MYOTIS gives the appearance of a facial mask, and several tail vertebrae extend past the edge of the tail membrane. CALIFORNIAN MYOTIS generally does not have a pronounced facial mask and does not have tail vertebrae extending beyond the tail membrane, setting it apart. The length of the naked area on the snout of DARK-NOSED SMALL-FOOTED MYOTIS is about one and a half times the width at the nostrils (rectangular); the bare snout of CALIFORNIAN MYOTIS is relatively square, with equal width and length (see images in key on page 102). The thumb (including the claw) of CALIFORNIAN MYOTIS is relatively short (average 3.8, range 3–5 millimetres), versus the longer thumb of DARK-NOSED SMALL-FOOTED MYOTIS (average 5.0, range 4–6.5 millimetres). Finally, the skull of CALIFORNIAN MYOTIS has a more steeply sloped forehead than that of DARK-NOSED SMALL-FOOTED MYOTIS (see Appendix 2).

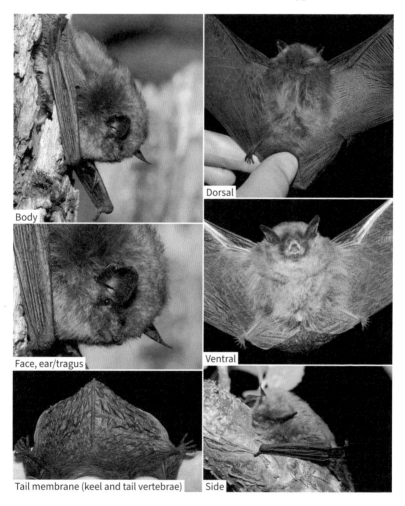

Body

Dorsal

Face, ear/tragus

Ventral

Tail membrane (keel and tail vertebrae)

Side

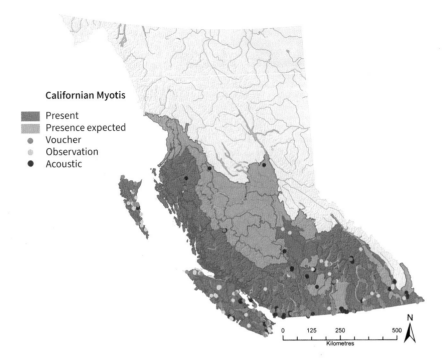

Californian Myotis

- ■ Present
- ▨ Presence expected
- ● Voucher
- ○ Observation
- ⬤ Acoustic

N

0   125   250   500
Kilometres

DISTRIBUTION

CALIFORNIAN MYOTIS occurs in western North America, where its range extends from southern Mexico to mainland BC and southeastern Alaska. In BC, it is also known from various coastal islands, including Vancouver Island and Haida Gwaii, the coastal mainland north to the Skeena River valley, and the Interior north to Wells Grey Provincial Park and east to Kootenay National Park and the Flathead River valley. Acoustic calls have been recorded in the Atlin area (not shown on map), suggesting that the species might occur there, but physical capture would be needed to confirm this. Lausen has also acoustically recorded this species at the Akamina Pass in Waterton Lakes National Park in Alberta, suggesting that its range may extend into the Rocky Mountain Foothills of Alberta. An inconclusive genetic sample from guano taken from a cave in southwestern Alberta in 2020, as part of WCS Canada's BatCaver program, adds further support to this hypothesis.

ACOUSTIC CHARACTERISTICS

45–50 kilohertz. CALIFORNIAN MYOTIS is one of Canada's highest-frequency bats. Like YUMA MYOTIS, CALIFORNIAN MYOTIS produces calls that typically end at or above 45 kilohertz, though CALIFORNIAN MYOTIS can dip to 43 kilohertz in open environments. This frequency guild sets these two species apart acoustically from other myotis. Its acoustic tendencies are consistent with other long-eared

ZERO-CROSS RECORDINGS

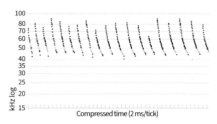

A sequence of calls showing progressively less response to clutter, suggesting that the bat is flying into open airspace.

FULL-SPECTRUM RECORDINGS

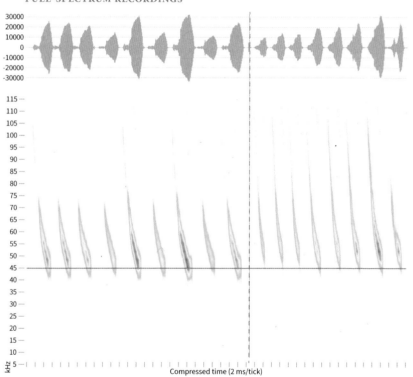

An open environment recording in left pane, and a higher-clutter sequence in right.

myotis bats. CALIFORNIAN MYOTIS gleans insect prey from surfaces, and even in open environments produces relatively steep calls. In open space, calls may drop to frequencies approaching 40 kilohertz, inviting confusion with other myotis species. As CALIFORNIAN MYOTIS is highly manoeuvrable in flight, it is often found foraging among clutter, producing extremely steep calls.

ACOUSTICALLY SIMILAR SPECIES

YUMA MYOTIS, DARK-NOSED SMALL-FOOTED MYOTIS. CALIFORNIAN and YUMA MYOTIS are difficult to differentiate in cluttered environments because of similar minimum frequencies, but their echolocation calls often differ when both species are flying in open (uncluttered) space. CALIFORNIAN MYOTIS retains steeper and often rounder or smoother calls, with the indistinct elbow of the call occurring near the end of the steep frequency sweep. This characteristic is diagnostic and sets these bats apart from YUMA MYOTIS, which tends toward lower-sloped calls in the open and often produces an abrupt change in the rate of decline in frequency (i.e., a distinct elbow in the call) partway through the broadband sweep of the call.

Recordings of CALIFORNIAN MYOTIS made in open habitats may be confused with recordings of DARK-NOSED SMALL-FOOTED MYOTIS. DARK-NOSED SMALL-FOOTED MYOTIS produces echolocation calls that end at approximately 39 to 43 kilohertz; CALIFORNIAN MYOTIS typically produces calls that end at 43 to 50 kilohertz, but in the open they may shift their calls low enough to generate confusion between the two species.

In high clutter, differentiating any of the 40 kilohertz myotis (NORTHERN, DARK-NOSED SMALL-FOOTED, LITTLE BROWN and LONG-LEGGED MYOTIS) from the 45–50 kilohertz myotis (YUMA and CALIFORNIAN MYOTIS) can be difficult, because bats tend to use high frequencies in extreme levels of clutter. High-clutter EASTERN RED BAT calls may also be confused with these species. In that context, a long sequence of uniform calls ending above 45 kilohertz can be attributed to either YUMA or CALIFORNIAN MYOTIS.

ROOSTING
In BC, CALIFORNIAN MYOTIS inhabits arid grasslands, humid coastal forests and montane forests. Altitude limits range from sea level on the coast to 1,280 metres in Glacier National Park. Rock crevices, tree cavities, openings under tree bark, mine tunnels, buildings, bat boxes and bridges are all used for summer day roosts. CALIFORNIAN MYOTIS roosts alone or in small maternity colonies. In BC, roosts are most often in tree cavities or under bark, although the BC Community Bat Program has occasionally documented them in bat boxes (Sunshine Coast and Southern Vancouver Island/Salt Spring Island). Both males and females show fidelity to roosts, with multiple banded individuals being recaptured across seasons at a mine in the West Kootenay.

CALIFORNIAN MYOTIS is particularly flexible in its choice of night roosts, and it will exploit almost any natural or man-made shelter. Males roost separately from females during the summer months and appear to change their roosting locations often.

FEEDING

As CALIFORNIAN MYOTIS has low wing loading and aspect ratio (see page 16), it is slow flying and highly manoeuvrable. It frequently forages close to the ground, often among foliage, likely gleaning insects from vegetation in addition to hawking insects in the air. Food items likely include moths and dipterans; in the Okanagan, the diet is caddisflies, moths, dipterans and beetles.

REPRODUCTION

For most BC bat species, mating probably occurs largely in autumn; however, free-flying CALIFORNIAN MYOTIS captured in November through March in the West Kootenay provide evidence of mating later in the fall and throughout the winter. Additionally, more than half of the males captured in March in the West Kootenay have their sperm stores depleted; by April and May, captured males have no remaining stored sperm, suggesting that mating has been completed by this time. Some males in the Okanagan-Thompson region show descended swollen testes (for sperm production) as early as late May, but in most of the southern part of the province, males are not scrotal until late July.

As with most other bats in BC, females produce a single young pup in the spring. The timing of reproduction in BC has been recorded for Haida Gwaii and West Kootenay, where parturition was documented in early to mid-July and lactation continued into August. Across southern BC, bats are noticeably pregnant by early June, although in some years pregnancy continues into late July. Lactation typically occurs throughout July, with weaning occurring by late August across southern BC.

MIGRATION AND WINTER

CALIFORNIAN MYOTIS periodically arouses from hibernation and, like many hibernating bats, will fly during the hibernation period. Lausen and others have captured and radio-tracked these bats using temperature-sensitive radio transmitters in the West Kootenay; they have been shown to remain in hibernation for an average of 16 days (with torpor bouts ranging from several days to a full month), often arousing for several hours before lowering their body temperature back into a state of torpor. This is repeated throughout the winter, with more than half of all arousals involving flight either outside or within the hibernaculum.

Museum specimens of CALIFORNIAN MYOTIS have been collected in the winter, from Hope (January) and Rogers Pass in Glacier National Park (January), as well as an increasing number of winter reports from across southern BC, including one of an individual found on the snow covered in sap and unable to fly (Mirror Lake in the West Kootenay [February]). There were also reports of numerous individuals killed by a cat throughout the winter at a talus slope near a home in Fletcher Falls (in the West Kootenay), and a cat kill at Sandspit, Haida Gwaii (February). Although it can be difficult to distinguish this species acoustically from YUMA MYOTIS, winter acoustic records suggest that this species hibernates as far north as Prince Rupert, Terrace and Lava Beds Provincial Park along the Nass River. CALIFORNIAN MYOTIS is often reported roosting on the outside of buildings in autumn in the West Kootenay.

In southern and coastal BC, CALIFORNIAN MYOTIS is the most likely to be acoustically recorded during the winter when temperatures hover close to freezing. It has been detected acoustically in all months of the year on Haida Gwaii and in West Kootenay, especially near rock crevices. Doug Burles documented substantial CALIFORNIAN MYOTIS activity on Haida Gwaii throughout January 2014, recording over 60 bat passes per hour on some nights. Much of this activity coincided with observations of abundant craneflies; Burles hypothesized that CALIFORNIAN MYOTIS were foraging on these mid-winter insect hatches, because he recorded substantial numbers of feeding buzzes (a record number of 266 feeding buzzes were recorded on just one night). On Haida Gwaii, CALIFORNIAN MYOTIS may overwinter in crevices during colder periods but use tree cavities or go under bark during warmer periods. This strategy is successful if suitable tree cavities typically remain above freezing in winter, as is the case on Haida Gwaii. Similarly, Lausen has recorded CALIFORNIAN MYOTIS in all winter months at MacMillan Provincial Park on Vancouver Island (elevation 200 metres) where old-growth WESTERN REDCEDAR provide the only obvious roosts.

Mid-winter radio-tracking of CALIFORNIAN MYOTIS in the West Kootenay by Lausen and others indicates that these bats use a combination of mines and rock crevices, switching between these two options occasionally throughout the winter. This species has also been observed in mixed species clusters (with SILVER-HAIRED BAT; see image on page 204 in SILVER-HAIRED BAT species account) hibernating in a mine during particularly cold winter temperatures. The mine microclimate ranged from 6°C to 7°C and 83% or greater humidity. One CALIFORNIAN MYOTIS was discovered roosting outside the mine in the same rock crevice as a hibernating SILVER-HAIRED BAT. The temperature in this rock crevice fell to below freezing, and although the bats tried to leave the roost, the entrance had iced over and both bats succumbed to freezing. Another CALIFORNIAN MYOTIS was radio-tracked in January, switching roosts from a mine to the root wad of an uprooted tree.

In the low-elevation West Kootenay mines, where Lausen and others have conducted substantial winter research, CALIFORNIAN MYOTIS was almost always recorded acoustically at night during the winter, yet daytime visual examinations of these mines usually failed to detect roosting bats. This led to the hypothesis that CALIFORNIAN MYOTIS might be flying into mines at night during winter, but not necessarily roosting in them during the day. To test this, researchers placed a bat detector with dual microphones inside a mine near Ainsworth, providing the first evidence that this species visits mines without hibernating in them. We found that the bats entered mines during winter nights, flew for short time periods inside the mines, and often then exited. Plastic laid in the bottom of mines to collect guano was used to test the hypothesis that the bats might be feeding mid-winter on arthropods that overwinter in low-elevation mines. However, despite substantial guano collected, genetic analyses by Elizabeth Clare indicated that the pellets contained only residual insect prey consumed in the fall. We concluded that guano production by CALIFORNIAN MYOTIS in December and January in the West Kootenay does not provide conclusive evidence of winter foraging. Instead, bats do not fully digest insects consumed in the fall just prior to hibernation until mid-winter during arousals, when warm body temperatures enable final digestion. We don't know why these bats are flying around inside mines for brief periods of the night in the winter.

On the south coast, there are several winter records from Vancouver Island and the Vancouver area. The single Vancouver record describes an active individual flying inside a building in January at the University of British Columbia. Insect remains were present in its stomach, suggesting it may have fed recently. In coastal Washington and Oregon, where CALIFORNIAN MYOTIS frequently hibernates in buildings, there is considerable evidence that it occasionally emerges from torpor to feed. Feeding buzzes were recorded in the winter months in coastal Washington, and at Sandspit, Haida Gwaii. Laura Matthias, Peter Ommundsen and others have acoustically recorded CALIFORNIAN MYOTIS throughout the winter months on Salt Spring Island (2014 to 2020).

CONSERVATION STATUS

A widespread and common bat in BC occupying a range of habitats, CALIFORNIAN MYOTIS is considered secure by conservation agencies. Potential threats are removal of tree roosts by commercial forest harvesting and disturbance of winter hibernacula. Its susceptibility to white-nose syndrome is unknown.

TAXONOMY AND VARIATION

Although CALIFORNIAN MYOTIS is morphologically distinct from DARK-NOSED SMALL-FOOTED MYOTIS, their mitochondrial DNA sequences are similar. Four subspecies are recognized, but they differ primarily in pelage colour and there have been no genetic studies confirming their validity. Two subspecies are found in the province:

> *Myotis californicus californicus* (Audubon and Bachman)—A pale subspecies that inhabits parts of the western United States east of the Cascade Range and the southern Interior of BC.

> *Myotis californicus caurinus* Miller—A dark coastal subspecies ranging from California to Alaska. In BC, it occupies the southern coastal mainland and various coastal islands, including Vancouver Island and Haida Gwaii. The type specimen for this race is from Masset, Haida Gwaii.

MEASUREMENTS

Mass of adults varies throughout the year: March–April, 4.3 grams (3.6–5.4; n = 42); May–June, 4.5 grams (3.8–5.4; n = 61); July–August, 4.8 grams (3.0–6.9; n = 192); September–November, 6.2 grams (4.3–7.0; n = 101); December–February, 5.3 grams (4.1–6.6; n = 83). Bats are approximately 25% heavier in fall than in spring. Bats in the western part of the province are significantly smaller than those in the east (see graph on page 77). Females are larger than males (see table on page 76).

Total length (mm):	80	(65–95)	n = 75
Tail vertebrae length (mm):	36	(26–41)	n = 77
Hind foot (mm):	6	(5–9)	n = 80
Ear (mm):	12	(7–15)	n = 72
Tragus (mm):	6.3	(4–9)	n = 67
Forearm (mm):	33.0	(30.0–35.8)	n = 553
Wingspan (mm):	222	(209–251)	n = 28
Mass (g):	5.0	(3.0–7.0)	n = 479

REMARKS

CALIFORNIAN MYOTIS is a common bat in BC. We don't know what restricts it to the southern half of the BC Interior, but its small size may limit it to overwintering in areas that experience mild winters, especially if this species does not move long distances seasonally.

On Salt Spring Island, a CALIFORNIAN MYOTIS was found dead next to a LONG-EARED MYOTIS, entangled in the spines of a FULLER'S TEASEL.

REFERENCES

Barclay and Brigham (2001), Brigham et al. (1997), Burles et al. (2014), Constantine (1998), Cowan (1942), Falxa (2007), Grindal et al. (1992), Krutzsch (1954), Norberg and Rayner (1987), Ommundsen (2020), Rodriguez and Ammerman (2004), Simpson (1993), Woodsworth (1981).

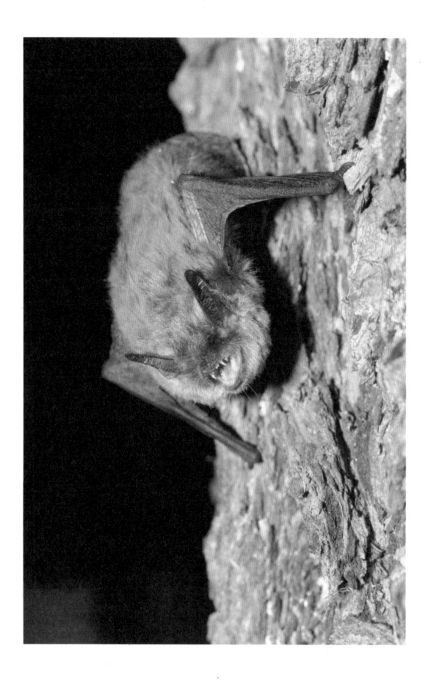

Long-Eared Myotis

Myotis evotis

DESCRIPTION

LONG-EARED MYOTIS is the longest-eared myotis species, with ears typically 18 millimetres or longer. Though a small keel can sometimes be present on the calcar, it is most often either indistinct or lacking. Dorsal fur colour is extremely variable, ranging from yellowish brown in the BC Interior to dark brown or nearly black in coastal populations. Blackish-brown shoulder patches are evident on paler individuals due to the bicoloured nature of the fur, with the dark base of the hairs most visible at the bend of the shoulders. The outer edge of the tail membrane has a sparse fringe of tiny hairs that is often seen only with a hand lens, except in young-of-year, where these hairs can be more obvious. The ears and flight membranes are nearly black and usually contrast sharply with the paler fur. The tragus is long and slender, with a small lobe at its base.

MORPHOLOGICALLY SIMILAR SPECIES

FRINGED MYOTIS, NORTHERN MYOTIS. The absence of a distinct keel on the calcar is usually enough to distinguish LONG-EARED MYOTIS from the three obviously keeled myotis species (LONG-LEGGED MYOTIS, CALIFORNIAN MYOTIS, and DARK-NOSED SMALL-FOOTED MYOTIS), but the obviously long dark ears can also help with this differentiation.

There are two other myotis with long ears in BC: FRINGED MYOTIS and NORTHERN MYOTIS. FRINGED MYOTIS features a prominent fringe of hairs on the tail membrane that is easily visible with the naked eye, though LONG-EARED

MYOTIS, especially in young-of-year, can have a sparse fringe of more widely spaced hair on the edge of the tail membrane. FRINGED MYOTIS generally has a longer forearm (greater than 40 millimetres) than LONG-EARED MYOTIS. Because of the more robust skull of FRINGED MYOTIS, measuring the width of the snout at the hairline can help differentiate: LONG-EARED MYOTIS has a narrow rostrum, ranging from 3 to 7 millimetres but on average 5.3 millimetres (n = 62), whereas FRINGED MYOTIS has a significantly wider rostrum, ranging from 6 to 8 millimetres, on average 6.6 millimetres (n = 7).

NORTHERN MYOTIS has a long, narrow, sharply pointed tragus and typically has shorter ears than LONG-EARED MYOTIS. The ears of NORTHERN MYOTIS are the same colour as the fur, which is typically dark brown. NORTHERN MYOTIS has a more restricted range in BC, although both species co-occur throughout much of the northern Interior.

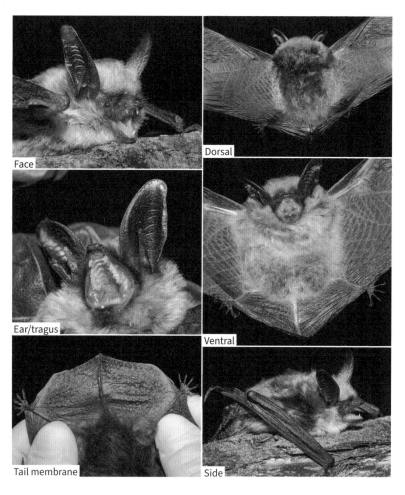

Face

Dorsal

Ear/tragus

Ventral

Tail membrane

Side

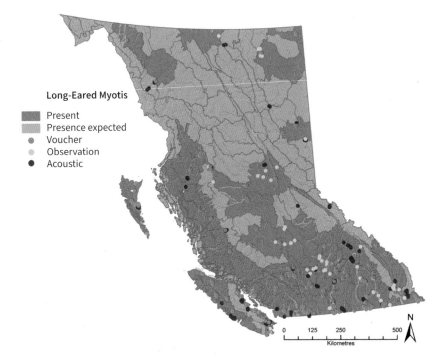

Long-Eared Myotis

- ▨ Present
- ▨ Presence expected
- ● Voucher
- ◉ Observation
- ● Acoustic

0 125 250 500
Kilometres

N

DISTRIBUTION

In BC, LONG-EARED MYOTIS is found across the province, including near Fort Nelson, at Atlin in the northwest, and on some coastal islands, including Haida Gwaii, Vancouver Island and several Gulf Islands (Denman, Cortes).

ACOUSTIC CHARACTERISTICS

30–35 kilohertz. As a long-eared gleaning species, the calls of LONG-EARED MYOTIS sweep through a broadband of frequencies very quickly, giving its spectrogram a relatively steep, almost vertical, appearance when viewed in a standard magnification. In zero-crossing format at a division ratio of 8 or higher, moderate- to high-clutter calls (like other LONG-EARED MYOTIS calls) are represented by few dots on the spectrogram because of the fast-changing sweep through frequencies, especially for the first portion of the call (see right panel in zero-cross recording, next page). Even when navigating in an open environment, this species tends toward short-duration broadband calls, though in these spaces it sweeps through frequencies somewhat more slowly, producing calls with slight curvature (see left panel in zero-cross recording, next page). Minimum frequencies of calls are typically 30 to 35 kilohertz but can be as high as 40 kilohertz, especially in coastal areas when the bat is flying in high clutter.

ZERO-CROSS RECORDINGS

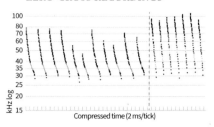

Open environment pulse shapes in left pane; sequence in right pane consists of high-clutter pulses.

FULL-SPECTRUM RECORDINGS

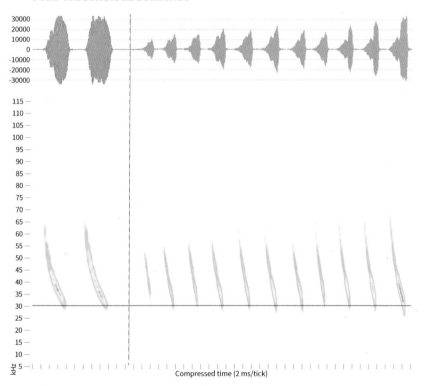

Left pane is an open environment recording; bat-kiting in right pane shows high-clutter pulse shapes.

ACOUSTICALLY SIMILAR SPECIES

FRINGED MYOTIS, PALLID BAT, BIG BROWN BAT. FRINGED MYOTIS and LONG-EARED MYOTIS share a high-clutter pulse shape even when foraging in open environments; FRINGED MYOTIS calls typically end at 20 to 25 kilohertz, lower than the 30 to 35 kilohertz of LONG-EARED MYOTIS. PALLID BAT and BIG BROWN BAT typically end around 25 kilohertz but in high clutter can have rather steep calls that end at 30 kilohertz, inviting some potential confusion with LONG-EARED MYOTIS.

ROOSTING

In BC, LONG-EARED MYOTIS inhabits diverse habitat types, from the arid grasslands and PONDEROSA PINE forests of the southern Interior to humid coastal and montane forests along the coast and boreal forests in northern BC. This is one of the few bats found consistently at high elevations in western Canada. Known altitudinal records extend from sea level on the coast up to 1,775 metres in the Selkirk Mountains at Stagleap Provincial Park (based on acoustic recordings by Lausen in June). Intermediate elevations include Manning Provincial Park (1,220 metres) in the Cascades, and Kootenay National Park (1,250 metres) in the Rocky Mountains. In the Kananaskis region of the Rocky Mountains in Alberta, summer populations of both sexes live at 1,350 to 2,050 metres. This contrasts with LITTLE BROWN MYOTIS, for which only the males live at higher elevations.

Summer day roosts are typically found under the bark of trees, in mines or caves, in stumps, or in rock crevices. Caves and mine adits are also used as temporary night roosts. Radio-tracking of LONG-EARED MYOTIS in the West Kootenay revealed extensive day roosting in large-diameter stumps by males and females within clear-cuts, with roost cavities most often facing southwest. Roost microclimates were stable and did not reach high temperatures relative to cavities in randomly available stumps.

A rock crevice maternity colony on Hot Springs Island, Haida Gwaii, is mixed with LITTLE BROWN MYOTIS, where bats are in roosts warmed by the natural hot spring. Doug Burles measured roost temperatures in summer as high as 34°C, stabilized by the warm water of the hot spring. Because of the nearby hot spring, the roost was also quite humid. Curiously, this roost is situated near the high tide line, and for several weeks each month it would be submerged for several hours at high tide. During these periods of high tides, the roost is evidently abandoned. Numbers at this maternity colony have fluctuated over the years and appear to be correlated with presence of NORTHERN SAW-WHET OWLS. In 2012 an earthquake changed the water availability in the hot spring temporarily, also reducing colony numbers at these rock roosts. Emergence counts since 1998 suggest that LONG-EARED MYOTIS population numbers fluctuate; Burles reported a peak emergence count in 2007 of 82, and as few as five in 2012.

Maternity colonies in buildings are generally small (5 to 30 individuals) and may contain a few adult males as well. The BC Community Bat Program has confirmed four maternity roosts for LONG-EARED MYOTIS in anthropogenic roost sites in BC: two are in bat boxes (one in the Kootenay region and another in the Skeena region), where species identification was confirmed using a combination of genetics and capture; two others are in buildings and are mixed maternity roosts with LITTLE BROWN MYOTIS on the Sunshine Coast and southern Vancouver Island. Cory Olson confirmed a building roost of LONG-EARED MYOTIS in Kootenay National Park, where a maternity colony of five females was roosting on a concrete block chimney.

FEEDING

Few studies of LONG-EARED MYOTIS food habits have been conducted in BC, but elsewhere moths are the major prey item, with beetles, flies and spiders also taken. In the southwestern area of the province, the species is most often detected in low-elevation cottonwood and WESTERN REDCEDAR–WESTERN HEMLOCK stands, with more activity in areas of increasing forest age. In the Merritt area, WESTERN SPRUCE BUDWORM moths and caterpillars were detected in the diet of several bat species, including LONG-EARED MYOTIS.

These bats glean prey from the ground or vegetation. They use a combination of visual and echolocation cues, but it has been well documented that they listen for prey-generated sounds to locate non-flying insects. In natural situations, LONG-EARED MYOTIS is quite flexible in its feeding behaviour, eating airborne insects while in flight as well as gleaning prey from vegetation or the ground. In southwestern Alberta, Lausen has captured LONG-EARED MYOTIS with cactus spines in their noses, confirming this foraging behaviour. It has been determined that because of the high energy expenditure associated with gleaning, LONG-EARED MYOTIS is likely to forage throughout the night, even when cool temperatures result in few insects flying. Gleaning enables this bat to keep foraging when aerial insects become inactive, but the energetic demands of this behaviour seem to necessitate longer feeding bouts than those of other bats in the same area. This means that during the cooler mid to late portion of the night, LONG-EARED MYOTIS are likely to still be active, while other bats night roost. This flexible feeding behaviour also likely enables females to breed successfully in cool high-elevation sites, where flying insects are scarce.

The quiet, short-duration, high-pitched echolocation calls are an adaptation for hunting in habitats with heavy vegetation, and these calls are not readily detected by most moths. When closing in to attack, LONG-EARED MYOTIS often stops calling and listens for sounds produced by its prey. The rustling noises created by fluttering moth wings may make these insects especially vulnerable to predation by this bat. The gleaning behaviour of LONG-EARED MYOTIS may explain why it has been found in insect pheromone funnel traps

The small orange dots visible (in the lower part of the ear) on this LONG-EARED MYOTIS are ectoparasites commonly seen on bats (see Disease and Bats, page 52).

on several occasions in BC, suggesting that escape ramps for bats may be needed in insect traps.

REPRODUCTION

There is a scattering of reproduction records across the province for LONG-EARED MYOTIS. In the southern Okanagan area, males begin to become scrotal and females show signs of early pregnancy by late May. Females with near-term fetuses have been found in the same area in late June, and nursing females were observed from early July to mid-August. In the town of Whistler (elevation 650 metres), LONG-EARED MYOTIS in early pregnancy were captured in mid-June in a stand of old-growth WESTERN REDCEDAR. In the Kootenay region, pregnant and lactating females and early-stage scrotal males were captured in the last half of July. In Hazelton, females captured in mid-July were still pregnant. Post-lactating females and scrotal males have been captured in early August in southern BC. A capture of an adult female and a single flying young in Atlin in mid-August suggests lactation may be later at the northern extent of the range. As with most other BC bat species, females give birth to a single pup. Newborn LONG-EARED MYOTIS are naked, with a mass of 1.0 to 1.5 grams.

Mating presumably occurs in autumn or early winter. This is supported by the capture of males with stored sperm in late August, and substantially diminished levels of stored sperm by late September and early October.

Insect pheromone trap checked by Erin McLeod as part of Nakusp and Area Community Forest DOUGLAS-FIR BEETLE monitoring. PHOTO: FRANCES SWAN

LONG-EARED MYOTIS have been found in these narrow traps, unable to escape because of the slippery inside surfaces. Erin McLeod reported that seven bats were found; four of the nine traps deployed for 13 to 15 weeks each summer for two years were discovered to contain bats. PHOTO: ERIN MCLEOD

MIGRATION AND WINTER

Winter records for BC are lacking, and this bat's winter biology is poorly documented throughout its range. On southern Vancouver Island in winter, Lausen recorded LONG-EARED MYOTIS flying in and out of mines, and in a building attic roost. Several caves on Vancouver Island are also thought to be hibernacula for this species, based on early fall presence. Lausen has recorded calls of LONG-EARED MYOTIS in winter at low-elevation mines (approximately 500 to 700 metres) in the West Kootenay. No definitive recordings of LONG-EARED MYOTIS have been made in the south Okanagan, despite acoustic monitoring during winter.

In the western United States, a few individuals have been found hibernating in caves and mines. There is also a December record from coastal Oregon of an individual LONG-EARED MYOTIS found hibernating in a garage.

CONSERVATION STATUS

This species is considered secure by BC conservation agencies. In 2003, COSEWIC designated coastal populations as Data Deficient under the species name KEEN'S MYOTIS. Forest harvesting and disturbance to roosting sites in caves were considered potential threats, but the uncertain taxonomy prompted the listing of Data Deficient. LONG-EARED MYOTIS has been found with white-nose syndrome. With KEEN'S MYOTIS now reduced to a coastal subspecies of LONG-EARED MYOTIS, an updated COSEWIC assessment that includes all Canadian populations of LONG-EARED MYOTIS is needed.

TAXONOMY AND VARIATION

Myotis evotis now includes the former species KEEN'S MYOTIS. This recent taxonomic revision was proposed because no genetic differences were found between these two purported species in the northern half of the LONG-EARED MYOTIS range, including the entire range of the formerly recognized KEEN'S MYOTIS. Mitochondrial DNA has proven uninformative in several genetic studies of LONG-EARED MYOTIS, and examination of breeding patterns using nuclear DNA revealed widespread interbreeding and no genetic structure.

Based on skull morphology and pelage colour, six subspecies are recognized, with two found in BC. Nonetheless, a genetic study across the entire range is required to assess the validity of these races.

➤ *Myotis evotis pacificus* Dalquest—A small, dark coastal subspecies ranging from coastal California, Oregon, Washington and western BC to as far north as the Stikine River and Atlin. According to subspecies taxonomy of Richard Manning, populations previously classified as KEEN'S MYOTIS would be assigned to this race.

➤ *Myotis evotis chrysonotus* (J.A. Allen)—A paler, larger subspecies that inhabits most of the western United States and western Canada. In BC, it is found throughout the Interior.

MEASUREMENTS

A significant cline in forearm lengths exists for LONG-EARED MYOTIS, with longer forearms documented in southeast BC and progressively shorter average forearm lengths moving west and north in the province.* The shortest forearm length is found in the farthest northwest locations, where substantial numbers of measurements have been collected (Haida Gwaii, Hazelton). Females are larger than males (see table on page 76).

Total length (mm):	92	(74–103)	n = 54
Tail vertebrae length (mm):	42	(31–50)	n = 51
Hind foot (mm):	9	(7–11)	n = 51
Ear (mm):	18.5	(15–21)	n = 209
Tragus (mm):	10.4	(8–12.7)	n = 206
Forearm (mm):	37.9	(34.3–40.6)	n = 231
Wingspan (mm):	271	(243–294)	n = 21
Mass (g):	5.9	(4.3–8.9)	n = 202

REMARKS

With the recent taxonomic change, it's important to note that information for KEEN'S MYOTIS in the 1993 edition of this handbook, and various government reports, including the 2003 COSEWIC report, now apply to a subspecies of LONG-EARED MYOTIS. Several wildlife habitat areas have been designated in BC for KEEN'S MYOTIS, and for all but the most recent one, KEEN'S was a provincially Red-listed species when they were created.

Despite its widespread distribution in BC, remarkably little is known about the basic biology of LONG-EARED MYOTIS, particularly in coastal forest habitats.

There is a published record of a NORTH AMERICAN RACER from the Okanagan with a dead LONG-EARED MYOTIS in its mouth.

On Salt Spring Island, a CALIFORNIAN MYOTIS was found dead next to a LONG-EARED MYOTIS, entangled in the spines of a FULLER'S TEASEL.

REFERENCES

Barclay (1991); Carstens and Dewey (2010); Chruszcz and Barclay (2003); COSEWIC (2003); Davis et al. (1997); Dewey (2006); Faure and Barclay (1992); Fenton, Merriam and Holroyd (1983); Lausen et al. (2019); Luszcz and Barclay (2016); Manning (1993); Ommundsen (2020); Slough et al. (2022); Vonhof and Barclay (1997); Wilson (2004); Wilson and Barclay (2006).

---

*   See graph in Lausen et al. (2019), page 276.

Little Brown Myotis

Myotis lucifugus

DESCRIPTION

LITTLE BROWN MYOTIS is a medium-sized myotis bat with no keel. The fur colour of LITTLE BROWN MYOTIS is extremely variable, with the dorsal fur ranging from yellow or olive in populations from the dry Interior to blackish in coastal populations. LITTLE BROWN MYOTIS has "mouse-ears" that exemplify the assignation to the genus *Myotis* (*Myotis* comes from the Greek for "mouse-eared"). Fur on the dorsal surface is long and glossy, while fur on the undersides is lighter, ranging from light brown to tan. Wing membranes and ears are dark brown. The ears are medium-sized, reaching the nostrils when laid forward; the tragus is blunt and about half the ear length; and the shape of tragus can vary from somewhat club-shaped to notched or triangular.

MORPHOLOGICALLY SIMILAR SPECIES

YUMA MYOTIS. Confusion with other myotis species in BC is possible, but examining the ear length and the calcar will differentiate LITTLE BROWN from six BC myotis species. The absence of a keel on the calcar distinguishes LITTLE BROWN MYOTIS from LONG-LEGGED MYOTIS, CALIFORNIAN MYOTIS and DARK-NOSED SMALL-FOOTED MYOTIS. The other three myotis species can be excluded based on examination of the ear: the ear and tragus of LITTLE BROWN MYOTIS are smaller than those of FRINGED MYOTIS, NORTHERN MYOTIS and LONG-EARED MYOTIS.

Among BC myotis bats, only LITTLE BROWN MYOTIS and YUMA MYOTIS lack a keel *and* have small to medium-length ears. Where both YUMA and LITTLE BROWN MYOTIS co-occur, they can be extremely difficult to differentiate using relative differences in morphological traits. YUMA MYOTIS is typically smaller (forearm less than 36 millimetres) with duller, shorter fur and a forehead

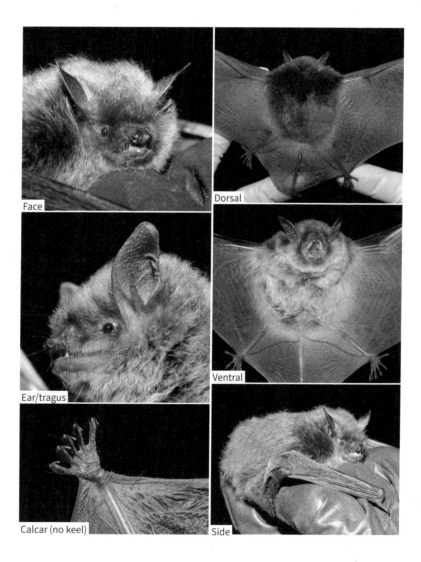

Face

Dorsal

Ear/tragus

Ventral

Calcar (no keel)

Side

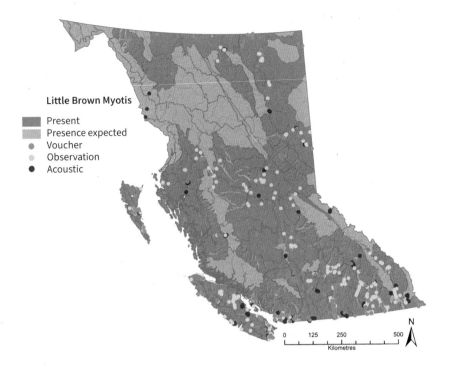

Little Brown Myotis

- Present
- Presence expected
- Voucher
- Observation
- Acoustic

0   125   250   500
Kilometres

N

that is steeply sloped relative to that of LITTLE BROWN MYOTIS. Although less than reliable, behavioural attributes may also be useful in identification, as LITTLE BROWN MYOTIS tends to be more defensive and audible than YUMA MYOTIS when handled. These two species are easily differentiated genetically, so a sample of DNA for mitochondrial DNA sequencing can provide the most conclusive identification.

Other than mitochondrial DNA genetic sequencing of a skin cell sample, the next most reliable way to differentiate YUMA MYOTIS from LITTLE BROWN MYOTIS is to conduct an acoustic bag test, which requires a bat detector, ideally one with a display of some form to visualize the calls while holding the bat. This is done by placing the bat in a small cotton bag and gently shaking it (move bag up and down) until it echolocates. The body of the calls (not including the toe) produced by YUMA MYOTIS will have a frequency of 45 kilohertz (or as low as 42 kilohertz). In contrast, the call of LITTLE BROWN MYOTIS will drop below 40 kilohertz, and sometimes as low as 30 kilohertz, providing a clear distinction between the species. A bag test result of approximately 40 to 42 kilohertz is uninformative and ambiguous, but by considering both forearm length and minimum call frequency together, you can usually differentiate these two species with a degree of confidence.

LITTLE BROWN MYOTIS bats, especially those found in the northern reaches of the province, can have ears 14 millimetres long or greater and may be

ZERO-CROSS RECORDINGS

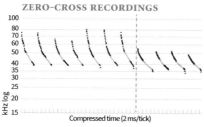

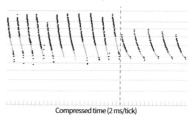

A. Low-clutter pulses, with the bat in the right pane tending toward lower frequencies; note the distinct elbow in the first, second and last pulses of the sequence in the left pane.

B. Higher-clutter pulses in left pane, and moderate-clutter pulses in right pane.

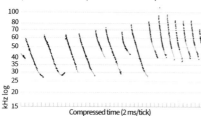

C. Low-frequency "grace notes" (second through fourth, sixth and eighth) produced within this sequence drop close to 25 kilohertz. (Recording by Karen Blejwas in Southeast Alaska.)

FULL-SPECTRUM RECORDINGS

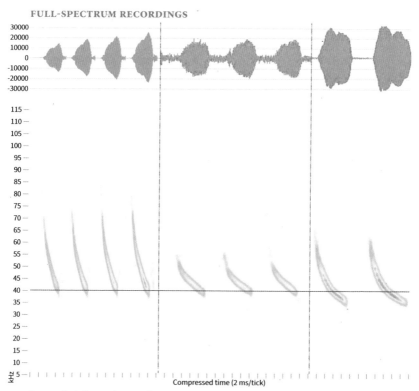

Progressively lower-clutter calls moving from left to right panes.

confused with NORTHERN MYOTIS where they co-occur. Both LITTLE BROWN MYOTIS and NORTHERN MYOTIS lack a keel and produce calls that end at 40 kilohertz, but NORTHERN MYOTIS has a longer, much pointier tragus and ears that are generally longer (though there can also be some overlap in ear length).

DISTRIBUTION

LITTLE BROWN MYOTIS is found throughout BC, including on the coastal islands of Haida Gwaii, Vancouver Island, Gulf Islands and various islands off the west coast of Vancouver Island. It is found throughout much of the United States and Canada.

ACOUSTIC CHARACTERISTICS

40 kilohertz. LITTLE BROWN MYOTIS shares echolocation call characteristics with three other bat species: NORTHERN MYOTIS, LONG-LEGGED MYOTIS and DARK-NOSED SMALL-FOOTED MYOTIS. Collectively this group of bats is referred to as the 40 kilohertz myotis bats, because calls are broadband but typically have minimum frequencies ranging from 35 to 42 kilohertz. Like YUMA MYOTIS, this species typically flies very close to calm water surfaces for an extended length of time (skimming; see spectrogram on page 276), and recordings made under these conditions may show sound wave interference patterns from reflected sound.

A wide variety of social sounds are made by LITTLE BROWN MYOTIS, though none can be identified as particularly diagnostic of the species. In some situations, LITTLE BROWN MYOTIS will produce one or several strangely low broadband sweeps among a normal echolocation call sequence ("grace notes" in zero-cross recording C); Lausen noted that a relatively higher portion of LITTLE BROWN MYOTIS recordings with these grace notes have come from northern BC or Yukon.

ACOUSTICALLY SIMILAR SPECIES

DARK-NOSED SMALL-FOOTED MYOTIS, LONG-LEGGED MYOTIS, NORTHERN MYOTIS, EASTERN RED BAT. The 40 kilohertz myotis bats are extremely difficult to differentiate acoustically in high clutter; however, when flying in an uncluttered environment, LITTLE BROWN MYOTIS typically reduces its call slope to well below that of a LONG-LEGGED, NORTHERN or DARK-NOSED SMALL-FOOTED MYOTIS flying in the open. LITTLE BROWN MYOTIS flying in the open will often produce calls of less than 60 octaves per second (and slopes may drop as low as 25 octaves per second). When flying in uncluttered spaces, LITTLE BROWN MYOTIS is more likely than other 40 kilohertz myotis to produce calls with a distinct knee (an abrupt change in call slope), often accompanied by a drop in minimum call frequency to 35 kilohertz.

EASTERN RED BAT can have similar minimum call frequency and low-sloped calls. While EASTERN RED BAT will usually show an undulating minimum frequency call pattern typical of a Lasiurine, this pattern is not always evident, especially if the call sequence is short. Additionally, an EASTERN RED BAT flying in clutter will have a call shape similar to that of a myotis flying in clutter, and will also have calls that end near 40 kilohertz, resulting in confusion with 40 kilohertz myotis species.

ROOSTING

LITTLE BROWN MYOTIS exploits a wide range of habitats in BC, from arid grassland and PONDEROSA PINE forest to humid coastal forest and northern boreal forest. With elevation records from sea level to 2,288 metres in the Rocky Mountains (Mount Assiniboine Provincial Park), LITTLE BROWN MYOTIS has the greatest altitudinal range of any BC bat. In the Alberta portion of the Rocky Mountains, males are more common than females at higher elevations. In the Cascade Mountains of western Washington, at elevations of 300 to 600 metres, few females were found, and none living at these elevations were reproductively active.

Summer roosts typically include buildings and other anthropogenic structures, including under tin roofs, under house siding, in bat boxes and in attic spaces. Natural summer roosts are in rock crevices, in cavities in trees, under tree bark and in caves. Cool roosts are typically used by males, while females seek warm roosts, especially late in gestation and while nursing when they congregate in large maternity colonies. Males rarely occupy nursery colonies, and in summer they can be found roosting singly or in small colonies, usually in sites that are cooler than the nurseries.

LITTLE BROWN MYOTIS arrive at maternity roosts in late spring, sometimes one to two months after YUMA MYOTIS have arrived at shared, mixed-species building or bat box maternity roosts. Females congregate in nursery colonies that may contain hundreds or even thousands of individuals. Reproductive females typically seek roosts with temperatures close to mammalian body temperature (37°C) or warmer while raising pups. This behaviour saves energy, as they don't need to generate heat to remain at active body temperature for milk production. Similarly, these warm roosts facilitate pup growth.

Several hundred LITTLE BROWN MYOTIS were discovered by cavers in an unusual natural site in a small cave on the Grayling River in northern BC. A hot (30°C), humid environment is maintained inside this cave by a nearby natural hot spring.

FEEDING

LITTLE BROWN MYOTIS are most frequently observed in old-growth mixed-wood forests and edge habitats adjacent to water; open areas are an attractive habitat element for LITTLE BROWN MYOTIS, allowing them to both drink and feed. One of few studies of food habit preferences done in BC comes from the southern Okanagan Valley. This study found that LITTLE BROWN MYOTIS hunted along the valley floor and nearby hills in PONDEROSA PINE forest, in openings between groups of trees, and over bluffs, lakes, rivers and irrigation flumes. Aquatic insects, such as midges, caddisflies and mayflies, are the major prey, although beetles, moths and other kinds of flies are also taken. The diet changes seasonally in response to insect abundance, with midges predominant in spring, and caddisflies and mayflies most important in summer. LITTLE BROWN MYOTIS can quickly adapt its hunting techniques to take advantage of local insect concentrations.

Most prey are captured in the air and eaten while flying. After an initial feeding period early in the night, individuals occupy temporary night roosts, which are most heavily used after temperatures have cooled (below 15°C) and aerial insect prey become less abundant. The selection of relatively warm night roost sites may allow LITTLE BROWN MYOTIS to avoid torpor, promoting rapid digestion of its meal. In Yukon, this species consumes a large number of spiders in its diet during periods of cold temperatures, suggesting the same may be true at the more northern BC locations with shorter growing seasons.

LITTLE BROWN MYOTIS is one of two species of bats in BC (in addition to YUMA MYOTIS) commonly observed flying just above the surface of the water for an extended period. Both species forage on insects on or above the water surface and occasionally dip down to the surface of the water with the bottom jaw open to drink water on the fly. Lausen has observed LITTLE BROWN MYOTIS skimming over ocean water, occasionally disturbing its surface, suggesting contact with salt water, although it is not known whether this is accidental or purposeful contact while foraging. Use of a spotlight to observe this water-skimming behaviour usually does not deter LITTLE BROWN MYOTIS, although YUMA MYOTIS will typically leave the area to avoid the bright light.

REPRODUCTION

Mating typically occurs in late summer and early fall during swarming, but may also occur in the winter, as males will mate with torpid females periodically. Like other myotis, females are presumed to store sperm during hibernation. If females have sufficient fat reserves in the spring, ovulation occurs, eggs are fertilized using stored sperm, and implantation occurs within a few days of emergence from hibernation. Examination of approximately 500 captures of adult females from across BC between June and early September revealed that 73% showed signs of being reproductive, having produced a pup either in the current year or in previous years. When reproduction was examined for success within a given year, 54% of adult females showed signs of having given birth to or nursed a pup.

Timing of parturition is variable and is determined at least in part by the timing of female arousal from hibernation. In the southern Okanagan Valley, females typically give birth between the second week of June and the second week of July. Young-of-year grow rapidly, nursed by lactating females. Lactating females generally return to the nursery roost several times per night.

By three weeks of age, the young are capable of flying, catching and consuming insect prey. Building and bat box roost monitoring studies across the province provide new fledging data yearly, though extrapolating data derived from studies of LITTLE BROWN versus YUMA MYOTIS may be unreliable because of the difficulty of identification. Captures of juvenile LITTLE BROWN MYOTIS in the Vancouver region found volant young-of-year starting in mid-July. There are a few reports of young-of-year fledging earlier: June 24 in the Flathead and June 20 at a Tranquille Creek barn roost near Kamloops. Populations living at higher elevations and northern latitudes also appear to spread out the birthing period over a longer time. Yukon studies report variation in when pups are born and become volant. Young-of-year LITTLE BROWN MYOTIS in bat boxes just north of Atlin were reported to fly by mid-July in 2013 and late July in 2014; near Watson Lake, Yukon, in 2006, LITTLE BROWN MYOTIS females didn't even give birth until mid-July and into early August.

MIGRATION AND WINTER

Adults leave nursery colonies in some areas as early as late July or early August. Before entering hibernation, there is a period in late summer and early autumn of swarming behaviour associated with mating. Gillian Sanders reported finding a banded adult female LITTLE BROWN MYOTIS in late September roosting in a building maternity roost at the north end of Kootenay Lake; it had been banded at a large bat box (a bat condominium) earlier that year in June, near Duck Lake, approximately 150 kilometres away.

East of the Rocky Mountains, LITTLE BROWN MYOTIS uses caves and abandoned mines for hibernation; however, few confirmed overwintering sites for this species have been reported west of the Rockies. This is likely due to sample bias, given that many winter records are observations in which bats have not been handled or genetically sampled to verify species. Unlike YUMA MYOTIS, which has a growing number of winter observations in buildings, LITTLE BROWN MYOTIS has only been confirmed in the winter at one house in the West Kootenay, where two females (one adult, November 7; one volant young-of-year November 27) were captured in mist-nets while free-flying outside a house roost where YUMA MYOTIS was already known to roost year-round and LITTLE BROWN MYOTIS was known to roost in the summer.

Hibernacula in caves in Alberta and the Northwest Territories host anywhere from several hundred to over 3,000 bats. Male bias in cave hibernacula suggests that reproductive adult females may seek out different hibernation features.

In BC, hibernation records are limited to a historic record of a single LITTLE BROWN MYOTIS hibernating with several TOWNSEND'S BIG-EARED BATS in a mine near Williams Lake on November 17. Locations of winter hibernacula for most of the BC population are otherwise unknown. A rocky outcrop feature in the Peace River region is suspected of housing hibernating LITTLE BROWN and NORTHERN MYOTIS. Underground cavities surrounding the roots of trees might provide extensive opportunities for bats to hibernate; Karen Blejwas used radiotelemetry and motion-sensing cameras to document LITTLE BROWN MYOTIS moving into tree root wads and crevices in talus slopes in southeast Alaska for the winter.

Hibernation likely begins in September or October, depending on the local climate, though this may not hold true in areas where insect activity continues well into the fall. Laura Matthias, Peter Ommundsen and others acoustically recorded LITTLE BROWN MYOTIS on Salt Spring Island from March 30 to November 4 (2014 to 2019 inventories). Male LITTLE BROWN MYOTIS readying for breeding (large testes producing sperm) have been reported flying in large numbers near cave entrances (e.g., Weymer Creek cave system) on Vancouver Island in late summer. By early October, these sites have few bats, suggesting that some may move to different sites for hibernation. Few reproductive females were reported at these caves, and none until early September, so they may mate at different sites. LITTLE BROWN MYOTIS are thought to hibernate in the Weymer Creek cave system, where the winter microclimates range from 2.4°C to 4°C at 100% relative humidity.

Hibernacula are generally in different locations than summer roosts. In Alberta, Dave Hobson used banding records to determine that LITTLE BROWN MYOTIS travel distances of up to 600 kilometres between summer and winter roosts. Although migration distances are unknown in BC, LITTLE BROWN MYOTIS may travel shorter distances in the more temperate climates of southern and coastal BC. Migration behaviour is also not known, though mortalities of this species under wind turbines in the Peace River region suggests that LITTLE BROWN MYOTIS in northeast BC may migrate between summer and winter locations. Lausen has acoustically recorded LITTLE BROWN MYOTIS at Kootenay Pass (1,775 metres) from May to September. Spikes of activity in August and September suggest migration.

In the BC Interior, hibernation probably lasts until April or early May. Male LITTLE BROWN MYOTIS remain in hibernation in Cadomin Cave, Alberta, until mid-May; however, in coastal regions this bat may arouse in late winter. LITTLE BROWN MYOTIS has been found feeding in coastal Oregon in mid-March.

CONSERVATION STATUS

Although population estimates are not available for LITTLE BROWN MYOTIS, it is considered one of the most abundant bats in BC; however, accurate estimates are likely confounded as a result of confusion in differentiating it from the morphologically and ecologically similar YUMA MYOTIS, and the tendency for these two species to roost in the same structures.

LITTLE BROWN MYOTIS was assessed as Endangered by COSEWIC in an emergency assessment completed in 2013 and is now listed under Canada's federal Species at Risk Act. The national listing was in response to large mortalities observed in populations in eastern Canada and in the United States from white-nose syndrome. Infection by the fungus results in high mortality rates for LITTLE BROWN MYOTIS during hibernation, with reported average declines in abundance at hibernacula of 73% within two years of infection. LITTLE BROWN MYOTIS has virtually disappeared from areas of eastern Canada because of mass mortality from white-nose syndrome, so it is possible that this may also occur in western Canada as the disease spreads.

Provincially this species is listed as secure. Other threats include the disturbance or displacement of maternity colonies from human-made structures, and fatalities at wind energy sites. At one wind energy site in northeastern BC, LITTLE BROWN MYOTIS accounted for 34% of bat fatalities. As with other bat species in BC that tend to raise young in colonies, LITTLE BROWN MYOTIS roosts in cavities of mature trees or snags, features reduced by commercial timber harvest; the impact of forestry on bats in BC is poorly understood.

TAXONOMY AND VARIATION

Six subspecies are traditionally recognized (mostly based on fur colour), with three found in BC:

> *Myotis lucifugus alascensis* Miller—A dark subspecies that ranges from California to southeast Alaska and is found throughout most of the province.

> *Myotis lucifugus carissima* Thomas—A pale subspecies that inhabits part of the western United States, southern Alberta, and the dry southern Interior of BC.

> *Myotis lucifugus lucifugus* (Le Conte)—A widespread subspecies that inhabits eastern and central North America, restricted to extreme northern BC.

Various authorities disagree on range boundaries of subspecies in the province. Moreover, genetic studies have produced controversy about their validity and classification. A recent study revealed extensive genetic exchange among LITTLE BROWN MYOTIS populations across western Canada and Alaska; this supports findings of extensive gene flow among two subspecies (*M. l. carissima* and *M. l. lucifugus*). These races were thought to have once been separated by glaciation but now fully interbreed as one population, roost together and cannot be differentiated using any morphological traits. Another genetic study recommended that, because the three subspecies represent distinct evolutionary lines, they be recognized as separate "phylogenetic species" regardless of gene flow (see What Is a Species?, page 6). The only LITTLE BROWN MYOTIS population in BC that exhibits some restriction in gene flow (i.e., geographically limited breeding) is the isolated population on Haida Gwaii.

MEASUREMENTS

As with many species, males are smaller than females (see table on page 76). Male LITTLE BROWN MYOTIS have significantly shorter forearm lengths than females in individuals captured west of the Continental Divide, in BC. The same significant size difference exists on the east side of the Continental Divide in BC and Alberta.

Examination of ear lengths for this species in BC and Yukon revealed that northern latitude (greater than 59°N) LITTLE BROWN MYOTIS have longer ears (mean 13.1 millimetres, range 11–15, n = 106) than southern individuals (less than 57°N; mean 12.0 millimetres, range 10–14, n = 145). This trend, together with increasing forearm length with latitude (see graph on page 77) supports the phenomenon referred to as Bergmann's rule, where animals are larger in colder environments. Although LITTLE BROWN MYOTIS is considered one breeding population across Canada, LITTLE BROWN MYOTIS at similar latitudes on either side of the Rocky Mountain Continental Divide differ significantly, with individuals having a longer forearm length on the eastern side (38.0 millimetres, range 34.2–41.6, n = 1,504) of the Rockies than on the western side (36.4 millimetres, range 32.7–40.8, n = 1,210).

Total length (mm):	86	(70–108)	n = 383
Tail vertebrae length (mm):	37	(25–59)	n = 379
Hind foot (mm):	10	(6–13)	n = 385
Ear (mm):	12.1	(10–15)	n = 161
Tragus (mm):	6.3	(4–9)	n = 155
Forearm (mm):	36.5	(32.5–40.2)	n = 706
Wingspan (mm):	248	(224–274)	n = 151
Mass (g):	6.7	(4.2–12.8)	n = 588

REMARKS

Although LITTLE BROWN MYOTIS is currently widespread and commonly encountered in BC, there is still much to be learned about the basic biology of this species. Detrimental population-wide effects from white-nose syndrome are anticipated to be significant, based on observed impacts in eastern North America. This species regularly occupies bat boxes throughout BC and into Yukon.

LITTLE BROWN MYOTIS has the longest recorded longevity of any BC bat, living up to 38 years (data from a banded bat in Alberta observed by Dave Hobson).

REFERENCES

Aldridge (1986), Barclay (1991), Burles et al. (2008, 2009), COSEWIC (2013), Davis et al. (1999), Davy et al. (2015, 2017), Fenton (1970), Fenton and Barclay (1980), Frick et al. (2010), Grindal et al. (1992), Herd and Fenton (1983), Humphrey and Cope (1976), Jobin (1952), Jung and Kukka (2014), Kaupas and Barclay (2017), Lausen et al. (2008), Morales and Carstens (2018), Schowalter, Gunson and Harder (1979), Talerico (2008), Thomas (1988).

Dark-Nosed Small-Footed Myotis *Myotis melanorhinus*

DESCRIPTION

DARK-NOSED SMALL-FOOTED MYOTIS is the smallest myotis species in BC. There is a distinct keel on the calcar and the foot is small (average 7 millimetres). Hairs are bicoloured (light and dark), and fur colour varies from pale tan to orange yellow on the dorsal surface; the ventral surface is paler, appearing buff. The black area around the eyes contrasts with paler fur, giving the appearance of a facial mask, and the ears are relatively long, reaching or extending past the tip of the nose when laid forward.

MORPHOLOGICALLY SIMILAR SPECIES

CALIFORNIAN MYOTIS, other myotis (e.g., YUMA MYOTIS, LITTLE BROWN MYOTIS, LONG-LEGGED MYOTIS), CANYON BAT. While other small- to medium-sized myotis may present some superficial similarity, DARK-NOSED SMALL-FOOTED MYOTIS has a keeled calcar and can be differentiated from YUMA and LITTLE BROWN MYOTIS on this trait alone. DARK-NOSED SMALL-FOOTED MYOTIS is one of only three myotis species in BC that features a prominent keel on the calcar (CALIFORNIAN and LONG-LEGGED MYOTIS are the other two myotis with a keel in BC). LONG-LEGGED MYOTIS has hairy armpits, and a much longer forearm (approximately 40 millimetres) than the smaller DARK-NOSED SMALL-FOOTED MYOTIS (forearm 29 to 35 millimetres).

Where they co-occur, DARK-NOSED SMALL-FOOTED MYOTIS and CALIFORNIAN MYOTIS are difficult to differentiate. The dark facial fur of DARK-NOSED SMALL-FOOTED MYOTIS gives the appearance of a facial mask, and several tail vertebrae extend past the edge of the tail membrane; CALIFORNIAN MYOTIS generally lacks a pronounced facial mask and does not have tail vertebrae extending beyond the tail membrane. The naked area on the snout of DARK-NOSED SMALL-FOOTED MYOTIS is rectangular, with a length about one and a half times the width at the nostrils, whereas the bare snout of CALIFORNIAN MYOTIS is relatively square, with equal width and length (see images in key on page 102). The thumb (including the claw) of CALIFORNIAN MYOTIS is relatively short (average 3.8 millimetres, range 3–5), while the thumb of DARK-NOSED SMALL-FOOTED MYOTIS is longer (average 5.0 millimetres, range 4–6.5). The forehead of CALIFORNIAN MYOTIS is more steeply sloped than that of DARK-NOSED SMALL-FOOTED MYOTIS (see Appendix 2).

Face

Dorsal

Ear/tragus

Ventral

Side

Tail membrane (keel and tail vertebrae)

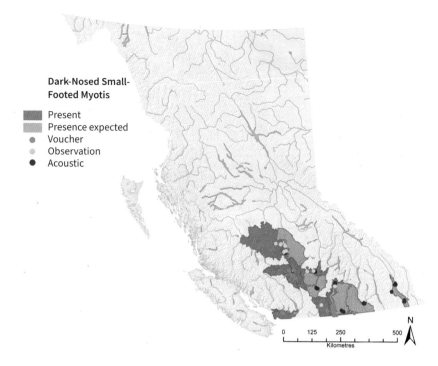

Dark-Nosed Small-Footed Myotis

- Present
- Presence expected
- Voucher
- Observation
- Acoustic

Although considered accidental in BC, CANYON BAT can be confused with DARK-NOSED SMALL-FOOTED MYOTIS. CANYON BAT also has a dark mask, but it is far more pronounced. Further, CANYON BAT has a round ear and a club-shaped tragus, unlike the pointier ear and tragus of DARK-NOSED SMALL-FOOTED MYOTIS.

DISTRIBUTION

DARK-NOSED SMALL-FOOTED MYOTIS range from Mexico north to BC, and west of the Great Plains in the United States. In BC, it occurs in the Okanagan and Similkameen valleys as far north as Oyama and Keremeos. DARK-NOSED SMALL-FOOTED MYOTIS also occurs throughout the lower-elevation grassland valley bottoms of the Thompson and Fraser River valleys and north to at least Sword Creek near Williams Lake. It is also found along the southern reaches of the Fraser River. Based on suitable habitat, and occurrences in the neighbouring states, it may also occur in the Trail, Creston and/or Cranbrook regions.

ACOUSTIC CHARACTERISTICS

40 kilohertz. DARK-NOSED SMALL-FOOTED MYOTIS is one of four 40 kilohertz myotis species, so it is difficult to differentiate acoustically from several other myotis. In high-clutter foraging situations (e.g., approaching vegetation), minimum call frequencies can be as high as 43 to 45 kilohertz. Its acoustic tendencies are consistent with other long-eared bats. It has been observed to

ZERO-CROSS RECORDINGS

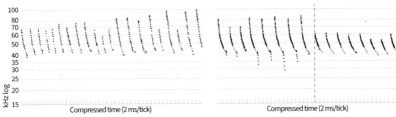

A. High-clutter pulses.

B. Moderate-clutter pulses in left pane and lower-clutter (open environment) calls in right pane.

FULL-SPECTRUM RECORDINGS

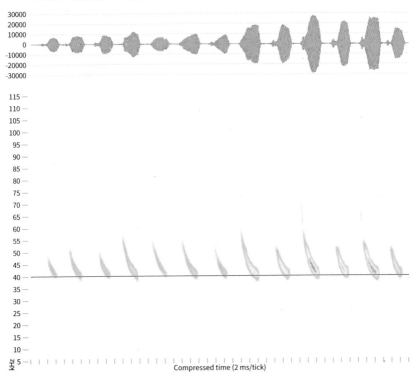

Open environment.

approach the ground and vegetation closely, probably to glean insect prey, and it produces relatively steep echolocation calls, even in open environments.

The tendency toward calls that sweep very quickly through a broad band of frequencies, even in open environments (i.e., grasslands), allows DARK-NOSED SMALL-FOOTED MYOTIS to be acoustically differentiated from LITTLE BROWN MYOTIS, which tends toward low-sloped and lower-frequency calls in the same environments, although confusion with LONG-LEGGED MYOTIS is still possible.

ACOUSTICALLY SIMILAR SPECIES

LONG-LEGGED MYOTIS, LITTLE BROWN MYOTIS, NORTHERN MYOTIS, CALIFORNIAN MYOTIS. Recordings of DARK-NOSED SMALL-FOOTED MYOTIS may be confused with any other 40 kilohertz myotis (LONG-LEGGED, LITTLE BROWN, NORTHERN MYOTIS) and occasionally with CALIFORNIAN MYOTIS. While CALIFORNIAN MYOTIS typically produces calls that end at 50 kilohertz, it can also produce calls as low as 43 kilohertz when foraging in uncluttered environments. In these instances, it might be confused with a DARK-NOSED SMALL-FOOTED MYOTIS foraging close to the ground, which sometimes produces higher minimum frequencies (i.e., both species may overlap in minimum frequencies around 43 kilohertz).

ROOSTING

DARK-NOSED SMALL-FOOTED MYOTIS is associated with cliffs and rock outcrops in arid valleys and badland habitats. Elevational records in BC range from 300 to 700 metres. Summer roosts have been found in cliffs, boulders, vertical banks, holes in the ground, talus slopes and under rocks on the ground. Roosting sites are usually situated in small, protected crevices where the environment is dry and hot (27°C to 33°C). One noteworthy roosting observation was of a mixed colony of males and pregnant female DARK-NOSED SMALL-FOOTED MYOTIS in California, under the wallpaper in the interior of an abandoned house. Small caves, abandoned mine adits and buildings can be used as night roosts.

In Alberta, the closely related WESTERN SMALL-FOOTED MYOTIS shows high fidelity to small roosting areas (approximately 100 metres straight-line distance across roosting area), regardless of sex. Radio-tracking, banding records (recaptures) and genetic studies near Empress, Alberta, confirm that male WESTERN SMALL-FOOTED MYOTIS return to natal areas and roost near mothers, with males roosting alone and females roosting alone, in pairs or in small clusters of up to five individuals. While natal philopatry is commonly observed among females of many bat species in North America, male natal philopatry is far less common.

FEEDING

Research near Vaseux Lake showed that DARK-NOSED SMALL-FOOTED MYOTIS fed primarily on caddisflies, though other flies, beetles and moths were also included in the diet. DARK-NOSED SMALL-FOOTED MYOTIS regularly hunts over the edge of rocky bluffs or grassy slopes, approaching the ground closely (within 1 metre); it also will forage over water, but generally only in areas where it does not co-occur with CALIFORNIAN MYOTIS. DARK-NOSED SMALL-FOOTED MYOTIS tends to forage in circles; in Alberta, Lausen commonly observed the closely related WESTERN SMALL-FOOTED MYOTIS circling cottonwood tree trunks in riparian areas and within eroded features (e.g., tunnels) of river valley walls.

REPRODUCTION

Mating presumably takes place in autumn, before hibernation. Scrotal males of the closely related WESTERN SMALL-FOOTED MYOTIS have been observed as early as mid-July in southern Alberta. Females usually have a single young, though there is a record of twins in WESTERN SMALL-FOOTED MYOTIS from South Dakota. In BC, pregnant females have been observed from June 21 to July 13 and nursing females from June 13 to August 3. This suggests that young are born from mid-June to mid-July. In Lillooet, volant juveniles were captured on August 4.

MIGRATION AND WINTER

DARK-NOSED SMALL-FOOTED MYOTIS hibernates during the winter in BC. Hibernating DARK-NOSED SMALL-FOOTED MYOTIS usually wedge themselves into tight crevices or depressions in the ceiling of the hibernaculum, with their undersides pressed against the ceiling and their heads facing outwards. These sites presumably provide a stable environment. Individuals tend to hibernate alone.

Mike Sarell and Cori Lausen observed a small number of individuals roosting in South Okanagan mines in mid-winter. In January 1992, DARK-NOSED SMALL-FOOTED MYOTIS was observed and photographed hibernating in a limestone cave near Williams Lake, where the temperature was 3°C.

The largest recorded number of hibernating DARK-NOSED SMALL-FOOTED MYOTIS (estimated at more than 40, mainly solitary, roosting individuals) was observed by Lausen and others at a mine between Grand Forks and Greenwood (elevation approximately 1,500 metres). Winter conditions there range from 0.5°C to 3°C and 60% to 97% relative humidity. Hundreds of TOWNSEND'S BIG-EARED BATS also hibernated at the site.

In the Okanagan, individuals have been recorded flying during the winter, along with other species that overwinter in this region, including BIG BROWN BAT and CALIFORNIAN MYOTIS.

DARK-NOSED SMALL-FOOTED MYOTIS is on the province's Blue List. Population trends are unknown, but the major threat is likely disturbance by cavers, hikers or geocachers, whose activities may negatively affect hibernating populations during the winter. A few known hibernacula in BC are gated to control access by humans. Summer roosts are situated in cliffs and rock faces; these may also be vulnerable to disturbance by rock climbers.

TAXONOMY AND VARIATION

In the 1993 edition of this handbook, DARK-NOSED SMALL-FOOTED MYOTIS was treated as the WESTERN SMALL-FOOTED MYOTIS, but in this edition we adopt the somewhat inconclusive taxonomic change to DARK-NOSED SMALL-FOOTED MYOTIS to follow batnames.org, the authority on bat taxonomy. Until recently, *Myotis melanorhinus* was classified as one of two subspecies of the WESTERN SMALL-FOOTED MYOTIS: *Myotis ciliolabrum ciliolabrum* in the Prairies and *Myotis ciliolabrum melanorhinus* west of the Great Plains. Various authorities now recognize the western populations as a distinct species, including the 2018 *Mammal Species of the World* database produced by the American Society of Mammalogists, and the IUCN Red List. However, both species of small-footed myotis are distinguished mainly by minor differences in pelage colour and a few differences in skull morphology. Genetic studies are needed to resolve the taxonomy of the small-footed myotis.

MEASUREMENTS

Total length (mm):	83	(72–90)	n = 44
Tail vertebrae length (mm):	38	(32–45)	n = 44
Hind foot (mm):	7	(6–8)	n = 44
Ear (mm):	13.0	(11–15)	n = 32
Tragus (mm):	6.6	(4–9)	n = 32
Forearm (mm):	32.2	(28.8–34.8)	n = 83
Wingspan (mm):	221	(205–245)	n = 25
Mass (g):	4.3	(2.6–6.1)	n = 55

REMARKS

DARK-NOSED SMALL-FOOTED MYOTIS occurs in the Okanagan and Similkameen valleys; captures along the Fraser River in Lillooet also confirm its presence in the Cariboo. A discovery of an individual DARK-NOSED SMALL-FOOTED MYOTIS hibernating at Williams Lake also suggests that this bat overwinters in parts of the Cariboo region in addition to the Okanagan/Similkameen regions. In

July 2020, an adult parous female DARK-NOSED SMALL-FOOTED MYOTIS was found less than 1 kilometre from the Fraser River in Maple Ridge. This is the first record of this species along the lower Fraser River. Seth Bennett, Emma Zinck and Chris Currie confirmed the identification using morphology.

Along the border of southern Alberta and north-central Montana, male and female WESTERN SMALL-FOOTED MYOTIS roost in closely related clusters (family units consisting of a mother and offspring), each geographically and genetically distinct from neighbouring clusters; related individuals roost singly or in small groups in rock crevices within approximately 100 metres of each other, along a length of river valley. This is in stark contrast to other prairie bat species roosting in river valleys, such as female BIG BROWN BATS, which roost in unrelated groups. Population genetics studies are needed for DARK-NOSED SMALL-FOOTED MYOTIS to determine if similar genetic structuring occurs.

REFERENCES

Arroyo-Cabrales and Álvarez-Castañeda (2017), Constantine (1998), Gannon et al. (2001), Genter (1986), Holloway and Barclay (2001), Lausen (2007), Lausen and Barclay (2006a), Mammal Diversity Database (2020), Metheny et al. (2008), Rodriguez and Ammerman (2004), Simmons (2005), Tuttle and Heaney (1974), van Zyll de Jong (1984), Woodsworth (1981).

Northern Myotis   *Myotis septentrionalis*

DESCRIPTION

NORTHERN MYOTIS is a medium-sized bat with no keel and uniformly coloured dark brown fur on the back (Alberta specimens may be lighter brown). Fur on the underside is paler, varying from tawny to pale brown. The ears and flight membranes are dark brown but not black. The ears are long, extending beyond the nose when laid forward; the tragus is a key diagnostic trait used to distinguish NORTHERN MYOTIS from four other non-keeled myotis species where their ranges overlap. In NORTHERN MYOTIS, the tragus is long, narrow and sharply pointed. The edge of the tail membrane is bare or with only a few sparsely spaced hairs. Some individuals have an indistinct keel on the calcar.

MORPHOLOGICALLY SIMILAR SPECIES

LONG-EARED MYOTIS, LITTLE BROWN MYOTIS. In BC, the range of NORTHERN MYOTIS overlaps with only one other myotis species that has long ears: LONG-EARED MYOTIS. NORTHERN MYOTIS can be distinguished from LONG-EARED MYOTIS by its relatively paler (brown) and shorter ears (less than 18 millimetres). NORTHERN MYOTIS also has a long, narrow (sharp-tipped) pointed tragus, unlike LONG-EARED MYOTIS, in which the tragus is blunt at the tip. The shoulder fur of NORTHERN MYOTIS, when gently blown to expose the base of the fur, is uniform in colour, while LONG-EARED MYOTIS typically has bicoloured shoulder hairs, with dark bases and lighter tips.

LITTLE BROWN MYOTIS, especially northern populations, can also have long ears, and this invites potential confusion with NORTHERN MYOTIS; however, the sharply pointed tragus of NORTHERN MYOTIS can be used to differentiate it from LITTLE BROWN MYOTIS, which has a blunt tragus.

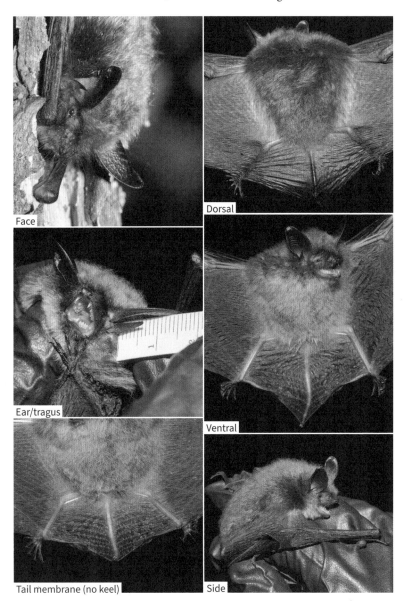

Face

Dorsal

Ear/tragus

Ventral

Tail membrane (no keel)

Side

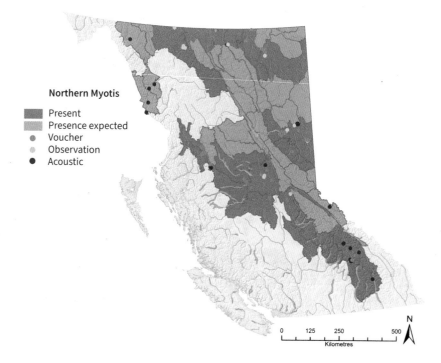

Northern Myotis
- Present
- Presence expected
- ● Voucher
- Observation
- ● Acoustic

0   125   250   500
Kilometres

N

DISTRIBUTION

Although largely considered an "eastern" bat species because most of its North American range occurs in the eastern United States and Canada, NORTHERN MYOTIS has been confirmed through captures in northern and eastern BC. The southernmost capture record in BC is in the West Kootenay at Staubert Lake, and captures have occurred at various locations in southeastern Yukon. We don't know how far west the range of NORTHERN MYOTIS extends; there are capture records in the Hazelton area, acoustic recordings by Lausen along the Stikine River, and some acoustic recordings in the Atlin area that are suggestive of this species. Capture of this species will be needed to confirm its presence in the northwest part of the province.

ACOUSTIC CHARACTERISTICS

40 kilohertz. NORTHERN MYOTIS is capable of gleaning insect prey from surfaces and is highly adapted to foraging in forested habitats. As such, it produces short-duration, high-frequency, low-intensity calls, and its perception distance is shorter than other bats with more aerial foraging habits (such as LITTLE BROWN MYOTIS). The broadband frequency sweeps emitted by NORTHERN MYOTIS typically end at 42–45 kilohertz, but minimum frequencies can drop below 40 kilohertz, especially in open environments. Its calls are typically short, often less than 2 milliseconds. A relatively high-clutter call pattern is produced

ZERO-CROSS RECORDINGS

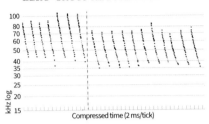

High-clutter pulses in left pane, with lower-clutter pulses as sequence progresses in right pane.

FULL-SPECTRUM RECORDINGS

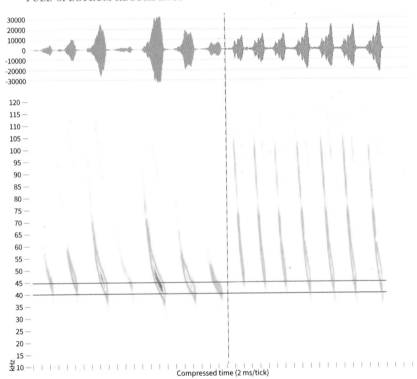

Free-flying hand-released bat in open environment in left pane, and higher-clutter calls during bat-kiting in right pane.

even when the bat flies in the open, indicative of its evolution as a forest bat. While the calls of this species appear highly linear in clutter, they can take on a noticeable curvature in an open environment.

Because these bats are typically focused on vegetative surfaces close to them as they navigate through clutter, their calls are often quiet, and they are therefore often under-represented in acoustic inventories. Additionally, acoustic inventories typically situate bat detectors in open environments to record low-clutter call types, maximizing the likelihood of identifying recordings to the level of species, rather than groups of species (e.g., myotis). NORTHERN MYOTIS may be under-represented in acoustic surveys because it spends much of its time flying within the forest under the canopy where bat detectors are not typically deployed.

ACOUSTICALLY SIMILAR SPECIES

LITTLE BROWN MYOTIS, LONG-LEGGED MYOTIS, YUMA MYOTIS, CALIFORNIAN MYOTIS. In a cluttered foraging environment, NORTHERN MYOTIS can be confused with the two other 40 kilohertz myotis species that have overlapping geographic ranges in BC: LITTLE BROWN MYOTIS and LONG-LEGGED MYOTIS. In open environments, call slopes decrease, and although slopes remain steeper than those of LITTLE BROWN MYOTIS, they can have considerable overlap with LONG-LEGGED MYOTIS. Additionally, there may be overlap with YUMA and CALIFORNIAN MYOTIS in clutter, as NORTHERN MYOTIS can produce end frequencies that approach 45 kilohertz, overlapping with these two high-frequency species. Recordings of bats flying in clutter are unlikely to yield confident identifications for any of these species. NORTHERN MYOTIS, if recorded when close to the microphone, is more likely than other myotis to produce calls that start as high as 120 kilohertz, and its calls are likely to sweep through the greatest bandwidth in the least amount of time relative to any of these other myotis species.

ROOSTING

NORTHERN MYOTIS is generally associated with boreal forests. Data on habitat use in BC are largely from Mount Revelstoke National Park and surrounding areas, where roosts were detected in mixed forests of WESTERN REDCEDAR and WESTERN HEMLOCK at approximately 700 to 800 metres, and from deciduous forests in the Liard and Peace areas. Nagorsen, Lausen and Doug Burles captured this species frequently in the Hazelton townsite in a small residual mixed forest stand composed of WESTERN REDCEDAR, TREMBLING ASPEN, mature BLACK COTTONWOOD and PAPER BIRCH. These observations provide evidence that NORTHERN MYOTIS does inhabit residential areas in the northern part of the province.

Tree roosts have been described in the Trout Lake area (Staubert Lake), the Liard area (near Fort Nelson), the Kiskatinaw River valley near Dawson Creek, and in Mount Revelstoke National Park. A non-reproductive adult female was captured at Staubert Lake and radio-tracked. This bat used a variety of tree roosts (WESTERN REDCEDAR snag, live WESTERN REDCEDAR and live WESTERN HEMLOCK) and foraged nightly within the old-growth patch of WESTERN REDCEDAR forest where it was initially captured.

A study near Fort Nelson found male and female tree roosts in mature stands of TREMBLING ASPEN and BALSAM POPLAR. Female roosts were mostly in the crevices of bark on tree trunks, usually low to the ground (less than 5 metres above ground) and contained between 1 and 58 bats. Males roosted alone and typically under loose bark. Similarly, Brian Paterson and others found that in the southern Peace River region, NORTHERN MYOTIS used decaying trembling aspen, 30 centimetres in diameter at breast height or larger, with longitudinal cracks from fire or frost.

Radio-tracking of reproductive females in the Liard area, near Fort Nelson, located two types of tree roosts—partly live TREMBLING ASPEN and BALSAM POPLAR. In total, six roost trees were found, all located in mature to old forest stands. Of the two tree roosts that could be accessed, at least five individual bats were seen roosting together. Similarly, Paterson in the southern Peace River region tracked females moving between a set of tree roosts, often switching daily and roosting in small groups (up to six bats) of variable membership.

In Mount Revelstoke National Park, radio-tracking of NORTHERN MYOTIS located nine roosts in WESTERN REDCEDAR, WESTERN HEMLOCK and WESTERN WHITE PINE trees. The roosts were all in large trees with extensive canopy cover; no roosts occurred in rock crevices.

FEEDING

NORTHERN MYOTIS hunts over small ponds and in forests under the tree canopy. Much of its hunting activity is 1 to 3 metres above the ground, just above the understorey but below the forest canopy and often in cluttered habitat. NORTHERN MYOTIS are most easily captured in mist-nets placed across narrow forest trails, as they search for food and glean insects from vegetation. A radio-tracking study conducted in Prince Edward Island reported that NORTHERN MYOTIS prefers to forage under forest canopy but will also forage in open areas less than 100 metres from the forest edge.

The diverse diet includes caddisflies, moths, beetles, flies and leafhoppers. Laboratory experiments demonstrate that the ears of at least some moth species are not sensitive to the high-frequency echolocation calls emitted by NORTHERN MYOTIS. NORTHERN MYOTIS listen for and use prey-generated sounds when gleaning; one study showed that cessation of sounds generated by a nocturnal katydid resulted in an aborted attack, suggesting that perched prey that remain silent are not detectable.

REPRODUCTION

Mating usually takes place at the hibernaculum in autumn; females produce single young. Pregnant females have been observed in mid to late June in southern portions of the range, and early pregnancy has been observed as late as early July in Hazelton.

MIGRATION AND WINTER

There are no confirmed winter records for BC. In other parts of North America, NORTHERN MYOTIS has been recorded hibernating in caves and abandoned mine tunnels. Swarming behaviour begins in late summer, or early fall, and researchers have documented movements of up to 56 kilometres between the hibernaculum and summer roost. This bat appears to be a relatively late hibernator, and in eastern Canada it arrives at hibernacula two to eight weeks after LITTLE BROWN MYOTIS first enters hibernation. NORTHERN MYOTIS hibernates alone or in small clusters, selecting tight crevices or drill holes where temperatures may be as cool as 1.6°C. Although NORTHERN MYOTIS often shares hibernacula with LITTLE BROWN MYOTIS in eastern Canada and in Alberta, the two species are rarely found hibernating in physical contact, and NORTHERN MYOTIS is more likely to be tucked into crevices, whereas LITTLE BROWN MYOTIS is more likely to be found on exposed rock surfaces in large clusters.

CONSERVATION STATUS

NORTHERN MYOTIS was assessed as Endangered by COSEWIC in an emergency assessment completed in 2013 and is now listed under Canada's Species at Risk Act. The federal listing was in response to a dramatic population decline in eastern Canada and the United States from white-nose syndrome. This species appears to be more susceptible to the disease than other myotis species.

Provincially, this species is on the Blue List. Given its strong association with trees for maternity and male day roosts, commercial forest harvesting practices are a concern. A few NORTHERN MYOTIS fatalities were recovered at two windfarms in northeastern BC, but the quantitative impact of wind energy site fatalities on the BC population is unknown.

TAXONOMY AND VARIATION

In older literature, NORTHERN MYOTIS was classified as a subspecies of KEEN'S MYOTIS, but substantial taxonomic revision based on morphology and genetics confirmed that NORTHERN MYOTIS is a distinct species. No subspecies are recognized. In eastern North America, populations of this species show little divergence in genetic structure, suggesting extensive gene flow. However, patterns of genetic variation across the full range, including western North America, have not been assessed. Females are larger than males (see table on page 76).

Total length (mm):	87	(80–94)	n = 18
Tail vertebrae length (mm):	39	(29–46)	n = 63
Hind foot (mm):	9	(7–11)	n = 61
Ear (mm):	15.6	(14.3–17.5)	n = 49
Tragus (mm):	9	(6.5–11.0)	n = 49
Forearm (mm):	36.3	(34.3–37.8)	n = 48
Wingspan (mm):	234		n = 1
Mass (g):	6.3	(5.2–7.5)	n = 33

REMARKS

Only three location records were listed for NORTHERN MYOTIS in the 1993 edition of this handbook, including Hudson's Hope and two areas near Revelstoke. Many new occurrences have been obtained in the past two decades, greatly expanding the known provincial distribution of this bat.

In northeastern Alberta, more than 15% of NORTHERN MYOTIS are incorrectly identified in the field as LITTLE BROWN MYOTIS, suggesting that genetic confirmation may be required to confirm species identification in areas where these two species overlap.

REFERENCES

Broders, Findlay and Zheng (2004); Caceres (1998); Caceres and Barclay (2000); Caire et al. (1979); COSEWIC (2013); Faure, Fullard and Dawson (1993); Fenton, Merriam and Holroyd (1983); Grindal, Stefan and Godwin-Sheppard (2011); Henderson and Broders (2008); Johnson et al. (2014); Jung et al. (2006); Kalcounis et al. (1999); Lausen, Jung and Talerico (2008); Lausen and Hill (2010); Lausen et al. (2019); Slough et al. (2022); Stadelmann et al. (2007); Ter Hofstede et al. (2008); van Zyll de Jong, Fenton and Woods (1980); Vonhof and Wilkinson (1999).

Fringed Myotis   *Myotis thysanodes*

DESCRIPTION

FRINGED MYOTIS is a large bat with pale-brown dorsal fur and even paler fur on the ventral surface. The calcar lacks a prominent keel, though a partial or indistinct keel could be present. The outer edge of the tail membrane has a distinct fringe of small, relatively densely and evenly spaced stiff hairs that can be seen with the naked eye. The ears are long, extending well beyond the nose when laid forward; this trait of long ears is shared with two other BC myotis species (LONG-EARED MYOTIS and NORTHERN MYOTIS). The tragus is long, slender and pointed.

MORPHOLOGICALLY SIMILAR SPECIES

LONG-LEGGED MYOTIS, LONG-EARED MYOTIS. Similarity in size might invite confusion with LONG-LEGGED MYOTIS; however, LONG-LEGGED MYOTIS can be identified by a prominent keel on its calcar, a thin layer of fur on the underwing extending to the knee and elbow, and a relatively short, round ear. Unlike FRINGED MYOTIS, it does not have a prominent fringe of hairs on the edge of its tail membrane.

FRINGED MYOTIS has a distinctive skull shape that appears narrower between the eyes and wider across the snout, giving it a more robust (or dog-like) appearance than LONG-EARED MYOTIS. Because of the more robust skull (see Appendix 2), measuring the width of the snout at the hairline can help differentiate: LONG-EARED MYOTIS has a narrow rostrum, ranging from 3 to 7 millimetres, on average 5.3 millimetres (n = 62), whereas FRINGED MYOTIS has a significantly wider rostrum, ranging from 6 to 8 millimetres, on average 6.6 millimetres (n = 7). The ears of FRINGED MYOTIS are generally shorter and the forearm is generally longer than those of LONG-EARED MYOTIS. Both species have dark shoulder patches when the fur is gently parted, due to hairs with dark bases.

LONG-EARED MYOTIS also lack the obvious dense "fringe" of stiff hairs along the edge of the tail membrane, though a sparse fringe of hairs is sometimes present on LONG-EARED MYOTIS (this is most conspicuous in young-of-year). Adding to the confusion is the fact that these two species have been documented to occasionally hybridize, including an unpublished record by Nagorsen and others of a July capture in Vancouver that presented as a hybrid based on population genetics, acoustics and morphology.

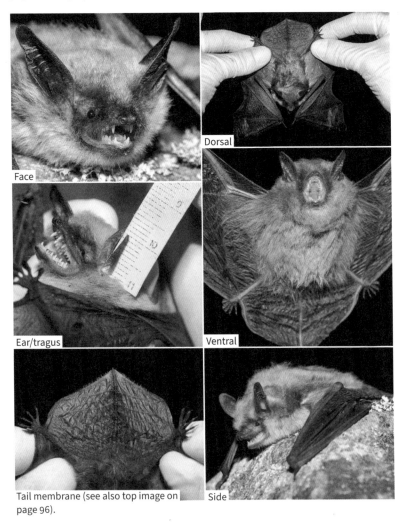

Face

Dorsal

Ear/tragus

Ventral

Tail membrane (see also top image on page 96).

Side

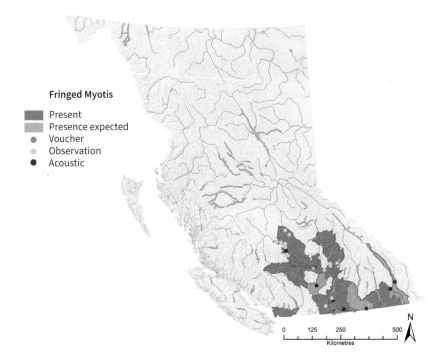

Fringed Myotis

- ■ Present
- ▨ Presence expected
- ● Voucher
- ◌ Observation
- ● Acoustic

0 125 250 500
Kilometres

N

DISTRIBUTION

FRINGED MYOTIS ranges from Mexico through the western United States to Canada (BC and Saskatchewan). In BC, it is associated with arid grasslands and PONDEROSA PINE–DOUGLAS-FIR forests. FRINGED MYOTIS occurs throughout most of these habitat types within the Okanagan, Similkameen, Thompson River and Fraser River valley bottom habitats, at least as far north as Sword Creek (a tributary of the Fraser River west of Williams Lake). This species is also occasionally found in the dry PONDEROSA PINE stands in the Creston Valley. Acoustic recordings through the North American Bat Monitoring Program and recordings made by Ian Adams and Hobbs have recently documented this species in the Kimberley-Cranbrook area, and Lausen has also detected FRINGED MYOTIS acoustically near Trail. Altitudinal records in the Okanagan Valley range from 300 to 700 metres and up to 1,250 metres in the Nicola and Thompson regions. In a study near Lillooet, FRINGED MYOTIS was the third most common species captured and was most common in open forested and grassland-forest interface habitats.

FRINGED MYOTIS occurs to some extent in coastal areas, although little is known about the coastal form. Acoustic recordings were made in the North American Bat Monitoring Program near Stave Lake, and Nagorsen and Doug Burles captured several FRINGED MYOTIS in the University of British Columbia's Malcolm Knapp Research Forest.

ZERO-CROSS RECORDINGS

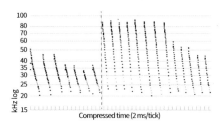

Sequence of search phase pulses in an open environment in left pane and high-clutter pulses in right pane.

FULL-SPECTRUM RECORDINGS

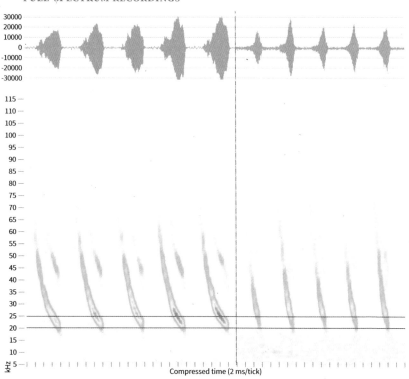

Open environment recording in left pane and higher-clutter pulses in right pane (recorded as part of the North American Bat Program). The presence of the second harmonic in each pane signifies that the bat has closely approached the microphone.

25 kilohertz. FRINGED MYOTIS is the only myotis species that produces such low-frequency calls, with minimum frequencies typically dropping to 20 to 25 kilohertz. As a long-eared species that gleans insects, this bat produces a high-clutter call shape, sweeping through a broad band of frequencies very quickly (less than 3 milliseconds call duration)—an extremely steep call. This characteristic call pattern is maintained even in open grassland environments. The breadth of frequencies produced by FRINGED MYOTIS can be impressive when the bat is close to the recorder, ranging from 120 kilohertz down to 20 kilohertz.

ACOUSTICALLY SIMILAR SPECIES
LONG-EARED MYOTIS, TOWNSEND'S BIG-EARED BAT, PALLID BAT, BIG BROWN BAT. LONG-EARED MYOTIS produces steep calls dropping to 30 kilohertz, while FRINGED MYOTIS regularly drops to 25 kilohertz; however, there is potential for overlap in call characteristics between these two species.

In native zero-crossing recordings, FRINGED MYOTIS calls are rarely confused with the calls of TOWNSEND'S BIG-EARED BAT, the other species that produces broadband short-duration calls ending at 25 kilohertz, as the latter species typically shows a split harmonic pattern, while FRINGED MYOTIS does not. However, in full spectrum, the similar intensity (decibels) recorded in first and second harmonics of TOWNSEND'S BIG-EARED BAT may be less obvious, inviting confusion with FRINGED MYOTIS. This confusion can be made worse by some post-recording zero-crossing conversion of full-spectrum recordings, where dominant harmonics are forced to show full instead of split regardless of peak energy, nullifying the split harmonic pattern as a trait to differentiate these species.

PALLID BAT, like FRINGED MYOTIS, typically produces steep echolocation calls even in open grassland habitats. As PALLID BAT produces calls that typically end at 25 kilohertz, it can potentially be confused with FRINGED MYOTIS, though PALLID BAT more typically has shorter-bandwidth, longer-duration calls, and show some call curvature, unlike FRINGED MYOTIS calls, which are more likely to have a linear shape. In high-clutter environments, BIG BROWN BAT can emit steep calls that end at 25 kilohertz, also inviting confusion with FRINGED MYOTIS.

ROOSTING
FRINGED MYOTIS is a colonial roosting bat that day roosts in tightly packed clusters, although considerable movement takes place in the roost in response to temperature changes. A colony of 30 to 40 adult female and immature FRINGED MYOTIS, found in the attic of a house in Vernon on July 19, 1937, is the only known nursery colony in a building in BC. All other roosts for this species in BC have been in PONDEROSA PINE or rock roosts (e.g., Creston, Lillooet). Generally, FRINGED MYOTIS roosts in caves, mines, rock crevices and

buildings for both day retreats and night roosts. Outside BC, nursery colonies with anywhere from 12 to 300 females and their young have been recorded in caves and buildings. In spring and summer, males roost separately and are rarely found in nursery colonies.

FEEDING

In the Okanagan, FRINGED MYOTIS is often netted in thickets along streams and rivers. It eats moths, flies, beetles, leafhoppers, lacewings, crickets and harvestmen. The presence of flightless insects in the diet suggests that some prey are gleaned from foliage.

REPRODUCTION

Detailed data on FRINGED MYOTIS reproduction for BC are lacking, but the nursery colony discovered at Vernon contained juveniles on July 19, suggesting that the young are born in late June or early July. Young-of-year males are usually not reproductively active in their first autumn; the age when females reach sexual maturity has not been determined. The young develop quickly and are capable of limited flight at 17 days old; by three weeks of age they have attained adult size.

MIGRATION AND WINTER

Until 2019, there were no confirmed winter records for this species in BC, although it had long been suspected that they hibernated in the Okanagan. Kirk Safford and Brian Paterson acoustically confirmed this species in Skaha Provincial Park in January. Surprisingly, there is little information available on the winter ecology of FRINGED MYOTIS from anywhere in its North American range. There are a few records of hibernating individuals in caves in South Dakota, Oregon and Montana, where these bats appear to hibernate solitarily. There is some circumstantial evidence from the southwestern United States that FRINGED MYOTIS moves only a short distance from its summer range to winter hibernation sites.

In BC, Lausen has recorded spikes of activity of this bat in the Creston Valley in September, but none have been detected during the winter in this area. FRINGED MYOTIS has been acoustically detected in the southern Okanagan as late as October 13 and as early as April 12. Similarly, Lausen and others have recorded FRINGED MYOTIS in early to mid-April in Lillooet and Grand Forks.

CONSERVATION STATUS

FRINGED MYOTIS is on the province's Blue List, with disturbance at night roosts in caves or mines identified as a possible threat. A federal COSEWIC assessment in 2004 designated this bat as Data Deficient, noting that the lack of data on population trends, range extent, habitat and hibernation sites prohibited a determination of its conservation status.

TAXONOMY AND VARIATION

Three subspecies of FRINGED MYOTIS are recognized in North America; one occurs in BC. However, genetic analysis suggests little genetic divergence among the three. Although BC individuals are traditionally classified as a single subspecies, the recently discovered coastal population in southwestern BC could be *Myotis thysanodes vespertinus*, a small, dark subspecies described from coastal Oregon. FRINGED MYOTIS captured by Nagorsen and Doug Burles in coastal forest habitat at the University of British Columbia's Malcolm Knapp Research Forest had darker pelage than Interior FRINGED MYOTIS. In a study of LONG-EARED BATS in BC by Lausen, Nagorsen, Burles and others, a lack of genetic information for coastal FRINGED MYOTIS precluded a proper genetic analysis, but population genetics using microsatellites to compare coastal captures with Interior populations of FRINGED and LONG-EARED MYOTIS suggested that FRINGED MYOTIS was the appropriate species identification. Some hybridization with LONG-EARED MYOTIS was suspected based on the results. A single museum specimen from Quinault Lake on the Olympic Peninsula in Washington may also represent the coastal subspecies.

➤ *Myotis thysanodes thysanodes* Miller—A subspecies widely distributed in Mexico and the western United States, reaching its northern limits in BC.

MEASUREMENTS

Total length (mm):	88	(78–93)	n = 10
Tail vertebrae length (mm):	40	(35–44)	n = 10
Hind foot (mm):	10	(8–11)	n = 10
Ear (mm):	17.2	(16 – 19)	n = 36
Tragus (mm):	9.5	(7–11)	n = 34
Forearm (mm):	42.1	(38.1–44.5)	n = 76
Wingspan (mm):	279	(250–295)	n = 31
Mass (g):	7.5	(4.8–10.6)	n = 70

REMARKS

A FRINGED MYOTIS banded at a mine near Oliver on August 6, 1982, was recaptured at this same site on April 7, 1990.

REFERENCES

Carstens and Dewey (2010); COSEWIC (2004a); Hill, Clarke and Stent (2007); Hobbs et al. (2011); Hobbs et al. (2015); Lausen and Hill (2012); Martin and Hawks (1972); Maslin (1938); O'Farrell and Studier (1973); O'Farrell and Studier (1980); Wilson (2004).

Long-Legged Myotis

Myotis volans

DESCRIPTION

Based on forearm length, LONG-LEGGED MYOTIS is one of the largest myotis species in BC and one of only three species in BC that features a prominent keel on the calcar (a trait shared with CALIFORNIAN MYOTIS and DARK-NOSED SMALL-FOOTED MYOTIS). Fur colour varies from reddish brown to nearly black, with juveniles being particularly dark. Among BC's three bat species with a prominent keel, LONG-LEGGED MYOTIS is unique in possessing hairy (i.e., furred) armpits: the hair on the belly extends onto the undersides of the wing membranes as far as the knees and elbows. The ears are rounded and relatively short, barely reaching the nose when laid forward; the tragus is long and narrow.

MORPHOLOGICALLY SIMILAR SPECIES

DARK-NOSED SMALL-FOOTED MYOTIS, CALIFORNIAN MYOTIS. While myotis bats can appear similar in photos or in hand, the prominent keel of LONG-LEGGED MYOTIS prevents it being confused with the five non-keeled myotis species. This narrows potential confusion to the two other myotis species that have a keel: CALIFORNIAN MYOTIS and DARK-NOSED SMALL-FOOTED MYOTIS. The obviously short round ears, hairy armpits and much longer forearm of LONG-LEGGED MYOTIS differentiate it from the other two.

CANYON BAT and BIG BROWN BAT also have a keel; however, CANYON BAT is readily distinguished by its tricoloured dorsal fur, blunt, club-shaped tragus and different dental formula, and it has a restricted range in BC. BIG BROWN BAT is readily distinguishable by its larger size (see species account).

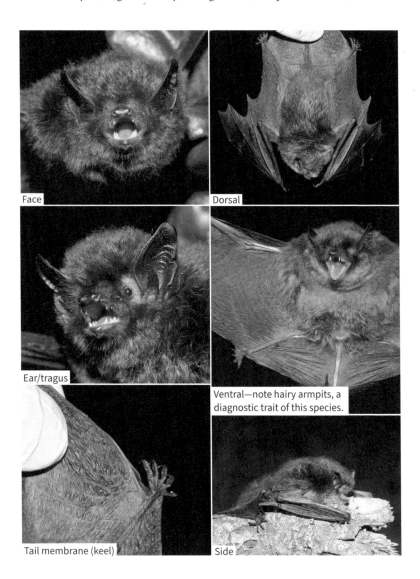

Face

Dorsal

Ear/tragus

Ventral—note hairy armpits, a diagnostic trait of this species.

Tail membrane (keel)

Side

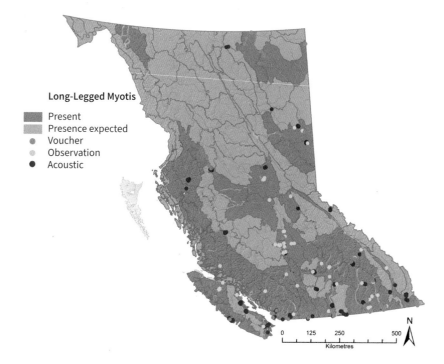

Long-Legged Myotis

■ Present
▪ Presence expected
● Voucher
○ Observation
● Acoustic

0   125   250   500

Kilometres

N

DISTRIBUTION

LONG-LEGGED MYOTIS inhabits western North America, where it ranges from southeastern Alaska and western Canada to Mexico. In coastal BC, it is found on Vancouver Island and the Gulf Islands (Mayne, Salt Spring, Cortes and Hornby). LONG-LEGGED MYOTIS also occurs in the Lower Mainland, as well as the southern Coast Mountains and Kitimat. In the Interior, there are records as far north as Atlin and the Yukon border in northeastern BC. This species ranges all the way to the Rocky Mountains in the east and is frequently observed in the Flathead River valley.

ACOUSTIC CHARACTERISTICS

40 kilohertz. LONG-LEGGED MYOTIS is extremely difficult, and in many cases impossible, to differentiate from other 40 kilohertz myotis. In high clutter, its minimum frequency can exceed 40 kilohertz. Even in low clutter, LONG-LEGGED MYOTIS echolocates with a fairly rapid sweep through a broad spectrum of frequencies, producing steeper-looking calls than LITTLE BROWN MYOTIS would produce in the same air space. In moderate clutter, however, call slope is the same between these two species and other 40 kilohertz myotis.

There is some speculation that an upsweep into the start of the call (similar to the upsweep into some TOWNSEND'S BIG-EARED calls' social component) may be a social component of LONG-LEGGED MYOTIS's repertoire and could

ZERO-CROSS RECORDINGS

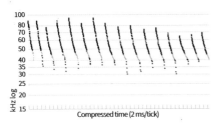

A couple of relatively high-clutter pulses start this sequence, but it quickly shifts into lower-clutter pulse shapes. In most cases, acoustic guilds are defined based on where the call body (shown in blue) ends, not where the toes end, which is important in a recording like this where the toes are excessively long, dipping to nearly 30 kilohertz. But this is not diagnostic, and LONG-LEGGED MYOTIS is a 40 kilohertz species, based on its characteristic frequency.

FULL-SPECTRUM RECORDINGS

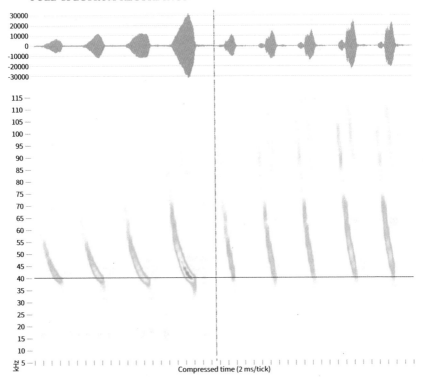

Free-flying, hand-released bat in open environment in left pane, and higher-clutter calls during bat-kiting in right pane.

set it apart from other myotis species; however, this remains unconfirmed, and Lausen has observed similar upsweeps from hand-released LITTLE BROWN MYOTIS. Special caution should be taken when viewing zero-crossing files derived from full-spectrum recordings made at 196 kilohertz sampling frequency; aliasing from clipped signals (when the bat is too close to the microphone) may superficially resemble an upsweep into a high-frequency call.

ACOUSTICALLY SIMILAR SPECIES
DARK-NOSED SMALL-FOOTED MYOTIS, LITTLE BROWN MYOTIS, NORTHERN MYOTIS, EASTERN RED BAT. LONG-LEGGED MYOTIS can easily be confused with any of the other 40 kilohertz myotis in BC (DARK-NOSED SMALL-FOOTED MYOTIS, LITTLE BROWN MYOTIS and NORTHERN MYOTIS). In high clutter, EASTERN RED BAT may also present confusion, especially if short or poor-quality sequences are recorded. In low clutter, LITTLE BROWN MYOTIS is likely to take on lower-sloped calls, and may be distinguishable from the other 40 kilohertz myotis, but there are no diagnostic echolocation call characteristics that will differentiate LONG-LEGGED MYOTIS (with the possible exception of a social component occasionally present, as described above).

ROOSTING
In BC, LONG-LEGGED MYOTIS inhabits a diversity of habitat types, occurring in arid rangelands of the Interior, humid coastal and montane forests, and boreal forests in northern BC. The few available altitudinal records extend from sea level to 1,440 metres (in Manning Provincial Park). Known summer maternity roosts in BC include several buildings, a park information booth in the Kootenay region, a building roost shared with LITTLE BROWN MYOTIS near Williams Lake, under cedar roofing shingles on Mayne Island, a bat box on Salt Spring Island, and under a highway bridge near Kispiox. A male from the Kispiox Valley was found in the crack of a dead BALSAM POPLAR tree in July, and a juvenile male was observed in a YUMA MYOTIS maternity colony in the attic of a church near Squilax in August.

In the western United States, buildings, crevices in rock cliffs, fissures in the ground, and cracks in the bark of trees have been reported as summer day roost structures. Maternity colonies have been found in attics, fissures in the ground, and under the bark of trees. In Alberta, maternity colonies occur in the crevices of hoodoos and in buildings. In both structures, LONG-LEGGED MYOTIS have been found to cohabit with LITTLE BROWN MYOTIS. Maternity colonies may be large, consisting of hundreds of females. Caves and abandoned mine tunnels are commonly used as night roosts.

FEEDING

LONG-LEGGED MYOTIS emerges at dusk and remains active throughout much of the night. It is an opportunistic hunter that takes aerial prey while foraging in a variety of habitats, including over water, under the forest canopy and along cliff faces. Research on foraging LONG-LEGGED MYOTIS in Idaho showed that males and females do not differ in diet, eating mainly beetles and moths. Other studies point to substantial consumption of moths and suggest that LONG-LEGGED MYOTIS may specialize on moths. Wing shape and large tail membrane affords this species a high degree of manoeuvrability.

REPRODUCTION

LONG-LEGGED MYOTIS share reproductive characteristics with many other species in BC. Mating begins in late August or September, before hibernation. In Alberta, males have been documented breeding in their first autumn. Pups are born in late June (in Flathead) or early July (other records), and young are likely to be volant in early August. Scrotal males are observed in late July. Recoveries of banded individuals indicate that LONG-LEGGED MYOTIS can live at least 21 years in the wild.

MIGRATION AND WINTER

LONG-LEGGED MYOTIS hibernates in small clusters in caves and mines. In BC, it has been found overwintering in caves on Vancouver Island and near Prince George, and in a mine in the West Kootenay. Inge-Jean Hansen and Brian Paterson found multiple individuals overwintering in the cellar of a house in the Charlie Lake area, near Fort St. John, BC. In Alberta, LONG-LEGGED MYOTIS hibernate at Cadomin and Wapiabi caves in the central part of the province; these caves are also used by LITTLE BROWN MYOTIS and NORTHERN MYOTIS (Cadomin only). Swarming of males at caves has been observed to begin on Vancouver Island in mid-August, and by late September some individuals have been observed hibernating in these caves. In the West Kootenay, LONG-LEGGED MYOTIS bats have been captured in late October flying into a mine at 1,280 metres elevation, where they are suspected to overwinter. Few data are available for the environmental conditions required by this species during hibernation but there are records in BC of LONG-LEGGED MYOTIS roosting at 2°C to 4°C in nearly 100% humidity.

Average wing loading and low aspect ratio (see page 16) suggests that LONG-LEGGED MYOTIS is relatively slow-flying and unlikely to migrate long distances—in contrast to LITTLE BROWN MYOTIS, which has lower wing loading but higher aspect ratio, and which is known to migrate several hundreds of kilometres seasonally (see LITTLE BROWN MYOTIS species account). We do not know if LONG-LEGGED MYOTIS migrate seasonally in BC.

Considered secure by conservation agencies, this species has not been assessed by COSEWIC. Potential threats are disturbance at winter hibernation sites and fatalities at wind energy sites. As with other bat species in BC that raise young in colonies in mature tree cavities, LONG-LEGGED MYOTIS may be impacted by commercial timber harvest in BC, but this threat is poorly understood.

TAXONOMY AND VARIATION
There has been no study of genetic variation across the range extent of LONG-LEGGED MYOTIS. Based mostly on fur colour, two subspecies are recognized in North America, with one occurring in BC.

> *Myotis volans longicrus* (True)—This subspecies is defined based on minor pelage colour differences and inhabits the Pacific coast of the United States and western Canada.

MEASUREMENTS

Total length (mm):	94 (83–105)	n = 33
Tail vertebrae length (mm):	43 (37–54)	n = 33
Hind foot (mm):	9 (7–10)	n = 31
Ear (mm):	11.9 (9–15)	n = 35
Tragus (mm):	6.1 (5–7.5)	n = 29
Forearm (mm):	38.5 (34.0–44.0)	n = 166
Wingspan (mm):	253 (215–272)	n = 25
Mass (g):	7.8 (5.6–10.3)	n = 99

REMARKS
The common name of this bat is LONG-LEGGED MYOTIS, and indeed this bat does have a longer tibia (average 19.3 millimetres, range 18–20.5 millimetres) than other similar myotis; however, tibia length is rarely used to differentiate it from other species, given that furred armpits are more obvious and definitive and don't require a measuring tool to assess.

It is difficult to differentiate this species from other 40 kilohertz myotis based solely on acoustic recordings, so direct observations (captured individuals) or genetic information (derived from guano) are typically needed to confirm the species' presence.

REFERENCES

Bininda-Emonds and Russell (1994); Dalquest and Ramage (1946); Davis et al. (1997); Fenton et al. (1980); Johnson, Lacki and Baker (2007); Norberg and Rayner (1987); Saunders (1989); Saunders and Barclay (1992); Schowalter (1980); Warner and Czaplewski (1984).

Yuma Myotis

Myotis yumanensis

DESCRIPTION

YUMA MYOTIS is a medium-sized bat. Dorsal fur varies from pale brown to nearly black, while the fur is paler on the underside. Its fur is short and dull (not glossy), and the wing membranes and ears are dark brown. It has pointed, medium-length ears, reaching the nostrils when laid forward, and the tragus is blunt and about half the length of the ear. The calcar lacks a keel, an important diagnostic trait.

MORPHOLOGICALLY SIMILAR SPECIES

YUMA MYOTIS is very similar to LITTLE BROWN MYOTIS. Note that confusion with six other myotis species in BC is also possible, but these can usually be ruled out based on the presence of a keel and/or ear length.

The absence of a keel on the calcar distinguishes YUMA MYOTIS from LONG-LEGGED MYOTIS, CALIFORNIAN MYOTIS and DARK-NOSED SMALL-FOOTED MYOTIS. Three other myotis species (FRINGED MYOTIS, NORTHERN MYOTIS and LONG-EARED MYOTIS) can be excluded based on their longer ears. YUMA MYOTIS is likely to be confused with LITTLE BROWN MYOTIS based on morphological characteristics. YUMA MYOTIS is typically smaller (forearm less than 36 millimetres), with duller, shorter fur and a relatively steep-sloped forehead; nonetheless, forearm lengths can overlap, and in some parts of the province these two species are extremely difficult to distinguish, especially in places where they cohabit the same roosts. Although unreliable, behavioural attributes may also assist in identification, as LITTLE BROWN MYOTIS tends to be more defensive when handled.

Other than sequencing mitochondrial DNA, the most reliable way to differentiate YUMA MYOTIS from LITTLE BROWN MYOTIS is to conduct an acoustic bag test. This requires a bat detector, ideally with a display of some form so you can see the calls while holding the bat. The test is conducted by placing the bat in a small cotton bag and gently shaking it up and down until it echolocates. The body of the calls (not including the toe) produced by YUMA MYOTIS will have a frequency of 45 kilohertz (as low as 42 kilohertz) or higher; the call produced by LITTLE BROWN MYOTIS will drop below 40 kilohertz, and sometimes as low as 30 kilohertz, providing clear differences between the species. A bag test result of approximately 40 to 42 kilohertz is uninformative, but by considering both forearm length and minimum call frequency together, you can usually differentiate these two species with a high degree of confidence.

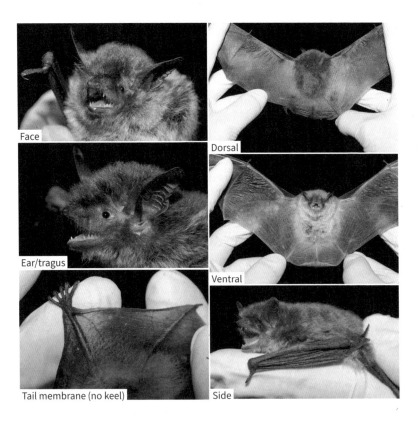

Face

Dorsal

Ear/tragus

Ventral

Tail membrane (no keel)

Side

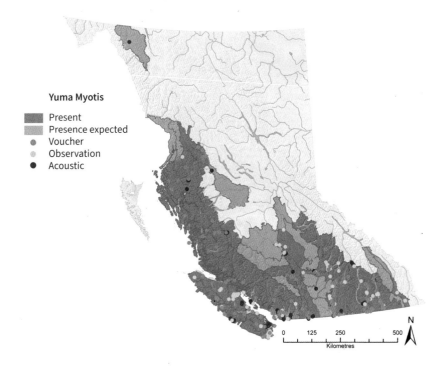

Yuma Myotis

- Present
- Presence expected
- Voucher
- Observation
- Acoustic

0 125 250 500
Kilometres

N

DISTRIBUTION

YUMA MYOTIS is found across western North America, from Mexico to southern BC. In BC, it is known from across the southern part of the province, including Vancouver Island, the Gulf Islands, Bowen Island, and Goose, King and Princess Royal islands in the Great Bear Rainforest. The species is also found in southeast Alaska, and thus presumably occurs along the entire BC coast; however, it has not been captured on Haida Gwaii. On the mainland it ranges as far north as Terrace, Smithers, Prince Rupert and the Nass Valley, and as far east as Elko. It was also recorded acoustically in Atlin. Curiously, there are no records of this species to date in the Rocky Mountain Trench in East Kootenay, despite genetic sampling of at least one guano pellet at numerous building roosts as part of the Kootenay Community Bat Project. There is abundant habitat for this species in the Columbia River Valley, suggesting additional inventory may yield this species. Found in the Flathead River valley of Montana, it may also occur in the northern reaches of the Flathead River valley in BC, but little survey effort has occurred there.

ACOUSTIC CHARACTERISTICS

45–50 kilohertz. YUMA MYOTIS is Canada's highest-frequency bat, although CALIFORNIAN MYOTIS can produce calls that also have minimum frequencies as high as 50 kilohertz. Both species produce calls that typically end at or above

ZERO-CROSS RECORDINGS

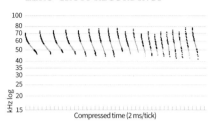

Pulses in the first half of this sequence reflect low to no clutter, with the pulses taking on a distinct elbow/knee. This sequence progresses to steeper calls as the bat approaches an object or surface.

FULL-SPECTRUM RECORDINGS

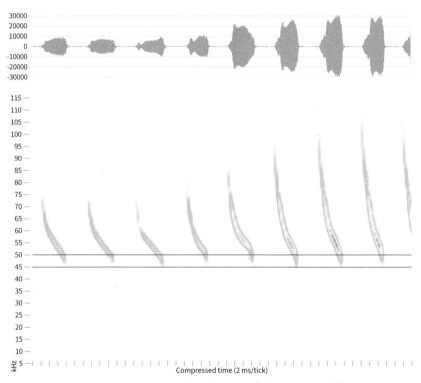

Pulses show the bat approaching the microphone, starting the sequence with low-clutter search phase calls; then, as the bat gets closer, higher-clutter pulse shapes and higher frequencies are recorded, including part of the second harmonic. (Recording made as part of the North American Bat Monitoring Program.)

45 kilohertz, setting them apart acoustically from other myotis species in BC. Like LITTLE BROWN MYOTIS, YUMA MYOTIS typically forages very close to calm water surfaces (water skimming); recordings made under these conditions may show interference patterns due to reflected sound (see next page).

ACOUSTICALLY SIMILAR SPECIES

CALIFORNIAN MYOTIS. CALIFORNIAN MYOTIS and YUMA MYOTIS occasionally drop their frequencies below 45 kilohertz minimum frequency, although CALIFORNIAN MYOTIS is more likely to do this. YUMA MYOTIS is most likely to produce calls that end at 50 kilohertz. These two species are especially difficult to differentiate in clutter. When flying in open space, however, their echolocation calls change in slope and call shape, which sets YUMA MYOTIS apart: when not reacting to clutter, YUMA MYOTIS typically produces calls that sweep more slowly through a broad band of frequencies, abruptly changing rate of decreasing frequencies mid-pulse, producing a far more distinct "elbow" or "knee" (a bend mid-call; see facing page), than would be produced by CALIFORNIAN MYOTIS.

In high clutter, differentiating any of the 40 kilohertz myotis (Northern, DARK-NOSED SMALL-FOOTED, LITTLE BROWN and LONG-LEGGED MYOTIS) from the 45 to 50 kilohertz myotis (YUMA and CALIFORNIAN MYOTIS) can be difficult, because bats tend to use high frequencies in extreme levels of clutter. High-clutter EASTERN RED BAT calls are also similar. Generally, a long uniform sequence of calls ending above 45 kilohertz can be attributed to either YUMA or CALIFORNIAN MYOTIS. However, in areas where CANYON BAT occurs, long sequences of low-sloped 45 to 50 kilohertz calls could indicate this species—see the CANYON BAT species account, page 295, for an acoustic description of CANYON BAT's call.

ROOSTING

YUMA MYOTIS was once considered a low-elevation species (sea level to 520 metres) in BC, but more widespread acoustic monitoring detected the species in spring and summer at 1,775 metres elevation (Bridal Lake in Stagleap Provincial Park). YUMA MYOTIS inhabits coastal forests, PONDEROSA PINE–DOUGLAS-FIR forests and arid grasslands. It has been found roosting in rock crevices near Vaseux Lake in the Okanagan Valley, but summer day roosts are usually in buildings and other anthropogenic structures close to water. Various anthropogenic structures, such as porches of houses, abandoned cabins, and bridges, also serve as night roosts.

Maternity colonies in buildings can be enormous, with more than 5,000 adult females recorded in a single colony. Examples of these high-occupancy roosts include a heritage building at Deas Island Regional Park in Delta, a large bat condominium built on the Creston Valley Wildlife Management Area that replaced a collapsing barn reported to have housed more than 7,000 bats, and

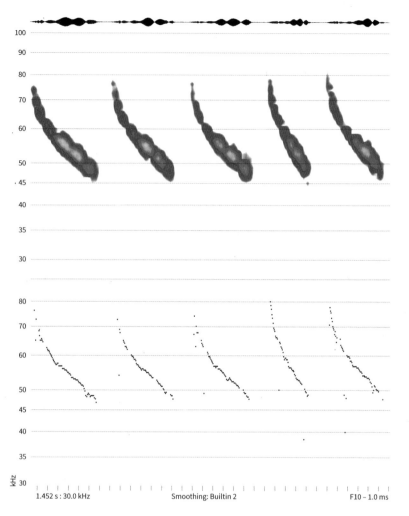

100
90
80
70
60
50
45
40
35
30

80
70
60
50
45
40
35
30

kHz

1.452 s : 30.0 kHz   Smoothing: Builtin 2   F10 – 1.0 ms

A YUMA MYOTIS as it forages above a calm water surface. In zero-cross (bottom spectrogram), the pulses look ragged and are often broken by gaps where bands of frequencies are missing. Because the bat is so close to the water, the echo from the water is only slightly delayed, so it mostly overlaps the bat's original signal. The signal and echo then interfere with each other, resulting in the microphone receiving alternating peaks and nulls as the frequency changes, so the signal can drop below the threshold of detection for the zero-crossing, causing the raggedness. The full-spectrum view (top spectrogram) shows the broken signal as a series of beads, also reflected in the oscillogram. (Recording near Bishop, California, by Chris Corben. Visualized in Insight software [Titley Scientific].)

the Peachland Visitor Centre (which promotes its maternity colony as a visitor attraction). Many YUMA MYOTIS maternity colonies are found in buildings and bat boxes in the Creston Valley and along Kootenay Lake between Creston and Crawford Bay, and it is in this region that YUMA MYOTIS activity is recorded year-round, including captures of bats overwintering in buildings. Small numbers of adult females have also been observed using tree hollows as summer roosts.

YUMA MYOTIS females return to maternity roosts earlier in spring than LITTLE BROWN MYOTIS females—a roost in Delta has had female YUMA MYOTIS observed as early as March 12, similar to the mid-March returns observed at the Creston Valley Wildlife Management Area's bat condominium.

During the nursing season, males roost separately from females, either singly or in small groups. In some areas, such as Metro Vancouver, adult females leave the maternity roosts by mid to late August, but in other areas, including the Creston Valley Wildlife Management Area north to Boswell, YUMA MYOTIS remain common year-round, and males begin to show up at maternity roosts in mid to late August.

FEEDING

At dusk, YUMA MYOTIS emerges from its daytime retreat to hunt over lakes, rivers and streams. Individuals from some colonies travel at least 4 kilometres from the roost to forage over rivers and lakes. In the Okanagan Valley, its diet has been found to consist of mayflies, caddisflies and midges. Midges are predominant in the spring; mayflies and caddisflies are the dominant food items in summer. Although food habits have not been studied in other parts of the province, aquatic insects are probably the major prey, given this species' tendency to hunt over water. An efficient hunter, YUMA MYOTIS can fill its stomach in 10 to 15 minutes on a productive summer's night. After feeding, these bats retreat to a night roost near the feeding area.

YUMA MYOTIS is one of two bat species in BC (in addition to LITTLE BROWN MYOTIS) commonly observed flying just above the surface of the water for extended periods, foraging on insects on or just above the water's surface, and occasionally dipping down to the surface of the water with the bottom jaw to drink on the wing. Use of a spotlight to observe this "water skimming" behaviour usually does not deter LITTLE BROWN MYOTIS, but YUMA MYOTIS tend to avoid the light and leave the area.

REPRODUCTION

In the Interior of southern BC, YUMA MYOTIS young are born between early June and mid-July. A large number of pregnant females sampled at a maternity colony near Haney on May 25 suggests that coastal populations bear young around the same time. As is true for many bats in BC, the parturition period can be extremely variable, even within a colony. Females measured on the same day in the Haney colony demonstrated various stages of pregnancy; some were in early pregnancy, with tiny embryos, and others carried well-developed fetuses, near birth. In the large YUMA MYOTIS colony at Squilax (a colonial roost in an old church building, which has since burned down), parturition dates ranged from June 5 to July 21, with most births falling between June 18 and July 7. Similar timing has been reported at mixed species roosts shared with LITTLE BROWN MYOTIS in the Creston Valley.

Some studies have reported near 100% reproductive rates at YUMA MYOTIS maternity colonies, leading to the conclusion that most YUMA MYOTIS females reproduce in their first year of life; Lausen found that 11% of approximately 500 female YUMA MYOTIS adults captured between June and early September in BC over several years showed no signs of having ever reproduced, suggesting they were yearlings that did not get pregnant in their first year of life. In contrast, Lausen found 27% of a similar number of adult female LITTLE BROWN MYOTIS were non-reproducing in their first year, supporting the conclusion that YUMA MYOTIS females are more likely to reproduce in their first than other building-roosting myotis species. Regardless of whether a female was a yearling or older, in any given year, approximately 80% of YUMA MYOTIS females are reproductive: pregnant, lactating or having weaned a pup. This is higher than the reproductive rate for adult female LITTLE BROWN MYOTIS, which averages just over 50%.

At the Creston Valley Wildlife Management Area bat condominium, adult male YUMA MYOTIS with stored sperm in cauda epididymides and testes that have ascended back into the body cavity are captured regularly, along with reproductive adult females and young. Levels of stored sperm in captured males throughout August to October show sperm depletion during this period, which is confirmation of mating activity. Lausen and others found that 87% of males captured at this maternity roost in April (n = 80) had stored sperm remaining in the cauda epididymides (5% to 90%), suggesting that mating continues in spring; 15% of males were non-reproductive yearlings, suggesting that males may return to their natal roosts.

These data suggest that YUMA MYOTIS mates in late summer, fall and spring, unlike most species, which are thought to mate only in late summer or autumn. This may partly explain why YUMA MYOTIS females are more likely to reproduce in their first year. Despite a great deal of capture effort at some major YUMA MYOTIS roosts, no juvenile male YUMA MYOTIS with descended testes have been reported, suggesting that males may not reproduce in their first year.

MIGRATION AND WINTER

Locations of winter hibernacula for YUMA MYOTIS are largely unknown. Despite the local abundance of this species throughout most of its range, no natural winter hibernacula have been confirmed in the province, though a number of building roosts have been found to house YUMA MYOTIS year-round. In coastal Washington, a few individuals have been found hibernating in caves, and it is possible that similar sites are used as natural hibernacula in BC.

By radio-tracking YUMA MYOTIS in October through December in the Creston Valley, Lausen and others confirmed extensive use of building and rock crevice roosts in the same area as summer roosts. Use of these roost sites continued until just prior to snowfall, when some of the bats left their summer roosting areas, presumably to relocate to hibernacula outside the area. Rock crevice roosting was not confirmed during the winter in the Creston Valley, but use of two building maternity roosts continued. Radio-tagged bats were documented to fly outside in mid-winter. In both building roosts, which were not occupied by humans during winter, bats concentrated along brick chimneys that retained low levels of heat from electric baseboard heaters. Of 26 mid-winter captures of free-flying bats outside these building roosts, 69% were young-of-year and 65.5% were males. One of these buildings has since been sold and renovated to exclude the bats.

One adult male YUMA MYOTIS was radio-tracked to under a train-car–sized boulder in an east-facing boulder field at 1,700 metres elevation across from Kuskanook, BC, in early November. It is not known if the bat spent the winter at this location, but if it did, it would have been covered by metres of snow; it is possible that this bat was en route to a different hibernaculum, and just day roosted under this large, high-elevation boulder, leaving the transmitter under the boulder in the process. This can occur if the bat's movement against the rock surface pries the glued transmitter off its back. Lausen acoustically recorded YUMA MYOTIS on Kootenay Pass (1,775 metres) from May to September, with only a small number of passes in summer, but spikes of activity starting in early September suggest some level of migration. At the Creston Valley Wildlife Management Area bat condominium, YUMA MYOTIS usually arrive back in March, suggesting a relatively short hibernation period (December through March).

Laura Matthias, Peter Ommundsen and others have acoustically recorded YUMA MYOTIS throughout the winter months on Salt Spring Island (2014 to 2020).

CONSERVATION STATUS

One of the most common bats in southern BC, YUMA MYOTIS is considered secure by conservation agencies. However, because LITTLE BROWN MYOTIS account for the largest number of cases of white-nose syndrome in the east, and because of the ecological similarities between YUMA and LITTLE BROWN MYOTIS, we anticipate that YUMA MYOTIS may be heavily impacted by this fungal disease as it spreads in the west. The threat of displacement from building maternity roosts (which provide optimal microclimates for raising young) could reduce the resiliency of populations and negatively impact future recovery of colonies following anticipated mortalities from white-nose syndrome. As with other bat species in BC that tend to raise young in colonies, YUMA MYOTIS roosts in cavities of mature trees or snags, features reduced by commercial timber harvest in BC; research is needed to understand the impact of the forestry industry on this bat.

TAXONOMY AND VARIATION

Although YUMA MYOTIS is sufficiently similar in morphology to LITTLE BROWN MYOTIS to present identification problems, genetic studies based on DNA have shown that the two species are not closely related and represent different genetic clades within the *Myotis* genus. Six subspecies of YUMA MYOTIS are recognized, based mostly on pelage colour, with two found in BC. There has been no study of genetic variation across the range of this species.

> *Myotis yumanensis saturatus* Miller—A dark coastal subspecies ranging from California to BC, where it occupies the coastal mainland and various islands, including Vancouver Island and the Gulf Islands.

> *Myotis yumanensis sociabilis* H.W. Grinnell—A paler subspecies found in the western United States and the Interior of BC.

MEASUREMENTS

In the West Kootenay, a large number of adult YUMA MYOTIS bats have been captured in spring and fall, with season-specific adult masses as follows: April, 5.4 grams (4.0–6.8; n = 398), May to June, 5.3 grams (4.1–7.4; n = 265), July to August, 5.5 grams (4.1–7.6; n = 351); September to November, 5.8 grams (3.6–7.8; n = 310). This suggests a reasonably small mass gain prior to hibernation (i.e., September to November masses are only 4% higher on average than summer masses. Fall masses are on average 9% greater than spring masses. Females are larger than males (see the table on page 76).

Total length (mm):	82	(60–99)	n = 322
Tail vertebrae length (mm):	36	(27–45)	n = 324
Hind foot (mm):	9	(6–13)	n = 323
Ear (mm):	11.4	(10–14)	n = 159
Tragus (mm):	5.6	(4–8)	n = 154
Forearm (mm):	34.7	(31.25–37.50)	n = 1,382
Wingspan (mm):	238	(205–260)	n = 208
Mass (g):	5.5	(3.60–7.78)	n = 1,324

REMARKS

In many locations, YUMA MYOTIS is the most common species captured in mist-nets set across water, due to the species' habit of foraging over the water surface.

YUMA MYOTIS and LITTLE BROWN MYOTIS are the most likely bats to take up residence in bat boxes in BC and will often form mixed-species colonies. They pack into bat boxes tightly, which may preclude escape during overheating events; there have been observations of mass mortality events during heat waves in Creston, Port Coquitlam and the Okanagan.

REFERENCES

Aldridge (1986); Barclay and Brigham (1994); Braun et al. (2015); Brigham, Aldridge and Mackey (1992); Dalquest (1947); Herd and Fenton (1983); Luszcz et al. (2016); Milligan and Brigham (1993); Schalk and Brigham (1995); Slough et al. (2022).

PHOTO: CORI LAUSEN

BIG-FREE TAILED BAT. PHOTO: MICHAEL DURHAM/MINDEN PICTURES (BAT CONSERVATION INTERNATIONAL)

Accidental Species

The following three species are currently considered "accidental," as there is no current evidence of breeding populations or captures to confirm their presence in BC.

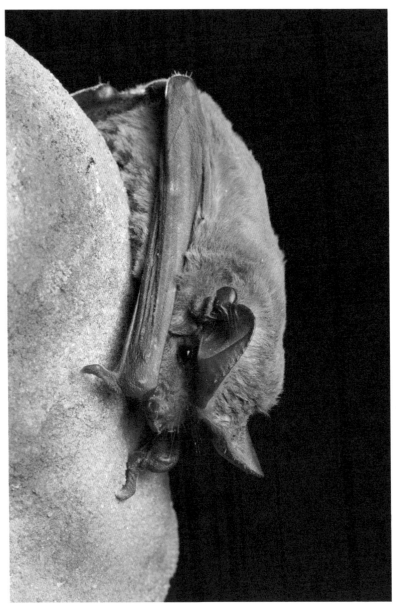

BRAZILIAN FREE-TAILED BAT. PHOTO: MICHAEL DURHAM/
MINDEN PICTURES (BAT CONSERVATION INTERNATIONAL)

Brazilian Free-Tailed Bat   *Tadarida brasiliensis*

DESCRIPTION

BRAZILIAN FREE-TAILED BAT is one of two members of the family Molossidae that have been detected in BC (to the other is BIG FREE-TAILED BAT). Both are considered accidental. As a Molossid, BRAZILIAN FREE-TAILED BAT has large, flattened ears; long, narrow wings built for speed; a short tail membrane and tail that extends well beyond the edge of the tail membrane. Its ears do not extend much beyond the end of the nose when laid forward and do not join at the midline of the head. It has deep vertical grooves (wrinkles) on the upper lip, which are thought to allow its mouth to open widely to more effectively capture prey during flight, compensating for its high-speed, low-manoeuvrability flight. Its fur is uniform in colour, but the exact shade of grey-brown depends on the time since moult.

BRAZILIAN FREE-TAILED BAT is medium-sized, with a body mass of 10 to 15 grams, a total length of 85 to 109 millimetres and a forearm length of 36 to 46 millimetres.

MORPHOLOGICALLY SIMILAR SPECIES

BIG FREE-TAILED BAT. As a Molossid, this species has unique morphological traits, as described above; it is unlikely to be confused with other BC bat species. BRAZILIAN FREE-TAILED BAT can be differentiated from the other accidental

ZERO-CROSS RECORDINGS

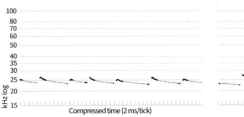

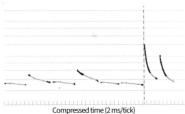

A. Flat pulses in open environment. This BC recording is indicative of the call shapes that have helped confirm this species' presence in the province.

B. Left pane shows sequence with diagnostic erratic pattern of low-sloped calls intermingled with a few higher-frequency and higher-sloped calls. Right pane shows two pulses of broad bandwidth. Recordings from California.

FULL-SPECTRUM RECORDINGS

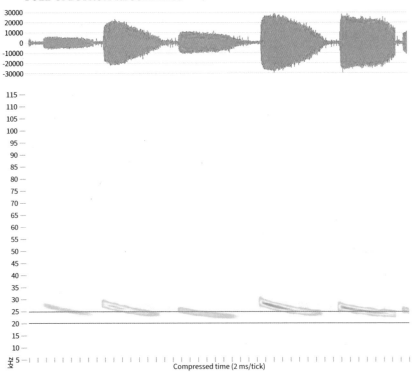

Spotlighted in January flying in an open environment in California. The oscillogram shows pulses that are somewhat carrot-shaped and that may aid in species identification, given that SILVER-HAIRED BATS are thought to produce this amplitude pattern less often.

Molossid in BC, BIG FREE-TAILED BAT, by size, as BIG FREE-TAILED BAT has a forearm longer than 50 millimetres. BIG FREE-TAILED BAT's ears also join at the midline of the head (see images in key on page 98).

DISTRIBUTION

BRAZILIAN FREE-TAILED BAT is expanding its range in North America. It is found in all southern US states, and in the west there are captures or carcasses from Idaho (three records confirmed by Rita Dixon), Oregon, Wyoming, Nevada, Utah and Colorado. There are no captures for BC or Washington, but several acoustic monitoring efforts (by the regional BC Community Bat Program on Salt Spring Island, by some consulting firms, and as part of the North American Bat Monitoring Program) have provided confirmed acoustic recordings (diagnostic for the species—see Acoustic Characteristics, below). Diagnostic recordings have been made in the summer in southwestern BC, including on Salt Spring Island, Texada Island, southern Vancouver Island (Duncan), Vancouver (by Hemmera in Brownsville Park and Maplewood Flats; by Julia Craig along several mobile acoustic bike transects) and Sumas (Aimee Mitchell). The nearest confirmed capture records of this species are from Oregon.

ACOUSTIC CHARACTERISTICS

20–25 kilohertz. BRAZILIAN FREE-TAILED BAT is a fast-flying bat with a variety of echolocation calls, ranging from nearly constant frequency, which produces flat-looking calls (A), to steep, broad-bandwidth calls (B, right pane). Unlike most bats, the minimum frequency does not typically decrease with degree of clutter; instead, this bat can produce almost flat-looking low-clutter calls at any frequency in the range of 20 to 28 kilohertz. Similarly, its broadband frequency sweep calls do not always correspond to high clutter, and it is common to see this bat randomly produce a call that is of higher frequency and/or higher slope within a sequence of otherwise flat-looking calls (B). These "out-of-place" calls that do not seem to fit the pattern of the rest of the sequence can be useful in species identification.

ACOUSTICALLY SIMILAR SPECIES

BIG BROWN BAT, SILVER-HAIRED BAT, HOARY BAT. Similar to SILVER-HAIRED BAT, BRAZILIAN FREE-TAILED BAT can produce flatter calls (5 octaves per second or less) than BIG BROWN BAT (greater than 5 and usually greater than 8 octaves per second). The presence of random "out-of-place" calls that break up the uniformity of the sequence (B) can help differentiate BRAZILIAN FREE-TAILED BAT from SILVER-HAIRED BAT when examining an unknown sequence of semi-constant frequency calls at or above 25 kilohertz. Only BRAZILIAN FREE-TAILED BAT produces flat or near-flat calls between 20 and 25 kilohertz, a call pattern that can be used to differentiate it from other bats. In clutter or in response to ambient noises, BRAZILIAN FREE-TAILED BAT will alter its calls and can produce calls that sweep through many frequencies, often ending around 25 kilohertz, which potentially invites confusion with SILVER-HAIRED BAT, BIG BROWN BAT or even HOARY BAT in moderate to high clutter.

ROOSTING

BRAZILIAN FREE-TAILED BAT is well known for its large colonies, with numbers of individuals sometimes in the millions (e.g., Bracken Cave and Austin's Congress Avenue Bridge, Texas). It roosts in caves, cliff faces and other rock crevices, and in anthropogenic structures, including buildings and bridges. As this bat has not been captured in BC, the types of roosts used in the province are not known.

FEEDING

BRAZILIAN FREE-TAILED BAT is capable of fast flight (greater than 60 kilometres/ hour), and has been documented flying long distances (greater than 50 kilometres) one way to forage. It often makes these long nightly commutes by flying at high altitudes (3,000 metres), where it often skips wing-beats and glides; large groups of these bats have been detected on weather-surveillance radar. Acoustic evidence suggests that it also forages at high altitudes, where it can hunt nocturnally migrating noctuid moths and other insects. BRAZILIAN FREE-TAILED BAT feeds mainly on moths and beetles, and several studies have demonstrated its economic value to agriculture through its consumption of corn-ear worm moths and other crop pests.

REPRODUCTION

BRAZILIAN FREE-TAILED BAT gives birth to a single pup. Because these bats may roost in colonies numbering in the millions, mother-pup recognition is important, and it has been shown that in addition to spatial memory, adult females produce "directive" calls to locate pups, and pups produce isolation calls to communicate with the mother. Mothers also locate pups using scent; a lactating female will mark her pup with odour from her glands.

Unlike hibernating bat species, neither male nor female BRAZILIAN FREE-TAILED BATS store sperm. Mating is in spring, when females are receptive (onset of estrus), and this coincides with the production of sperm (spermatogenesis).

MIGRATION AND WINTER

This species is largely considered to be a non-hibernating, migratory bat. Not all populations of BRAZILIAN FREE-TAILED BAT migrate, but western populations demonstrate a north-south migration. Migration distances of almost 2,000 kilometres have been documented. Despite the behaviour differences in migratory and non-migratory groups of BRAZILIAN FREE-TAILED BATS, no genetic differentiation has been found, suggesting widespread gene flow.

REMARKS

BRAZILIAN FREE-TAILED BAT is also referred to as Mexican free-tailed bat in some publications. Given the long-range movements of this species, it is not inconceivable that it could appear in various regions of southern BC.

Until genetic evidence or captures have confirmed BRAZILIAN FREE-TAILED BAT here, it is likely to remain listed as accidental, despite reports from Peter Ommundsen that diagnostic acoustic recordings of this species are on the rise on Salt Spring Island. To date it is known only from southwestern BC, but given its presence in Idaho, it may appear in other areas of southern BC, especially areas with rocky cliff habitat.

REFERENCES

Balcombe and McCracken (1992); Best and Geluso (2003); Genoways, Freemand and Grell (2000); Gillam and McCracken (2007); Gustin and McCracken (1987); Krutzsch, Fleming and Crichton (2002); Lee and McCracken (2005); McCracken (1999); McCracken et al. (2016); Ommundsen, Lausen and Matthias (2017); Russell, Medellín and McCracken (2005); Whitaker (1980); Wilkins (1989); Williams et al. (1973).

BRAZILIAN FREE-TAILED BAT. PHOTO: BRUCE D. TAUBERT (BAT CONSERVATION INTERNATIONAL)

BRAZILIAN FREE-TAILED BAT. PHOTO: MICHAEL DURHAM/MINDEN PICTURES
(BAT CONSERVATION INTERNATIONAL)

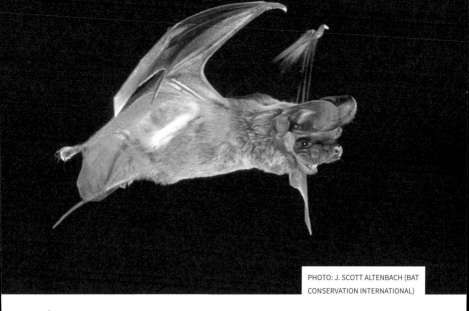

Big Free-Tailed Bat   *Nyctinomops macrotis*

DESCRIPTION

BIG FREE-TAILED BAT is a large bat with a tail that extends well beyond the tail membrane and is thus free to move, hence its common name. As a Molossid, this is a migratory bat with large ears (which nearly reach the end of the snout when laid forward) and long, narrow wings built for speed. Dorsal fur can vary from pale reddish brown to dark brown and blackish. The ears are joined at the midline of the head, and the sides of the lips have grooves (wrinkles).

BIG FREE-TAILED BAT is known from a single specimen in BC, measuring a total length of 139 millimetres, with tail vertebrae 52 millimetres, hind foot 13 millimetres, and forearm 60.9 millimetres. Elsewhere, this species ranges from 145 to 160 millimetres (males) or 120 to 139 millimetres (females) in total length, with a tail length ranging from 40 to 57 millimetres, and a mass of 22 to 30 grams.

MORPHOLOGICALLY SIMILAR SPECIES

BRAZILIAN FREE-TAILED BAT. As a Molossid, this species has unique morphological traits, as described above; it is unlikely to be confused with any other BC bat species. BIG FREE-TAILED BAT can be differentiated from the other accidental Molossid in BC, BRAZILIAN FREE-TAILED BAT, by size, as BIG FREE-TAILED

ZERO-CROSS RECORDINGS

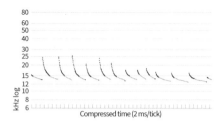

Low-clutter pulse shapes progressing to more moderate-clutter pulses, each ending near 12 kilohertz. (Recorded by Chris Currie on the Sunshine Coast.)

kHz log

Compressed time (2 ms/tick)

PHOTO: MICHAEL DURHAM/MINDEN PICTURES (BAT CONSERVATION INTERNATIONAL)

BAT has a forearm length of 58 to 64 millimetres, much greater than that of BRAZILIAN FREE-TAILED BAT (46 millimetres or less). BIG FREE-TAILED BAT's ears join at the midline of the head, while BRAZILIAN FREE-TAILED BAT's ears do not (see page 98).

DISTRIBUTION

BIG FREE-TAILED BAT is found in the southwestern United States through to South America. It is sparsely distributed within its range. It has been captured at elevations of more than 2,400 metres. Accidental occurrences have been reported as far north as BC and as far east as South Carolina. In BC, it is known from a male specimen (possibly immature) that was captured after it flew into an open hospital window at Essondale, Coquitlam, in November 1938. There is also a recent acoustic record from the Sunshine Coast.

ACOUSTIC CHARACTERISTICS

Audible. Most of the echolocation produced by BIG FREE-TAILED BAT is below 20 kilohertz and is thus considered audible to humans (it sounds like a series of clicks). Open-environment commuting calls can be very low-sloped calls ending between 10 and 12 kilohertz, with clutter calls sweeping through frequencies starting above 25 kilohertz and ending at 12 to 16 kilohertz, though they can end as high as 18 kilohertz in high clutter.

ACOUSTICALLY SIMILAR SPECIES

HOARY BAT. In BC, the only other bat species that echolocates in the range of BIG FREE-TAILED BAT is HOARY BAT. However, these two species are unlikely to ever be confused because HOARY BAT's lowest frequency range (approximately 15 kilohertz) is associated with flat, near-constant frequency calls, coinciding with an open flying environment. In contrast, calls produced by BIG FREE-TAILED BAT ending at this same frequency would be very steep-looking broadband sweeps, corresponding to high clutter.

ROOSTING

BIG FREE-TAILED BAT is found in rugged terrain, mainly near cliffs. It will roost in buildings, caves and occasionally trees. Males and females roost separately. Maternity colonies can range from less than six to hundreds of individuals. Radio-telemetry in northern Arizona at 1,200 metres elevation identified southeast-facing rock crack roosts approximately 130 metres above ground level on a cliff, ranging from 18 to 30 metres in length and 0.3 to 0.9 metres wide.

The BC acoustic detection by Chris Currie was made at the bottom of a rugged, narrow, steep-sided north-south coastal valley, with many exposed rock faces.

FEEDING

This bat has been captured at large ponds and will travel more than 25 kilometres one way from its roost to forage. It feeds on a variety of insects but relies heavily on moths as a preferred prey item.

REPRODUCTION

Females typically give birth to single young, but little is known about mating and reproduction.

MIGRATION AND WINTER

BIG FREE-TAILED BAT is a fast-flying bat that does not hibernate. Flight speeds of more than 60 kilometres per hour have been estimated based on radiotelemetry studies. Most individuals in the southwestern United States migrate into Mexico during winter months.

REMARKS

Six acoustic recordings (each 15 seconds) were made by Chris Currie in the Upper Clowhom Watershed on the Sunshine Coast, between 21:47 and 21:49 on July 14, 2014.

The nearest known population is in California. BIG FREE-TAILED BAT is a large bat, and as with Molossids in general, its high aspect ratio and moderate wing loading (see page 16), similar to that of small birds, make it capable of long-distance flight. There are other reports of this species outside its usual range, suggesting that it is a transient migrant in BC and not likely to be found regularly.

REFERENCES

Corbett, Chambers and Herder (2008); Cowan (1945); Milner, Jones and Jones (1990); Norberg (1981); Parish and Jones (1999); van Zyll de Jong (1985).

Canyon Bat   *Parastrellus hesperus*

DESCRIPTION

CANYON BAT is a small bat. The black coloration of the snout and the area around the eyes gives it an extensive facial mask. Its fur is generally pale in colour, composed of hairs that have a black base and a grey or buff brown-yellow tip. Its calcar is keeled. It has a unique, club-shaped tragus, with a slight curve and a blunt end.

Adult mass is 3 to 6 grams, with a wingspan of 19 to 23 centimetres and a forearm of 26 to 33 millimetres.

MORPHOLOGICALLY SIMILAR SPECIES

DARK-NOSED SMALL-FOOTED MYOTIS. CANYON BAT and DARK-NOSED SMALL-FOOTED MYOTIS are both small bats with light-coloured pelage, facial masks and keeled calcars; however, CANYON BAT is readily distinguished by its blunt, club-shaped tragus. It also has a different dental formula: instead of the 38 teeth of myotis species, it has only 34, with one less premolar per jaw quadrant.

DISTRIBUTION

CANYON BAT is found throughout western North America, from Mexico to Washington. This species is associated with arid desert/grassland landscapes but is also found in rocky low-elevation areas in mixed conifer forests in California and Arizona. Its occurrence in BC is not confirmed but is suspected based on

ZERO-CROSS RECORDINGS

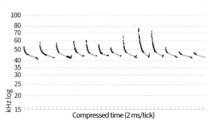

Moderate- to low-clutter pulses, recorded in Arizona.

FULL-SPECTRUM RECORDINGS

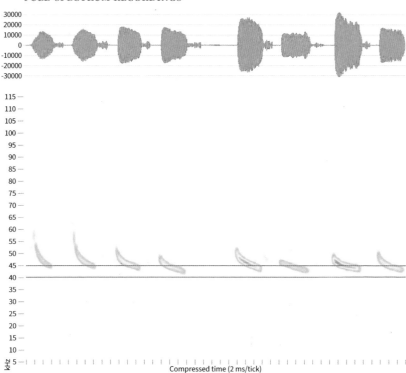

Spotlighted in Arizona, this CANYON BAT flew away from a hedgerow, so the two pulses on the left are relatively high-clutter pulses, and then the pulses lowered in slope and frequency as the bat flew into the open.

an acoustic recording made June 2013 (by Mike Sarell) in a rocky canyon of the dry grasslands southwest of Osoyoos, and several May and June recordings by Kirk Safford in the rocky cliffs of Skaha Provincial Park and Okanagan Mountain Park (acoustically analyzed by Mike Sarell, Cori Lausen, Brian Paterson and Bill Haas). The nearest known capture location for this species is in central Washington, directly south of the BC recordings, and recent acoustic monitoring in the Little Pend Oreille National Wildlife Refuge in northeast Washington detected this species in both summer and winter. Both sites are within 225 kilometres of BC recording sites.

ACOUSTIC CHARACTERISTICS

45 kilohertz. Although its minimum frequencies can approach 40 kilohertz, CANYON BAT more typically produces calls that end at 45 kilohertz, though they can end at a higher frequency, especially in the presence of conspecifics (individuals of the same species). In open environments, the calls have low slopes, often with a gentle curvature on the bottom and sometimes with an upward hook, resembling the upturned toes of Lasiurine bats (see species accounts for HOARY and EASTERN RED BAT). Unlike the Lasiurines, CANYON BAT produces a uniform sequence of pulses, and even in clutter, spectrograms show a relatively narrow bandwidth, giving the pulses a rather short appearance.

ACOUSTICALLY SIMILAR SPECIES

YUMA MYOTIS, CALIFORNIAN MYOTIS. In BC, the only bat species producing calls that end at around 45 kilohertz are CANYON BAT, YUMA MYOTIS and CALIFORNIAN MYOTIS, although EASTERN RED BAT cannot be completely ruled out, as its calls can approach 45 kilohertz when flying in high clutter. Unlike red bats (eastern and western), which as Lasiurines produce undulating minimum-frequency call patterns, CANYON BAT produces sequences of calls that uniformly end at the same minimum frequency, as do YUMA and CALIFORNIAN MYOTIS. To differentiate CANYON BAT from the myotis species in low clutter, call shape is used: CANYON BAT spectrograms typically show a narrower bandwidth (and thus calls are of relatively short duration despite their low slope) and calls that can flatten to a constant frequency near the end. YUMA MYOTIS spectrograms typically show calls that sweep through a broader range of frequencies, and although they may have a low slope following an abrupt change in slope (elbow/knee), they do not have a constant frequency (flat) component as CANYON BAT would. While both canyon and myotis bats can have downward-facing toes on their calls, the presence of upward hooks at the end of CANYON BAT calls can be used to differentiate this species from myotis, although this can present confusion with WESTERN RED BAT (not found in BC).

Outside BC, in areas where this species is common, a spotlight can be useful in helping identify this bat because of its "fluttering" flight pattern.

ROOSTING

CANYON BAT's name stems from its association with rocky areas, where it roosts in small crevices, although it has also been suggested that it may roost under rocks or in holes in the ground. It roosts near permanent water sources. In Arizona, it has been found roosting in exterior crevices of houses with swimming pools.

FEEDING

This small bat flies slowly and somewhat erratically, resembling a large moth in flight. It is often documented emerging before dusk to feed and is thus observed in relatively high light levels compared with other bats. The three primary food sources of CANYON BAT are small moths, leafhoppers and flying ants, although it has also been found to eat caddisflies, stoneflies, mosquitoes and flies.

A genetic study of guano in Texas identified a large range of arthropod prey—representing 8 orders and 27 species—expanding the known prey base for this species to include two new substantial components (FALSE CHINCH BUG and two species of ground beetles). It was found that males and females had different diets, but young-of-year bats did not differ in diet from adults. Diet also did not differ with stage of female reproduction.

REPRODUCTION

Females typically give birth to twins in late May through June, and the mothers with their young may roost alone or in small groups (approximately 12 individuals).

MIGRATION AND WINTER

CANYON BAT has low aspect ratio and wing loading, similar to CALIFORNIAN MYOTIS, and is thus slow-flying and considered non-migratory. It is known to hibernate in crevices or mines, and to forage during the daylight on mild winter days in some areas; it is one of the most active bats at night in winter in Nevada.

REMARKS

CANYON BAT was classified as a species of pipistrelle (*Pipistrellus hesperus*, WESTERN PIPISTRELLE) in most publications. However, a study of morphological and genetic data in 2006 revealed that it is not related to the pipistrelle bats and classified it as the sole member of the genus *Parastrellus*.

In a genetic study of the rabies virus, it was found that CANYON BAT has a unique rabies virus variant, different from the variants carried by SILVER-HAIRED BAT and TRICOLORED BAT, which are the variants most commonly associated with human rabies in the United States. When rabid, CANYON BAT is typically aggressive, engaging in seemingly unprovoked attacks on other bats.

REFERENCES

Adams (2003), Barbour and Davis (1969), Barnett and Collins (2019), B.C. Conservation Data Centre (2015), Demere (2016), Franka et al. (2006), Hayes and Wiles (2013), Hoofer et al. (2006), Norberg and Rayner (1987), O'Farrell and Bradley (1970), Sidner (1999).

Acknowledgements

For creation of range maps, we thank the Ministry of Environment and Climate Change Strategy: Jacqueline Clare, Data and Information Management Unit Lead, B.C. Conservation Data Centre; and Orville Dyer, Bat Specialist. We also thank Jason Rae of Wildlife Conservation Society Canada.

For data contributions, we thank Erin Fraser, Public Health Veterinarian, Communicable Diseases and Immunization Service, BC Centre for Disease Control; Government of Northwest Territories; Parks Canada—Wood Buffalo National Park; and Wildlife Conservation Society Canada and BC Parks for contribution of North American Bat Monitoring Program acoustic recordings. We draw on observations and data from the original handbook, and we have updated the text with unpublished data or observations made by Aimee Mitchell, Audrey Lauzon, Elizabeth Clare, Brian Paterson, Kirk Safford, Doug Burles, Bill Haas, Inge-Jean Hansen, Tim Ennis, Brock Fenton, Daniella Rambaldini, Dave Hobson, Doug Burles, Francis Iredale, Gillian Sanders, Greg Falxa, Ian Adams, Ian McTaggart-Cowan, Inge-Jean Hansen, John Saremba, Jeff Clerc, Karen Blejwas, Ken Racey, Leah Rensel, Michelle Evelyn, Mike Sarell, Peter Ommundsen, Richard Manning, Todd Manning, Frank Doyle, Scott Grindal, Susan Dulc, Susan Holroyd, Tanya Luszcz, Tory Rhoads, Vanessa Craig, Cory Olson, Laura Matthias, Rodney Polden, John Boulanger, David Paetkau, Joseph Poissant, Lisa Tedesco, Heather Gates, Jessica Holden, Emily de Freitas, Kim Frederiksen, Purnima Govindarajulu, Mike Farley, Julia Craig, Chris Currie, Jackie McQuillan, Kyle Nelson and Neil Tracey.

For contribution of photos, we thank Florian Graner (Sealife Productions), Jared Grummer (ArcoIris Photography), J. Scott Altenbach and Bruce Taubert (Bat Conservation International), Michael Durham (Minden Pictures/Bat Conservation International), José Martinez (Northern Arizona University), Erin McCleod, Leah Rensel, Michael Proctor, Cory Olson, Christian Engelstoft, Ian Routley, John Saremba, Mike Sarell, Nathan deBruyn, Laura Finn, Susan Dulc, Steve Latour, Heather Gates, Francis Swan, Hildegard Gerlach, Mathieu Lauriault, Ken Dzinbal, Hunter Causey and Chris Currie.

For contribution of acoustic recordings, we thank Chris Corben, Chris Currie, Bill Haas and Karen Blejwas.

For reviewing and/or formatting parts of this second edition handbook manuscript we thank: Brian Paterson, Emily de Freitas, Mike Sarell and Wildlife Conservation Society Canada's Jason Rae, Dana Blouin and Heather Gates.

For facilitating recordings, photos and data collection, we thank Dave Johnston (H.T. Harvey & Associates), Bat Conservation International (Mylea Bayless, Javier Folgar and Corey Anklam), Martin Davis (Island Karst Research), Mandy Kellner (BC Community Bat Program), Sigi Liebmann (International Timberframes) and Jillian Kusch (Saskatchewan Conservation Data Centre).

Appendix 1: Other Species Referred to in Text

Common name used in book	Scientific name
ALFALFA WEEVIL	*Hypera postica*
ANTELOPE BRUSH	*Purshia tridentata*
BAT FLY	*Trichobius corynorhini*
BALSAM POPLAR	*Populus balsamifera*
BELTED KINGFISHER	*Megaceryle alcyon*
BIG SAGEBRUSH	*Artemisia tridentata*
BLACK COTTONWOOD	*Populus trichocarpa*
BTI	*Bacillus thuringiensis israelensis*
CALIFORNIAN LEAF-NOSED BAT	*Macrotus californicus*
COLUMBIA PLATEAU POCKET MOUSE	*Perognathus parvus*
DOUGLAS-FIR	*Pseudotsuga menziesii*
DOUGLAS-FIR BEETLE	*Dendroctonus pseudotsugae*
EASTERN SMALL-FOOTED MYOTIS	*Myotis leibii*
FALSE CHINCH BUG	*Nysius raphanus*
FULLER'S TEASEL	*Dipsacus fullonum*
GRAY-HEADED FLYING FOX	*Pteropus poliocephalus*
JERUSALEM CRICKET	*Stenopelmatus fuscus*
KEEN'S MYOTIS	*Myotis keenii*
NORTH AMERICAN RACER	*Coluber constrictor*
NORTHERN SAW-WHET OWL	*Aegolius acadicus*
PACIFIC MARTEN	*Martes caurina*
PAPER BIRCH	*Betula papyrifera*
PD (WHITE-NOSE FUNGUS)	*Pseudogymnoascus destructans*
PONDEROSA PINE	*Pinus ponderosa*
RABBIT BRUSH	*Chrysothamnus nauseosus*
RED-STEM CEANOTHUS	*Ceanothus sanguineus*
SHORT-EARED OWL	*Asio flammeus*
SPECTACLED FLYING FOX	*Pteropus conspicillatus*
TREMBLING ASPEN	*Populus tremuloides*
TRICOLORED BAT	*Perimyotis subflavus*
WESTERN HEMLOCK	*Tsuga heterophylla*
WESTERN PIPISTRELLE (previous classification of CANYON BAT)	*Pipistrellus hesperus*
WESTERN REDCEDAR	*Thuja plicata*
WESTERN SCREECH OWL	*Megascops kennicottii*
WESTERN SMALL-FOOTED MYOTIS	*Myotis ciliolabrum*
WESTERN SPRUCE BUDWORM	*Choristoneura occidentalis*
WESTERN TOAD	*Bufo boreas*
WESTERN RED BAT	*Lasiurus blossevillii*
WESTERN WHITE PINE	*Pinus monticola*

Appendix 2: Key to Skulls and Dental Traits of BC Bats

Based on cranial and dental characters, this key will assist in the identification of skulls of the province's 15 resident and three accidental bat species. It is designed to be used on cleaned skulls—either museum specimens or skulls found in caves or owl pellets. You will require a hand lens or binocular dissecting microscope for viewing dentition, and vernier calipers to measure skulls or tooth rows. Different types of teeth referred to in the key are identified.

The four types of teeth are as follows:

I	upper incisors	i	lower incisors
C	upper canine	c	lower canine
P	upper premolars	p	lower premolars
M	upper molars	m	lower molars

Skull measurements are illustrated as follows:

$A-A^1$ skull length
$B-B^1$ postorbital width
$C-C^1$ width across last upper molars
$D-D^1$ length from the last upper premolar to last upper molar
$E-E^1$ length of the upper toothrow

The key is dichotomous, with the diagnostic characteristics arranged into couplets; each couplet offers you two mutually exclusive choices (labelled a or b). To identify a bat, begin with **couplet 1** and select **a** or **b**. This will give you either a species name or direct you to another couplet in the key. By working through the various steps in the key, you will arrive at an identification. A table summarizing the dental formula of each bat species follows the key.

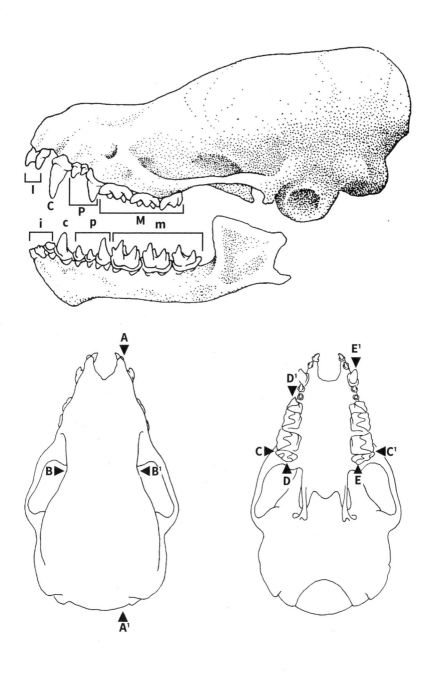

1	**1a**	One upper incisor on each side of skull: Go to **2** 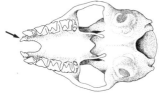
	1b	Two upper incisors on each side of skull: Go to **6** 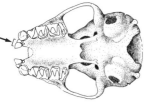
2 (L1)	**2a**	Palate extends well behind third upper molars: Go to **3**
	2b	Palate extends only slightly beyond third upper molars: Go to **4**
3 (L2)	**3a**	Skull length greater than 20 mm: BIG FREE-TAILED BAT (p. 291)
	3b	Skull length less than 20 mm: BRAZILIAN FREE-TAILED BAT (p. 285)
4 (L2)	**4a**	One upper premolar on each side of skull: PALLID BAT (p. 135) 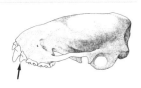
	4b	Two upper premolars on each side of skull: Go to **5** 
5 (L4)	**5a**	Skull length greater than 15 mm: HOARY BAT (p. 187)
	5b	Skull length less than 15 mm: EASTERN RED BAT (p. 179)
6 (L5)	**6a**	One upper premolar on each side of skull: BIG BROWN BAT (p. 159)
	6b	More than one upper premolar on each side of skull: Go to **7**

| 7 (⊥6) | 7a | Two upper premolars on each side of skull: Go to **8** | |
| | 7b | Three upper premolars on each side of skull: Go to **11** | |

| 8 (⊥7) | 8a | Three lower premolars on each side of mandible: Go to **9** |
| | 8b | Two lower premolars on each side of mandible: Go to **10** |

| 9 (⊥8) | 9a | Postorbital width greater than 4 mm: SILVER-HAIRED BAT (p. 197) |
| | 9b | Postorbital width less than 4 mm: TOWNSEND'S BIG-EARED BAT (p. 147) |

| 10 (⊥8) | 10a | Skull length greater than 14 mm: SPOTTED BAT (p. 169) |
| | 10b | Skull length less than 14 mm: CANYON BAT (p. 295) |

| 11 (⊥7) | 11a | Postorbital width less than 3.4 mm: Go to **12** |
| | 11b | Postorbital width greater than 3.4 mm: Go to **13** |

| 12 (⊥11) | 12a | Forehead with steep slope: CALIFORNIAN MYOTIS (p. 207) | |
| | 12b | Forehead with gradual slope: DARK-NOSED SMALL-FOOTED MYOTIS (p. 239) | |

| 13 (⊥11) | 13a | Ratio of postorbital width/upper toothrow length greater than 0.7 mm: Go to **14** |
| | 13b | Ratio of postorbital width/upper toothrow length less than 0.7 mm: Go to **16** |

| **14** (ᴌ13) | **14a** | Braincase strongly elevated: LONG-LEGGED MYOTIS (p. 263) | 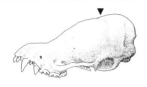 |

| | **14b** | Braincase not strongly elevated: Go to **15** |  |

| **15** (ᴌ14) | **15a** | Forehead with steep slope; skull length usually less than 14.0 mm: YUMA MYOTIS (p. 271) |
| | **15b** | Forehead with gradual slope; skull length usually greater than 14.0 mm: LITTLE BROWN MYOTIS (p. 227) |

| **16** (ᴌ13) | **16a** | Length across upper molars and last upper premolar (P^4–M^3) greater than 4.2 mm: Go to **17** |
| | **16b** | Length across upper molars and last upper premolar (P^4–M^3) less than 4.2 mm: NORTHERN MYOTIS (p. 247) |

| **17** (ᴌ16) | **17a** | Width across last upper molars (M^3–M^3) greater than 6.2 mm: FRINGED MYOTIS (p. 255) |
| | **17b** | Width across last upper molars (M^3–M^3) less than 6.2 mm: LONG-EARED MYOTIS (p. 217) |

Dental Formulae of BC Bats

The table below gives the number of each kind of tooth on one side of the upper and lower bat jaws. For example, PALLID BAT has 1 incisor in each half of the upper jaw and 2 incisors in each half of the lower jaw (mandible).

Species	Incisors	Canines	Premolars	Molars
Vespertilionidae				
PALLID BAT	1/2	1/1	1/2	3/3
TOWNSEND'S BIG-EARED BAT	2/3	1/1	2/3	3/3
BIG BROWN BAT	2/3	1/1	1/2	3/3
SPOTTED BAT	2/3	1/1	2/2	3/3
EASTERN RED BAT	1/3	1/1	2/2	3/3
HOARY BAT	1/3	1/1	2/2	3/3
SILVER-HAIRED BAT	2/3	1/1	2/3	3/3
CALIFORNIAN MYOTIS	2/3	1/1	3/3	3/3
DARK-NOSED SMALL-FOOTED MYOTIS	2/3	1/1	3/3	3/3
LONG-EARED MYOTIS	2/3	1/1	3/3	3/3
LITTLE BROWN MYOTIS	2/3	1/1	3/3	3/3
NORTHERN MYOTIS	2/3	1/1	3/3	3/3
LONG-LEGGED MYOTIS	2/3	1/1	3/3	3/3
FRINGED MYOTIS	2/3	1/1	3/3	3/3
YUMA MYOTIS	2/3	1/1	3/3	3/3
CANYON BAT	2/3	1/1	2/2	3/3
Molossidae				
BIG FREE-TAILED BAT	1/2	1/1	2/2	3/3
BRAZILIAN FREE-TAILED BAT	1/2 or 1/3	1/1	2/2	3/3

Appendix 3: Reference Table for Species Morphology

Bat species identification at a glance. This is not meant to be a key so much as a way to narrow down which species accounts to consult. There is also a dichotomous key for identifying species using morphological descriptions and measurements (page 97).

Species	Primary body fur colour	Ear description	Tail membrane, if important for identification	Keeled calcar?	Other diagnostic traits
SPOTTED BAT	black	big	n/a	no keel	3 white spots on back; pinkish ears
PALLID BAT	pale	big	n/a	no keel	pig-like nose; large eyes
TOWNSEND'S BIG-EARED BAT	pale	big	n/a	no keel	projections/ folds on each side of nose
HOARY BAT	grey (with frosted white tips)	short, round	dorsal side heavily furred	long, narrow keel	yellow-brown fur around head
EASTERN RED BAT	red	short, round	dorsal side heavily furred	indistinct	n/a
SILVER-HAIRED BAT	black or dark brown	short, round	dorsal side furred near body, less fur toward tip	no keel	most will have silver-tipped hairs on dorsal side (variable depending on age/moult)
BIG BROWN BAT	brown	short, round	n/a	keeled	swollen gland features on side of snout
LONG-LEGGED MYOTIS	brown	short, round	n/a	keeled	hairy armpits

Species	Primary body fur colour	Ear description	Tail membrane, if important for identification	Keeled calcar?	Other diagnostic traits
CALIFORNIAN MYOTIS	brown	medium length, pointed	unlike the similar-sized DARK-NOSED SMALL-FOOTED MYOTIS, tail does not extend beyond edge of tail membrane	keeled	n/a
DARK-NOSED SMALL-FOOTED MYOTIS	brown	medium length, pointed	unlike the similar-sized CALIFORNIAN MYOTIS, tail extends several vertebrae beyond edge of tail membrane	keeled	n/a
YUMA MYOTIS	brown	medium length, pointed	n/a	no keel	similar to LITTLE BROWN MYOTIS— consult species accounts
LITTLE BROWN MYOTIS	brown	medium length, pointed	n/a	no keel	similar to YUMA MYOTIS— consult species accounts
LONG-EARED MYOTIS	brown	long	edge of tail membrane may have sparse hairs (especially in young-of-year)	indistinct if present	ears are longer than NORTHERN and FRINGED MYOTIS
NORTHERN MYOTIS	brown	long	n/a	n/a	long, narrow, very sharp tragus
FRINGED MYOTIS	brown	long	thick fringe of hairs on edge of tail membrane	indistinct if present	n/a

Species	Primary body fur colour	Ear description	Tail membrane, if important for identification	Keeled calcar?	Other diagnostic traits
CANYON BAT	brown	short, round	n/a	keeled	paddle-like tragus (blunt, short, wide and leaning slightly forward); dark eye mask
BRAZILIAN FREE-TAILED BAT	dark brown/ grey	big, oriented forward	approximately one-third of tail dangles free (not in tail membrane)	n/a	ears do not meet at forehead; deeply wrinkled top lip
BIG FREE-TAILED BAT	brown-black	big, oriented forward	approximately one-third of tail dangles free (not in tail membrane)	n/a	base of ears join at forehead; deeply wrinkled top lip

Appendix 4: Acoustic Species Summary Table

This table provides descriptions of BC bat species' call characteristics. The general frequency category in the left column of the table is the description or approximate range of frequencies at which the calls for each species typically end in a low-clutter flying environment.

Caveats

It is important to note that call parameters for each species are provided as a guideline only. The acoustic descriptions provided in each species' profile and summarized in the table do not fully describe the entire repertoire of BC bat species, as recordings have not been made across the provincial ranges of all species. These qualitative and quantitative descriptions simply provide an overview of acoustic characteristics for each species based on recordings collected to date.

In addition, due to the functional nature of bat echolocation and the effect that context has on the parameters of calls and sequence patterns, species-specific call identification may not be accurate or even possible. No reference call library for a species is ever complete, and the species-specific parameters that underpin descriptions in this table may not fully reflect the acoustic breadth of each species, leaving room for error in identification. It is generally good practice to have an acoustic expert review your assessment, and where possible, to use additional methods of identification, such as mist-net capture or genetic identification from guano. Other acoustic resources in this book include the individual species accounts and a dichotomous key in Acoustics: Echolocation and Species Identification (page 125). Acoustics terminology is also explained in that section and in the glossary.

General frequency category	Species	Other bats this can be confused with in BC
Audible	SPOTTED BAT	
Distinctive because of its audible frequency calls, often dropping to 8 kilohertz or lower. Even in low clutter this species maintains a relatively steep call. Diagnostic social calls at approximately 15 kilohertz consist of a series of narrow-bandwidth calls between echolocation pulses.		None—but note that grass being ruffled in the wind, insects and other sources of sound in the 5–12 kilohertz range can mask this bat's presence.

General frequency category	Species	Other bats this can be confused with in BC
10–18 kilohertz	BIG FREE-TAILED BAT	

This bat is in the audible range for humans with good hearing. The minimum frequency produced by BIG FREE-TAILED BAT when flying in an open environment is as low as 10 kilohertz—at this low frequency, the pulses are low in slope. These flatter calls make it easily distinguished from SPOTTED BAT (whose calls are always steep), the only other audible bat in BC. The high-clutter calls of BIG FREE-TAILED BAT typically end at a frequency in the range of 12–16 kilohertz. At 15–16 kilohertz, call frequencies overlap with the lowest frequencies produced by HOARY BAT. However, when HOARY BAT produces calls with minimum frequency as low as 15 kilohertz, these are low-clutter and thus low-sloped calls, contrasting with the steeper slopes of BIG FREE-TAILED BAT calls at this frequency. Because of these obvious differences in pulse shape, the BIG FREE-TAILED BAT, which is accidental in BC, can be acoustically distinguished from all other bat species in BC.

None.

| **15–30 kilohertz** | HOARY BAT | |

Distinguishable from other low-frequency bats when flying in open environments due to low (15–20 kilohertz) calls that tend toward flat (low to no bandwidth). These low-frequency, low-clutter calls used when commuting are generally of long duration (e.g., 20–30 milliseconds) and can have one second between calls. When calls are above a minimum frequency of 20 kilohertz (moderate- to high-clutter scenarios), the call duration and time between calls is substantially less, introducing potential confusion with other species (see right-hand column); however, a sufficiently long recording will typically reveal an erratic undulating pattern of minimum call frequencies and a tendency toward upward-turned toes at the ends of calls, differentiating it from other 25 kilohertz bats. This undulating minimum frequency pattern of hooked calls is typical of the Lasiurines. Note that SILVER-HAIRED and BIG BROWN BATS can occasionally show a slight upturned toe/hook but will produce a uniform sequence of calls.

In moderate to high clutter, this bat's calls drop only to 25–30 kilohertz, causing potential confusion with BIG BROWN, SILVER-HAIRED and BRAZILIAN FREE-TAILED BATS.

General frequency category	Species	Other bats this can be confused with in BC
20–25 kilohertz	BRAZILIAN FREE-TAILED BAT	BIG BROWN BAT, SILVER-HAIRED BAT, HOARY BAT

Calls can be highly variable, even within a sequence (i.e., lack of uniformity in shape and frequency between consecutive calls), providing a basis for differentiation from other 25 kilohertz bats in a sufficiently long recording. Flat or low-sloped calls can be produced as low as 20 or as high as 30 kilohertz. In low clutter, this bat tends toward flat calls, leading to confusion with SILVER-HAIRED BAT. Flat calls falling between 20 and 25 kilohertz differentiate it from SILVER-HAIRED, BIG BROWN and HOARY BATS.

General frequency category	Species	Other bats this can be confused with in BC
25 kilohertz	PALLID BAT	FRINGED MYOTIS, LONG-EARED MYOTIS; in moderate to high clutter, BIG BROWN BAT, SILVER-HAIRED BAT

This species will produce high-clutter-type (broad-bandwidth) calls even in apparently open environments as it searches the ground for food, inviting confusion with other 25 kilohertz bats flying in clutter. Its steepest calls can lead to confusion with FRINGED MYOTIS flying in open environments but tend to have some curvature at the end of the pulse and lower energy in the higher frequencies than FRINGED MYOTIS (see below). PALLID BAT has a social directive call that resembles a stretched-out S or zigzag extending from the end of the call; this long, low social component sets it apart from BIG BROWN BAT, but BIG BROWN BATS have been documented producing a wavy extension from their calls that could have a resemblance to PALLID BAT's directive (though much shorter in duration and bandwidth).

General frequency category	Species	Other bats this can be confused with in BC
25 kilohertz	BIG BROWN BAT	SILVER-HAIRED BAT, BRAZILIAN FREE-TAILED BAT, HOARY BAT; in moderate to high clutter, PALLID BAT

Calls typically drop to 30 kilohertz in higher clutter, and as low as 20 kilohertz in open environments. Moderate- and high-clutter calls overlap extensively with SILVER-HAIRED BAT and PALLID BAT (see PALLID BAT, above). Recordings of bats in moderate to high clutter can include loud high frequencies that start above 65 kilohertz; this feature may help differentiate it from SILVER-HAIRED BAT (see below). In uncluttered flight conditions, calls may drop as low as 20 kilohertz, but their slope never approaches zero; these traits may also be used to differentiate it from SILVER-HAIRED BAT (see below). Search phase calls show uniformity, and this may help differentiate it from BRAZILIAN FREE-TAILED BAT (see above).

General frequency category	Species	Other bats this can be confused with in BC
25 kilohertz	SILVER-HAIRED BAT	

Calls typically drop to 30 kilohertz in higher clutter, and as low as 23 kilohertz in open or moderate-clutter environments. Calls overlap extensively with BIG BROWN BAT. In uncluttered flight conditions, calls are typically flat, remaining above 25 kilohertz—traits that can be used to differentiate it from BIG BROWN BAT, which does not produce a flat call shape. As with BIG BROWN BAT, search phase calls show uniformity, and this may help differentiate them from the calls of BRAZILIAN FREE-TAILED and HOARY BATS (see above). In full-spectrum recordings in moderate to high clutter, the presence of a second harmonic may aid in differentiating from BIG BROWN BAT; a starting frequency of less than 50–55 kilohertz in the first harmonic when a second harmonic is visible is typical of SILVER-HAIRED BAT. (A BIG BROWN BAT in clutter, when approaching a microphone closely enough to record a second harmonic, starts its first harmonic at frequencies in excess of 65 kilohertz.)

Other bats this can be confused with in BC: BIG BROWN BAT, BRAZILIAN FREE-TAILED BAT, HOARY BAT; in moderate to high clutter, PALLID BAT

| 25 kilohertz | TOWNSEND'S BIG-EARED BAT | |

This species tends to put more energy into its second harmonic than most other species, which often results in the recording of both first and second harmonics; in zero-crossing analysis, this appears as split harmonics, and in full spectrum, similar amplitude would be displayed for both first and second harmonics. Overall, this bat has low-amplitude echolocation, requiring it to approach bat detectors more closely to be recorded than most other species. First harmonic calls drop to 20–25 kilohertz, but in zero-crossing analysis these look truncated, with a split-second harmonic ending at 40–50 kilohertz. Pulses may occasionally show a slower rate of frequency change early in the call, giving it a subtly unique shape. *Corynorhinus* species can also produce a component at the start of their echolocation pulses that consists of an upward sweep into the echolocation pulse and may be used in social communication.

Other bats this can be confused with in BC: Especially in full-spectrum recordings, FRINGED MYOTIS

General frequency category	Species	Other bats this can be confused with in BC
25 kilohertz	FRINGED MYOTIS	

This bat produces a steep high-clutter call type with substantial bandwidth, even in uncluttered environments, as it closely approaches surfaces to glean prey. Calls tend to drop to 20–25 kilohertz. If the bat is close to the microphone, calls can start as high as 120 kilohertz, resulting in very long frequency sweeps.

In high clutter, LONG-EARED MYOTIS; in poor-quality recording, possible confusion with PALLID BAT; in full-spectrum recording, possible confusion with TOWNSEND'S BIG-EARED BAT

| 30 kilohertz | LONG-EARED MYOTIS | |

Calls are generally steep, even in low-clutter environments, with minimum frequency ranging from 30 to 35 kilohertz but as high as 40 kilohertz, especially in the western portion of their BC range. At these higher frequencies, LONG-EARED MYOTIS can overlap with NORTHERN MYOTIS, another long-eared species (see below).

FRINGED MYOTIS, PALLID BAT; in high clutter, BIG BROWN BAT; in clutter, possible confusion with NORTHERN MYOTIS, especially in northwestern areas, where ranges may overlap

| 30–45 kilohertz | EASTERN RED BAT | |

Wide variability in frequency and slope of calls. In uncluttered environments, low-sloped calls, generally long in duration, dropping as low as 30 kilohertz; in cluttered environments, steep calls, short in duration, ending as high as 45 kilohertz. As a Lasiurine (see HOARY BAT, above), EASTERN RED BATS typically have an erratic call pattern showing undulating minimum call frequencies, and calls have a hook or upturned toe. An undulating, Lasiurine pattern between 30 and 45 kilohertz is diagnostic when produced. Steeper calls (in clutter) without undulation can be impossible to differentiate from some myotis species, particularly LITTLE BROWN MYOTIS.

In moderate to high clutter, and in short or poor-quality recordings, possible confusion with myotis species, particularly LITTLE BROWN MYOTIS

General frequency category	Species	Other bats this can be confused with in BC

35–40 kilohertz   LITTLE BROWN MYOTIS

Although classified as a 40 kilohertz myotis, this bat regularly echolocates as low as 35 kilohertz in open environments. Low-clutter calls are low in slope and often associated with a bend or elbow/knee in the call as it rapidly changes slope. This low frequency and bent shape allows it to be differentiated from other myotis and EASTERN RED BATS. Unlike EASTERN RED BATS, LITTLE BROWN BATS typically show uniformity of calls in a sequence, and toes of calls often turn down rather than upward, though slightly upturned toes/hooks are possible. Like YUMA MYOTIS, this species typically flies very close to calm water surfaces for an extended length of time (skimming), and recordings made under these conditions may show sound wave interference patterns due to reflected sound.

Other 40 kilohertz myotis: NORTHERN, DARK-NOSED SMALL-FOOTED, LONG-LEGGED; in high clutter and poor-quality recording, EASTERN RED BAT

40 kilohertz   NORTHERN MYOTIS

In low clutter, calls are often less steep than for other long-eared bats. Characteristic call frequencies range from approximately 38 to 45 kilohertz, but considering a toe, minimum frequencies can extend lower than this. When in close range of the microphone, calls can start as high as 120 kilohertz. High-clutter calls can be very steep (short duration) and often quiet (low energy). In general, they produce steep calls with large bandwidth, but in low clutter have obvious call curvature.

Especially in northwestern areas, LONG-EARED MYOTIS; in clutter, LONG-LEGGED MYOTIS and LITTLE BROWN MYOTIS

40 kilohertz   DARK-NOSED SMALL-FOOTED MYOTIS

Difficult to differentiate from other 40 kilohertz myotis. In high clutter, minimum frequency can be 45 kilohertz. As a relatively long-eared bat that takes insect prey from surfaces, it produces relatively steep calls even in low-clutter environments.

LITTLE BROWN MYOTIS, LONG-LEGGED MYOTIS; possibly YUMA or CALIFORNIAN MYOTIS

General frequency category	Species	Other bats this can be confused with in BC
40 kilohertz	LONG-LEGGED MYOTIS	

Difficult to differentiate from other 40 kilohertz myotis. In high clutter, minimum frequency can exceed 40 kilohertz. There is some speculation that a social component may exist for this species that sets it apart from other myotis—an upsweep into the start of the call. (See species account for more detail.)

Other 40 kilohertz myotis: NORTHERN, DARK-NOSED SMALL-FOOTED, LITTLE BROWN

45 kilohertz	CANYON BAT	

Short-bandwidth calls uniformly ending at 45 kilohertz. Call shape has a low slope and often an upturned toe. Although this species has similar call features to WESTERN RED BAT (not described here), there are no BC species that this bat can be confused with, as long as a recording of sufficient quality has been made. YUMA MYOTIS calls can have relatively low slope at the same frequency, but CANYON BAT has shorter bandwidth and a tendency for the toes to turn up.

YUMA MYOTIS

45–50 kilohertz	YUMA MYOTIS	

Minimum call frequency is typically higher than 45 kilohertz, up to 50 kilohertz in higher clutter. In open environments, calls take on a shallower slope, often with a distinct bend (elbow/knee), setting it apart from CALIFORNIAN MYOTIS, the other 50 kilohertz species. Like LITTLE BROWN MYOTIS, this species typically flies very close to calm water surfaces for an extended length of time (skimming), and recordings made under these conditions may show sound wave interference patterns due to reflected sound.

CALIFORNIAN MYOTIS

45–50 kilohertz	CALIFORNIAN MYOTIS	

In high clutter, this bat is indistinguishable from YUMA MYOTIS, the other BC species that produces calls dropping to 45–50 kilohertz. As a bat with relatively long ears and a tendency to glean insects from a surface, this bat produces steep high-clutter call shapes even in low clutter. As such, this bat can be distinguished from YUMA MYOTIS in low-clutter recording environments, where CALIFORNIAN MYOTIS typically does not take on the low-sloped or distinctly elbowed pulse shape of YUMA MYOTIS and may dip to frequencies a few kilohertz below 45 kilohertz.

YUMA MYOTIS; in low clutter and where ranges overlap, DARK-NOSED SMALL-FOOTED MYOTIS

Appendix 5: Fun Bat Facts

Species	Interesting facts
SPOTTED BAT	SPOTTED BAT is the only bat in Canada that does not use ultrasound to echolocate. Its echolocation calls can be heard by the human ear, resembling a series of clicking sounds. With large pink ears and three white spots on its back, this species is by far the most recognizable of BC's bats.
BIG BROWN BAT	BIG BROWN BAT appears to be BC's hardiest bat in the cold, with mid-winter flights outside of hibernacula recorded as far north as the Dawson Creek area. In Alberta and BC, this species flies at temperatures well below freezing.
CALIFORNIAN MYOTIS	Despite being the second smallest bat in the province, CALIFORNIAN MYOTIS is commonly recorded flying on cold winter nights throughout southern BC. It is recorded during winter flying in and out of shallow low-elevation mines at night, although its roosts are often in nearby rock crevices, where it will hibernate for weeks at a time before arousing to make another short flight.
CANYON BAT, BRAZILIAN FREE-TAILED BAT and BIG FREE-TAILED BAT	We don't know much about these species in BC. In this book we consider them to be "accidental," but CANYON BAT and BRAZILIAN FREE-TAILED BAT have been acoustically recorded multiple times, suggesting they may be new residents just waiting to be confirmed. By contrast, BIG FREE-TAILED BAT, a strong flyer, occasionally shows up well outside of its southwestern US range, and the two records in BC are thought to be truly accidental.
DARK-NOSED SMALL-FOOTED MYOTIS	Weighing in at less than the mass of a nickel, DARK-NOSED SMALL-FOOTED MYOTIS is BC's smallest bat. It can be found roosting alone in small gaps among rocks on the ground in the dry Interior of BC. Previously, this bat was known as the WESTERN SMALL-FOOTED MYOTIS, but populations west of the Rocky Mountains were renamed based on morphology.
EASTERN RED BAT	We did not know that we had EASTERN RED BAT in BC until the first carcass was found under a wind turbine in the northeast, having been struck by a fast-turning blade. Common in eastern North America, this species has been expanding its range westward.
FRINGED MYOTIS	FRINGED MYOTIS produces the lowest echolocation frequencies of all myotis species. It is distinct from LONG-EARED MYOTIS, but there is evidence in BC of some hybridization between these two species. Typically associated with the dry PONDEROSA PINE habitats of southern BC, a coastal form has also been documented, though little is known about it.
HOARY BAT	When HOARY BAT feels threatened, it produces a series of clicking sounds and hisses somewhat like a snake. The long-term outlook for HOARY BAT populations in North America is dire—the wind energy industry is predicted to devastate this species, as wind turbines kill these high-flying migratory bats along their migration corridors each year.

Species	Interesting facts
LITTLE BROWN MYOTIS	LITTLE BROWN MYOTIS commonly roosts in the same buildings or bat boxes as YUMA MYOTIS, and the two species are often confused (even by bat biologists), as they look almost identical, even though they are not genetically similar. Within each roost, however, these two species partition the space and are typically not clustered together.
LONG-EARED MYOTIS	LONG-EARED MYOTIS used to be considered taxonomically separate from the similar-looking coastal species, KEEN'S MYOTIS, which was Red-listed in BC. It was recently determined that these represent one breeding population and now all are considered just one species: LONG-EARED MYOTIS.
LONG-LEGGED MYOTIS	Although LONG-LEGGED MYOTIS is small and brown like all of the other myotis species, it is unique in having hairy armpits.
NORTHERN MYOTIS	NORTHERN MYOTIS is one of the quietest echolocating bats, foraging among trees and rarely emerging into open areas. It is thought to be dependent on old-growth trees for raising young in BC.
PALLID BAT	Although all bats in Canada eat insects, PALLID BAT is unique in its ability to also feed on scorpions. It is capable of echolocating using reflected ultrasound to find insects in the air, just as other bats do, but large ears and prominent eyes are indicative of its tendency to hunt for prey on the ground without use of echolocation. PALLID BAT uses its ears to listen for prey-generated sounds, such as the scurry of a beetle's feet, and on well-lit nights uses its eyes to aid in hunting.
SILVER-HAIRED BAT	Although many people assume that all bats are black, SILVER-HAIRED BAT is the only species in BC that is truly black, although older individuals look dark brown. In southern BC, they are commonly found overwintering in firewood piles and are known to also use trees, rock crevices and some large mines for hibernation.
TOWNSEND'S BIG-EARED BAT	When it roosts, TOWNSEND'S BIG-EARED BAT rolls its long ears up beside its head, so they look like a ram's horns. When it flies, it keeps its ears erect above its head, and while hovering can use them as funnels to listen carefully for prey-generated sounds, such as the flutter of a moth on a leaf.
YUMA MYOTIS	There are building attics in BC that house thousands of YUMA MYOTIS individuals. Like LITTLE BROWN MYOTIS, this species commonly flies just above the surface of calm water, foraging on insects at the water's surface. You can often catch glimpses of these bats when you shine a flashlight out over the water; unlike LITTLE BROWN MYOTIS, though, YUMA will typically shy away from the beam of your flashlight.

Glossary

adit—A horizontal (or nearly horizontal) entrance to an underground mine.

aerial hawking—Foraging behaviour in which prey is pursued and caught in flight.

aerodynamic—Having a shape that reduces drag in air.

altricial—Having young born, or hatched, in an undeveloped state and requiring parental care and feeding.

amplitude (of a sound wave)—The extent to which air particles are displaced; sound amplitude is experienced as the loudness of sound.

anthropogenic—Human-made.

approach (in echolocation)—A change in call structure (often an increase in frequency sweep coinciding with a decrease in call duration) that occurs when a bat receives and responds to echoes off a surface or object. This phase in a call **sequence** often precedes a **buzz**. (See also **search phase call**.)

aspect ratio—A measure of wing shape calculated as wing length divided by width.

auto-identification—Identification of bat calls or call **sequences** by software that uses a statistical procedure to match unknown pulses to known calls from reference libraries. Auto-identification software typically provides a measure of confidence associated with species-level identification.

bag test—An identification tool in which a bat is held in a cloth holding bag and gently moved up and down in close proximity to a bat detector that records and displays ultrasonic signals. Some bat species that are otherwise difficult to tell apart using morphometrics can be differentiated based on the frequencies they emit. This can be more effective for differentiating LITTLE BROWN MYOTIS from YUMA MYOTIS than recording echolocation of a bat released from the hand.

bandwidth—The range of frequencies through which an echolocation call sweeps. Narrow bandwidth calls sweep through a few frequencies over time, whereas broad bandwidth calls sweep through many frequencies.

bat box—A human-built structure that is typically small (approximately 1 metre or less in height) erected well above the ground to provide a **roost** for bats. Also called a bat house. See **bat condominium**.

bat condominium—A large structure built exclusively for bats to roost in, typically 4 metres by 4 metres, with corner posts, and generally placed at least 4–5 metres above the ground. It has a series of chambers similar to those in bat boxes, with various entry/exit points. Also referred to as a condo, with smaller-scale versions referred to as mini-condos.

bat detector—Electronic equipment capable of detecting ultrasonic sounds (echolocation calls) produced by bats that are normally above the range of human hearing. The bat detector may produce audible sounds so that bat echolocation can be heard by the user. Many also allow for these sounds to be recorded.

BatCaver—A Wildlife Conservation Society Canada program that engages cavers in bat conservation. See batcaver.org.

BC Community Bat Program—A network of smaller community bat programs across BC that provide outreach and education under the slogan "Got Bats?" See bcbats.ca.

Bergmann's rule—An ecogeographical rule that states that within a broadly distributed taxon, populations have a larger body size in colder environments and smaller body size in warmer regions.

Blue List—One of three provincial conservation status lists for organisms in BC. The Blue List includes species that are not immediately threatened but are of concern because of characteristics that make them particularly sensitive to human activities or natural events. See env.gov.bc.ca/wld/documents /ranking.pdf.

British Columbia Bat Action Team (BC BAT)—An ad hoc group of professional biologists, academic researchers, veterinarians, environmental educators, students, naturalists, wildlife rehabilitators, government biologists and others who are interested in bat conservation in BC. BC BAT is modelled after Canada's first bat working group, the Alberta Bat Action Team (ABAT), and is under the Western Bat Working Group umbrella along with western US state bat working groups. See bcbat.ca.

broadband (versus narrowband)—Broad **bandwidth** calls sweep through many frequencies, whereas narrow bandwidth calls sweep through a few frequencies over time.

buzz—The terminal phase of a bat echolocation **sequence** that results in numerous rapidly produced pulses during the approach to a potential prey item (feeding buzz) or a water surface (drinking buzz). The pulses are so closely spaced that, to the human ear, the output from a detector sounds like a buzz.

calcar—A cartilaginous spur, unique to bats, that is attached to the heel bone and extends into the tail membrane.

call—A brief continuous emission of sound produced by a bat when echolocating; see also **pulse**.

call body—The flattest part of a bat **call** or **pulse** when viewed in a frequency-versus-time **spectrogram**. This part of the call is where frequencies are not changing as rapidly with time as they do in the rest of the call. The zero-cross spectrograms in this book show this call parameter in blue.

cauda epididymides—(*sing.* epididymis) Tubes in the male reproductive system, one on each side of the body, that function as a sperm storage reservoir. These can be seen on either side of the tail in the tail membrane, close to the body, in male bats. (Also referred to as "epididymides.")

characteristic frequency—The last **frequency** produced in the **call body** of a **pulse**.

civil twilight—The period after sunset or before sunrise when the sun is six degrees below the horizon.

clutter—Objects or surfaces that produce reflected sound to an echolocating bat. These obstacles affect the recordings of bats: **ultrasound** may be scattered and attenuated sounds captured by the **bat detector**, and/or bats may change their search phase calls in response to the clutter, changing call parameters. Clutter can refer to almost anything that reflects sound and is within the hearing distance of bats, including other bats.

clutter continuum—The full range of call shapes that bats are capable of making. The continuum refers to the differing calls from bats flying in an open environment versus responding to **clutter**. Some species dramatically change their call structure between open environment search phase calls and calls produced in high clutter (e.g., HOARY BAT), while others show less variation in call shapes, with varying degrees of clutter (e.g., NORTHERN MYOTIS). This terminology was made popular in bat acoustics by Chris Corben, maker of Anabat.

colony—A group or cluster of bats. If a colony consists of females who are largely reproductive, it is referred to as a **maternity colony**.

COSEWIC—The Committee on the Status of Endangered Wildlife in Canada, a national committee of experts that assesses conservation status of Canadian wildlife.

cryptic—Having the tendency to hide.

dipterans—Flies of the taxonomic Order Diptera.

division ratio—A setting on a **bat detector** that records zero-cross files so you can listen to bats using **frequency** division, or in a software program that converts sound to a zero-cross format. The value of the division ratio represents the nth wave that is used in the process. For example, a division ratio of 8 on a frequency division detector divides the sound's frequencies by 8 so that an input sound from a bat that is 24 kilohertz has an output sound of 3 kilohertz, making it audible to a human ear; a zero-cross detector or acoustic software set at a division ratio of 4 means that the time elapsed for four sound waves can be used for a frequency calculation, and a series of these x (time), y (frequency) measurements can be graphed to produce a zero-cross **spectrogram**.

dorsal—On the back or upper side of an animal.

echolocation—An orientation system used by bats, based on generating sounds and listening to their returning echoes to locate obstacles and prey.

ectoparasite—A parasite, such as a flea, that lives on the outside of its host.

epididymides—See **cauda epididymides**.

epiphyseal gap—The noncalcified part of a growing long bone (at the ends); in a bat's finger joint, this cartilaginous zone appears translucent when illuminated from behind.

fast Fourier transform (FFT)—As applied to enabling a full-spectrum bat recording to be presented as a **spectrogram** (**frequency** versus time representation), FFT is a mathematical algorithm that is used to transform the signal from its original time domain to a representation in the frequency domain. Sound is a mixture of frequencies of different **amplitudes**, and FFT dissects these sounds, producing the average frequency content of a signal over the time that the signal was acquired.

free-flying—Flying through the air, as opposed to being held in the hand (i.e., captured) or sitting on a surface (i.e., roosting).

frequency—The number of sound waves that pass a given point in a given amount of time, measured in hertz (1 wave per second) or kilohertz (1,000 hertz). Frequency is equal to the reciprocal of the **period** (the duration of time of one sound wave).

frequency-modulated (FM) call—A type of **echolocation** call that varies or "modulates" in **frequency** throughout the call with no pulse-echo overlap. Low duty cycle.

full-spectrum—Full-spectrum **bat detectors** record all desirable information about the sounds in the environment, including multiple frequencies and amplitude, such that resulting **spectrograms** allow multiple **harmonics** to be dissected and visualized (see **fast Fourier transform**).

fundamental frequency—Frequency of the first harmonic, also called the **fundamental harmonic**.

fundamental harmonic—The lowest **frequency** of a periodic waveform (see also **harmonics**).

gate—A grate used to close off an underground hole/tunnel (typically an abandoned mine but can also be used on caves) to keep humans out for safety. The gate is "bat-friendly" if the horizontal bars are spaced appropriately for bats to fly through.

gestation period—The length of time that a fetus is developing in the uterus (from conception to birth).

glean—To capture insect prey from vegetation surfaces or the ground.

Gloger's rule—An ecogeographical rule stating that within a species of endotherm, more heavily pigmented forms tend to be found in more humid environments (usually nearer to the equator).

guano—Bat feces.

harmonics—Frequencies that are integer multiples of the **fundamental frequency**. Sometimes referred to as overtones, they can be used to assist in pinpointing an insect's location. Some bats alter the **amplitude** of harmonics by selective filtering during sound production.

harp trap—A device used to capture bats, with strings of fishing line strung vertically inside a generally square or rectangular frame. Strings are typically arranged in two offset lines, so that as a bat tries to manoeuvre through one line of strings, it runs into the second. It then drops into a bag below the frame of vertical strings, where there is usually a plastic flap that prevents the bat from crawling out.

hibernacula—(*sing.* hibernaculum) Sites where hibernation occurs (i.e., winter roosting).

isotherm—A line on a map that delineates areas of similar temperature.

isotope analysis—The analysis of an isotopic signature. Isotopes are variants of a chemical element (often carbon, nitrogen, oxygen, hydrogen or sulphur) that differ in neutron number in the atomic nucleus and vary in the environment in a predictable way. Because animals incorporate stable isotopes into their tissues through food and water consumption, the ratio of the isotopic variants (heavy:light) in a sample can be used to trace what foods have been consumed or where the animal has been.

keel—A flap of skin that may protrude from a bat's tail membrane in association with the **calcar**, near the ankle.

kilohertz (kHz)—The most common unit of measure of the **frequency** of sound; the equivalent of 1,000 hertz.

knee or elbow (in spectrograms)—**Pulses** of sound produced by bats can be visualized as a **spectrogram** showing **frequency** changes over time. The shape of these pulses can differ between and within individuals and species, and is affected by structures in the environment (see **clutter** and **clutter continuum**). If a bat slows the rate of change of its frequencies mid-pulse, this abrupt change appears as an angle and may be referred to as a knee or elbow. The presence of this feature in a pulse can be useful in differentiating some species.

lactation—Production of milk by a mother for her young. Bats nurse young during the lactation period in summer.

Lasiurine—Of the genus *Lasiurus*. In BC this includes EASTERN RED BAT and HOARY BAT.

maternity colony—A group of female bats that cluster together to raise young. Bats may cluster into other types of **colonies**, such as bachelor colonies of males, or mixed ages and sexes during hibernation.

maternity roost—A **roost** used by a female bat or group of female bats and their young during pregnancy and/or **lactation**. During lactation, the maternity roost may be specifically referred to as a nursery roost.

microsatellites—Sections of DNA that have a repetitive sequence of nucleotides (the building blocks of DNA). The length of a microsatellite is an allele (a form of a gene) that can be inherited. Microsatellites are used in studies of breeding patterns (population genetics). For example, ATATATAT is a repeat of the two nucleotides adenosine and thymine, and if there are 50 repeats of this on a chromosome, then this is a different allele than a chromosome with 40 repeats. At this specific microsatellite location on the two chromosomes, this individual would be described as 50, 40 (a genotype). These alleles are individually passed along to offspring through the sex cells (egg, sperm).

minimum frequency (of a pulse)—The lowest **frequency** produced in a **frequency-modulated (FM) call**.

mist-net—A device used to capture bats. They are typically made of nylon or polyester mesh and suspended between two poles, resembling a fine mesh badminton net.

mitochondrial DNA/**genome**—A circular strand of DNA found in the mitochondrion of most eukaryotic cells, which encodes for some proteins used in cellular metabolism. Passed along in an egg but typically not the sperm, mitochondrial DNA is considered to generally follow a maternal inheritance pattern. Mitochondrial DNA is a small portion of the DNA in a cell, with most genetic material residing in the nucleus (see **nuclear** DNA).

morphometrics—Measurements that describe the size and shape of a form.

narrowband (versus broadband)—See **broadband**.

natal philopatry—The tendency of animals to return to their birthplace.

native zero-crossing—When the **zero-crossing** analysis of a signal is done by a **bat detector** and the files are saved in this format—in contrast to a zero-crossing analysis of **full-spectrum** recordings performed by acoustic software.

niche—A species' interactions with its environment, including biotic factors, such as animals and plants, and non-living factors, such as landscape characteristics.

noctuid—A moth belonging to the family Noctuidae; a type of **tympanate moth**.

nubby ear—A phenomenon seen in some bats, especially LITTLE BROWN and YUMA MYOTIS, where one or both ears appear to have been damaged at the tip and are thus shorter in length. Also called "square ear." The cause of this is unknown.

nuclear DNA—Linear DNA contained in the nucleus of eukaryote cells (as chromosomes), accounting for most of the genetic material in the cell (see **mitochondrial** DNA). There are typically copies of chromosomes, and nuclear DNA is typically inherited equally from both parents—both characteristics in contrast to mitochondrial DNA.

nuclear genetic marker—A genetic marker is a gene or DNA sequence. Nuclear genetic markers have a known location on a nuclear chromosome (see **nuclear** DNA).

octaves per second (OPS)—Rate of decrease of **frequency** with respect to time. This is a measurement of **slope** in a bat pulse used by some acoustic software packages. The main advantage of using OPS over a standard **kilohertz**/seconds slope is that because OPS is logarithmic, a certain value can be used to describe a "low slope." For bat calls, when Sc (the slope of the **call body**) is less than 10 OPS, it is low, approaching flat. A steep call would have OPS values of several hundred. This applies to bats of any frequency. Another advantage is that when using OPS, different **harmonics** have the same slope. OPS between two points is calculated as $\log_2 (F1 / F2) / (T2 - T1)$ where the first point is at time T1 with frequency F1 and the second point is at T2 with frequency F2. The frequency units are irrelevant, but the time is in seconds. $\log_2$ means the logarithm to base 2. See hoarybat.com.

oscillogram—A two-dimensional graphical display of sound **amplitude** as a function of time. In this book, all full-spectrum spectrograms include this along the top of each recording, shown in blue.

parturition—Birth.

PIT (passive integrated transponder) tag—Small tags, about the size of a grain of rice, that can be inserted just under the skin of bats for individual identification. PIT tags can be automatically read and individual identification numbers logged by readers, enabling the presence of a bat to be known without capturing it again.

population vital rates—Birth rates and death rates, which determine whether a population is increasing or decreasing. Reflects fecundity, health and age composition of the population.

prey-generated sounds—Sounds made by potential prey items (e.g., insects) that are used by bats to locate, identify and capture them.

pulse (sound)—Another term used for a bat **call**. A single burst of sound produced by a bat.

pup—A young bat that cannot yet fly.

radio-tagged—When a bat has a **radio transmitter** attached so it can be radio-tracked.

radiotelemetry/radio-tracking—A means of detecting radio signals using receiving equipment for monitoring animals. In the case of bats, a small **radio transmitter** is glued to a bat.

radio transmitter—A device used to track animals in a process called **radiotelemetry** or **radio tracking**. It emits a very high frequency (VHF) signal, which is detected using a radio receiver equipped with an antenna. In bats, these are small, typically 5% or less of their body mass so as to not interfere with flight, and most often are attached to the bat's back using non-toxic glue.

Red List—One of three provincial conservation status lists for organisms in BC. The Red List refers to species that have been legally designated as Endangered or Threatened under the provincial Wildlife Act, are extirpated or are candidates for designation. See env.gov.bc.ca/wld/documents/ranking.pdf.

roost—Daytime retreats or nighttime resting sites used by bats.

scrotal—In bats, testes undergo a seasonal migration between the abdomen and the scrotal pouches in the upper part of the tail membrane, where they can produce sperm at a slightly cooler temperature; **scrotal** refers to when the testes are swollen, producing sperm in these scrotal pouches on either side of the tail. The **cauda epididymides** are permanently located in the scrotal pouches of the tail, where they store sperm produced in the testes. When sperm production has completed, the testes shrink in size and migrate upward into the abdomen.

search phase call (in echolocation)—The type of **echolocation call** emitted by bats when commuting or searching for prey (foraging); characterized by regular consistent call characteristics. Acoustic identification of species typically uses search phase calls.

sequence—Two or more **echolocation calls** or **pulses** generated by the same individual.

slope (in acoustics)—The change of frequencies over time during a bat **pulse**. While slope might be measured in units of hertz/seconds, it may also be measured in **octaves per second**. Slopes of various parts of a bat pulse can be compared between pulses; although slope is usually affected by **clutter**, it is an important call parameter used in species identification.

snout—The entire muzzle protruding from the face. In bats this includes the mouth and nostrils. The snout also includes the nose, which is at the tip of the snout, where the nostrils are located.

snag—A standing dead or dying tree.

Species at Risk Act (SARA)—Canadian federal legislation that came into force in 2002, with the goal of protecting endangered or threatened organisms and their habitats.

spectrogram—A way of visualizing a spectrum of **frequencies** over time. Acoustic software used for bat **echolocation** analysis allows you to see spectrograms of bat recordings. Sometimes also referred to as a sonogram.

split harmonic—A **zero-crossing** analysis phenomenon in which **spectrograms** show parts of more than one **harmonic** for a single **pulse**. This occurs when the strongest **amplitude** of the signal within a pulse shifts from **frequencies** in the **fundamental harmonic** to frequencies in a higher harmonic. Because zero-crossing analysis represents only the loudest frequency at a point in time, the pulse appears to break at the point where the highest **amplitude** frequency of the signal shifts between harmonics.

swarming—Behaviour associated with nocturnal flights that are made at potential **hibernacula** by aggregations of bats in late summer or fall.

talus—Broken rock fragments, also referred to as scree, at the base of crags, mountain cliffs, volcanoes or valley shoulders that has accumulated through periodic rockfall from adjacent cliff faces.

tibia—The large-diameter long bone of the lower leg, connecting the knee with the ankle.

time between calls (TBC)—The amount of time a bat is silent between **echolocation calls** or **pulses**. For bats that use **frequency-modulated** echolocation, this time is when the bat is listening for echoes.

toe (in spectrograms)—**Frequencies** produced after the **call body** in a **pulse**. Not all pulses have toes, and in some cases the toe may be low in **amplitude**

and thus not recorded. If there is no toe, the **characteristic frequency** is the same as the **minimum frequency**. If there is a toe, it may turn up or down.

torpor—A short-term (daily) state of inactivity associated with a reduction in metabolic rate leading to a lowering of body temperature to conserve energy. Seasonally extended bouts of torpor are called hibernation. Bats in torpor are torpid.

tragus—A thin, erect, fleshy structure attached to the base of the ear, used in **echolocation**.

tympanate moth—A moth that possesses simple ears (tympanic membranes).

ulna—The stabilizing long bone making up the forearm; articulates with the larger-diameter humerus at the elbow joint.

ultrasound—Sounds above the range of hearing of the human ear (normally above 20 **kilohertz**).

ventral—On the underside of an animal.

volant—Able to fly.

voucher—For the purpose of creating the maps in this book, vouchers are species occurrences based on museum specimens, live captures identified from a DNA sequence, or photographs of species that are reliably identified from a photograph.

wavelength—The distance travelled in one wave cycle. It also equals the speed of sound divided by **frequency**.

white-nose syndrome (WNS)—A fungal disease that has killed millions of bats in North America. Named for a distinctive growth of *Pseudogymnoascus destructans* around the muzzle and on the wings of hibernating bats. First identified in 2006 near Albany, New York.

wildlife habitat areas (WHA)—Mapped areas designating sensitive habitats and habitat elements within which activities are managed through legislation to protect impacts on specific species.

wildlife habitat features (WHF)—Includes discrete features deemed to require special management, including nests of certain bird species, significant mineral licks, and bat **hibernacula** and **maternity roosts**. At the time of writing this book, WHFs were designated only for a specific and limited set of species ("Identified Wildlife") in the Kootenay Boundary region.

wing loading—Wing area relative to the size of the bat; calculated by dividing the mass of the bat by its wing area.

young-of-year—Juvenile bats that are less than a year old as they were born in the current summer.

zero-crossing (analysis)—The calculation of **frequencies** made by measuring the time between moments of zero sound pressure, which corresponds to the period of the wave. By nature of this counting technique, zero-crossing analysis can only respond to the loudest frequency, that with the most energy (**amplitude**). See also **native zero-crossing** and **division ratio**.

References

Adams, J., P. Roby, P.S. Sewell, J. Schwierjohann, M. Gumbert and M. Brandenburg. 2015. "Success of BrandenBark™, an Artificial Roost Structure Designed for Use by Indiana Bats (*Myotis sodalis*)." *Journal of the American Society of Mining and Reclamation* 4, no. 1: 1–15.

Adams, R.A. 2003. *Bats of the Rocky Mountain West: Natural History, Ecology, and Conservation*. Boulder: University Press of Colorado.

Adams, R.A. 2010. "Bat Reproductive Declines When Conditions Mimic Climate Change Projections for Western North America." *Ecology* 9, no. 8: 2437–45.

Adams, R.A., S.C. Pedersen, K.M. Thibault, J. Jadin and B. Petru. 2003. "Calcium as a Limiting Resource to Insectivorous Bats: Can Water Holes Provide a Supplemental Mineral Source?" *Journal of Zoology* 260, no. 2: 189–94.

Aldridge, H. 1986. "Manoeuvrability and Ecological Segregation in the Little Brown (*Myotis lucifugus*) and Yuma (*M. yumanensis*) Bats (Chiroptera: Vespertilionidae)." *Canadian Journal of Zoology* 64, no. 9: 1878–82.

Altringham, J., and G. Kerth. 2016. "Bats and Roads." In *Bats in the Anthropocene: Conservation of Bats in a Changing World*, edited by Christian C. Voigt and Tigga Kingston, 35–62. Cham, Switzerland: Springer.

Amelon, S.K., S.E. Hooper and K.M. Womack. 2017. "Bat Wing Biometrics: Using Collagen–Elastin Bundles in Bat Wings as a Unique Individual Identifier." *Journal of Mammalogy* 98, no. 3: 744–51.

Ancillotto, L., M.T. Serangeli and D. Russo. 2013. "Curiosity Killed the Bat: Domestic Cats as Bat Predators." *Mammalian Biology-Zeitschrift für Säugetierkunde* 78, no. 5: 369–73.

Anderson, M.E., and P.A. Racey. 1991. "Feeding Behaviour of Captive Brown Long-eared Bats, *Plecotus auritus*." *Animal Behaviour* 42, no. 3: 489–93.

Andrusiak, L. 2008. "An Unusual Roosting Location of a Hoary Bat (*Lasiurus cinereus*) in British Columbia." *Wildlife Afield* 5, no. 2: 211–14.

Arlettaz, R., G. Jones and P.A. Racey. 2001. "Effect of Acoustic Clutter on Prey Detection by Bats." *Nature* 414, no. 6865: 742.

Arnett, E., and E.F. Baerwald. 2013. "Impacts of Wind Energy Development on Bats: Implications for Conservation." In *Bat Evolution, Ecology, and Conservation*, edited by R.A. Adams and S.C. Pedersen, 435–56. New York: Springer.

Arnold, B.D., and G.S. Wilkinson. 2011. "Individual Specific Contact Calls of Pallid Bats (*Antrozous pallidus*) Attract Conspecifics at Roosting Sites." *Behavioral Ecology and Sociobiology* 65: 1581–93.

Arroyo-Cabrales, J., and S.T. Álvarez-Castañeda. 2017. "*Myotis melanorhinus*." *The IUCN Red List of Threatened Species* 2017: e.T136784A22033542.

Baerwald, E.F. 2015. "Movement Ecology and Conservation of the Migratory Bats *Lasiurus cinereus* and *Lasionycteris noctivagans*." PhD diss., University of Calgary, Alberta.

Baerwald, E.F., and R.M.R. Barclay. 2011. "Patterns of Activity and Fatality of Migratory Bats at a Wind Energy Facility in Alberta, Canada." *Journal of Wildlife Management* 75, no. 5: 1103–14.

Bailey, L., R.M. Brigham, S.J. Bohn, J.G. Boyles and B. Smit. 2019. "An Experimental Test of the Allotonic Frequency Hypothesis to Isolate the Effects of Light Pollution on Bat Prey Selection." *Oecologia* 190, no. 2: 367–74.

Baird, A.B., J.K. Braun, M.A. Mares, J.C. Morales, J.C. Patton, C.Q. Tran and J.W. Bickham. 2015. "Molecular Systematic Revision of Tree Bats (Lasiurini): Doubling the Native Mammals of the Hawaiian Islands." *Journal of Mammalogy* 96, no. 6: 1255–74.

Balcombe, J.P., and G.F. McCracken. 1992. "Vocal Recognition in Mexican Free-Tailed Bats: Do Pups Recognize Mothers?" *Animal Behaviour* 43, no. 1: 79–87.

Ball, L.C. 1998. "Roosting Behavior of Pallid Bats (*Antrozous pallidus*): Energetic and Ecological Mechanisms." PhD diss., University of Nevada, Reno.

Baker, R.J., and R.D. Bradley. 2006. "Speciation in Mammals and the Genetic Species Concept." *Journal of Mammalogy* 87, no. 4: 643–62.

Barbour, J.R., and W.H. Davis. 1969. *Bats of America.* Lexington: University Press of Kentucky.

Barclay, R.M.R. 1984. "Observations on the Migration, Ecology and Behavior of Bats at Delta Marsh, Manitoba." *Canadian Field-Naturalist* 98, no. 3: 331–36.

Barclay, R.M. 1985. "Long- versus Short-Range Foraging Strategies of Hoary (*Lasiurus cinereus*) and Silver-Haired (*Lasionycteris noctivagans*) Bats and the Consequences for Prey Selection." *Canadian Journal of Zoology* 63, no. 11: 2507–15.

Barclay, R.M. 1986. "The Echolocation Calls of Hoary (*Lasiurus cinereus*) and Silver-Haired (*Lasionycteris noctivagans*) Bats as Adaptations for Long- versus Short-range Foraging Strategies and the Consequences for Prey Selection." *Canadian Journal of Zoology* 64, no. 12: 2700–2705.

Barclay, R.M. 1989. "The Effect of Reproductive Condition on the Foraging Behavior of Female Hoary Bats," *Lasiurus cinereus. Behavioral Ecology and Sociobiology* 24, no. 1: 31–37.

Barclay, R.M. 1991. "Population Structure of Temperate Zone Insectivorous Bats in Relation to Foraging Behaviour and Energy Demand." *Journal of Animal Ecology* 60, no. 1: 165–78.

Barclay, R.M. 1999. "Bats Are Not Birds—A Cautionary Note on Using Echolocation Calls to Identify Bats: A Comment." *Journal of Mammalogy* 80, no. 1: 290–96.

Barclay, R.M.R., and R.M. Brigham. 1994. "Constraints on Optimal Foraging: A Field Test of Prey Discrimination by Echolocating Insectivorous Bats." *Animal Behaviour* 48, no. 5: 1013–21.

Barclay, R.M.R., and R.M. Brigham. 2001. "Year-to-Year Re-use of Tree-Roosts by California Bats *(Myotis californicus)* in Southern British Columbia." *American Midland Naturalist* 146, no. 1: 80–85.

Barclay, R.M., P.A. Faure and D.R. Farr. 1988. "Roosting Behavior and Roost Selection by Migrating Silver-Haired Bats (*Lasionycteris noctivagans*)." *Journal of Mammalogy* 69, no. 4: 821–25.

Barnett, J.K., and G.H. Collins. 2019. "Species Richness and Seasonality of Bat Occupancy on Northwestern National Wildlife Refuges." *Journal of Fish and Wildlife Management* 10, no. 2: 468–79.

Bat Conservation International. 2020. batcon.org.

Baxter, D.J., J.M. Psyllaki, M.P. Gillingham and E.L. O'Brien. 2006. "Behavioural Response of Bats to Perceived Predation Risk While Foraging." *Ethology* 112, no. 10: 977–83.

Bell, G.P. 1982. "Behavioral and Ecological Aspects of Gleaning by a Desert Insectivorous Bat *Antrozous pallidus* (Chiroptera: Vespertilionidae)." *Behavioral Ecology and Sociobiology* 10, no. 3: 217–23.

Bell, G.P. 1985. "The Sensory Basis of Prey Location by the California Leaf-Nosed Bat *Macrotus californicus* (Chiroptera: Phyllostomidae)." *Behavioral Ecology and Sociobiology* 16, no. 4: 343–47.

Best, T.L., and K.N. Geluso. 2003. "Summer Foraging Range of Mexican Free-Tailed Bats (*Tadarida brasiliensis mexicana*) from Carlsbad Cavern, New Mexico." *Southwestern Naturalist* 48, no. 4: 590–96.

Betts, B.J. 1998. "Effects of Inter-Individual Variation in Echolocation Calls on Identification of Big Brown and Silver-Haired Bats." *Journal of Wildlife Management* 62, no. 3: 1003–10.

Bideguren, G.M., A. López-Baucells, X. Puig-Montserrat, M. Mas, X. Porres and C. Flaquer. 2019. "Bat Boxes and Climate Change: Testing the Risk of Over-Heating in the Mediterranean Region." *Biodiversity and Conservation* 28, no. 1: 21–35.

Bininda-Emonds, O.R.P., and A.P. Russell. 1994. "Flight Style in Bats as Predicted from Wing Morphometry: The Effects of Specimen Preservation." *Journal of Zoology* 234, no. 2: 275–87.

Blejwas, K.M., M.L. Kohan, L.O. Beard and G.W. Pendleton. 2021. "The Milieu Souterrain Superficiel (MSS) as Hibernation Habitat for Bats: Implications for White-Nose Syndrome." *Journal of Mammalogy* 102, no. 4 (August): 1110–27.

Blejwas, K.M., C.L. Lausen and D. Rhea-Fournier. 2014. "Acoustic Monitoring Provides First Records of Hoary bats (*Lasiurus cinereus*) and Delineates the Distribution of Silver-Haired Bats (*Lasionycteris noctivagans*) in Southeast Alaska." *Northwestern Naturalist* 95, no. 3: 236–50.

Bohn, S.J. 2017. "Tall Timber: Roost Selection of Reproductive Female Silver-Haired Bats (*Lasionycteris noctivagans*)." Master's thesis, University of Regina, Saskatchewan.

Bonwitt, J., H. Oltean, M. Lang, R.M. Kelly and M. Goldoft. 2018. "Bat Rabies in Washington State: Temporal-Spatial Trends and Risk Factors for Zoonotic Transmission (2000–2017)." *PLOS ONE* 13, no. 10: e0205069.

Booher, C.M. 2008. "Effects of Calcium Availability on Reproductive Output of Big Brown Bats." *Journal of Zoology* 274, no. 1: 38–43.

Boyle, C., L. Lavkulich, H. Schreier and E. Kiss. 1997. "Changes in Land Cover and Subsequent Effects on Lower Fraser Basin Ecosystems from 1827–1990." *Environmental Management* 21, no. 2: 185–96.

Boyles, J.G., P.M. Cryan, G.F. McCracken and T.H. Kunz. 2011. "Economic Importance of Bats in Agriculture." *Science* 332, no. 6025: 41–42.

Brass, D.A. 1994. *Rabies in Bats: Natural History and Public Health Implications*. Ridgefield, CT: Livia Press.

Braun, J.K., B. Yang, S.B. González-Pérez and M.A. Mares. 2015. "*Myotis yumanensis* (Chiroptera: Vespertilionidae)." *Mammalian Species* 47, no. 918: 1–14.

Brigham, R.M. 1987. "The Significance of Winter Activity by the Big Brown Bat (*Eptesicus fuscus*): The Influence of Energy Reserves." *Canadian Journal of Zoology* 65, no. 5: 1240–42.

Brigham, R.M. 1990. "Prey Selection by Big Brown Bats (*Eptesicus fuscus*) and Common Nighthawks (*Chordeiles minor*)." *American Midland Naturalist* 124, no. 1: 73–80.

Brigham, R.M. 1991. "Flexibility in Foraging and Roosting Behaviour by the Big Brown Bat (*Eptesicus fuscus*)." *Canadian Journal of Zoology* 69, no. 1: 117–21.

Brigham, R.M., H.D.J.N. Aldridge and R.L. Mackey. 1992. "Variation in Habitat Use and Prey Selection by Yuma Bats (*Myotis yumanensis*)." *Journal of Mammalogy* 73, no. 7: 640–45.

Brigham, R.M., and M.B. Fenton. 1987. "The Effect of Roost Sealing as a Method to Control Maternity Colonies of Big Brown Bats." *Canadian Journal of Public Health* 78, no. 1: 47–50.

Brigham, R.M., and M.B. Fenton. 1991. "Convergence in Foraging Strategies by Two Morphologically and Phylogenetically Nocturnal Aerial Insectivores." *Journal of Zoology* 223, no. 3: 475–89.

Brigham, R.M., E.K.V. Kalko, G. Jones, S. Parson and H.J.G.A. Limpens. 2002. *Bat Echolocation Research—Tools, Techniques and Analysis*. Austin, TX: Bat Conservation International.

Brigham, R.M., M.J. Vonhof, R.M.R. Barclay and J.C. Gwilliam. 1997. "Roosting Behavior and Roost-Site Preferences of Forest-Dwelling California Bats (*Myotis californicus*)." *Journal of Mammalogy* 78, no. 4: 1231–39.

British Columbia Community Bat Program. 2020. "Community Bat Programs Help People Help Bats." bcbats.ca.

British Columbia (B.C.) Conservation Data Centre. 2015. "Species Summary: *Parastrellus hesperus*." a100.gov.bc.ca/pub/eswp/speciesSummary.do?id=35726.

British Columbia Ministry of Environment. 2013. *Management Plan for the Spotted Bat (Euderma maculatum) in British Columbia*. Victoria: Ministry of Environment.

British Columbia Ministry of Environment. 2016. *Recovery Plan for the Pallid Bat (Antrozous pallidus pallidus) in British Columbia*. Victoria: Ministry of Environment.

British Columbia Ministry of Environment, Lands and Parks. 1998. *Inventory Methods for Bats: Standards for Components of British Columbia's Biodiversity, No. 20*. Victoria, BC: Resources Information Committee. gov.bc.ca/assets/gov/environment/natural-resource-stewardship/nr-laws-policy/risc/bats.pdf.

Broders, H.G., C.S. Findlay and L. Zheng. 2004. "Effects of Clutter on Echolocation Call Structure of *Myotis septentrionalis* and *M. lucifugus*." *Journal of Mammalogy* 85, no. 2: 273–81.

Brokaw, A.F., J. Clerc, and T.J. Weller. 2016. "Another Account of Interspecific Aggression Involving a Hoary Bat (*Lasiurus cinereus*)." *Northwestern Naturalist* 97, no. 2: 130–34.

Brühl, C.A., L. Despres, O. Frör, C.D. Patil, B. Poulin, G. Tetreau and S. Allgeier. 2020. "Environmental and Socioeconomic Effects of Mosquito Control in Europe Using the

Biocide *Bacillus thuringiensis* subsp. *israelensis* (BTI)." *Science of the Total Environment* 724: 137800.

Brunet-Rossinni, A.K., and G.S. Wilkinson. 2009. "Methods for Age Estimation and the Study of Senescence in Bats." In *Ecological and Behavioral Methods for the Study of Bats,* edited by T.H. Kunz and S. Parsons. Baltimore, MD: Johns Hopkins University Press.

Bunkley, J.P., and J.R. Barber. 2015. "Noise Reduces Foraging Efficiency in Pallid Bats (*Antrozous pallidus*)." *Ethology* 121, no. 11: 1116–21.

Burgin, C.J., J.P. Colella, P.L. Kahn and N.S. Upham. 2018. "How Many Species of Mammals Are There?" *Journal of Mammalogy* 99, no. 1: 1–14.

Burles, D.W., R.M. Brigham, R.A. Ring and T.E. Reimchen. 2008. "Diet of Two Insectivorous Bats, *Myotis lucifugus* and *Myotis keenii*, in Relation to Arthropod Abundance in a Temperate Northwest Pacific Rainforest Environment." *Canadian Journal of Zoology* 86, no. 12: 1367–75.

Burles, D.W., R.M. Brigham, R.A. Ring and T.E. Reimchen. 2009. "Influence of Weather on Two Insectivorous Bats in a Temperate Northwest Pacific Rainforest." *Canadian Journal of Zoology* 87, no. 2: 132–38.

Burles, D.W., M.B. Fenton, R.M.R. Barclay, R.M. Brigham and D. Volkers. 2014. "Aspects of the Winter Ecology of Bats on Haida Gwaii, British Columbia." *Northwestern Naturalist* 95, no. 3: 289–99.

Caceres, M.C. 1998. "The Summer Ecology of Myotis Species in the Interior Wet-Belt of British Columbia." MSc thesis, University of Calgary, Alberta.

Caceres, M.C., and R.M.R. Barclay. 2000. "*Myotis septentrionalis*." *Mammalian Species* 634: 1–4.

Caire, W., R.K. LaVal, M.L. LaVal and R. Clawson. 1979. "Notes on the Ecology of *Myotis keenii* (Chiroptera, Vespertilionidae) in Eastern Missouri." *American Midland Naturalist* 102, no. 2: 404–7.

Carstens, B.C., and T.A. Dewey, 2010. "Species Delimitation Using a Combined Coalescent and Information-Theoretic Approach: An Example from North American Myotis Bats." *Systematic Biology* 59, no. 4: 400–414.

Chambers, C., M. Herder, K. Yasuda, D. Mikesic, S. Dewhurst, W. Masters and D. Vleck. 2011. "Roosts and Home Ranges of Spotted bats (*Euderma maculatum*) in Northern Arizona." *Canadian Journal of Zoology* 89, no. 12: 1256–67.

Chapman, K., K. McGuiness and R.M. Brigham. 1994. *Status of the Pallid bat in British Columbia.* Wildlife Working Report No. WR-61.

Chruszcz, B.J., and R.M. Barclay. 2003. "Prolonged Foraging Bouts of a Solitary Gleaning/ Hawking Bat, *Myotis evotis*." *Canadian Journal of Zoology* 81, no. 5: 823–26.

Constantine, D.G. 1998. "An Overlooked External Character to Differentiate *Myotis californicus* and *Myotis ciliolabrum* (Vespertilionidae)." *Journal of Mammalogy* 79, no. 2: 624–30.

Constantine, D.G. 2003. "Geographic Translocation of Bats: Known and Potential Problems." *Emerging Infectious Diseases* 9, no. 1: 17–21.

Constantine, D.G., and D.S. Blehert. 2009. *Bat Rabies and Other Lyssavirus Infections*. Circular 1329. Reston, VA: US Geological Survey National Wildlife Health Center.

Corben, C. 2020. "Anabat." users.lmi.net/corben/anabat.htm#Anabat%20Contents.

Corbett, R.J.M., C.L. Chambers and M.L. Herder. 2008. "Roosts and Activity Areas of *Nyctinomops macrotis* in Northern Arizona." *Acta Chiropterologica* 10, no. 2: 323–29.

Corcoran, A.J., J.R. Barber and W.E. Conner. 2009. "Tiger Moth Jams Bat Sonar." *Science* 325, no. 5938: 325–27.

Corcoran, A.J., and W.E. Conner. 2014. "Bats Jamming Bats: Food Competition through Sonar Interference." *Science* 346, no. 6210: 745–47.

Corcoran, A.J., and T.J. Weller. 2018. "Inconspicuous Echolocation in Hoary Bats (*Lasiurus cinereus*)." *Proceedings of the Royal Society B* 285, no. 1878: 20180441.

Committee on the Status of Endangered Wildlife in Canada (COSEWIC). 2003. COSEWIC Assessment and Update Status Report on Keen's Long-eared Bat Myotis keenii in Canada. Ottawa, ON: COSEWIC.

COSEWIC. 2004a. COSEWIC *Assessment and Update Status Report on the Fringed Bat* Myotis thysanodes *in Canada*. Ottawa, ON: COSEWIC.

COSEWIC. 2004b. COSEWIC *Assessment and Update Status Report on the Spotted bat* Euderma maculatum *in Canada*. Ottawa, ON: COSEWIC.

COSEWIC. 2010. COSEWIC *Status Appraisal Summary on the Pallid bat* Antrozous pallidus *in Canada*. Ottawa, ON: COSEWIC.

COSEWIC. 2013. COSEWIC *Assessment and Update Status Report on the Little Brown Myotis,* Myotis lucifugus, *Northern Myotis,* Myotis septentrionalis, *Tri-Colored Bat,* Perimyotis subflavus, *in Canada*. Ottawa, ON: COSEWIC.

Cowan, I. McTaggart. 1933. "Some Notes on the Hibernation of *Lasionycteris noctivagans*." *Canadian Field-Naturalist* 48: 74–75.

Cowan, I. McTaggart. 1942. "Notes on the Winter Occurrence of Bats in British Columbia." *Murrelet* 23: 61.

Cowan, I. McTaggart. 1945. "The Free-tailed Bat, *Tadarida macrotis*, in British Columbia." *Canadian Field-Naturalist* 59, no. 4: 149.

Cowan, I. McTaggart and C.J. Guiguet. 1960. *The Mammals of British Columbia*. Victoria, BC: British Columbia Provincial Museum.

Crichton, E.G., and P.H. Krutzsch. 2000. *Reproductive Biology of Bats*. New York: Academic Press.

Cryan, P.M. 2003. "Seasonal Distribution of Migratory Tree Bats (*Lasiurus* and *Lasionycteris*) in North America." *Journal of Mammalogy* 84, no. 2: 579–93.

Cvikel, N., E. Levin, E. Hurme, I. Borissov, A. Boonman, E. Amichai and Y. Yovel. 2015. "On-Board Recordings Reveal No Jamming Avoidance in Wild Bats." *Proceedings of the Royal Society B* 282, no. 1798: 2014–74.

Dalquest, W.W. 1947. "Notes on the Natural History of the Bat *Corynorhinus rafinesquii* in California." *Journal of Mammalogy* 28, no. 1: 17–30.

Dalquest, W.W., and M.C. Ramage. 1946. "Notes on the Long-legged Bat (*Myotis volans*) at Old Fort Tejon and Vicinity, California." *Journal of Mammalogy* 27, no. 1: 60–63.

Davis, M., A.D. Vanderberg, T.A. Chatwin and M.H. Mather. 1997. *Bat Usage of the Weymer Creek Cave Systems on Northern Vancouver Island.* Science Council of British Columbia.

Davis, M.J., A.D. Vanderberg, T.A. Chatwin and M.H. Mather. 1999. "Bat Usage of the Weymer Creek Cave Systems on Northern Vancouver Island." In *Proceedings of a Conference on the Biology and Management of Species and Habitats at Risk, Kamloops, BC, 15–19 Feb. 1999. Volume 1,* edited by L.M. Darling, 305–12. Victoria and Kamloops, BC: Ministry of Environment, Lands and Parks, and University College of the Cariboo.

Davy, C.M., M.E. Donaldson, Y. Rico, C.L. Lausen, K. Dogantzis, K. Ritchie, C.K.R. Willis, D.W. Burles, T.S. Jung, S. McBurney and A. Park. 2017. "Prelude to a Panzootic: Gene Flow and Immunogenetic Variation in Northern Little Brown Myotis Vulnerable to Bat White-Nose Syndrome." *FACETS* 2, no. 2: 690–714.

Davy, C.M., F. Martinez-Nunez, C.K.R. Willis and S.V. Good. 2015. "Spatial Genetic Structure among Bat Hibernacula along the Leading Edge of a Rapidly Spreading Pathogen." *Conservation Genetics* 16, no. 5: 1013–24.

Demarchi, D.A. 2011. *An Introduction to the Ecoregions of British Columbia* (3rd ed.). Victoria, BC: Ministry of Environment.

Demere, K.D. 2016. "Molecular Analysis of the Diet of *Parastrellus hesperus,* the American Parastrelle." MSc thesis, Angelo State University, San Angelo, TX.

Dewey, T.A. 2006. "Systematics and Phylogeography of North American Myotis *(Chiroptera: Vespertilionidae)."* PhD diss., University of Michigan.

Dokuchaev, N.E. 2015. "Uropatagium Venation Pattern in Bats as Diagnostic Character (by the Example of Genus Myotis)." *Russian Journal of Theriology* 14, no. 2: 129–32.

Dunbar, M.B., and R.M. Brigham. 2010. "Thermoregulatory Variation among Populations of Bats along a Latitudinal Gradient." *Journal of Comparative Physiology B* 180, no. 6: 885–93.

Environment and Climate Change Canada. 2017. *Recovery strategy for the Pallid Bat (*Antrozous pallidus*) in Canada 2017.* Species at Risk Act Recovery Strategy Series. Ottawa, ON: Environment and Climate Change Canada. canada.ca/en/environment-climate -change/services/species-risk-public-registry/recovery-strategies/pallid-bat-2017.html.

Falxa, G. 2007. "Winter Foraging of Silver-Haired Bat and California Myotis Bats in Western Washington." *Northwestern Naturalist* 88, no. 2: 98–100.

Faure, P.A., and R.M.R. Barclay. 1992. "The Sensory Basis of Prey Detection by the Long-Eared Bat, *Myotis evotis,* and the Consequences for Prey Selection." *Animal Behaviour* 44, no. 1: 31–39.

Faure, P.A., J.H. Fullard and J.W. Dawson. 1993. "The Gleaning Attacks of the Northern Long-Eared Bat, *Myotis septentrionalis,* Are Relatively Inaudible to Moths." *Journal of Experimental Biology* 178, no. 1: 173–89.

Fenton, M.B. 1970. *Population Studies of* Myotis lucifugus: *(Chiroptera: Vespertilionidae) in Ontario.* Toronto, ON: Royal Ontario Museum.

Fenton, M.B. 1982. "Echolocation, Insect Hearing, and the Feeding Ecology of Insectivorous Bats." In *Ecology of Bats,* edited by T.H. Kunz, 261–85. New York: Plenum Press.

Fenton, M.B. 2011. "The World through a Bat's Ear." *Science* 333, no. 6042: 528–29.

Fenton, M.B., and R.M.R. Barclay. 1980. "*Myotis lucifugus.*" *Mammalian Species* 142: 1–8.

Fenton, M.B., A.C. Jackson, and P.A. Faure. 2020. "Bat Bites and Rabies: The Canadian Scene." *FACETS* 5, no. 1: 367–80.

Fenton, M.B., H.G. Merriam and G.L. Holroyd. 1983. "Bats of Kootenay, Glacier, and Mount Revelstoke National Parks in Canada: Identification by Echolocation Calls, Distribution, and Biology." *Canadian Journal of Zoology* 61, no. 11: 2503–8.

Fenton, M.B., D.G. Streicker, P.A. Racey, M.D. Tuttle, R.A. Medellin, M.J. Daley, S. Recuenco, and K.M. Bakker. 2020. "Knowledge Gaps about Rabies Transmission from Vampire Bats to Humans." *Nature Ecology and Evolution* 4, no. 4: 517–18.

Fenton, M.B., C.G. Van Zyll de Jong, G.P. Bell, D.B. Campbell and M. Laplante. 1980. "Distribution, Parturition Dates, and Feeding of Bats in South-Central British Columbia." *Canadian Field-Naturalist* 94, no. 4: 416–20.

Findley, J.S., and C. Jones. 1964. "Seasonal Distribution of the Hoary bat." *Journal of Mammalogy* 45, no. 3: 461–70.

Firman, M. 2003. *Townsend's Big-Eared Bat in the East Kootenays: Updated Report.* Athalmer, BC: Columbia Basin Fish and Wildlife Compensation Program.

Flaquer, C., X. Puig, A. López-Baucells, I. Torre, L. Freixas, M. Mas, X. Porres and A. Arrizabalaga. 2014. "Could Overheating Turn Bat Boxes into Death Traps?" *Barbastella, Journal of Bat Research* 7, no. 1: 46–53.

Franka, R., D.G. Constantine, I. Kuzmin, A. Velasco-Villa, S.A. Reeder, D. Streicker, L.A. Orciari, A.J. Wong, J.D. Blanton and C.E. Rupprecht. 2006. "A New Phylogenetic Lineage of Rabies Virus Associated with Western Pipistrelle Bats (*Pipistrellus hesperus*)." *Journal of General Virology* 87, no. 8: 2309–21.

Fraser, E.E., D. Brooks and F.J. Longstaffe. 2017. "Stable Isotope Investigation of the Migratory Behavior of Silver-Haired Bats (*Lasionycteris noctivagans*) in Eastern North America." *Journal of Mammalogy* 98, no. 5: 1225–35.

Fraser, E.E., A. Silvis, R.M. Brigham and Z.J. Czenze. 2020. *Bat Echolocation Research: A Handbook for Planning and Conducting Acoustic Studies* (2nd edition). Austin, TX: Bat Conservation International.

Frick, W.F., E.F. Baerwald, J.F. Pollock, R.M.R. Barclay, J.A. Szymanski, T.J. Weller, A.L. Russell, S.C. Loeb, R.A. Medellin and L.P. McGuire. 2017. "Fatalities at Wind Turbines May Threaten Population Viability of a Migratory Bat." *Biological Conservation* 209: 172–77.

Frick, W.F., P.A. Heady III and J.P. Hayes. 2009. "Facultative Nectar-Feeding Behavior in a Gleaning Insectivorous Bat (*Antrozous pallidus*)." *Journal of Mammalogy* 90, no. 5: 1157–64.

Frick, W.F., T. Kingston J. and Flanders. 2019. "A Review of the Major Threats and Challenges to Global Bat Conservation." *Annals of the New York Academy of Sciences* 1469, no. 1: 5–25.

Frick W.F., J.F. Pollock, A.C. Hicks, K.E. Langwig, D.S. Reynolds, G.G. Turner, C.M. Butchkoski and T.H. Kunz. 2010. "An Emerging Disease Causes Regional Population Collapse of a Common North American Bat Species." *Science* 329, no. 5992: 679–82.

Frick, W.F., S.J. Puechmaille, J.R. Hoyt, B.A. Nickel, K.E. Langwig, J.T. Foster, K.E. Barlow, T. Bartonička, D. Feller, A.J. Haarsma and C. Herzog. 2015. "Disease Alters Macroecological Patterns of North American Bats." *Global Ecology and Biogeography* 24, no. 7: 741–49.

Fullard, J.H. 1987. "Sensory Ecology and Neuroethology of Moths and Bats: Interactions in a Global Perspective." In *Recent Advances in the Study of Bats,* edited by M.B. Fenton, P. Racey and J.M.V. Rayner, 244–72. Cambridge, UK: Cambridge University Press.

Fullard, J.H., and J. Dawson. 1997. "The Echolocation Calls of the Spotted bat *Euderma maculatum* Are Relatively Inaudible to Moths." *Journal of Experimental Biology* 200, no. 1: 129–37.

Fullard, J.H., M.B. Fenton, and C.L. Furlonger. 1983. "Sensory Relationship of Moths and Bats Sampled from Two Nearctic Sites." *Canadian Journal of Zoology* 61, no. 8: 1752–57.

Fullard, J.H., and J.E. Yack. 1993. "The Evolutionary Biology of Insect Hearing." *Trends in Ecology and Evolution* 8, no. 7: 248–52.

Fuzessery, Z.M., P. Buttenhoff, B. Andrews and J.M. Kennedy. 1993. "Passive Sound Localization of Prey by the Pallid Bat (*Antrozous p. pallidus*)." *Journal of Comparative Physiology A* 171, no. 6: 767–77.

Gannon, W.L., R.E. Sherwin, T.N.D.E. Carvalho and M.J. O'Farrell. 2001. "Pinnae and Echolocation Call Differences between *Myotis californicus* and *M. ciliolabrum* (Chiroptera: Vespertilionidae)." *Acta Chiropterologica* 3, no. 1: 77–91.

Genoways, H.H., P.W. Freeman, and C. Grell. 2000. "Extralimital Records of the Mexican Free-Tailed Bat (*Tadarida brasiliensis mexicana*) in the Central United States and Their Biological Significance." *Transactions of the Nebraska Academy of Sciences* 26: 85–96.

Genter, D.L., 1986. "Wintering Bats of the Upper Snake River Plain: Occurrence in Lava-Tube Caves." *Great Basin Naturalist* 46, no. 2: 241–44.

Gillam, E.H., and G.F. McCracken. 2007. "Variability in the Echolocation of *Tadarida brasiliensis*: Effects of Geography and Local Acoustic Environment." *Animal Behaviour* 74, no. 2: 277–86.

Gonsalves, L., B. Law, C. Webb and V. Monamy. 2013. "Foraging Ranges of Insectivorous Bats Shift Relative to Changes in Mosquito Abundance. *PLOS ONE* 8, no. 1: e64081.

Green, D.M., L.P. McGuire, M.C. Vanderwel, C.K.R. Willis, M.J. Noakes, S.J. Bohn, E.N. Green and R.M. Brigham. 2020. "Local Trends in Abundance of Migratory Bats across 20 years." *Journal of Mammalogy* 101, no. 6: 1542–47.

Griffin, D.R. 1958. *Listening in the Dark: The Acoustic Orientation of Bats and Men.* New Haven, CT: Yale University Press.

Griffiths, S.R. 2021. "Overheating Turns a Bat Box into a Death Trap." *Pacific Conservation Biology*: doi.org/10.1071/PC20083

Grindal, S.D., and R.M. Brigham. 1998. "Effects of Small Scale Habitat Fragmentation on Activity by Insectivorous Bats." *Journal of Wildlife Management* 62, no. 3: 996–1003.

Grindal, S.D., and R.M. Brigham. 1999. "Impacts of Forest Harvesting on Habitat Use by Foraging Insectivorous Bats at Different Spatial Scales." *Écoscience* 6, no. 1: 25–34.

Grindal, S.D., T.S. Collard and R.M. Brigham. 1991. "Evidence for a Breeding Population of Pallid Bats, *Antrozous pallidus* (Chiroptera: Vespertilionidae), in British Columbia." *Contributions to Natural Science* 14. Victoria, BC: Royal British Columbia Museum.

Grindal, S.D., T.S. Collard, R.M. Brigham and R.M.R. Barclay. 1992. "The Influence of Precipitation on the Reproduction by Myotis Bats in British Columbia." *American Midland Naturalist* 128, no. 2: 339–44.

Grindal, S., C.I. Stefan and C. Godwin-Sheppard. 2011. "Diversity, Distribution, and Relative Abundance of Bats in the Oil Sands Regions of Northeastern Alberta." *Northwestern Naturalist* 92, no. 3: 211–20.

Gunnell, G.F., and N.B. Simmons. 2005. "Fossil Evidence and the Origin of Bats." *Journal of Mammalian Evolution* 12, no. 1: 209–46.

Gustin, M.K., and G.F. McCracken. 1987. "Scent Recognition between Females and Pups in the Bat *Tadarida brasiliensis mexicana*." *Animal Behaviour* 35, no. 1: 13–19.

Haase, C.G., N.W. Fuller, Y.A. Dzal, C.R. Hranac, D.T. Hayman, C.L. Lausen, K.A. Silas, S.H. Olson, S.H. and R.K. Plowright. 2021. "Body Mass and Hibernation Microclimate May Predict Bat Susceptibility to White-Nose Syndrome." *Ecology and Evolution* 11, no. 1: 506–15.

Hall, M.C. 1929. "Arthropods as Intermediate Hosts of Helminths." *Smithsonian Miscellaneous Collections* 81, no. 15: 1–81.

Hallmann, C.A., M. Sorg, E. Jongejans, H. Siepel, N. Hofland, H. Schwan, W. Stenmans, A. Müller, H. Sumser, T. Hörren, D. Goulson and H. de Kroon. 2017. "More Than 75 Percent Decline over 27 Years in Total Flying Insect Biomass in Protected Areas." *PLOS ONE* 12, no. 10: e0185809.

Halsall, A.L., J.G. Boyles and J.O. Whitaker Jr. 2012. "Body Temperature Patterns of Big Brown Bats during Winter in a Building Hibernaculum." *Journal of Mammalogy* 93, no. 2: 497–503.

Hardy, R. 1941. "Some Notes on Utah Bats." *Journal of Mammalogy* 22, no. 3: 289–95.

Hayes, G., and G.J. Wiles. 2013. *Washington Bat Conservation Plan.* Olympia: Washington Department of Fish and Wildlife.

Hein, C., P.P. Garcia, Bat Conservation International Inc. and NRG Systems Inc. 2017. Ultrasonic Bat Deterrent System. U.S. Patent Application 15/211,916.

Hemmera. 2013, 2014. Quality Wind Project: Bird and Bat Monitoring 2013 and 2014 Annual Reports. File 670–002.09. (Request report from: https://www.hemmera.com /project/quality-wind-energy-project/.)

Henderson, L.E., and H.G. Broders. 2008. "Movements and Resource Selection of the Northern Long-Eared Myotis (*Myotis septentrionalis*) in a Forest-Agriculture Landscape." *Journal of Mammalogy* 89, no. 4: 952–63.

Herd, R.M., and M.B. Fenton. 1983. "An Electrophoretic, Morphological, and Ecological Investigation of a Putative Hybrid Zone between *Myotis lucifugus* and *Myotis yumanensis* (Chiroptera: Vespertilionidae)." *Canadian Journal of Zoology* 61, no. 9: 2029–50.

Hermanson, J.W., and T.J. O'Shea. 1983. "*Antrozous pallidus*." *Mammalian Species* 213: 1–8.

Hill, T.J., R. Clarke and P. Stent. 2007. "2007 West Kootenay Fringed myotis Project." Nelson, BC: Fish and Wildlife Compensation Program—Columbia Basin. http://www .sgrc.selkirk.ca/bioatlas/pdf/WK_Fringed_Bat_2007.pdf.

Hill, T.H., A. Reid, R. Clarke, J. Krebs and J. Gwilliam. 2006. *West Kootenay Townsend's Big-Eared (Corynorhinus townsendii) Project: Final Report.* Nelson, BC: Fish and Wildlife Compensation Program—Columbia Basin. http://www.sgrc.selkirk.ca/bioatlas/pdf/West_Kootenay_Townsends_Big-eared_Bat_Project_Final_Report.pdf

Hobbs, J., S. Gidora, T. Katamay-Smith and C. Lausen. 2015. "Bridge and Seton Watersheds: Grassland Bat Management Project." Prepared for Fish and Wildlife Conservation Program. Bridge Coastal Area. (Request report from B.C. Conservation Data Centre.)

Hobbs, J., M. Sarell. T. Hill and F. Iredale. 2011. "Bridge River Bat Assessment 2010." Prepared for Fish and Wildlife Conservation Program. Bridge Coastal Area. (Request report from B.C. Conservation Data Centre.)

Holderied, M.W., and O. Von Helversen. 2003. "Echolocation Range and Wingbeat Period Match in Aerial-Hawking Bats." *Proceedings of the Royal Society of London B* 270, no. 1530: 2293–99.

Holloway, G.L., and R.M. Barclay. 2001. "*Myotis ciliolabrum.*" *Mammalian Species*, 670: 1–5.

Hoofer, S.R., R.A. Van Den Bussche and I. Horáče. 2006. "Generic Status of the American Pipistrelles (Vespertilionidae) with Description of a New Genus." *Journal of Mammalogy* 87, no. 5: 981–92.

Hranac, C., C. Haase, N. Fuller, M. McClure, J. Marshall, C.L. Lausen, L. McGuire, S. Olson and D. Hayman. 2021. "What Is Winter? Modelling Spatial Variation in Bat Host Traits and Hibernation and Their Implications for Overwintering Energetics." *Ecology and Evolution*, 10.1002/ece3.7641.

Humphrey, S.R., and J.B. Cope. 1976. *Population Ecology of the Little Brown Bat,* Myotis lucifugus, *in Indiana and North-Central Kentucky.* American Society of Mammologists, Special Publication 4.

Humphries, M.M., D.W. Thomas and J.R. Speakman. 2002. "Climate-Mediated Energetic Constraints on the Distribution of Hibernating Mammals." *Nature* 418, no. 6895: 313–16.

Jakobsen, L., S. Brinkløv and A. Surlykke. 2013. "Intensity and Directionality of Bat Echolocation Signals." *Frontiers in Physiology* 4: 89.

Jakobsen, L., J. Hallam, C.F. Moss and A. Hedenström. 2018. "Directionality of Nose-Emitted Echolocation Calls from Bats without a Nose Leaf (*Plecotus auritus*)." *Journal of Experimental Biology* 221, no. 3: p.jeb171926.

Jobin, L. 1952. "New Winter Records of Bats in British Columbia." *Murrelet* 33: 42.

Johnston, D.S., and M.B. Fenton. 2001. "Individual and Population-Level Variability in Diets of Pallid bats (*Antrozous pallidus*)." *Journal of Mammalogy* 82, no. 2: 362–73.

Johnson, J.B., J.H. Roberts, T.L. King, J.W. Edwards, W.M. Ford and D.A. Ray. 2014. "Genetic Structuring of Northern Myotis (*Myotis septentrionalis*) at Multiple Spatial Scales." *Acta Theriologica* 59, no. 2: 223–31.

Johnson, J.S., M.J. Lacki and M.D. Baker. 2007. "Foraging Ecology of Long-Legged Myotis (*Myotis volans*) in North-Central Idaho." *Journal of Mammalogy* 88, no. 5: 1261–70.

Johnson, J.S., J.J. Treanor, A.C. Slusher, M.J. Lacki. 2019. "Buildings Provide Vital Habitat for Little Brown Myotis (*Myotis lucifugus*) in a High-Elevation Landscape." *Ecosphere* 10: e02925.

Jones, G. 1999. "Scaling of Echolocation Call Parameters in Bats." *Journal of Experimental Biology* 202, no. 23: 3359–67.

Jones, G., D.S. Jacobs, T.H. Kunz, M.R. Willig and P.A. Racey. 2009. "Carpe Noctem: The Importance of Bats as Bioindicators." *Endangered Species Research* 8, no. 1–2: 93–115.

Jung, T.S. 2014. "Attempted Predation of a Diurnally Active Spotted bat (*Euderma maculatum*) by a Belted Kingfisher (*Megaceryle alcyon*)." *Canadian Field-Naturalist* 127, no. 4: 346–47.

Jung, T.S., and P.M. Kukka. 2014. *Conserving and Monitoring Little Brown Bat (*Myotis lucifugus*) Colonies in Yukon: 2013 Annual Report*. Report PR-14–03. Whitehorse, YK: Yukon Fish and Wildlife Branch.

Jung, T.S., and P.M. Kukka. 2016. *Conserving and Monitoring Little Brown Bat (Myotis lucifugus) Colonies in Yukon: 2014–2015 Annual Report*. Whitehorse, YK: Yukon Environment.

Jung, T.S., C.L. Lausen, J.M. Talerico and B.G. Slough. 2011. "Opportunistic Predation of a Little Brown Bat (*Myotis lucifugus*) by a Great Horned Owl (*Bubo virginianus*) in Southern Yukon." *Northwestern Naturalist* 92, no. 1: 69–72.

Jung, T.S., B.G. Slough, D.W. Nagorsen, T.A. Dewey, and T. Powell. 2006. "First Records of the Northern Long-Eared Bat, *Myotis septentrionalis*, in the Yukon Territory." *Canadian Field-Naturalist* 120, no. 1: 39–42.

Kalcounis, M.C., K.A. Hobson, R.M. Brigham and K.R. Hecker. 1999. "Bat Activity in the Boreal Forest: Importance of Stand Type and Vertical Strata." *Journal of Mammalogy* 80, no. 2: 673–82.

Kaupas, L.A., and R.M.R. Barclay. 2017. "Temperature-Dependent Consumption of Spiders by Little Brown Bats (*Myotis lucifugus*), but Not Northern Long-eared Bats (*Myotis septentrionalis*), in Northern Canada." *Canadian Journal of Zoology* 96, no. 3: 261–68.

Kellner, A.M.E., and A.S. Harestad. 2005. "Diets of Bats in Coastal Rainforests on Vancouver Island, British Columbia." *Northwestern Naturalist* 86, no. 2: 45–48.

Klüg-Baerwald, B.J., and R.M. Brigham. 2017. "Hung Out to Dry? Arid Adaptation in Hibernating Big Brown Bats (*Eptesicus fuscus*)." *Oecologia* 183, no. 4: 977–85.

Klüg-Baerwald, B.J., L. Gower, C.L. Lausen and R.M. Brigham. 2016. "Environmental Correlates and Energetics of Winter Flight by Bats in Southern Alberta, Canada." *Canadian Journal of Zoology* 94, no. 12: 829–36.

Klüg-Baerwald, B.J., C.L. Lausen, C.K.R. Willis and R.M. Brigham. 2017. "Home Is Where You Hang Your Bat: Winter Roost Selection by Prairie-Living Big Brown Bats." *Journal of Mammalogy* 98: 752–60.

Klüg-Baerwald, B.J., C.L. Lausen, B. Wissel and R.M. Brigham. 2021. "Meet You at the Local Watering Hole? Evidence of Dehydration in and Use of an Artificial Water Resource by Hibernating Bats in the Prairies." *Acta Chiropterologica*, in press.

Krutzsch, P.H. 1954. "Notes on the Habits of the Bat, *Myotis californicus*." *Journal of Mammalogy* 35, no. 4: 539–45.

Krutzsch, P.H., T.H. Fleming and E.G. Crichton. 2002. "Reproductive Biology of Male Mexican Free-Tailed Bats (*Tadarida brasiliensis mexicana*)." *Journal of Mammalogy* 83, no. 2: 489–500.

Kunz, T.H., 1982. "*Lasionycteris noctivagans*." *Mammalian Species* 172: 1–5.

Kunz, T.H., and R.A. Martin. 1982. "*Plecotus townsendii.*" *Mammalian Species* 175: 1–6.

Kunz, T.H., and S. Parsons (eds). 2009. *Ecological and Behavioral Methods for the Study of Bats*. Baltimore, MD: Johns Hopkins University Press.

Kurta, A., G. Auteri, J. Hofmann, J. Mengelkoch, J. White, J. Whitaker, T. Cooley and J. Melotti. 2018. "Influence of a Large Lake on the Winter Range of a Small Mammal: Lake Michigan and the Silver-Haired Bat (*Lasionycteris noctivagans*)." *Diversity* 10, no. 2: 24.

Kurta, A., and G.G. Kwiecinski. 2007. "The Square-Eared Anomaly in New World Myotis." *Acta Chiropterologica* 9, no. 2: 495–501.

Lack, J.B., and R.A. Van Den Bussche. 2010. "Identifying the Confounding Factors in Resolving Phylogenetic Relationships in Vespertilionidae." *Journal of Mammalogy* 91, no. 6: 1435–48.

Lausen, C.L. 2001. "Thermoregulation and Roost Selection by Reproductive Big Brown Bats (*Eptesicus fuscus*) Roosting in the South Saskatchewan River Valley, Alberta: Rock-Roosting and Building-Roosting Colonies." MSc thesis, University of Calgary, Alberta.

Lausen, C. 2005. "Appendix 4: Tissue Sampling Protocol for Genetic Study of Bats." In *Handbook of Inventory Methods and Standard Protocols for Surveying Bats in Alberta*, edited by M. Vonhof (2002, revised 2005). Edmonton, AB: Alberta Sustainable Resource Development.

Lausen, C.L. 2007. "Roosting Ecology and Landscape Genetics of Prairie Bats." PhD diss., University of Calgary, Alberta.

Lausen, C.L., and R.M.R. Barclay. 2002. "Roosting Behaviour and Roost Selection of Female Big Brown Bats (*Eptesicus fuscus*) Roosting in Rock Crevices in Southeastern Alberta." *Canadian Journal of Zoology* 80, no. 6: 1069–76.

Lausen, C.L., and R.M.R. Barclay. 2003. "Thermoregulation and Roost Selection by Reproductive Female Big Brown Bats (*Eptesicus fuscus*) Roosting in Rock Crevices." *Journal of Zoology* 260, no. 3: 235–44.

Lausen, C.L., and R.M.R. Barclay. 2006a. "Winter Bat Activity in the Canadian Prairies." *Canadian Journal of Zoology* 84, no. 8: 1079–86.

Lausen, C.L., and R.M.R. Barclay. 2006b. "Benefits of Living in a Building: Big Brown Bats (*Eptesicus fuscus*) in Rocks versus Buildings." *Journal of Mammalogy* 87, no. 2: 362–70.

Lausen, C.L., I. Delisle, R.M.R. Barclay and C. Strobeck, C. 2008. "Beyond mtDNA: Nuclear Gene Flow Suggests Taxonomic Oversplitting in the Little Brown Bat (*Myotis lucifugus*)." *Canadian Journal of Zoology* 86, no. 7: 700–713.

Lausen, C.L., and T.J. Hill. 2010. *A Summary of Bat Work in 2009 in the Columbia Basin as Part of the Provincial Taxonomic Study of Long-Eared Bats in B.C.* Nelson, BC: Fish and Wildlife Compensation Program—Columbia Basin.

Lausen, C.L., and T.J. Hill. 2012. *Identifying and Securing Hibernation Habitat for Bats in the Columbia Basin in Response to Risk of White-Nose Syndrome*. Year 1 Summary Report. Nelson, BC: Fish and Wildlife Compensation Program—Columbia Basin.

Lausen, C.L., T.S. Jung and J.M. Talerico. 2008. "Range Extension of the Northern Long-Eared Bat (*Myotis septentrionalis*) in the Yukon." *Northwestern Naturalist* 89, no. 2: 115–17.

Lausen, C.L., and D. Player. 2014. "Eastern Red Bat (*Lasiurus borealis*) Occurrence in Northern Alberta." *Northwestern Naturalist* 95, no. 2: 219–27.

Lausen, C.L., M. Proctor, D.W. Nagorsen, D. Burles, D. Paetkau, E. Harmston, K. Blejwas, P. Govindarajulu and L. Friis. 2019. "Population Genetics Reveal *Myotis keenii* (Keen's Myotis) and *Myotis evotis* (Long-Eared Myotis) to Be a Single Species." *Canadian Journal of Zoology* 97, no. 3: 267–79.

Lausen, C.L., J.W. Waithaka and D.P. Tate. 2014. "Bats of Nahanni National Park Reserve and Surrounding Areas, Northwest Territories." *Northwestern Naturalist* 95, no. 3: 186–96.

Lee, Y.F., and G.F. McCracken. 2005. "Dietary Variation of Brazilian Free-Tailed Bats Links to Migratory Populations of Pest Insects." *Journal of Mammalogy* 86, no. 1: 67–76.

Leonard, M.L., and M.B. Fenton. 1983. "Habitat Use by Spotted Bats (*Euderma maculatum*, Chiroptera: Vespertilionidae): Roosting and Foraging Behaviour." *Canadian Journal of Zoology* 61, no. 7: 1487–91.

Leslie, M.J., W. Messenger, R.E. Rohde, J. Smith, R. Cheshier, C. Hanlon and C.E. Rupprecht. 2006. "Bat-Associated Rabies Virus in Skunks." *Emerging Infectious Diseases* 12, no. 8: 1274.

Lewis, S.E. 1994. "Night Roosting Ecology of Pallid Bats (*Antrozous pallidus*) in Oregon." *American Midland Naturalist* 132, no. 3219–26.

Lewis, S.E. 1996. "Low Roost-Site Fidelity in Pallid Bats: Associated Factors and Effect on Group Stability." *Behavioral Ecology and Sociobiology* 39, no. 5: 335–44.

Loeb, S.C., T.J. Rodhouse, L.E. Ellison, C.L. Lausen, J.D. Reichard, K.M. Irvine, T.E. Ingersoll, J.T. Coleman, W.E. Thogmartin, J.R. Sauer and C.M. Francis. 2015. *A Plan for the North American Bat Monitoring Program (NABat)*. General Technical Report SRS-208. Asheville, NC: US Department of Agriculture Forest Service.

Luszcz, T.M., and R.M.R. Barclay. 2016. "Influence of Forest Composition and Age on Habitat Use by Bats in Southwestern British Columbia." *Canadian Journal of Zoology* 94, no. 2: 145–53.

Luszcz, T.M., J.M. Rip, K.J. Patriquin, L.M. Hollis, J.M. Wilson, H.D. Clarke, J. Zinck and R.M.R. Barclay. 2016. "A Blind-Test Comparison of the Reliability of Using External Morphology and Echolocation-Call Structure to Differentiate between the Little Brown Bat (*Myotis lucifugus*) and Yuma Myotis (*Myotis yumanensis*)." *Northwestern Naturalist* 97, no. 1: 13–24.

Maclaughlan, L. 2017. *Southern Interior Area Forest Health Program Pest Management Plan 2017–2021–4*. Kamloops, BC: Ministry of Forests, Lands and Natural Resource Operations.

Mammal Diversity Database. 2020. "*Myotis melanorhinus*." ASM Mammal Diversity Database #136784.

Manning, R.W. 1993. "Systematics and Evolutionary Relationships of the Long-Eared Myotis, *Myotis evotis* (Chiroptera: Vespertilionidae)." PhD diss., Texas Tech University. *The Museum*, Special Publications 37: 1–58.

Marín, G., D. Ramos-H, D. Cafaggi, C. Sierra-Durán, A. Gallegos, A. Romero-Ruiz and R.A. Medellín. 2021. "Challenging Hibernation Limits of Hoary bats: The Southernmost Record of *Lasiurus cinereus* Hibernating in North America." *Mammalian Biology* 101, no. 3: 287–91.

Martin, R.A., and B.G. Hawks. 1972. "Hibernating Bats of the Black Hills of South Dakota: Distribution and Habitat Selection." *Bulletin of the New Jersey Academy of Science* 17: 24–30.

Maslin, T.P. 1938. "Fringe-Tailed Myotis Bat in British Columbia." *Journal of Mammalogy* 19, no. 3: 373.

McClure, M.L., D. Crowley, C.G. Haase, L.P. McGuire, N.W. Fuller, D.T. Hayman, C.L. Lausen, R.K. Plowright, B.G. Dickson and S.H. Olson. 2020. "Linking Surface and Subterranean Climate: Implications for the Study of Hibernating Bats and Other Cave Dwellers." *Ecosphere* 11, no. 10: e03274.

McCracken, G.F. 1999. "Brazilian Free-Tailed Bat, *Tadarida brasiliensis*." In *North American Mammals*, edited by E.B.D.E. Wilson and S. Ruff, 127–29. Washington, DC: Smithsonian Institute.

McCracken, G.F., K. Safi, T.H. Kunz, D.K. Dechmann, S.M. Swartz, and M. Wikelski. 2016. "Airplane Tracking Documents the Fastest Flight Speeds Recorded for Bats." *Royal Society Open Science* 3, no. 11: 160–398.

McGuire, L.P., N.W. Fuller, Y.A. Dzal, C.G. Haase, B.J. Klüg-Baerwald, K.A. Silas, R.K. Plowright, C.L. Lausen, C. Willis and S.H. Olson. 2022. "Interspecific Variation in Evaporative Water Loss, and Not Metabolic Rate, among Hibernating Bats." *Scientific Reports*, in press.

McGuire, L.P., N.W. Fuller, Y.A. Dzal, C.G. Haase, K.A. Silas, C.K. Willis, S.H. Olson and C.L. Lausen. 2021. "Similar Hibernation Physiology in Bats across Broad Geographic Ranges." *Journal of Comparative Physiology B.* doi.org/10.1007/s00360-021-01400-x.

Mead, J.I., and D.G. Mikesic. 2001. "First Fossil Record of *Euderma maculatum* (Chiroptera: Vespertilionidae), Eastern Grand Canyon, Arizona." *Southwestern Naturalist* 46, no. 3: 380–83.

Meredith, R.W., J.E. Janečka, J. Gatesy, O.A. Ryder, C.A. Fisher, E.C. Teeling, A. Goodbla, E. Eizirik, T.L.L. Simão, T. Stadler, D.L. Rabosky, R.L. Honeycutt, J.J. Flynn, C.M. Ingram, C. Steiner, T.L. Williams, T.J. Robinson, A. Burk-Herrick, M. Westerman, N.A. Ayoub, M.S. Springer and W.J. Murphy. 2011. "Impacts of the Cretaceous Terrestrial Revolution and KPg Extinction on Mammal Diversification." *Science* 334, no. 6055: 521–24.

Messenger, S.L., C.E. Rupprecht and J.S. Smith. 2003. "Bats, Emerging Virus Infections, and the Rabies Paradigm." In *Bat Ecology*, edited by T.H. Kunz and M.B. Fenton, 622–79. Chicago: University of Chicago Press.

Messenger, S.L., J.S. Smith and C.E. Rupprecht. 2002. "Emerging Epidemiology of Bat-Associated Cryptic Cases of Rabies in Humans in the United States." *Clinical Infectious Diseases* 35: 738–47.

Metheny, J.D., M.C. Kalcounis-Rüppell, K.A. Kolar, C.K.R. Willis and R.M. Brigham. 2008. "Genetic Relationships of Roost-Mates in a Fission-Fusion Society of Tree-Roosting Big Brown Bats." *Behavioral Ecology and Sociobiology* 62, no. 7: 1043–51.

Miller, L.A., and A. Surlykke. 2001. "How Some Insects Detect and Avoid Being Eaten by Bats: Tactics and Countertactics of Prey and Predator." *BioScience* 51, no. 7: 570–81.

Milligan, B.N., and R.M. Brigham. 1993. "Sex Ratio Variation in the Yuma Bat (*Myotis yumanensis*)." *Canadian Journal of Zoology* 71, no. 5: 937–40.

Milner, J., C. Jones and J.J. Jones, 1990. "*Nyctinomops macrotis*." *Mammalian Species* 351: 1–4.

Mineau, P., and C. Callaghan. 2018. *Neonicotinoid Insecticides and Bats: An Assessment of the Direct and Indirect Risks*. Canadian Wildlife Federation.

Morales, A.E., and B.C. Carstens. 2018. "Evidence That *Myotis lucifugus* 'subspecies' Are Five Nonsister Species, Despite Gene Flow." *Systematic Biology* 67, no. 5: 756–69.

Morningstar, D.E., C.V. Robinson, S. Shokralla and M. Hajibabaei. 2019. "Interspecific Competition in Bats and Diet Shifts in Response to White-Nose Syndrome." *Ecosphere* 10, no. 11: e02916.

Murrant, M.N., J. Bowman, C.J. Garroway, B. Prinzen, H. Mayberry and P.A. Faure. 2013. "Ultrasonic Vocalizations Emitted by Flying Squirrels." *PLOS ONE* 8, no. 8.

Myers, R.F. 1960. "*Lasiurus* from Missouri Caves." *Journal of Mammalogy* 41, no. 1: 114–17.

Nagorsen, D.W., A.A. Bryant, D. Kerridge, G. Roberts, A. Roberts and M.J. Sarell. 1993. "Winter Bat Records for British Columbia." *Northwestern Naturalist* 74, no. 3: 61–66.

Nagorsen, D.W., and B. Paterson. 2012. "An Update on the Status of Red Bats, *Lasiurus blossevillii* and *Lasiurus borealis*, in British Columbia." *Northwestern Naturalist* 93, no. 3: 235–37.

Nagorsen, D.W., I. Robertson and D. Manky. 2014a. "Acoustic Evidence for Hoary Bat Migration in the Coast Mountains of British Columbia." *Northwestern Naturalist* 95, no. 3: 50–54.

Nagorsen, D.W., I. Robertson and M. Sarell. 2014b. "Pre-construction Bat Activity at Four Wind Energy Sites in Northeastern British Columbia." *Northwestern Naturalist* 95, no. 3: 300–311.

Navo, K.W., J.A. Gore and G.T. Skiba. 1992. "Observations on the Spotted bat, *Euderma maculatum*, in Northwestern Colorado." *Journal of Mammalogy* 73, no. 3: 547–51.

Neubaum, D.J., T.J. O'Shea and K.R. Wilson. 2006. "Autumn Migration and Selection of Rock Crevices as Hibernacula by Big Brown Bats in Colorado." *Journal of Mammalogy* 87, no. 3: 470–79.

Norberg, U.M. 1981. "Allometry of Bat Wings and Legs and Comparison with Bird's Wings." *Philosophical Transactions of the Royal Society B* 292, no. 1061: 359–98.

Norberg, U.M. 1987. "Wing Form and Flight Mode in Bats." In *Recent Advances in the Study of Bats*, edited by M.B. Fenton, P. Racey and J.M.V. Rayner, 335–427. Cambridge, UK: Cambridge University Press.

Norberg, U.M., and R.Å. Norberg. 2012. "Scaling of Wingbeat Frequency with Body Mass in Bats and Limits to Maximum Bat Size." *Journal of Experimental Biology* 215, no. 5: 711–22.

Norberg, U.M., and J.M. Rayner. 1987. "Ecological Morphology and Flight in Bats (Mammalia: Chiroptera): Wing Adaptations, Flight Performance, Foraging Strategy and Echolocation. *Philosophical Transactions of the Royal Society B* 316, no. 1179: 335–427.

O'Farrell, M.J., and W.G. Bradley. 1970. "Activity Patterns of Bats over a Desert Spring." *Journal of Mammalogy* 51, no. 1: 18–26.

O'Farrell, M.J., C. Corben, and W.L. Gannon. 2000. "Geographic Variation in the Echolocation Calls of the Hoary Bat (*Lasiurus cinereus*)." *Acta Chiropterologica* 2, no. 2: 185–96.

O'Farrell, M.J., and E.H. Studier. 1970. "Fall Metabolism in Relation to Ambient Temperatures in Three Species of Myotis." *Comparative Biochemistry and Physiology* 35, no. 3: 697–703.

O'Farrell, M.J., and E.H. Studier. 1973. "Reproduction, Growth, and Development in *Myotis thysanodes* and *M. lucifugus* (Chiroptera: Vespertilionidae)." *Ecology* 54, no. 1: 18–30.

O'Farrell, M.J., and E.H. Studier. 1980. "*Myotis thysanodes*." *Mammalian Species* 137: 1–5.

Olson, C.R., and R.M.R. Barclay. 2013. "Concurrent Changes in Group Size and Roost Use by Reproductive Female Little Brown Bats (*Myotis lucifugus*)." *Canadian Journal of Zoology* 91, no. 3: 149–55.

Ommundsen, P. 2020. "Myotis Bat Mortality Caused by the Plant Fuller's Teasel (*Dipsacus fullonum*)." *Western Wildlife* 7: 22–23.

Ommundsen, P., C. Lausen and L. Matthias. 2017. "First Acoustic Records of the Brazilian Free-Tailed Bat (*Tadarida brasiliensis*) in British Columbia." *Northwestern Naturalist* 98, no. 2: 132–36.

Ormsbee, P.C., J.D. Kiser, S.I. Perlmeter. 2009. "Importance of Night Roosts to the Ecology of Bats." In *Bats in Forests: Conservation and Management*, edited by M.J. Lacki, J.P. Hayes and A. Kurta, 129–51. Baltimore, MD: Johns Hopkins University Press.

Orr, R.T. 1954. "Natural History of the Pallid Bat, *Antrozous pallidus* (LeConte)." *Proceedings of the California Academy of Science* 28: 165–246.

Painter, M.L., C.L. Chambers, M. Siders, R.R. Doucett, J.O. Whitaker Jr. and D.L. Phillips. 2009. "Diet of Spotted Bats (*Euderma maculatum*) in Arizona as Indicated by Fecal Analysis and Stable Isotopes." *Canadian Journal of Zoology* 87, no. 10: 865–75.

Parish, D.A., and C. Jones. 1999. "Big Free-Tailed Bat, *Nyctinomops macrotis*." In *North American Mammals*, edited by D.E. Wilson and S. Ruff, 130–31. Washington, DC: Smithsonian Institute.

Parker, R., D. McKay, C. Hawes, P. Daly, E. Bryce, P. Doyle, I. McKenzie, D. Roscoe, S. Weatherill, and D.M. Skowronski. 2003. "Human Rabies, British Columbia, January 2003." *Canada Communicable Disease Report* 29, no. 16: 137–38.

Parsons, H.J., D.A. Smith and R.F. Whittam. 1986. "Maternity Colonies of Silver-Haired Bats, *Lasionycteris noctivagans*, in Ontario and Saskatchewan." *Journal of Mammalogy* 67, no. 3: 598–600.

Patyk, K., A. Turmelle, J.D. Blanton, and C.E. Rupprecht. 2012. "Trends in National Surveillance Data for Bat Rabies in the United States: 2001–2009." *Vector-Borne and Zoonotic Diseases* 12, no. 8: 666–73.

Pavlinić, I., N. Tvrtković, and D. Holcer. 2008. "Morphological Identification of the Soprano Pipistrelle (*Pipistrellus pygmaeus* Leach, 1825) in Croatia." *Hystrix* 19, no. 1: 47–53.

Pearson, O.P., M.P. Koford and A.K. Pearson. 1952. "Reproduction of the Lump-Nosed Bat (*Corynorhinus rafinesquii*) in California." *Journal of Mammalogy* 33, no. 3: 273–320.

Perkins, J.M., and S.P. Cross. 1988. "Differential Use of Some Coniferous Forest Habitats by Hoary and Silver-Haired Bats in Oregon." *Murrelet* 69, no. 1: 21–24.

Player, D., C.L. Lausen, B. Zaitlin, J. Harrison, D. Paetkau and E. Harmston. 2017. "An Alternative Minimally Invasive Technique for Genetic Sampling of Bats: Wing Swabs Yield Species Identification." *Wildlife Society Bulletin* 41, no. 3: 590–96.

Poché, R.M. 1975. New Record of *Euderma maculatum* from Arizona. *Journal of Mammalogy* 56, no. 4: 931–33.

Poché, R.M. 1981. *Ecology of the Spotted Bat (*Euderma maculatum*) in Southwest Utah.* Publication no. 81–1. Utah Department of Natural Resources, Division of Wildlife Resources.

Preston, B.T., I.R. Stevenson, G.A. Lincoln, S.L. Monfort, J.G. Pilkington and K. Wilson. 2012. "Testes Size, Testosterone Production and Reproductive Behaviour in a Natural Mammalian Mating System." *Journal of Animal Ecology* 81, no. 1: 296–305.

Psyllakis, J.M., and R.M. Brigham. 2006. "Characteristics of Diurnal Roosts Used by Female Myotis Bats in Sub-boreal Forests." *Forest Ecology and Management* 223, no. 1–3: 93–102.

Pybus, M.J. 1986. "Rabies in Insectivorous Bats of Western Canada, 1979 to 1983." *Journal of Wildlife Diseases* 22, no. 3: 307–13.

Racey, K. 1933. "Pacific Pallid Bat in Canada." *Murrelet* 14: 18.

Racey, P.A. 1982. "Ecology of Bat Reproduction." In *Ecology of Bats*, edited by T.H. Kunz, 57–104. Boston: Springer.

Rambaldini, D.A., and R.M. Brigham. 2008. "Torpor Use by Free-Ranging Pallid Bats (*Antrozous pallidus*) at the Northern Extent of Their Range." *Journal of Mammalogy* 89, no. 4: 933–41.

Rambaldini, D.A., and R.M. Brigham. 2011. "Pallid Bat (Vespertilionidae: *Antrozous pallidus*) Foraging over Native and Vineyard Habitat in British Columbia, Canada." *Canadian Journal of Zoology* 89, no. 4: 816–22.

Rehorek, S.J., T.D. Smith and K.P. Bhatnagar. 2010. "The Orbitofacial Glands of Bats: An Investigation of the Potential Correlation of Gland Structure with Social Organization." *Anatomical Record* 293, no. 8: 1433–48.

Reid, A., T. Hill, R. Clarke, J. Gwilliam and J. Krebs. 2010. "Roosting Ecology of Female Townsend's Big-Eared Bats (*Corynorhinus townsendii*) in South-Eastern British Columbia: Implications for Conservation Management." *Northwestern Naturalist* 91, no. 2: 215–18.

Reimer, J.P., C.L. Lausen, R.M.R. Barclay, S. Irwin and M.K. Vassal. 2014. "Bat Activity and Use of Hibernacula in Wood Buffalo National Park, Alberta." *Northwestern Naturalist* 95, no. 3: 277–89.

Rintoul, J.L.P., and R.M. Brigham. 2014. "The Influence of Reproductive Condition and Concurrent Environmental Factors on Torpor and Foraging Patterns in Female *Eptesicus fuscus*." *Journal of Comparative Physiology B* 184, no. 6: 777–87.

Rodhouse, T.J., M.F. McCaffrey and R.G. Wright. 2005. "Distribution, Foraging Behavior, and Capture Results of the Spotted Bat (*Euderma maculatum*) in Central Oregon." *Western North American Naturalist* 65, no. 2: 10.

Rodhouse, T.J., R.M. Rodriguez, K.M. Banner, P.C. Ormsbee, J. Barnett and K.M. Irvine. 2019. "Evidence of Region-Wide Bat Population Decline from Long-Term Monitoring and Bayesian Occupancy Models with Empirically Informed Priors." *Ecology and Evolution* 9, no. 19: 11078–88.

Rodriguez, R.M., and L.K. Ammerman. 2004. "Mitochondrial DNA Divergence Does Not Reflect Morphological Difference between *Myotis californicus*, and *M. ciliolabrum*." *Journal of Mammalogy* 85, no. 5: 842–51.

Ross, A. 1961. "Biological Studies on Bat Ectoparasites of the Genus *Trichobius* (Diptera: Streblidae) in North America, North of Mexico." *Wasmann Journal of Biology* 19, no. 2: 229–46.

Rueegger, N. 2016. "Bat Boxes: A Review of Their Use and Application, Past, Present and Future." *Acta Chiropterologica* 18, no. 1: 279–99.

Russell, A.L., R.A. Medellín and G.F. McCracken. 2005. "Genetic Variation and Migration in the Mexican Free-Tailed Bat (*Tadarida brasiliensis mexicana*)." *Molecular Ecology* 14, no. 7: 2207–22.

Santana, S.E., T.O. Dial, T.P. Eiting and M.E. Alfaro. 2011. "Roosting Ecology and the Evolution of Pelage Markings in Bats." *PLOS ONE* 6, no. 10: p.e25845.

Saunders, M.B. 1989. "Resource Partitioning between Little Brown Bats (*Myotis lucifugus*) and Long-Legged Bats (*Myotis volans*) in Southern Alberta." MSc thesis, University of Calgary, Alberta.

Saunders, M.B., and R.M.R. Barclay. 1992. "Ecomorphology of Insectivorous Bat: A Test of Predictions Using Two Morphologically Similar Species." *Ecology* 73, no. 4: 1335–45.

Schalk, G.V., and R.M. Brigham. 1995. "Prey Selection by Insectivorous Bats: Are Essential Fatty Acids Important?" *Canadian Journal of Zoology* 73, no. 10: 1855–59.

Schowalter, D.B. 1980. "Swarming, Reproduction, and Early Hibernation of *Myotis lucifugus* and *M. volans* in Alberta, Canada." *Journal of Mammalogy* 61, no. 2: 350–54.

Schowalter, D.B., W.J. Dorward and J.R. Gunson. 1978. "Seasonal Occurrence of Silver-Haired Bats (*Lasionycteris noctivagans*) in Alberta and British Columbia." *Canadian Field-Naturalist* 92, no. 3: 288–91.

Schowalter, D.B., J.R. Gunson and L.D. Harder. 1979. "Life History Characteristics of Little Brown Bats (*Myotis lucifugus*) in Alberta." *Canadian Field-Naturalist* 93, no. 3: 243–51.

Schowalter, T. 2001. *Distribution and Relative Abundance of Small Mammals of the Western Plains of Alberta as Determined from Great Horned Owl Pellets*. Alberta Species at Risk Report No. 17. Edmonton, AB: Alberta Sustainable Resource Development, Fisheries and Wildlife Management Division.

Shankar, V., R.A. Bowen, A.D. Davis, C.E. Rupprecht and T.J. O'Shea. 2004. "Rabies in a Captive Colony of Big Brown Bats (*Eptesicus fuscus*)." *Journal of Wildlife Diseases* 40, no. 3: 403–13.

Sherwin, H.A., W.I. Montgomery and M.G. Lundy. 2013. "The Impact and Implications of Climate Change for Bats." *Mammal Review* 43, no. 3: 171–82.

Shump, K.A., and A.U. Shump. 1982. "*Lasiurus borealis*." *Mammalian Species* 183: 1–6.

Siders, M.S., M.J. Rabe, T.K. Snow and K. Yasuda. 1999. "Long Foraging Distances in Two Uncommon Bat Species (*Euderma maculatum* and *Eumops perotis*) in Northern

Arizona." In *Proceedings of the Fourth Biennial Conference of Research on the Colorado Plateau*, 113–22. Flagstaff, AZ: US Geological Survey.

Sidner, R. 1999. "Western Pipistrelle." In *North American Mammals*, edited by D.E. Wilson and S. Ruff, 113–14. Washington, DC: Smithsonian Institute.

Simmons, N.B. 2005. "Order Chiroptera." In *Mammal Species of the World*, edited by D.E. Wilson and D.M. Reeder, 312–529. Baltimore, MD: Johns Hopkins University Press.

Simmons, N.B., and A.L. Cirranello. 2020. *Bat Species of the World: A Taxonomic and Geographic Database*. batnames.org.

Simmons, N.B., K.L. Seymour, J. Habersetzer and G.F. Gunnell. 2008. "Primitive Early Eocene Bat from Wyoming and the Evolution of Flight and Echolocation." *Nature* 451, no. 7180: 818–21.

Simpson, M.R. 1993. "*Myotis californicus*." *Mammalian Species* 248: 1–4.

Slough, B.G., and T.S. Jung. 2008. "Observations on the Natural History of Bats in the Yukon." *Northern Review* 29 (Fall): 127–50.

Slough, B.G., T.S. Jung and C.L. Lausen. 2014. "Acoustic Surveys Reveal Hoary Bat (*Lasiurus cinereus)* and Long-Legged Myotis (*Myotis volans*) Occurrence in Yukon." *Northwestern Naturalist* 95, no. 3: 176–85.

Slough, B.G., C.L. Lausen, I.J. Hansen, B. Paterson, J.P. Thomas, P.M. Kukka, T.S. Jung, D. Van de Wetering and J. Rae. 2022. "New Records Increase Knowledge of Bat Diversity and Distribution in Northwestern Canada." *Northwestern Naturalist*: in press.

Solick, D.I., and R.M.R. Barclay. 2007. "Geographic Variation in the Use of Torpor and Roosting Behaviour of Female Western Long-Eared Bats." *Journal of Zoology* 272, no. 4: 358–66.

Solick, D.I., R.M.R. Barclay, L. Bishop-Boros, Q.R. Hays and C.L. Lausen. 2020. "Updated Distributions of Eastern and Western Red Bats in Western North America." *Western North American Naturalist* 80, no. 1: 90–97.

Solick, D.I., J.C. Gruver, M.J. Clement, K.L. Murray and Z. Courage. 2012. "Mating Eastern Red Bats Found Dead at a Wind-Energy Facility." *Bat Research News* 53, no. 2: 15–18.

Stadelmann, B., L.K. Lin, T.H. Kunz, and M. Ruedi. 2007. "Molecular Phylogeny of New World Myotis (Chiroptera, Vespertilionidae) Inferred from Mitochondrial and Nuclear DNA genes." *Molecular Phylogenetics and Evolution* 43, no. 1: 32–48.

Stone, E.L., S. Harris and G. Jones. 2015. "Impacts of Artificial Lighting on Bats: A Review of Challenges and Solutions." *Mammalian Biology* 80, no. 3: 213–19.

Storz, J.F. 1995. "Local Distribution and Foraging Behavior of the Spotted bat (*Euderma maculatum*) in Northwestern Colorado and Adjacent Utah." *Great Basin Naturalist* 55, no. 1: 78–83.

Straka T.M., S. Greif, S. Schulz, H.R. Goerlitz, C.C. Voigt. 2020. "The Effect of Cave Illumination on Bats." *Global Ecology and Conservation* 21: e00808.

Swartz, S.M., and N. Konow. 2015. "Advances in the Study of Bat Flight: The Wing and the Wind." *Canadian Journal of Zoology* 93, no. 12: 977–90.

Straka, T.M., M. Wolf, P. Gras, S. Buchholz and C.C. Voigt. 2019. "Tree Cover Mediates the Effect of Artificial Light on Urban Bats." *Frontiers in Ecology and Evolution* 7: 91.

Szewczak, J. 2011. *Echolocation Call Characteristics of Western US Bats.* Arcata, CA: Humboldt State University Bat Lab.

Tacutu, R., D. Thornton, E. Johnson, A. Budovsky, D. Barardo, T. Craig, E. Diana, G. Lehmann, D. Toren, J. Wang, V.E. Fraifeld and J.P. de Magalhaes. 2018a. "Human Ageing Genomic Resources: New and Updated Databases—An Age Entry for *Antrozous pallidus.*" *Nucleic Acids Research* 46, no. D1: 1083–1090. genomics.senescence.info /species/entry.php?species=Antrozous_pallidus.

Tacutu, R., D. Thornton, E. Johnson, A. Budovsky, D. Barardo, T. Craig, E. Diana, G. Lehmann, D. Toren, J. Wang, V.E. Fraifeld and J.P. de Magalhaes. 2018b. "Human Ageing Genomic Resources: New and Updated Databases—An Age Entry for *Lasiurus cinereus.*" *Nucleic Acids Research* 46, no. D1: 1,083–1,090. genomics.senescence.info /species/entry.php?species=Lasiurus_cinereus.

Talerico, J.M. 2008. "The Behaviour, Diet and Morphology of the Little Brown Bat (*Myotis lucifugus*) Near the Northern Extent of Its Range in Yukon, Canada." PhD diss., University of Calgary, Alberta.

Ter Hofstede, H.M., J.M. Ratcliffe and J.H. Fullard. 2008. "The Effectiveness of Katydid (*Neoconocephalus ensiger*) Song Cessation as Antipredator Defence against the Gleaning Bat *Myotis septentrionalis.*" *Behavioral Ecology and Sociobiology* 63, no. 2: 217–26.

Tessler, D.F., M.L. Snively and T.A. Gotthardt, 2014. "New Insights on the Distribution, Ecology, and Overwintering Behavior of the Little Brown Myotis (*Myotis lucifugus*) in Alaska." *Northwestern Naturalist* 95, no. 3: 251–64.

Thapa, V., G.G. Turner and M.J. Roossinck. 2021. "Phylogeographic Analysis of *Pseudogymnoascus destructans* Partitivirus-pa Explains the Spread Dynamics of White-Nose Syndrome in North America. *PLOS Pathogens* 17, no. 3: p.e1009236.

Thomas, D.W. 1988. "The Distribution of Bats in Different Ages of Douglas-fir Forests." *Journal of Wildlife Management* 52, no. 4: 619–26.

Thomas, D.W., M. Dorais and J.M. Bergerson. 1990. "Winter Energy Budgets and Cost of Arousals for Hibernating Little Brown Bats, *Myotis lucifugus.*" *Journal of Mammalogy* 71, no. 3: 475–79.

Turmelle, A.S., F.R. Jackson, D. Green, G.F. McCracken and C.E. Rupprecht. 2010. "Host Immunity to Repeated Rabies Virus Infection in Big Brown Bats." *Journal of General Virology* 91 (Pt 9): 2360–2366.

Turmelle, A.S., T.H. Kunz and M.D. Sorenson. 2011. "A Tale of Two Genomes: Contrasting Patterns of Phylogeographic Structure in a Widely Distributed Bat." *Molecular Ecology* 20, no. 2: 357–75.

Tuttle, M.D., and L.R. Heaney. 1974. "Maternity Habits of *Myotis leibii* in South Dakota." *Bulletin of the Southern California Academy of Sciences* 73, no. 2: 80–83.

van Zyll de Jong, C.G. 1984. "Taxonomic Relationships of Nearctic Small-footed Bats of the *Myotis leibii* Group (Chiroptera: Vespertilionidae)." *Canadian Journal of Zoology* 62, no. 12: 2519–26.

van Zyll de Jong, C.G. 1985. *Handbook of Canadian Mammals: Bats.* Ottawa, ON: National Museum of Canada.

van Zyll de Jong, C.G., M.B. Fenton and J.G. Woods. 1980. "Occurrences of *Myotis californicus* at Revelstoke and a Second Record of *Myotis septentrionalis* from British Columbia." *Canadian Field-Naturalist* 94, no. 4: 455–56.

Verant, M.L., J.G. Boyles, W. Waldrep Jr., G. Wibbelt and D.S. Blehert. 2012. "Temperature-Dependent Growth of *Geomyces destructans*, the Fungus That Causes Bat White-Nose Syndrome. *PLOS ONE* 7, no. 9.

Voigt, C.C., and T. Kingston, eds. 2016. *Bats in the Anthropocene: Conservation of Bats in a Changing World.* Springer Science.

Vonhof, M.J., and R.M.R. Barclay. 1996. "Roost-Site Selection and Roosting Ecology of Forest-Dwelling Bats in Southern British Columbia." *Canadian Journal of Zoology* 74, no. 10: 1797–805.

Vonhof, M.J., and R.M.R. Barclay. 1997. "Use of Tree Stumps as Roosts by the Western Long-Eared Bat." *Journal of Wildlife Management* 61, no. 3: 674–84.

Vonhof, M.J., and A.L. Russell. 2015. "Genetic Approaches to the Conservation of Migratory Bats: A Study of the Eastern Red Bat (*Lasiurus borealis*)." *PeerJ* 3: 983.

Vonhof, M.J., and L. Wilkinson. 1999. *Roosting Habitat Requirements of Northern Long-Eared Bats (*Myotis septentrionalis*) in the Boreal Forests of Northeastern British Columbia: Year 2.* Fort St. John, BC: Ministry of Environment, Lands and Parks.

Wai-Ping, V., and M.B. Fenton. 1989. "Ecology of Spotted Bat (*Euderma maculatum*) Roosting and Foraging Behavior." *Journal of Mammalogy* 70, no. 3: 617–22.

Walker, F.M., C.H. Williamson, D.E. Sanchez, C.J. Sobek and C.L. Chambers. 2016. "Species from Feces: Order-Wide Identification of Chiroptera from Guano and Other Non-Invasive Genetic Samples." *PLOS ONE* 11, no. 9.

Warner, R.M., and N.J. Czaplewski. 1984. "*Myotis volans.*" *Mammalian Species* 224: 1–4.

Watkins, L.C. 1977. "*Euderma maculatum.*" *Mammalian Species* 77: 1–4.

Weaver, S. 2019. "Understanding Wind Energy Impacts to Bats and Testing Reduction Strategies in South Texas." PhD diss., Texas State University, Dallas.

Webb, P.I., J.R. Speakman and P.A. Racey. 1996. "How Hot Is a Hibernaculum? A Review of the Temperatures at Which Bats Hibernate." *Canadian Journal of Zoology* 74, no. 4: 761–65.

Weyandt, S.E., and R.A. Van Den Bussche. 2007. "Phylogeographic Structuring and Volant Mammals: The Case of the Pallid Bat (*Antrozous pallidus*)." *Journal of Biogeography* 34, no. 7: 1233–45.

Wheeler, Q.D., and R. Meier. 2000. *Species Concepts and Phylogenetic Theory: A Debate.* New York: Columbia University Press.

Whitaker, J.O., Jr. 1980. *The Audubon Society Field Guide to North American Mammals.* New York: Chanticleer.

Wildlife Conservation Society Canada. 2021. *WCS Bats.* wcsbats.ca.

Wilkins, K.T. 1989. "*Tadarida brasiliensis.*" *Mammalian Species* 331: 1–10.

Williams, T.C., L.C. Ireland and J.M. Williams. 1973. "High Altitude Flights of the Free-Tailed Bat, *Tadarida brasiliensis,* Observed with Radar." *Journal of Mammalogy* 54, no. 4: 807–21.

Willis, C.K.R., and R.M. Brigham. 2003. "New Records of the Eastern Red Bat, *Lasiurus borealis*, from Cypress Hills Provincial Park, Saskatchewan: A Response to Climate Change?" *Canadian Field-Naturalist* 117, no. 4: 651–54.

Willis, C.K.R., and R.M. Brigham. 2004. "Roost Switching, Roost Sharing and Social Cohesion: Forest-Dwelling Big Brown Bats (*Eptesicus fuscus*) Conform to the Fission-Fusion Model." *Animal Behaviour* 68, no. 3: 495–505.

Willis, C.K.R., and R.M. Brigham. 2005. "Physiological and Ecological Aspects of Roost Selection by Reproductive Female Hoary Bats (*Lasiurus cinereus*)." *Journal of Mammalogy* 86, no. 1: 85–94.

Willis, C.K.R., and R.M. Brigham. 2007. "Social Thermoregulation, Not Cavity Microclimate, Explains Forest Roost Preferences in a Cavity-Dwelling Bat." *Behavioral Ecology and Sociobiology* 62, no. 1: 97–108.

Willis, C.K.R., R.M. Brigham and F. Geiser. 2006. "Deep, Prolonged Torpor by Pregnant, Free-Ranging Bats." *Naturwissenschaften* 93, no. 2: 80–83.

Wilson, J.M. 2004. "Foraging Behaviour of Insectivorous Bats during an Outbreak of Western Spruce Budworm." MSc thesis. University of Calgary, Alberta.

Wilson, J.M., and R.M.R. Barclay. 2006. "Consumption of Caterpillars by Bats during an Outbreak of Western Spruce Budworm." *American Midland Naturalist* 155, no. 1: 244–50.

Wine, M., C.A. Bowen and D.M. Green. 2019. "Interspecific Aggression between a Hoary Bat (*Lasiurus cinereus*) and a Tricolored Bat (*Perimyotis subflavus*) in Northern Arkansas." *Southeastern Naturalist* 18, no. 4: N37–N40.

Woodsworth, G.C., 1981. "Spatial Partitioning by Two Species of Sympatric Bats, *Myotis californicus and Myotis leibii*." PhD diss., Carleton University, Ottawa, ON.

Woodsworth, G.C., G.P. Bell and M.B. Fenton. 1981. "Observations of the Echolocation, Feeding, Behaviour, and Habitat Use of *Euderma maculatum* (Chiroptera: Vespertilionidae) in Southcentral British Columbia." *Canadian Journal of Zoology* 59, no. 6: 1099–102.

Ziegler, A.C., F.G. Howarth and N.B. Simmons. 2016. "A Second Endemic Land Mammal for the Hawaiian Islands: A New Genus and Species of Fossil Bat (Chiroptera: Vespertilionidae)." *American Museum Novitates* 3854: 1–52.

Zimmerling, J.R., and C.M. Francis. 2016. "Bat Mortality Due to Wind Turbines in Canada." *Journal of Wildlife Management* 80, no. 8: 1360–69.

Index

Figures and illustrations indicated by page numbers in **bold**

canyon bat (continued)
reproduction, 298; roosting, 298; skull and dental traits key, 305; taxonomy and nomenclature, 6, 298; tragus, 96–97
capturing bats, 73. *See also* harp traps; mist-nets
cars, collisions with, 69, **69**
cattle drinking tanks, 67
cauda epididymides, 29, 79–81, **80**, **81**, 322
Ceanothus sanguineus (red-stem ceanothus), 196
cedar, western red- (*Thuja plicata*), 51, 192, 204, 213, 222, 251–52
Chambers, Carol, 176
characteristic frequency, 108, **109**, 322
chigger mites, **54**
Chiroptera (order), 3, 4
Choristoneura occidentalis (western spruce budworm), 26, 222
Cirranello, Andrea: *Bats of the World* (with Simmons), 6
civil twilight, 26, 323
Clare, Elizabeth, 214
classification, 3. *See also* taxonomy
Clerc, Jeff, 202–3
climate, 9, 11. *See also* temperature
climate change, 11, 68, 70–71
clutter, definition, 323
clutter continuum, 110, **111–12**, 112–13, **114**, 323
colony, definition, 323
colour, of fur, 20, **21**, 97
Coluber constrictor (North American racer), 226
Committee on the Status of Endangered Wildlife in Canada (COSEWIC): definition, 323; eastern red bat and, 58; fringed myotis and, 260–61; hoary bat and, 58; little brown myotis and, 65, 236; long-eared myotis and, 225, 226; long-legged myotis and, 269; northern myotis and, 65, 253; pallid bat and, 143; silver-haired bat and, 58; spotted bat and, 176; Townsend's big-eared bat and, 157

conservation: advocacy and education, 71; Blue List, 61, 157, 176, 245, 253, 260, 322; endangered bat species, 57, 61; habitat protection, 65; Red List, 61, 143, 226, 327; roosting sites, 39–40, 61; Species at Risk Act, 57, 143, 176, 236, 253, 328. *See also* threats
conservation status, specific species: big brown bat, 166; Californian myotis, 214; dark-nosed small-footed myotis, 61, 245; eastern red bat, 58, 184; fringed myotis, 61, 260–61; hoary bat, 58, 195, 318; little brown myotis, 57, 59, 235–36; long-eared myotis, 225; long-legged myotis, 269; northern myotis, 57, 59, 61, 253; pallid bat, 57, 61, 143; silver-haired bat, 58, 205; in species accounts, 132; spotted bat, 57, 61, 176; Townsend's big-eared bat, 61, 157; Yuma myotis, 279–80
Corynorhinus (genus), 116, 314
Corynorhinus townsendii. See Townsend's big-eared bat
Corynorhinus townsendii townsendii, 157
cottonwood, black (*Populus trichocarpa*), 153, 251
Craig, Vanessa, 153
Craseonycteris thonglongyai (bumblebee bat), 1
cricket, Jerusalem (*Stenopelmatus fuscus*), 141
cryptic, definition, 323
Currie, Chris, 246, 293, 294
Czenze, Z.J.: *Bat Echolocation Research* (with Fraser, Silvis and Brigham), 87

dark-nosed small-footed myotis (*Myotis melanorhinus*), 239–46; acoustically similar species, 211, 231, 243, 267, 275, 316, 317; acoustic characteristics, **123**, 241–43, **242**, 316; acoustic key to, 127; conservation status, 61, 245; dental formulae, 307; description, 239, **240**, 309; distribution, 241, **241**, 245–46; feeding, 244; fun facts, 318; genetic identification and, 91; head coloration, 97; keeled calcar, 95; measurements,

characteristics, **123**, **258**, 259, 315; 318; conservation status, 61, 260–61; dental formulae, 307; description, 255, **256**, 309; distribution, 257, **257**; and ear and tragus measurement, 93–94; feeding, 260; foot length, 94; fun facts, 318; hair fringe, 96; hybridization with long-eared myotis, 256, 261, 318; measurements, 261; migration and winter, 260; morphological key to, 100; morphologically similar species, 217–18, 228, 255–56, 271; parenting, 30; photographs, **255**, **262**; remarks, 261; reproduction, 260; roosting, 61, 259–60; sexual maturity, 30; skull and dental traits key, 306; snout measurement, 95; taxonomy and variation, 261, 318; white-nose syndrome and, 59; wildlife habitat areas and, 65

fuller's teasel (*Dipsacus fullonum*), 67, 215, 226

full-spectrum, definition, 324

fundamental frequencies, 22, 103, 115, 324

fundamental harmonic, 113, 115, 324

fur: about, 13, 20; colour, 20, **21**, 97; hair fringe, 96, **96**

gates, 62, 324. *See also* mines

Gates, Heather, 18

genetics: male-mediated gene flow, 142; nuclear DNA, 6, 225, 326; nuclear genetic marker, 167, 326; sampling, 121, **136**; for species identification, 91, 93, 98, 229; taxonomy and, 6, 7. *See also* mitochondrial DNA/genome

genetic species concept, 7

genitalia, 77, **78**, **79**

Geomyces destructans, 59. *See also* white-nose syndrome

George, Alison, 25

gestation period, 29, 324. *See also* pregnancy; reproduction

gleaning, 22, 23, 103, 324

global warming. *See* climate change

Gloger's rule, 20, 324

Govindarajulu, Purnima, 194

gray-headed flying fox (*Pteropus poliocephalus*), **viii**

Grindal, Scott, 64

guano: collecting, 85; definition and overview, 39, **40**, 324; studying, 73; Townsend's big-eared bat, **153**, 158

habitat: loss of, 62, 64, 143; protection of, 65

Haida Gwaii: bat species, 9; California myotis, 209, 212, 213, 214, 215; little brown myotis, 221, 231, 237; long-eared myotis, 219, 221; silver-haired bat, 199; winter bat activity, 50

hair. *See* fur

handling bats, 56, 85, 90, 91

Hansen, Inge-Jean, 268

harmonics, 113, 115–18, **116**, **117**, 324

harp traps, 73, **74**, 121, 324–25. *See also* mist-nets

head, 97. *See also* skulls

hearing, sense of, 22

hemlock, western (*Tsuga heterophylla*), 222, 251, 252

Herd, Robert, 144

hibernation: arousal, 46, 47, 48; climate and climate change, 11, 70–71; energy reserves and metabolism, 45–46; in mines, 62, **63**, 156; roosting sites (hibernacula), 46–47, 51–52, 325; roost switching, 47–48. *See also* migration and winter

hind legs, 16

histoplasmosis (*Histoplasma capsulatum*), 53

hoary bat (*Lasiurus cinereus*), 187–96; acoustically similar species, 163, 192, 201–2, 288, 293, 313, 314; acoustic characteristics, 22, 112, 123, **123**, **190**, 191, 312; acoustic key to, 125; aspect ratio and wing loading, 16; burdock entanglement, 67; clutter continuum, 113; conservation status, 58, 195, 318; dental formulae, 307; description, 187, **188**, 308; distribution, 9, 11, 130, 189, **189**; dorsal surface hairy, 96; drinking water, 27; easily identified, 92; feeding,

hoary bat (continued)
192–93; fun facts, 318; fur colour, 20, **21**; mammary glands, 77; measurements, 196; migration and winter, 45, 194–95; morphological key to, 99, **99**; morphologically similar species, 187, 189, 198; photograph, **187**; remarks, 196; reproduction, 28, **193**, 194; roosting, 37, 192; sexual maturity, 30; skull and dental traits key, 304; taxonomy and variation, 195; wind turbine fatalities, 57–58, 191, 195, 318; zip-lining, 87

Hobbs, Jared, **74**, **75**, **86**, 174, 176, 181, 257
Hobson, Dave, 45, 60, 235, 237
Holden, Jessica, 176
Holroyd, Susan, 78, 153
horseshoe bat, **115**
humans: rabies and, 55–56; roosting and, 39; as threat to bats, 67, 144, **145**
hunting. *See* feeding
Hypera postica (alfalfa weevil), 26

identification: introduction, 91–92; acoustic characteristics key, 124–27; genetic tools, 91, 93, 98, 229; morphological key, 97–102; skulls and dental traits key, 302–6. *See also* acoustic analysis; in-hand differentiation
Identified Wildlife list, 65
in-hand differentiation, 92–102; introduction, 91–92; diagnostic external features, 92, 95–97; ear and tragus length, **93**, 93–94; ear and tragus shape, **96**, 96–97, **97**; foot length, 94, **94**; forearm length, 93, **93**; head, 97; morphological key, 97–102; morphometrics, 92, 93–95; photography tips, 92–93; snout length and width, 94–95; tail membrane, 95–96; thumb length, 95; tibia length, 94, **94**; wing membrane, 96
insects, 23, 24, 62. *See also* feeding
insect traps, 67, 222–23, **224**
Integrated Pest Management Plan, 62
International Union for Conservation of Nature, 57
invasive plants, **66**, 67, 215, 226

Iredale, Francis, 174, 176
isolation calls, 32, 288
isotherm, definition, 325
isotope analysis, 83, 85, 325

jamming, 23
Jerusalem cricket (*Stenopelmatus fuscus*), 141

keel, 16, **17**, 95, **95**, 325
Keen's myotis (*Myotis keenii*), 6, 225, 226, 253, 319. *See also* long-eared myotis; northern myotis
keystone species, 1
kilohertz (kHz), definition, 325
kingfisher, belted (*Megaceryle alcyon*), 177
Klüg-Baerwald, Brandon, **49**
knee/elbow (spectrograms), 107, **109**, 325
Kootenay Community Bat Project, 28, 273
Kunz, T.H.: *Ecological and Behavioral Methods for the Study of Bats* (with Parsons), 90

lactation, 33, 325
larynxes, 113, 115
Lasionycteris noctivagans. See silver-haired bat
Lasiurines (*Lasiurus* genus): acoustic characteristics, 112, 123, 163; definition, 325; furry tail, 179, 187, 197; mammary glands, 77; roosting, 37, 183
Lasiurus blossevillii (western red bat), 125, 181, 183, 185, 317
Lasiurus borealis. See eastern red bat
Lasiurus cinereus. See hoary bat
Latour, Steve, 68
Lausen, Cori: acoustic analysis by, **128**, 130, 139; on big brown bat, 32, 53, 139; on Californian myotis, 209, 212, 213; on canyon bat, 297; on dark-nosed small-footed myotis, 244; on fringed myotis, 257, 260, 261; on hibernacula, 47, 51, **63**, 156; on hoary bat, 192, 194; inspecting teeth, 79; on little brown myotis, 233, 235; on long-eared myotis, 222, 225; migration and winter activity, 45, 48, 49, **49**, 50; netting bats, **74**, **75**; on

northern myotis, 251; on nubby ears, 18; on rabies, 53; radiotelemetry and, **86**; on reproduction, 28, 32; on silver-haired bat, 45, 199, 203, 204, 205; on spotted bat, 175; on Townsend's big-eared bat, 154, 156, 157; on Yuma myotis, 278, 279; zip-lining, **88**

Lausen, Leroy, **49**

Lauzon, Audrey, 64

legs, hind, 16

Liebmann, Sigi, **63**

lifespans, 32

light pollution, 68

little brown myotis (*Myotis lucifugus*), 227–37; acoustically similar species, 183, 211, 231–32, 243, 251, 267, 275, 315, 316, 317; acoustic bag test, 101, 229, 272, 321; acoustic characteristics, **123**, **230**, 231, 265, 267, 316; acoustic key to, 127; bat boxes and, 281; burdock entanglement, **66**; calcar, 95; car collisions, 69; catching a glimpse of over water, 277, 319; conservation status, 57, 59, 235–36; dental formulae, 307; description, 227, **228**, 309; distribution, 9, 11, **229**, 231; feeding, 25, 26, 232–33; foot length, 94; forearm length, 75, **76**, 77; forehead, 97; fun facts, 319; genetic identification and, 91; guano, **40**; lifespan, 32, 237; measurements, 237; migration and winter, 45, 46–47, 48, 49, 50, 51, 52, 234–35, 253, 268; morphological key to, 101; morphologically similar species, 227–29, 231, 239, 248, 254, 271–72; netting, 73; nubby ear, 18; parenting, 30, 32; photographs, **227**, **238**; pup, **29**; remarks, 237; reproduction, 28, 233–34, 278; roosting, 34, **38**, 39, 43, 221, 232, 267, 281; sexual maturity, 30; skull and dental traits key, 306; taxonomy and variation, 5, 7, 236–37; teats, **82**; tragus, 96; white-nose syndrome and, 59, 60, 61, 236, 237, 279; wildlife protection measures and, 65; wind turbine fatalities, 58, 235, 236; Yuma myotis and, 98, 281, 319

long-eared myotis (*Myotis evotis*), 217–26; acoustically similar species, 139, 221, 259, 313, 315, 316; acoustic characteristics, **123**, 219, **220**, 315; acoustic key to, 126; bat-kiting, 87; conservation status, 225; dental formulae, 307; description, 217, **218**, 309; distribution, 9, 11, 219, **219**; and ear and tragus measurement, 93–94; ectoparasites, **223**; feeding, 222–23; foot length, 94; forearm length, 75, **76**; fun facts, 319; genetic identification and, 91; hair fringe, 96; head coloration, 97; hybridization with fringed myotis, 256, 261, 318; insect traps and, 67, 222–23, **224**; invasive plants and, 67, 215, 226; keeled calcar, 95; measurements, 226; migration and winter, 52, 225; morphological key to, 101, **101**; morphologically similar species, 217–18, 228, 247, 255–56, 271; netting, **74**; nubby ear, 18; photograph, **217**; remarks, 226; reproduction, 223; roosting, 39, 221–22; sense of hearing, 22; skull and dental traits key, 306; snout measurement, 95; taxonomy and variation, 6, 225, 226, 319; tooth wear, **79**; white-nose syndrome and, 59, 225

long-legged myotis (*Myotis volans*), 263–69; acoustically similar species, 211, 231, 243, 251, 267, 275, 316; acoustic characteristics, **123**, 265–67, **266**, 317; acoustic key to, 127; conservation status, 269; dental formulae, 307; description, 263, **264**, 308; distribution, 9, 11, 265, **265**; and ear and tragus measurement, 94; ears, 18, 97; feeding, 268; foot length, 94; forearm length, **76**; fun facts, 319; hairy armpits, 96, 263, **264**, 269, 319; identification considerations, 269; keeled calcar, 95; measurements, 269; migration and winter, 45, 51, 52, 268; morphological key to, 101; morphologically similar species, 207, 217, 227, 239, 255, 263–64, 271; photographs, **263**, **270**; remarks, 269; reproduction, 268; roosting, 39, 267;

long-legged myotis (continued)
sexual maturity, 30; skull and dental
traits key, 306; taxonomy and variation,
269; tibia length, 94, 269; wings, 96
low duty cycle (frequency-modulated
[FM] calls), 23, 106, 324
Luszcz, Tanya, **41**, 142

Macrotus californicus (Californian leaf-
nosed bat), 116, 118
male-mediated gene flow, 142
mammary glands, 77, 81, **82**
Manning, Richard, 225
Manning, Todd, 64
marking, 82–83, **84**
Martes caurina (Pacific marten), 158
Martinez, Felix, 26
maternity colonies and roosts: big brown
bat, 32, 164; big free-tailed bat, 293;
definitions, 325; gender and, 30; little
brown myotis, 11, 221, 232; long-eared
myotis, 221, 222; long-legged myotis,
267; nubby ear and, 18; roost destruction
and disturbance, 61; roosting sites,
37–39, **38**, 40, 43, 65; spotted bat, 174;
Townsend's big-eared bat, 152, 153–54;
Yuma myotis, 275, 277
mating. *See* reproduction
Matthias, Laura, 203, 214, 235, 279
McLeod, Erin, **224**
McTaggart-Cowan, Ian, 144
measurements: approach to, 132–33;
big brown bat, 167; Californian
myotis, 215; dark-nosed small-
footed myotis, 245; eastern red
bat, 185; fringed myotis, 261; hoary
bat, 196; little brown myotis, 237;
long-eared myotis, 226; long-legged
myotis, 269; northern myotis, 254;
pallid bat, 143–44; silver-haired bat,
205–6; spotted bat, 176; Townsend's
big-eared bat, 157; Yuma myotis, 280.
See also descriptions, specific species;
morphology
Megaceryle alcyon (belted kingfisher), 177
Megachiroptera (megabats), 3

Megascops kennicottii (western screech
owl), 32
metabolism, 33, 34, 46
Mexican free-tailed bat. *See* Brazilian
free-tailed bat
micro-calls, 191
Microchiroptera (microbats), 3
microsatellites, 261, 325–26
migration and winter: approach to, 132;
flight during winter, 48–50; migration
overview, 45; mines and, 48–49, 52,
213–14; torpor, 33, 34, 45, 46, 47, 329.
See also hibernation
migration and winter, specific species:
big brown bat, 45, 48, 51, 52, 165–66,
244; big free-tailed bat, 294; Brazilian
free-tailed bat, 288–89; Californian
myotis, 45, 46, 47–48, 48–49, 51, 52, **204**,
204–5, 212–14, 244, 318; canyon bat, 298;
dark-nosed small-footed myotis, 45, 52,
244; eastern red bat, 45, 184; fringed
myotis, 260; hoary bat, 45, 194–95;
little brown myotis, 45, 46–47, 48, 49,
50, 51, 52, 234–35, 253, 268; long-eared
myotis, 52, 225; long-legged myotis, 45,
51, 52, 268; northern myotis, 235, 253,
268; pallid bat, 45, 142–43; silver-haired
bat, 45, 46, 47–48, 49, 50, 51, 52, 203–5,
204, 213; spotted bat, 175; Townsend's
big-eared bat, 45, 46, 47, 49, 52, **155**,
156–57, 235, 244; Yuma myotis, 45, 46,
51, 52, 234, 278–79
mines, 48–49, 52, 62, **63**, 156, 213–14
minimum frequency (pulse), 108, **109**,
123; definition, 326
mist-nets: definition and overview, 73,
326; northern myotis and, 252; setting
up, **72**, **74**, **75**; for species differentiation,
121; spotted bat and, 174; Townsend's
big-eared bat and, 158; Yuma myotis
and, 281. *See also* harp traps
mitochondrial DNA/genome: big brown
bat, 167; Californian myotis, 91, 214;
dark-nosed small-footed myotis, 91,
214; definition, 326; eastern red bat,
185; little brown myotis, 7, 91, 229;

Populus tremuloides (trembling aspen), 204, 251, 252

Populus trichocarpa (black cottonwood), 153, 251

predation on bats, 32

pregnancy, 81. *See also* gestation period; reproduction

prey-generated sounds, 3, 22, 67, 68, 103, 327

Proctor, Michael, **89**

Pseudogymnoascus destructans, 59. *See also* white-nose syndrome

Pseudotsuga menziesii (Douglas-fir), **10**, 51, 171, 192, 204, 257, 275

Pteropodidae (family), 3, 13. *See also* flying foxes

Pteropus conspicillatus (spectacled flying fox), 68

Pteropus poliocephalus (gray-headed flying fox), **viii**

pulses (acoustic), 106, 327. *See also* acoustic analysis; acoustic characteristics; echolocation

pups: definition and overview, 30, 327; little brown myotis, **29**; nubby ears and, 18; parenting, 30–32, **31**; post-weaning, 34; roosting and, 33; wing finger joints, 81–82, **83**

Quamme, Darcie, **63**

rabies, 53, 55–57, 206, 298

racer, North American (*Coluber constrictor*), 226

Racey, Ken, 144

radio-tagged, definition, 327

radiotelemetry/radio-tracking: big brown bat, 48; big free-tailed bat, 293, 294; Californian myotis, 48, 51, 212, 213; dark-nosed small-footed myotis, 243; definition and overview, 85–87, **86**, 327; little brown myotis, 50, 235; long-eared myotis, 221; northern myotis, 252; pallid bat, 140; roosting studies and, 43, 51, 65; silver-haired bat, 48, 51, 204; spotted bat, 173–74, 174–75; Townsend's

big-eared bat, 153, 154, 156, 157; Yuma myotis, 279

radio transmitters, 48, 51, 86, **86**, 327

Rambaldini, Daniella, 140

red bats. *See* eastern red bat; western red bat

Red List, 61, 143, 226, 327

red-stem ceanothus (*Ceanothus sanguineus*), 196

Rensel, Leah, 18, 44, 70

reproduction, 28–30; approach to, 132; assessing status, 78–81; cauda epididymides, 29, 79–81, **80**, **81**, 322; genitalia, 77, **78**, **79**; gestation period, 29, 324; lactation, 33, 325; mating habits, 28, 49; parturition, 30, 327; pregnancy, 81; roosting and, 33, 42–43; scrotal state, 29, 79–81, **80**, 327–28; sexual maturity, 30; sperm production, 29; testes, 29, 78–81, **80**. *See also* maternity colonies and roosts; pups

reproduction, specific species: big brown bat, 165; big free-tailed bat, 294; Brazilian free-tailed bat, 288; Californian myotis, 28, 212; canyon bat, 298; dark-nosed small-footed myotis, 244; eastern red bat, 28, 184; fringed myotis, 260; hoary bat, 28, **193**, 194; little brown myotis, 28, 233–34, 278; long-eared myotis, 223; long-legged myotis, 268; northern myotis, 253; pallid bat, 142; silver-haired bat, 28, 202–3; spotted bat, 175; Townsend's big-eared bat, 28, 154; Yuma myotis, 28, 277–78

Rhoads, Tory, 60

roosting: "artificial bark" roosts, **63**, 64; bat boxes (*see* bat boxes); bat condominiums, **38**, 39, 43, 321; conflict with humans, 39; conservation considerations, 61; counting bats emerging from roosts, 73; definition, 327; distribution and, 11, 36; eviction from, 39–40, 43; habitat protection measures, 65; little brown myotis and Yuma myotis, 319; maternity colonies and roosts (*see* maternity colonies and roosts);

roosting (continued)

natal philopatry, 37, 243, 326; night roosts, 26, 36, **37**, 39; overheating, 42, 43, 44, 68, 70, **70**, 281; site selection, 33–34, 42–43; summer sites, **35**, **36**, 36–44; types of sites, 36–37; winter sites (hibernacula), 46–47, 47–48, 51–52, 325

roosting, specific species: approach to, 132; big brown bat, 34, 37, **37**, 39, 40, 43, 164, 246; big free-tailed bat, 293; Brazilian free-tailed bat, 288; Californian myotis, 39, 42, 211–12; canyon bat, 298; dark-nosed small-footed myotis, 43, 243, 246; eastern red bat, 37, 183; fringed myotis, 61, 259–60; hoary bat, 37, 192; little brown myotis, 34, **38**, 39, 43, 221, 232, 267, 281; long-eared myotis, 39, 221–22; long-legged myotis, 39, 267; northern myotis, **35**, 251–52; pallid bat, 61, 139–40; silver-haired bat, 202; spotted bat, 173–74; Townsend's big-eared bat, 39, 61, 152–54; Yuma myotis, 34, **38**, 39, 275, 277, 281

Safford, Kirk, 260, 297

Sanders, Gillian, 68, 234

Sarell, Mike, 140, 142–43, 144, 174, 176, 244, 297

Saremba, John, 44, 70

scorpions, 4, 319

scrotal males, 29, 79–81, **80**, 327–28

search phase call (echolocation), 106, 123, 328

sequence, 106, 328

sexual maturity, 30

short-eared owl (*Asio flammeus*), 32

Shryry, Darcey, **74**

silver-haired bat (*Lasionycteris noctivagans*), 197–206; acoustically similar species, 124, 139, 163, 192, 201–2, 287–88, 312, 313; acoustic characteristics, **123**, 199, **200**, 314; acoustic key to, 126; burdock entanglement, 67; clutter continuum, 113, **114**; conservation status, 58, 205; dental formulae, 307; description, 197, **198**, 308; distribution, 9, 11, 161, 199,

199; dorsal surface hairy, 96; feeding, 202; forearm length, **76**; fun facts, 319; fur colour, 20; measurements, 205–6; migration and winter, 45, 46, 47–48, 49, 50, 51, 52, 203–5, **204**, 213; morphological key to, 100, **100**; morphologically similar species, 147, 197–98; nubby ear, 18; in old-growth forests, 206; photograph, **197**; rabies and, 55–56, 206; remarks, 206; reproduction, 28, 202–3; roosting, 202; sexual maturity, 30; skull and dental traits key, 305; taxonomy and variation, 205; white-nose syndrome and, 59; wind turbine fatalities, 57–58, 203, 205

Silvis, A.: *Bat Echolocation Research* (with Fraser, Brigham and Czenze), 87

Simmons, Nancy: *Bats of the World* (with Cirranello), 6

skin, 13

skin samples, 85

skulls, key for identifying BC bats, 302–6

slope (acoustics), 107, 108, **109**, 328

snag, definition, 328

snout, 94–95, 328

social calls, 139, 151, 173, 191

species, concept of, 6–7

Species at Risk Act (SARA), 57, 143, 176, 236, 253, 328

spectacled flying fox (*Pteropus conspicillatus*), 68

spectrograms: bat detectors and, 92, 113, 121, **122**; definition, 328; example, **105**; knee/elbow, 107, **109**, 325; toe, 107–8, **108**, **109**, 328–29. *See also* acoustic analysis; echolocation

sperm, 29, 79–81, **81**. *See also* cauda epididymides; testes

spiders, 24

split harmonic, 115, **117**, 119, **150**, 151, 328

spotted bat (*Euderma maculatum*), 169–77; acoustically similar species, 173; acoustic characteristics, 22, 23, 104, **123**, 171–73, **172**, 311, 318; acoustic key to, 125; capturing, 73, 174, 176–77; conservation status, 57, 61, 176; daytime flying for drinking, 177; dental formulae, 307; description, 169, **170**, 308; distribution, 130, 132, 171, **171**; ears, 16, **17**; easily identified, 92; feeding, 174–75; fun facts, 318; fur colour, 20; measurements, 176; migration and winter, 175; morphological key to, 99; morphologically similar species, 147, 169; mummified remains, 177; photographs, **169**, **177**, **178**; radiotelemetry and, **86**; recording calls of, 119; remarks, 176–77; reproduction, 175; roosting, 173–74; sightings and reports, 176; skull and dental traits key, 305; taxonomy and variation, 176; teats, **82**; tragus, **19**; wildlife habitat areas and, 65; wing swab sampling, **85**

squirrels, flying, 192

Stenopelmatus fuscus (Jerusalem cricket), 141

studying bats, 73–90; assessing age, 77–78, 82; assessing reproductive status, 78–81; calls (*see* acoustic analysis; acoustic characteristics; echolocation); capturing bats for, 73, **74**, **75**; collecting samples, 83, 85, **85**; direct and indirect methods, 73; forearm length, 75, **76**, **77**; handling best practices, 56, 85, 90, 91; isotope analysis, 83, 85, 325; marking, 82–83, **84**; morphological traits for species differentiation, 77 (*see also* in-hand differentiation); pups, 81–82; radiotelemetry/radio-tracking, 43, 51, 85–87, **86**, 327

subspecies, 5

summer, 11

swarming, 166, 233, 234, 253, 268, 328

Tadarida brasiliensis. See Brazilian free-tailed bat

tail membrane, 13, 16, 20, **21**, 25, 29, 92, 95–96

talus, definition, 328

tapeworms, 193

taxonomy, 4–6, 7

taxonomy, specific species: approach to, 132; big brown bat, 167; Californian myotis, 214–15; canyon bat, 298; dark-nosed small-footed myotis, 6, 245, 318; eastern red bat, 184–85; fringed myotis, 261, 318; hoary bat, 195; little brown myotis, 5, 7, 236–37; long-eared myotis, 6, 225, 226, 319; long-legged myotis, 269; northern myotis, 6, 253–54; pallid bat, 143; silver-haired bat, 205; spotted bat, 176; Townsend's big-eared bat, 5, 6, 157; Yuma myotis, 280

teasel, Fuller's (*Dipsacus fullonum*), 67, 215, 226

teats (nipples), 77, 81, **82**

teeth: about, 19–20; assessing age and, 78, **79**; formulae overview, 307; key for identifying BC bats, 302–6; in pups, 19, 30

temperature, 11, 20, 26, 46–47, 50. *See also* overheating

testes, 29, 78–81, **80**

testosterone, 29

tethering techniques, 87, **88**, **89**

threats, 57–71; introduction, 57; barbed wire, 67; car collisions, 69, **69**; climate change, 68, 70–71; forestry practices, 62, 64, 67, 205, 214, 225, 236, 253, 269, 280; habitat loss, 62, 64, 143; human activity, 67, 144, **145**; invasive plants, **66**, 67, 215, 226; light pollution, 68; noise pollution, 67–68, 141–42; pesticide poisoning, 61–62. *See also* conservation; white-nose syndrome; wind turbine fatalities

Thuja plicata (western redcedar), 51, 192, 204, 213, 222, 251–52

thumbs: clawed, 13; length, 95

tibia: definition, 328; length, 94, **94**, 269

tiger moths, 23

time between calls (TBC), 106, 191, 328

toe (spectrograms), 107–8, **108**, **109**, 328–29

torpor, 33, 34, 45, 46, 47, 329

Wildlife Rescue Association, 171

wind turbine fatalities: about, 57–59, **59**; big brown bat, 166; eastern red bat, 57–58, 181, 184, 318; hoary bat, 57–58, 191, 195, 318; little brown myotis, 59, 235, 236; long-legged myotis, 269; northern myotis, 59, 253; silver-haired bat, 57–58, 203, 205

wings: about, 13–14; aspect ratio, 16, 321; as diagnostic feature, 96; finger joints, 82, **83**; flight and, **14**, 14–16, **15**; foraging and, 25; strength of, 32; swab sampling, 85, **85**; wingbeat-pulse synchronization, 108–9; wing loading, 16, 329

winter. *See* hibernation; migration and winter

About the Authors

Cori Lausen is director of bat conservation with Wildlife Conservation Society Canada (wcsbats.ca), based in Kaslo, BC. Cori started researching bats as an undergraduate in 1993 and went on to complete her master's (2001) and PhD (2007) degrees at the University of Calgary, focusing on bat ecology and using molecular genetics and bat acoustics as tools. Although she has worked with bats around the world, much of her career has focused on northwestern North America, where she has captured more than 15,000 bats, studying them in all seasons of the year. Cori has worked on bats in BC since 2006, when she moved to Kaslo to join forces with her husband, Michael Proctor, an independent research conservation biologist; he has helped her with bat captures, and she with his grizzly bear captures. With a strong interest in bat echolocation, she helped develop the North American Bat Monitoring Program and has taught acoustics courses to biologists around the world. She supervises graduate students and is an adjunct professor at Thompson Rivers University. Canoeing, snowmobiling, helicopters, mine exploration, hiking, and tens of thousands of kilometres of driving have enabled Cori to access remote sites across this beautiful province and study its amazing bats. An important focus of her research has been understanding what bats do in winter—hibernation ecology and physiology. Her early work to unravel the mysteries of winter bat flight was stimulated by her father, Leroy Lausen, who supported her research career in many ways—including building an elaborate hot-tub experiment to test whether bats flying in winter drink from open water sources (see image on page 49). For this and his support over the years, she dedicates this book to his memory.

David Nagorsen is a research associate at the Royal British Columbia Museum. David has more than 30 years of experience as a mammalogist, museum biologist and wildlife consultant, carrying out research, fieldwork, endangered species conservation, public education and environmental assessments. His interest in bats began in the 1970s, when he was working at the Royal Ontario Museum, where there was a strong research emphasis on tropical bats. He has authored or co-authored four handbooks on BC's mammals and many scientific papers and reports.

Mark Brigham is a professor of biology at the University of Regina. Mark has studied bats in BC since 1985. With his students, he seeks to understand how bats and nightjars use torpor and hibernation to save energy; he also studies the ecology and behaviour of bats to determine the reasons for and to reverse population declines. In 2006, Mark received the Gerrit S. Miller Jr. Award for lifetime contributions to bat biology from the North American Society for Bat Research. He is co-editor of the *Canadian Journal of Zoology* and a strong proponent of talking about science and research with the public; it was partly for this work that he received the 2008 Joseph Grinnell Award for long-term contribution to education about mammals from the American Society of Mammalogists.

Jared Hobbs is a Registered Professional Biologist and professional wildlife photographer based in Victoria, BC. Jared has worked as a biologist since 1994. Throughout his professional career, he has primarily focused on conservation of species at risk in BC, with a lesser focus on other areas, including Yukon, Alberta, Northwest Territories, Kauai, Alaska, Australia and Antarctica. Jared continues to work as an independent wildlife biologist (as the director and owner of J. Hobbs Ecological Consulting Ltd.), supporting conservation of species at risk, including bats, throughout Canada. He has also authored or co-authored several published scientific papers and reports. Jared also began photographing wildlife in 1994; today his images are represented by All Canada Photos, Alamy, Corbis and Getty Images, and they continue to be used by publishers, government agencies and environmental advocacy groups worldwide. His independent photographic publications include a book on spotted owls and several articles for *Canadian Geographic* and *British Columbia Magazine*.